# JORGE AMADO

# Latin American Studies
## David William Foster, *Series Editor*

# Jorge Amado
## New Critical Essays

Edited by Keith H. Brower
Earl E. Fitz
Enrique Martínez-Vidal

Routledge
New York & London

Published in 2001 by
Routledge
29 West 35th Street
New York, NY 10001

Published in Great Britain by
Routledge
11 New Fetter Lane
London EC4P 4EE

Routledge is an imprint of the Taylor & Francis Group.

Copyright © 2001 Routledge
Typesetting: Jack Donner

Library of Congress Cataloging-in-Publication Data

Jorge Amado : new critical essays / edited by Keith H. Brower, Earl E. Fitz [and] Enrique Martínez-Vidal.
    p. cm. – (Latin American studies series, v. 21)
    Includes bibliographical references and index.
    ISBN 0-8153-2083-3 (hardbound)    ISBN 0-8153-3932-1 (pbk.)
1. Amado, Jorge, 1912—Criticism and interpretation. I. Brower, Keith H. II. Fitz, Earl E. III. Martinez-Vidal, Enrique E. IV. Series.

PQ9697.A647 Z465          2000
869.3'41–dc21                        00-061735

# Contents

# Acknowledgments

We, the co-editors, would like to thank all of the many people who have helped make this book, the first of its kind on Jorge Amado and his works, a reality. We thank, among others, David William Foster, who recommended our proposal to Garland Publishing; Gary Kuris, of Garland, who believed in the project enough to offer us a contract; our contributors, who answered the call and have filled the book with their wonderful essays; the staff at Garland, and in particular James Morgan and Julie Ho, who have carefully led us through the many stages of the book's production; and last, but by no means least, our families—Lori and Alex Brower; Juli, Ezra, Caitlin, Dylan, and Duncan Fitz; and Diane and Alex Martínez-Vidal—without whose patience and support during this project and in all things we would be quite lost.

# Introduction

Long regarded as one of modern Brazilian literature's most renowned figures, Jorge Amado was born in 1912 on a cacao plantation in Bahia, one of the principal states in Brazil's Northeast. In 1931, as the Depression was enveloping Brazil, he travelled south to Rio de Janeiro to study law. He also published his first novel, the rather clumsy and doctrinaire *O país do carnaval [The land of carnival]*, in the same year. As a law student and aspiring novelist, Amado also found himself increasingly drawn to both journalism and politics, both of which come to figure prominently in his later work. He became a follower of Luís Carlos Prestes, the charismatic Communist and military officer of the 1930s and ended up writing his biography, *Vida de Luís Carlos Prestes, o cavaleiro da esperança [The life of Luís Carlos Prestes, the knight of hope]*. During the ensuing regime of the populist strong man, Getúlio Vargas, Amado was forced (because of his leftist political views) to exile himself and live, for a time (1941–1943), in Argentina. Later, after becoming disillusioned with the tyranny of the Soviet Union, the country that bestowed upon him in 1951 the Stalin International Peace Prize, he returned to his native land. In 1959 he was elected to the prestigious Academia Brasileira de Letras, and he steadily became one of its most prominent authors and public figures.

A prolific writer, Amado was also the first Brazilian to gain commercial success in the United States, where his 1958 novel, *Gabriela, cravo e canela [Gabriela, Clove and Cinnamon]*, became a best-seller and placed among the top twenty-five novels published in 1962. With his works currently translated into some thirty-three languages, Amado is undoubtedly Brazil's best-known author abroad, a fact which, ironically, has had both positive and negative repercussions at home. On the one hand, Amado is a tremendously popular writer with a long record of advocacy in favor of Brazil's economically disadvantaged and marginalized peoples and, as he demonstrated in *Tenda dos milagres [Tent of Miracles]* (1969), of its very important Afro-Brazilian culture, as well. At the same time, however, he has been accused, particularly in his post-1958 work, of sexism and sexual stereotyping, of utilizing too many scenes of excessive violence (especially against women), of romanticizing poverty, and (most would say unintentionally) of perpetuating what have been described as paternalistic racial views. The result is that Amado elicits very different responses from people; for some, he is a great ambassador of Brazilian culture and civilization around the world (and for this reason he has often been touted as a deserving recipient of the Nobel Prize for literature), while for others he is deprecated for writing not serious literature and for pandering to the worst aspects of popular culture.

What no one can deny, however, is the importance of Jorge Amado to the evolution of modern Brazilian narrative, where Amado's skills and charm as a storyteller merge Brazil's oral tradition with its written tradition. Indeed, it is not farfetched to say that, in terms of their structure and technique, many of Amado's most successful narratives are essentially attempts to recreate, or recast, this lively, colorful, and often comic oral tradition in the form of the modern novel. One's opinion of Amado's skill as a novelist, in fact, can change rather dramatically if one considers works like *Tent of Miracles, Home is the Sailor [Os velhos marinheiros ou o capitão de longo curso]*, or *A morte e a morte de Quincas Berro dágua [The Two Deaths of Quincas Wateryell]* as not exemplifying the traditional realistic novel but what we might think of as a new genre, the oral novel, or the oral tradition reconstituted in written novelistic form. Reading *Tent of Miracles,* for example, is very much akin to sitting in one's favorite bar listening to a master storyteller spin out a great, sprawling yarn, replete with fascinating characters, endless subplots, and a constant commentary on the story-telling process itself, including the role of the listener/reader in it.

It is commonly said that Amado's long career as a novelist (it currently spans seven decades) divides itself into two parts, with the funny, sexy and, in its own way, socially revolutionary *Gabriela, cravo e canela* serving as the point of division in 1958. The early works, however, may be further subdivided into two more categories, the cacao cycle novels (the aforementioned *O país do carnaval, Cacau [Cacao], Suor [Sweat]*, and, in 1943, *Terras do sem fim [The Violent Land]*) and the somewhat later urban novels of Salvador, the Bahian capital port city (*Jubiabá [Jubiabá], Mar Morto [Sea of Death]*, and *Capitães da areia [Captains of the Sands]*). If the cacao cycle novels are marked by a fairly crude style and a rather simplistic political vision (one in which evil capitalists ruthlessly exploit innocent workers), the more technically sophisticated urban novels, and especially *Jubiabá* (routinely considered, along with *Terras do sem fim* and *Mar Morto*, among Amado's best pre-*Gabriela* efforts), seek to awaken a sense of Marxist class consciousness among the proletariat of the city, the people Amado chooses to champion in his fiction.

Overall, however, certain characteristics of Amado's style or outlook can be ascertained, even in the more overtly political works of the 1930s and 1940s. Amado has always been a realist in terms of recreating the defining details, customs, and problems of the common people whom he chooses to depict in his writings, yet at the same time he manages, in his best works, to achieve a level of poetically rendered universality that makes him immediately accessible to readers everywhere. Like Colombian novelist and Nobel Prize winner Gabriel García Márquez, with whom he is sometimes compared, Amado knows how to make the local or particular express the universal. Indivisibly linked to the people of Bahia, their picturesque speech patterns, their culture and their struggles, Amado transforms the language of these unlettered people into poetry and achieves the fullest expression as a writer when, often by means of loose, digressive plots (again echoing the oral tradition), rich, pungent descriptions, and ironic metafictional commentary, he brings these characters to life and becomes their spokesperson, arguing for their just treatment in modern Brazilian society.

Although, as his critics maintain, Amado's work may be flawed and, at times, even crippled by the faults mentioned above, he remains an optimistic and forward-looking artist/intellectual, one who continues to exert a progressive force in both Brazilian fiction and Brazilian culture. It is our hope that the essays contained in this book will allow the individual reader to come to her or his own determination about this important, if controversial, twentieth-century Brazilian master.

# Religion and Revolution
## The Allegorical Subtexts of *Capitães da areia*

CATHLEEN E. ANDERSON

Jorge Amado's literary career spans over half a century, and as a consequence, some of his works receive less critical attention than others. It seems to be the case, however, that critics quickly dismiss his earlier novels, claiming that they are "to a greater degree social and political polemics rather than true novels" (Schlomann 74). Fred Ellison also comments on the socio-political views that are present in Amado's early novels, and the ramifications of including such views in literature: "From the strictly literary standpoint, however, it must be observed that such a philosophy, when projected in the novels, has grave consequences for art. Their frankly political aim requires some justification in literary works" (85). Although admitting that in the earlier works, especially those dealing with the city of Bahia, there are "moments of supreme artistry," Ellison amends his praise, adding "but, probably more often, moments when art is absent" (92). Ellison finds fault not only in the content of Amado's earlier works, but in the structure of these novels as well, which he sees as "a succession of episodes" which are "not always well integrated" (107–108). Further criticism arises from Amado's incorporation of popular culture, as well as for the fact that his "literature is repetitive, anti-intellectual, and offers little in the ways of innovation or literary genius" (Curran 3).

In many ways, these critics are correct in their assessment of Amado's earlier works. Amado himself has stated that his purpose in writing is to tell a story meant to be enjoyed by all, not to please critics: "Writing has to give pleasure and not just to a small circle of intellectuals" (Price 173). Even though he claims that his earlier writings are for the common man, Amado is cognizant of the literary or artistic defects that they contain. In the epilogue of *Capitães da areia [Captains of the Sands]*,[1] he discusses what he calls his "Bahian Novels," a series of six novels in which he attempts to capture the essence of Bahia (245). He admits that these novels contain flaws: "I know full well that this series of novels has nothing of genius or the miraculous about it. The work of a young man, it could not help but be full of defects." He justifies his writing of such novels, however, because they contain what is lacking in Brazilian works of art: "an absolute solidarity with and a great love for the humanity that lives in these books" (CS 247).

Despite the flaws of these novels, they do contain elements which deserve critical study. Due to the fact that they have been overlooked by early Amadian scholars, however, later critics also tend to shy away from them. As Bobby Chamberlain states in his introduction to *Jorge Amado*, he chooses to emphasize Amado's later works over the earlier ones due in part to his own personal preferences, although he notes that his choices "likewise correspond in large measure to the value judgments expressed by most previous Amadian scholars . . ." (x). Hence the cycle continues, and the earlier novels continue to be left behind by the critics.

The last novel of the Bahian cycle, *Capitães da areia*, published in 1937, is one such novel that has been, to a certain degree, ignored by the critics. Granted, this novel does include many of the aforementioned flaws replete in Amado's earlier works, such as an episodic structure, a strong socio-political bent, and even, as Chamberlain points out, "melodramatic proclivities and 'oversentimentalization' of the wretched plight of the Bahian masses" (22). If, however, this novel is looked at from Agnus Fletcher's perception of allegory, these so-called flaws turn into elements of a tightly structured literary work. Aside from the obvious lack of proper names in the narrative (with some exceptions), this novel contains other elements of allegory as described by Fletcher. According to his definition, an allegory includes "emblematic, isolated, mosaic imagery," "the lack of that perspective which would create a mimetic world" as well as "the microcosmic character of the imagery, where 'every single word must contain in itself the entire concept'" (171). The episodic structure of this novel serves to present the reader with a "mosaic imagery," in which certain aspects of the lives of the protagonists are highlighted. In the same way, the portrayal of the "wretched plight" of the people of Bahia is justified when seen as the "microcosmic character of the imagery," working to transmit a message in as few words as possible. In addition, the presence of progress, which can be understood as a "questing journey" (151), as well as the inclusion of a "battle form" (157) in a literary work add to its categorization as allegory. These concepts as presented in Amado's novel will be explored throughout this study.

*Capitães da areia* is the story of a group of orphans, abandoned by their parents, neglected by the city, and when placed in the care of the city, abused by the police and forced to endure the inhumane conditions of the state directed boy's reformatory. Although there are over fifty youngsters in the gang, only a few can be considered as main characters in the development of the novel. These include Sem-Pernas, a crippled boy; Gato, the "dandy" of the gang, who is more concerned with looking good and seducing older women than he is with improving the lot of the gang members; the Professor, who spends his time reading and drawing pictures on the sidewalk in order to earn some money; Volta-Seca, who dreams of joining the fighting legions of Lampião in the backlands; Pirulito, who has heard the call of God and wants to become a priest; and Pedro Bala, the leader of the pack of delinquents.[2] In order to survive, the Captains of the Sands, the name by which they are collectively known, as well as feared, live according to their wits. With no adult supervision and no stable home environment, they often go hungry. Their survival depends, therefore, on begging, gambling and stealing. They coerce people into believing that they are good and then turn around and rob from them. Although such a lawless group would seemingly have no need for, and even less tolerance of, religion, such is not the case. The Captains of the Sands, who have little or no respect for adults, embrace into their lives the Catholic priest Father José Pedro and the *mãe-de-santo* Don'Aninha. The importance of these two characters in the lives of the orphans serves to show the centrality of the theme of religion in the novel.

In his portrayal of Catholicism and the syncretic African religion practiced by Don'Aninha, Amado illustrates the good intentions of both religions, while simultaneously critiquing the people's belief that their religion will cure the ills of society. Rather than ignore completely the possible influence of these religions, however, Amado suggests that the combination of religion and politics is a way for the poor people of the novel (and by extension the real citizens of the city of Bahia) to rise above the poverty and squalor of their lives.

Don'Aninha, the *mãe-de-santo*, is a positive figure in the lives of the Captains of the Sands in that she is one of the few adults in whom they trust and confide. In fact, she is one of only two adults who have set foot in their hideout. She is a confidant not only of the Captains of the Sands, but a friend of all the poor as well: ". . . all blacks and all poor people in Bahia are friends of the great mãe-de-santo"(80–81) [". . . porque são amigos da grande mãe-de-santo todos os negros e todos os pobres da Bahia"] (80–81). Nevertheless, she (and by extension, her religion) is incapable of helping the Captains of the Sands improve their situation in life. There are times, in fact, when the opposite is true and the young orphans go to her aid. When the police raid a *candomblé* session and confiscate Ogun, a statue of one of the African deities, it is up to the Captains of the Sands, and specifically their leader Pedro Bala, to steal it back from the police. Rather than Don'Aninha's religion improving the lives of the Captains of the Sands, their blatant lawlessness comes to her aid. Another example of Don'Aninha's inability to change the lives of the Captains of the Sands is when Dora, the only female member of the gang and Pedro's sweetheart, falls deathly ill. Although the *mãe-de-santo* does what she can, she is incapable of saving young Dora's life. Once again, Don'Aninha is present in the lives and the crises of the orphans, but she is powerless to help them.

Various African deities also appear in this novel. Omolu, the goddess of smallpox, plays a central role. As Pedro is told, "Omolu isn't just a black folks' Saint. She's a Saint for all poor people" (72) ["Omolu não é só santo de negro. É santo dos pobres todos"] (90). As the protector of the poor, she foretells of the day of vengeance of her people and the downfall of the rich. During a *candomblé* held in Gantóis, she promises to plague the rich with an onslaught of smallpox, which would benefit the poor by eliminating the rich, thereby allowing the poor to be well-fed and happy (73). Unleash the smallpox she does, only to have her plans of decimating the rich people thwarted by their ability to vaccinate against the disease. Once released, however, the disease proves unstoppable, making its way to the poorer neighborhoods, whose residents are unable to vaccinate against it. Taking pity on the poor people, Omolu reduces the smallpox to milk pox, a milder version of the disease; despite this measure, the poor still suffer and die.

In his study of the African presence in the works of Amado, Russell Hamilton states that both Omolu and Don'Aninha serve as positive elements in this novel: "In *Capitães da areia* the cult priestess Don'Aninha emerges as a defender of the oppressed, along with Omolu, the god of smallpox, who would announce the day which the poor would be avenged" (245). If speaking of intentions, Hamilton's observations are valid, because both Don'Aninha and Omolu do indeed have the best interests of the poor and oppressed at heart. It is when one looks at the results brought about by these two figures that Hamilton's comments come into question. As Maria Nunes points out, "In recounting this episode [of the smallpox], the author's attitude toward the efficacy of African religion seems to be quite negative . . ." (95). The goddess of the poor people, rather than helping her followers, in fact works to destroy them. Part of the critique of Omolu (as well as of her disciples) is her lack of scientific knowledge: "Omolu didn't know about vaccines, Omolu was a goddess from the jungles of Africa, what could she know of vaccines and scientific things?" (125) ["Omolu não sabia da vacina. Omolu era uma deusa das floresta da África, que podia saber de vacinas e coisas científicas?"] (144). Although Don'Aninha is portrayed as defender of the poor, and Omolu does predict a day of vengeance for the poor, in reality Don'Aninha seeks help from those she supposedly defends, and Omolu, albeit unintentionally, inflicts disease and death upon the poor.

Catholicism, represented by the priest Father José Pedro, also faces criticism in this novel. Hamilton, for one, feels that the difference between the presentation of *candomblé* and Catholicism is significant: "The kindly Catholic priest José Pedro seeks to aid the abandoned children, but he is hampered by his superiors and the community in general. *Candomblé* offers an immediate and personal release, while the Church is distant and impersonal.

The cult priestess identifies with the people" (246). Although correct in his assessment of the forces that work against Father José Pedro, Hamilton fails to see the personal link that the priest establishes with the orphans. Like Don'Aninha, the Captains of the Sands befriend and trust him, and he is the other adult allowed to visit their hideout. Beyond that, he often faces an internal battle between the mandates of the Church and what he feels in his heart he should do in order to help the children. Although powerless to change their plight, he often disregards the teachings of the Church in his attempts to help the children. As a result of his deeds, not only is he reprimanded by his superiors and denied the parish that he has been awaiting so long, but the people to whom he ministers reject him and criticize him as well. The other priests also scorn him, fearing that his presence and adherence to the morals and ethics of the priesthood will put an end to the gifts and favors they have become accustomed to receiving. Throughout the novel, the lowly priest with the good intentions of helping the young orphans is praised; it is the institution of the Catholic Church which comes under fire.

Despite his good intentions, Father José Pedro constantly finds himself in trouble. Whereas in his mind a priest's mission is to serve, many of the older women in the parish feel it their duty to serve their priests and fawn over them. Aware that many other priests accept such lavish attention, Father José Pedro makes the conscious decision to reject them: "He knew that in reality the great majority of priests didn't revolt and got fine presents of chickens, turkeys, embroidered handkerchiefs, and sometimes even gold watches that had come down through generations in the same family. But Father José Pedro had a different idea of his mission, he thought the others were in error ..." (60) ["Em verdade ele sabia que a grande maioria dos padres não se revoltava e ganhava bons presentes de galinhas, perus, lenços bordados e por vezes até antigos relógios de ouro que passavam através de gerações na mesma família. Mas o padre José Pedro tinha outra idea da sua missão, pensava que os outros estavam errados ..."] (77). When the parishioners complain to their favorite confessor, the fat Father Clóvis, he calms them down, telling them that in time Father José Pedro will come around to their way of thinking. He expresses his true feelings (fears) as they leave however, worried that "These newly ordained priests will spoil everything ..." (61) ["—Esses padres recém-ordenados estragam a vida da gente ..."] (78). The difference between a priest true to his ministry and the priest comfortable in merely going through the priestly motions and happily accepting the doting of his parishioners is obvious.

Father José Pedro's conflicts extend beyond the parishioners and Father Clóvis, however. Many times his dealings with the Captains of the Sands force him into interior conflict, needing to choose between what he has been taught (the church as Institution) and what he himself feels in his heart to be the right decision. When one of the boys contracts the highly contagious milk pox, by law Father José Pedro must inform the city officials. The boys ask him not to, afraid that their friend will be taken to the pest house and die. As a result, Father José Pedro turns his back on his "duty" as defined by society, and, acting according to his intuition, he bows to the wishes of the boys.

The distinction between the unfeeling institution of the Church and the goodness and intuition of the poor priest is seen again when Father José Pedro appears before the canon Secretary of the Archbishop to answer the many complaints that have been lodged against him. Before words are even exchanged, the difference in the two men is obvious. The canon "was tall and thin, angular, with a clean cassock, what little hair he had left was carefully combed. His lips had a hard line . . . There was no human kindness in his face, in his hard features . . . They said he was quite intelligent, a great preacher, famous for the strictness of his habits" (133) ["Era alto e muito magro, angu- loso, com a batina muito limpa, os raros cabelos que lhe restavam muito bem penteados. Os lábios tinham uma linha dura. . . . Não havia nenhuma simpatia humana na sua figura, nos seus traços duros. . . . Diziam que era inteligentís- simo, grande orador sacro, célebre pela rigidez dos seus costumes"] (152–153). Father José Pedro stands in stark contrast to the canon: ". . . [a] short figure, his dirty cassock mended in two places, his frightened look, the lack of intelligence . . . mixed with goodness, was reflected on the priest's face" (133) [. . . a figura baixa do padre, a sua batina suja e remendada em dois lugares, o seu ar de medo, a falta de inteligência que de mistura com a bondade se reflectia na cara do padre"] (153). The differences between the two men extend beyond physical characteristics to their beliefs regarding what constitutes a priest's mission. Whereas Father José Pedro strives to improve the lot of the abandoned children and bring them closer to God, the canon concerns himself more with the outward appearances of the priests under his supervision, their reputation, as well as the gifts that the parish- ioners bestow on them. When he mentions a complaint made against the priest by one of the women of the parish, Father José Pedro attempts to tell the canon the truth of the matter; the canon reprimands him, tells him to be humble and respectful, and reminds him that "the widow Santos is one of the best supporters of religion in Bahia. . . . You should see her gifts . . ." (134) ["—O senhor sabe que a viúva Santos é uma das melhores protetoras da religião na Bahia? Não sabe dos donativos . . ."] (154).

Throughout the entire interview with the canon Father José Pedro holds onto the faith that his ministering to the Captains of the Sands is the right thing to do, regardless of what the canon thinks: "Father José Pedro had great faith in God's goodness. Many times he had thought that God approved what he was doing. He thought that now too. That thought had suddenly filled his heart" (135) ["O padre José Pedro tinha confiança na bondade de Deus. Muitas vezes pensara que Deus aprovava o que ele estava fazendo. Agora pensava isto também. Aquele pensamento tinha enchido seu coração de repente"] (155). Summoning up his courage, he finally battles back, justifying his actions while at the same time criticizing the hypocrisy of the rich parishioners. In his opinion, the rich are at least partly to blame for the plight of the Captains of the Sands: " 'They steal in order to eat because all these rich people who've got enough to throw away, to give to churches, forget that hungry children exist . . .' " (136) ["—Roubam para comer porque todos esses ricos que têm para botar fora, para dar para as igrejas, não se lembram que existem crianças com fome . . ."] (156). The canon responds by accusing the priest of being a communist and dismisses him with the admonition to forget his communist ideas and do penance for his sins. Father José Pedro leaves his meeting with the canon more confused than ever, yet still convinced in his heart that he is being true to his vocation. He even goes so far as to compare his ministry to that of Christ: "Suffer the little children to come unto me . . . Christ . . . He was a radiant and young figure. The priests had said he was a revolutionary too . . . He can't abandon them. Who can God be with? With the canon or with the poor priest? The widow . . . No, God is with the priest . . . He's with the priest" (136–138) ["Deixai vir a mim as criancinhas . . . Cristo . . . Era uma figura radiosa e moça. Os sacerdotes também disseram que ele era em revolucionário . . . Não pode abandoná-las. Com quem estará Deus? Com o cônego ou com o pobre padre? A viúva . . . Não, Deus está com o padre . . . Está com o padre"] (157–159). The good, although somewhat unconventional, intentions of the poor priest mean more to God than the false intentions espoused by the canon and the institution of the church.

Despite the many obstacles Father José Pedro encounters in his attempt to minister to the poor children, Amado does not completely negate the value of the Catholic Church in this novel. A change, however, needs to take place within the institution of the church. Father José Pedro, who often finds himself more allied with the Captains of the Sands than with the institution he represents, holds such a belief. He comes to the realization that his situation, that of ministering to a gang of delinquents, requires him to alter the manner in which he carries out his ministry. When Dora dies from the fever, for example, the boys and Don'Aninha make preparations to bury her at sea. Horrified at first, the priest refuses to allow them to commit such a sin. In the end, however, he again disregards the teachings of the church and allows his intuitions and feelings to guide him in his actions. Not only does he allow the boys to follow through with their burial plans, but he participates in the event. In a coming together of the two religions, Father José Pedro prays as Don'Aninha sends Dora off to meet Yemanjá.

In assessing the presence of African rites in his novels, Nunes observes that although Amado viewed them as an important element of the lives of the people he described, at the same time he "advocated political solutions to their problems" (101). She cites the episode of Omolu and the smallpox as proof of her argument, stating "The author's point of view seems to be that the hopes of the poor are best invested in political action. Even the gods of the lower classes cannot always be depended upon ..." (96). Although such observations are valid (*Capitães da areia* as well as several other of the early novels end with a strike scene in which the poor people actively seek equality), religion cannot be completely discounted in the solution sought by the poor. A combination of religion and politics is presented in this novel as a way for the poor and oppressed to improve their situation in life.

This politico-religious suggestion is seen in the words and actions of both Don'Aninha and Father José Pedro, as well as in the thoughts and actions of Pedro Bala, the leader of the Captains. Don'Aninha's sanctioning of a politico-religious solution is less obvious than that of the other two, but the seed is present. When she goes to the Captains of the Sands to enlist their aid in recovering the stolen Ogun, she comments on the negative impact of politics on her religion: " 'They [the police] don't even leave the poor people's God alone. Poor people can't dance, can't sing to their God, can't ask a favor of their God.' Her voice was bitter, a voice that didn't seem to be that of the priestess Don'Aninha. 'They're not content with killing poor people with hunger ... Now they take away poor people's saints' ... and she raised her fists" (81) ["—... Não deixam nem o deus dos pobres em paz. Pobre não pode dançar, não pode cantar pra seu deus, não pode pedir uma graça a seu deus.—Sua voz era amarga, uma voz que não parecia da mãe-de-santo Don'Aninha.—Não se contentam de matar os pobres à fome. Agora tiram os santos dos pobres ...—E alçava os punhos"] (99). Although not explicitly suggesting violence or any kind of power struggle, by raising her fists she implies that the poor people, in order to be treated equally, cannot just sit back; they need to take action. And that is what she asks of the Captains of the Sands when she condones their breaking the law in order to restore Ogun to his place on the altar. Although a seemingly insignificant occurrence, it foretells of more substantial actions to come.

The case of Father José Pedro is more involved as well as more explicit than that of Don'Aninha. Whereas she merely complains, raises her fists in anger and curses the rich and the police, Father José Pedro actually contemplates the implications of a power struggle and tries to justify such a radical action with the dogma that he has been taught and in turn is supposed to be teaching to his followers. As has already been shown, he doesn't think twice about breaking the law or even committing a sin (as in the case of Dora's burial at sea) if the reasons behind such transgressions are legitimate.

Although Father José Pedro breaks an occasional law, in his mind he justifies such actions. When he begins to contemplate revolution, however, he must reconsider everything that he has been taught. In his mind the lawless life led by the Captains of the Sands results not from their being inherently bad people, but rather from the injustices of life itself. He therefore tries to improve their lives in an attempt to change them into honest, hardworking men. His beliefs come into question when the dockworker João de Adão confronts him with opposing viewpoints; he believes that society and the rich are to blame for the situation of the Captains of the Sands: "... as long as nothing was changed the boys couldn't be men of goodness. And he said that Father José Pedro would never be able to do anything for them because the rich wouldn't let him" (95) ["... que enquanto tudo não mudasse, os meninos não poderiam ser homens de bem. E disse que o padre José Pedro nunca poderia fazer nada por eles porque os ricos não deixariam"] (113). Although the priest doesn't want to, he reluctantly admits that there might be some truth in what the dockworker says. He appreciates what João de Adão says, but he steadfastly clings to his trust and faith in God; the battle he faces has evolved from an internal one to one that is external. Upon further contemplation of João de Adão's dreams of revolution and equality for all, however, Father José Pedro agrees more and more with what the dockworker professes:

> The priest wanted to give houses, schools, love, and comfort to the children without revolution, without putting an end to the rich. But there was a barrier all around. He felt lost and asked God for inspiration. And with a certain terror he saw without wanting to that when he thought about the problem under consideration that the dockworker João de Adão was right. Then he was taken by fear, because that wasn't what they'd taught him, and he would pray for hours on end for God to give him illumination. (96)

> [O padre queria dar casa, escola, carinho e conforto aos meninos sem a revolução, sem acabar com os ricos. Mas de todos os lados era uma barreira. Ficava como perdido e pedia a Deus que o inspirasse. E com certo pavor via que, quando pensava no problema, dava, sem sequer o sentir, razão ao doqueiro João de Adão. Então era possuído de temor, porque não fora assim que lhe haviam ensinado, e rezava horas seguidas para que Deus o iluminasse]. (114)

He desperately searches for a way in which to reconcile the two seemingly opposite ideologies.

Father José Pedro finally finds such a reconciliation when he receives the parish assignment that he has waited so long for, and it is not in the city as he had expected, but rather in a desolate village lost in the backlands. His parishioners are not the rich hypocrites he had previously criticized, but rather *cangaceiros*, or bandits. Whereas the canon sees this assignment as a kind of punishment for the trouble caused by Father José Pedro, the assignment suits the priest. He compares his new charges to adult versions of the Captains, and as such he sees his new parish as a continuation of his mission of ministering to children. His service to these lawless bandits also affords Father José Pedro the opportunity to pursue his internal struggle between what he has been taught and the idea of revolution proposed by João de Adão. The priest leaves for the backlands, taking with him both his religious training and the revolutionary ideas of João de Adão, in search of an answer that will satisfy him. What he does with these two conflicting ideologies remains unsaid, leaving one to wonder which road he decides to follow. The lack of a resolution is significant because Amado does not tell his readers what they should do; he merely presents them with different possibilities, thereby allowing them to reach their own decisions.

While neither Don'Aninha nor Father José Pedro make any conscious decisions regarding the mixing of religion and politics, Pedro Bala, the leader of the Captains, does. A young boy of fifteen, living on the streets since the age of five, he commands the admiration and respect of his fellow gang members and the fear of the rest of the community. The only two adults that he respects are Don'Aninha and Father José Pedro: "The leader of the Captains of the Sands didn't get to *candomblés* very often, just as he didn't listen to Father José Pedro's lessons very much. But he was a friend of the priest as well as of the priestess and among the Captains of the Sands when one is a friend one acts like a friend" (81) ["O chefe dos Capitães da Areia ia pouco aos candomblés, como pouco ouvia as lições do padre José Pedro. Mas era amigo tanto do padre como da mãe-de-santo e entre os Capitães da Areia quando alguém é amigo serve ao amigo"] (99). Although not a staunch believer of the religious dogma preached by the priestess and the priest, he listens to them, absorbing the advice they give, as well as hearing their opinions of the world. As such, Don'Aninha's negative comments towards the rich and the police and the priest's affirmation that all people would be equal in heaven fill both Pedro's head and heart and aid in the formation of his opinions. Not surprisingly, the conclusions that he not only reaches but also acts upon are the same as those that Don'Aninha and Father José Pedro only thought about: combining revolution and religion.

Although Father José Pedro preached an eternal equality in the realm of heaven, Pedro's concerns lie with the here and now. "Poor people had nothing. Father José Pedro said that the poor would go to heaven one day, where God would be the same for everybody. But Pedro Bala's young reasoning didn't see justice in that. In the kingdom of heaven they would be equal. But they were unequal on earth now, the scale always tilted to one side" (81) ["Os pobres não tinham nada. O padre José Pedro dizia que os pobres um dia iriam para o reino dos Céus, onde Deus seria igual para todos. Mas a razão jovem de Pedro Bala não achava justiça naquilo. No reino do Céu seriam iguais. Mas já tinham sido desiguais na Terra, a balança pendia sempre para um lado"] (99). It is precisely this earthly inequality that prompts Pedro to question the calling of one of his compatriots, Pirulito, who aspires to serve God by becoming a priest. While Pedro respects Pirulito's decision, and even allows him to continue living with the gang after he abandons their lawless lifestyle, he has difficulty understanding his devotion, especially after seeing how futile the priest's efforts had been. Rather than looking to God for answers and solutions, Pedro searches in the solidarity of the people in hopes of finding redemption and salvation.

As the gang slowly breaks up and the members go their separate ways, finding their niches in life, Pedro remains behind, still searching for his place in society. Having been influenced by many in his life, including Father José Pedro and João de Adão, Pedro tries to find a place for himself in society that will allow him to realize his interior need for freedom: "Pedro feels the spectacle of men, he doesn't think this freedom is enough for the thirst of freedom he has inside. Nor does he feel the call of God as Pirulito felt it. For him, the preachings of Father José Pedro never said anything. He liked the priest as a good man. Only João de Adão's words found a place in his heart" (219) ["Pedro sente o espectáculo dos homens, acha que aquela liberdade não é suficiente para a sede de liberdade que tem dentro de si. Tampouco sente o chamado de Deus, como Pirulito o sentiu. Para ele, as pregações do padre José Pedro nunca disseram nada. Gostava do padre como de um homem bom. Só as palavras de João de Adão encontravam acolhida no seu coração"] (240–241). Pedro's feelings toward the priest are significant; he liked the goodness of Father José Pedro more so than his preachings. He liked the priest who went by his intuition rather than what the institution dictated he do. He liked the revolutionary priest, who rather than condemning the burial of Dora at sea, prayed as she went to meet the African goddess Yemanjá. This goodness combined with a revolutionary spirit that Pedro saw and liked in the priest helps him to realize his destiny: the revolution.

The calling to participate in the revolution that Pedro hears belongs not only to him, however. It is a calling from God, a calling as strong as that which pulled Pirulito away from a life of stealing into the service of God; it is a voice that comes from the drums that reverberate in the *candomblé* rites. It is a voice that comes from his former gang members, from the poor people of the city, and more importantly, a voice that comes from the two religious influences in his life: "A voice that even comes from Father José Pedro, a poor priest with fearful eyes as he sees the terrible destiny of the Captains of the Sands. A voice that comes from the *filhas-de-santo*, dancers of Don'Aninha's *candomblé* on the night the police took Ogun away" (241) ["Uma voz que vem mesmo do padre José Pedro, padre pobre de olhos espantados diante do destino terrível dos Capitães da Areia. Uma voz que vem das filhas-de-santo do candomblé de Don'Aninha, na noite que a polícia levou Ogum"] (262). It is a calling to finally take all that he has learned during his journey, during his years on the streets, and make a difference. But the difference must be not just in his life, but in the lives of those around him. It is a calling to make the difference that both Don'Aninha and Father José Pedro attempted to, but failed, to make.

Although Father José Pedro feels that his attempts to give the Captains of the Sands a new and better life were not successful, he realizes that his ministry was not a complete failure. If nothing else, he was able to provide them with the family they didn't have, the love that they lacked, and the solidarity they needed. And this religion that included giving family and support to those in need that the priest practiced mingles with the words of revolution spoken by João de Adão and in the new Pedro Bala, the revolutionary. Years after leaving the warehouse and the lawlessness of the gang, Pedro Bala still flees the police and lands in prison. There is not a feeling of pessimism or despair regarding the revolutionary, because Pedro, unlike Don'Aninha and Father José Pedro, has been successful in his endeavors to help the poor and the oppressed: "And the day he escaped, in numberless homes at the hour of their poor meal, faces lighted up when they heard the news. And in spite of the fact that the terror was out there, any one of those homes was a home that would be open for Pedro Bala, a fugitive from the police. Because the revolution is a homeland and a family" (244) ["E, no dia em que ele fugiu, em inúmeros lares, na hora pobre do jantar, rostos se iluminaram ao saber de notícia. E, apesar de que lá fora era o terror, qualquer daqueles lares era um lar que se abriria para Pedro Bala, fugitivo da polícia. Porque a revolução é uma pátria e uma família"] (266). Although in his youth Pedro professed not to believe in the teachings of the priest, years later in his work as a revolutionary he practices the tenets practiced by Father José Pedro. Combining the goodness of the poor priest and the defense of the poor shown by Don'Aninha with the political ideas espoused by João de Adão, Pedro Bala finally reaches the end of his quest. He is able to provide his followers, the poor and oppressed, with the same sense of family, solidarity and protection that Father José Pedro and Don'Aninha gave to the poor orphans living on the docks.

At first glance, this novel does indeed suffer from many of the flaws for which Amado's early novels have been criticized. The social criticism of the city bureaucracy, especially in regards to the forgotten and abandoned children, as well as the showcasing of the hypocrisy that is replete in the Catholic Church, cannot be ignored. This novel can also be considered a series of episodes, some of which come to less than satisfying conclusions. Considering Fletcher's commentaries regarding allegory, however, sheds new light on the novel.

In order to fully appreciate the workings of this novel as an allegory, two of the main characters, Father José Pedro and Pedro Bala, need to be looked at more closely. It is striking that of the many characters that appear in the novel, these two have proper names, as opposed to the symbolic names attributed to Pedro's companions. This is not to say, however, that Father José Pedro's and Pedro Bala's names are without meaning. If we look at the two elements of the priest's name, various biblical images come to mind. In the

New Testament, Joseph is the foster father of Christ, but Joseph is also an important figure in the book of Genesis. He is the dreamer, scorned by his brothers and eventually sent to a far off land. There, after suffering many trials and tribulations, he becomes not only a respected advisor to the Pharaoh, the main political force in the land, but one of his high ranking officials: "Now Joseph was governor over the land" (Genesis 42:6). Peter, in the New Testament, is the apostle chosen by Christ to found the new Church and become the first leader of His disciples: "And I also say to you that you are Peter, and on this rock I will build My church, and the gates of Hades shall not prevail against it" (Matthew 16:18). In bestowing these two names on the priest of this novel, the priest who finds himself caught between religion and politics, Amado suggests that the answer to the plight of the poor lies in the combination of the political aspects of the name José and the religious elements found in the name Pedro.

Pedro Bala's name carries the same message. Pedro, in a religious light once again, can be seen as the founder of a new church, whereas Bala, bullet, implies the use of force or violence. The fact that Pedro's name carries with it more of an allusion to violence than does the priest's fits in well with the actions taken by the two throughout the novel. In the end, it is Pedro who acts, while Father José Pedro travels to the far-off land to serve in whatever capacity is required of him.

For Fletcher, progress, sometimes seen as a journey involving "a sequence of steps in one main direction" (159), serves in allegory to show the growth of a character. Such growth often manifests itself as self-knowledge (151–152). These steps towards self-knowledge make up both Pedro Bala's and Father José Pedro's respective journeys. Pedro's quest began the moment he became an orphan and found himself on the streets. As Fletcher points out, the journey does not need to be a physical journey; what is required is that there be " . . . a constant forward motion, that it be unremittingly directed toward a goal, that it attempt an undeviating movement in a given direction" (154). Although Pedro's journey does not take him to strange and exotic lands, it does take him to a new point in his life, that of a leader, a revolutionary. All that he experienced on the streets growing up, including Father José Pedro's examples of love and compassion, lead him to his destiny. Father José Pedro's journey is more physical, because it takes him from the city of Bahia to the backlands, where he, like Pedro, will find his final destiny, which will be a ministering to a group of outlaws; again, the combination of religion and politics is clear.

The other element required in an allegory, according to Fletcher, is the presence of a battle. Again, he advises his readers not to take this term too literally: whereas it could refer to a battle that takes place on a battlefield, Fletcher informs his readers that other, "gentler permutations of this imagery

of conflict are the 'debate' and the 'dialogue' . . . where the war is verbal . . ."
(157–158). Both Pedro and Father José Pedro enter into a battle of sorts when
trying to figure out their destinies. Pedro's battle is a literal battle, when he
and his gang members fight against the strike-breakers, led by an American.
After this initial battle, he is considered a comrade, *um companheiro*, and his
destiny is decided.

The priest's battle is more of a figurative one, that takes place first within
himself, as he tries to reconcile what he feels he should do with what the
Church says he should do. His battle then turns into an external dialogue, as
he listens to the ideas of João de Adão and tries, intellectually and emotionally, to fight against them. This indecision on the part of Father José Pedro,
first internally and then with João de Adão, mirrors the back and forth movement of an actual battle: "The back and forth of battle, when translated to a
mental conflict or an ideological warfare, becomes the symmetrical presentation of first the argument on one side, then the argument on the other. The
debaters of the debate are presented in an equality, so that each side gets its
fair share of the action" (Fletcher 159). The back and forth action of the
priest's battle never comes to an end; the result of his battle is left unresolved.
Still confused, still unsure of what his role in the revolution, if any, should be,
José Pedro embarks upon his journey to the backlands, to minister to the *cangaceiros*. Along with the physical journey to the backlands, he continues
upon his inner quest for self-knowledge.

Whereas at first glance *Capitães da areia* is just a sub-par novel which
depends on an episodic structure to capture the attention and emotion of the
reader, when analyzed more closely, it becomes apparent that the novel is
much more than that. Amado employs an allegorical structure to this work
not just to tell a story, but to impart a message as well: in order for the poor to
improve their plight, they need to do more than rely on religion. A combination of the positive aspects of religion (compassion, love, sense of family and
solidarity) with the more practical aspects of revolution (equality and solidarity for all, protection for the poor) is what is needed to change things in not
only Bahia, but all of Brazil.

**NOTES**

1. This epilogue is found in the translation into English, not in the original Portuguese.
2. The fact that all of these characters, including Pedro Bala (Bala means "bullet" in
   Portuguese) have names that relate to their position within the gang adds to the
   argument that this novel can be considered an allegory.

## BIBLIOGRAPHY

Amado, Jorge. *Capitães da areia*. 3rd edition. Portugal: Publicações Europa-América, Lda., n.d.

————. *Captains of the Sands*. Trans. Gregory Rabassa. New York: Avon Books, 1988.

————. Interview. *Latin America: The Writer's Journey*. Greg Price. London: Hamish Hamilton, 1990. 169–179.

————. Postface. *Captains of the Sands*. Trans. Gregory Rabassa. New York: Avon Books, 1988.

Chamberlain, Bobby J. *Jorge Amado*. Boston: Twayne Publishers, 1990.

Curran, Mark. "Amado, Jorge." *A Dictionary of Contemporary Brazilian Authors*. Comp. David William Foster and Roberto Reis. Tempe: Center for Latin American Studies, ASU, 1981.

Ellison, Fred P. *Brazil's New Novel*. Berkeley: University of California Press, 1954.

Fletcher, Angus. *Allegory: The Theory of a Symbolic Mode*. Ithaca: Cornell University Press, Ltd., 1964.

Hamilton, Russell G. "Afro-Brazilian Cults in the Novels of Jorge Amado." *Hispania* 50 (1967): 242–252.

*The Holy Bible, The New King James Version*. Nashville: Thomas Nelson Publishers, 1983.

Nunes, Maria Luisa. "The Preservation of African Culture in Brazilian Literature: The Novels of Jorge Amado." *Luso-Brazilian Review* 10.1 (June 1973): 86–101.

Schlomann Lowe, Elizabeth. "The 'New' Jorge Amado." *Luso-Brazilian Review* 6.2 (Dec. 1969): 73–82.

# Ambiguity Lost

## Jorge Amado's *A morte e a morte de Quincas Berro Dágua* on Film

KEITH H. BROWER

Transferring fiction to film is always a tricky proposition. Filmmakers must determine at virtually every level, from dialogue and casting, to music, location and set design, how to adapt the work in question in such a way that it will faithfully convey not only the original's story, but also its look, its feel, and, of course, its meanings to the audience. Or the filmmakers may choose not to present what many might see as a faithful rendition of the work at all, and instead rely on their own, perhaps even deliberately controversial, interpretation of the original. Either way, like it or not, once their adaptation goes public, they must face both critics and the audience, and often the latter is a much more difficult group to satisfy. Included in this group are those who have never read the original and who have no opinion regarding the adaptation itself, but, far more importantly, are those who have read and perhaps even revered the original and so frequently come away saying, often at best, "Not bad, but the book was better." Adapting fiction for film under even the best of circumstances is fraught with difficulties and so often a recipe for at least relative failure (again, *"Not bad*, but the book was better"), but as Louis Giannetti writes, "the better the literary work, the more difficult the adaptation" (390). In fact, a wise filmmaker may choose to avoid a work considered by many to be any sort of a literary masterpiece altogether, as "[s]ome commentators believe that if a work of art has reached its fullest artistic expression in one form, an adaptation will inevitably be inferior" (390).

Given the above, even casual readers of Jorge Amado's *A morte e a morte de Quincas Berro Dágua* might well imagine the problems a filmmaker would encounter in bringing this particular work to the screen. Those who have gone so far as to study Amado's short gem, or who have read any of the many essays which address the novella's genius, may even be puzzled that anyone has so much as attempted to adapt it for film. But indeed a film adaptation, directed by Walter Avancini and aired on *Rede Globo,* and seen by few outside of Brazil, has been made, and the results are in many respects, given both the nature of the original and Giannetti's comments above, predictable, even disappointing, though the movie is not at all without its merits. Where the film falls short, however, may not be so much the fault of its production team, and in particular its director, as much as it serves as further testament to Amado's creativity, as well as to the unique qualities of the written word, especially in the hands of a true, albeit underrated, craftsman.

Clearly, the greatest difficulty in adapting *Quincas* to film involves the presentation of the original's ambiguity, which Earl Fitz has rightfully termed the novella's "defining characteristic" (228). As Fitz writes, the work's "uniqueness, indeed, its brilliance, lies in Amado's ability to counterbalance in an unobtrusive fashion events that are mimetically rendered with those that are utterly fantastic in nature" (221). So skillfully intertwined, however, are potential "fact" and potential "fiction" in this story that the reader, though left to make his or her own interpretation of what really happens, can never really be sure of which interpretation of the work's reality would be "correct." The result is an open-ended narrative in which Amado, as Bobby Chamberlain suggests, emphasizes "the relativity of truth" (50). There simply can be no definitive interpretation of what happens in the novella, of what is real and what, if anything, is wholly unreal in Quincas's world due to the ambiguous context of the story and, more importantly, the deliberately ambiguous language in which Amado so brilliantly tells it.

Ambiguity is woven into the fabric of the novella from start to finish, beginning with the story's less than authoritative and clearly second-hand, at best, narrator, who opens his telling of the tale with: "Até hoje permanece certa confusão em torno da morte de Quincas Berro Dágua. Dúvidas por explicar, detalhes absurdos, contradições no depoimento das testemunhas, lacunas diversas. Não há clareza sobre hora, local e frase derradeira" (15) ["A certain amount of confusion about the death of Quincas Wateryell persists even today. There are doubts to be explained away, ridiculous details, contradictory testimony from witnesses, divers gaps in the story. Time, place, and last words are uncertain"] (3). The shaky footing on which the "facts" of the story tread is later exacerbated by the potential influence of spiritualism and excessive room temperature (Quincas's daughter Vanda's encounter with her deceased father[1]), and, much more so, by the increasingly drunken state of Quincas's cronies as the story unfolds and the most ambiguous, and most unusual, to say the least, aspects of the tale are presented.[2] Even the narrator's parting comment concerning Quincas's last words suggests that determining the whole "truth" regarding Quincas's story presents a slippery slope at best: "Quanto à frase derradeira há versões variadas. Mas, quem poderia ouvir direito no meio daquele temporal?" (103) ["As for Quincas's last words, there are several different versions. But who could swear to what he had heard in the middle of a storm like that?"] (97).

At the center of the story's ambiguity, however, clearly, even famously, among the work's readers, is the section that portrays the deceased Quincas's post-mortem activities, the first significant phase of which is his "regeneration" in the company of his four loyal but inebriated friends, Curió, Cabo Martim, Negro Pastinha, and Pé-de-Vento. With his family gone home and Quincas left for the night with these four to watch over his body, the truly magical, truly bizarre, or truly gruesome–depending on one's perhaps evolving interpretation of the narrative–events begin, as the deceased's friends treat him as if he were alive, and perhaps he is; thus, the ambiguity. Cabo Martim, for example, offers Quincas, the corpse, a drink, hoping to win favor from his old friend in the competition to inherit the girlfriend Quincas has left behind. The four cronies pour *cachaça* into Quincas's mouth, but "[e]spalhou-se um pouco pela gola do paletó e o peito da camisa" (85) ["some of [the rum] spilled over his collar and down his shirtfront"] (74). Noticing Quincas's difficulty in drinking lying down, but not for a moment attributing it to his being dead–and again, perhaps he is not, at this point–the four prop him up in his coffin and try again: "Sentaram Quincas no caixão, a cabeça movia-se para um e outro lado. Com a gole de cachaça ampliara-se seu sorriso" (85) ["They adjusted Quincas to a sitting position in the coffin. His head bobbed from one side to the other, and after the swig of rum, his smile grew broader"] (75). Quincas, now "revived," or so it seems, begins to talk, calling his family, "Os homens, uns bestalhões. As mulheres, umas jararacas" (87) ["The men are jackasses and the women are vipers"] (77). He goes on to call a family aunt, Tia Marocas, "[u]m saco de peidos" (87) ["[a] sackful of shit"] (77).

This section also gives the reader a first look at the deliberately ambiguous language that Amado employs to describe a Quincas who could be either alive or dead. For example, following his friends' aborted version of the Lord's Prayer, "Quincas parecia indiferente à rez" (84) ["Quincas listened indifferently to the praying"] (73), while a few pages later, his friends argue over the physical virtues of the aforementioned Tia Marocas, but "Quincas, porém, nem ouvia" (87) ["Quincas was not even listening"] (77).

Both the ambiguous activities and the ambiguous language intensify in the next several pages of the novella, as the four friends venture out with their old and dear friend Quincas, who is either simply dead or "dead drunk," and everything that happens at this point, and the language used to describe it, serves not to clarify which of these two choices is correct for the confused reader, but instead makes choosing between the two virtually impossible. Out in the street, for example, Quincas, supported by his friends, "tentava passar rasteiras no Cabo e no Negro, estendia a língua para os transeuntes, enfiou a cabeça por uma porta para espiar, malicioso, um casal de namorados, pretendia, a cada passo, estirar-se na rua" (93) ["He tried to trip up Martim and the Negro, stuck out his tongue at passersby, put his head into a doorway to peer maliciously at a couple of lovers, and threatened to fall flat in the street at

every step"] (80). Later, someone suggests that it is Quincas's birthday, and
"[n]ão negou Quincas fosse seu anniversário" (94) ["Quincas did not deny
that it was his birthday. . ."] (81). When the people in the street shout to Quincas, "[e]le agradecia com a cabeça, como um rei de volta a seu reino" (96)
["He thanked them with courteous nods of his head to left and right, like a
monarch returning in triumph to his kingdom"] (85–86). Later, during a stopover at Quitéria's house, Quincas lies silently on his girlfriend's bed, before a
disgusted Quitéria announces to the mourners-turned-revelers that "O des-
graçado dormiu" (97) ["Old fool's gone to sleep"] (86).

Due again to Amado's linguistic sleight of hand, Quincas's true condition is not clear even when he helps start and appears to participate in a fight
in a neighborhood bar. Quincas, the corpse or the drunk, and the reader,
again, cannot be sure which, is seated in a chair, his legs fully extended, when
a passer-by angrily orders him to move his legs out of the way. Quincas "fez
que não ouviu" (98) ["Quincas pretended not to hear him"] (88). The passer-
by attacks Quincas and the latter "[d]eu-lhe. . .uma cabeçada, a inana
começou" (98) ["Quincas returned the blow with his head, and the fight was
on"] (88). When calm is restored, Quincas "encontrava-se estendido no chão,
levara uns socos violentos, batera com a cabeça numa laje do passeio" (99)
["he was stretched out unconscious on the floor, having absorbed some violent blows and hit his head on the tiles in the passageway"] (88). His girlfriend Quitéria comforts him with *cachaça*: "Quincas reanimou-se mesmo
foi com um bom trago. Continuava a beber daquela maneira esquisita: cus-
pindo parte da cachaça, num esperdício" (99) ["A good stiff drink finally
brought Quincas around. He still drank in that peculiar way of his, spitting
out part of the rum—a real waste of good liquor"] (89).

Quincas's visit to Mestre Manuel's boat and his subsequent demise there
(this is but one way to account for the two *mortes* in the title) are equally
ambiguous in content, if less consistently so in language than the previous
scenes. The reader is told that Quincas and Quitéria are the only ones not eating but instead lie in the stern of the boat, where Quitéria scolds Quincas for
giving her such a scare. Quincas, however, "[n]ão respondia, aspirava o ar
marítimo, uma de suas mãos tocava a água, abrindo um risco nas ondas"
(101) ["Quincas, breathing in the salt air, gave her no answer. One of his
hands trailed in the water, leaving a wake behind it"] (93). Later, during a
storm, the narrator states: "Ninguém sabe como Quincas se pôs de pé,
encostado à vela menor" (101) ["No one knows to this day how Quincas got
to his feet and leaned against the aftersail"] (93). Soon thereafter, those on
board "viram Quincas atirar-se e ouviram sua frase derradeira" (102) ["they
saw Quincas throw himself overboard and heard his last words"] (96).

In all of the above, Amado, and from start to finish in this work, including the unusual title, as Fitz states, is "acutely aware that language does considerably more in literary art than merely communicate some arbitrary,

conventional set of meanings. He is sensitive to the fact that words, especially as employed in literature, are arranged in such a way as to suggest the possibility of several meanings, all of which are at least potentially applicable to a given set of circumstances" (223). Fitz goes on to state that Amado is "completely in control not only of what he wants to say but, more importantly, how he wants to say it, [and he] preserves the central ambiguity of the action by balancing contrastive but equally 'appropriate' explanations of what is transpiring" (224).

So where does all this leave the artists who wish to adapt *Quincas* for film? With numerous difficulties, certainly. How does one take a story that involves a corpse that may or may not "regenerate" and tell it as ambiguously as Amado's narrator so that the audience is as deliberately confused as the reader, keeping in mind, one would think, that any rendering of the story in which both possible interpretations are not equally viable would not be seen as a faithful presentation of the story, and in fact would be deemed, in all likelihood, as a one-dimensional shell of the original? How, indeed?

The answer is quite simple: the filmmakers do not. In fact, it appears that they do not even attempt to consider, much less present, the ambiguity clearly present in Amado's narrative, and by extension, they do not seem to seek in any way to engender the confusion in their audience that Amado so purposely and skillfully instills in his reader. This does not mean that the filmmakers avoid presenting Qunicas's post-mortem comments and actions, for example, which contribute to the reader's thoughts they he may indeed be alive, but they do so in such a way that there is no question as to Quincas's state as a corpse. Add in the absence of Amado's shaky narrator and, far more importantly, the absence of the author's wonderfully flexible wording, as well as the addition of the audience's ability to see what transpires, and all of the ambiguity, and certainly all of the real genius, of Amado's gem of a novella is removed.

With it clear that Quincas is dead and not even possibly a mysteriously revived drunk, his "regeneration" in the company of his four friends and his last night on the town with them are at best fine examples of the humor that storytellers and filmmakers so often find in the illusions and behavior of drunkenness and at worst simply gruesome. In the film, just as in the original, Cabo Martim, Curió, Negro Pastinha, and Pé-de-Vento volunteer to sit with Quincas's body for the night and following a comically inept attempt at the Lord's Prayer, they begin to talk to their deceased friend, and soon thereafter offer him a drink of their *cachaça*. And just as in the original, Quincas spits it out. In the film, however, the audience can see that Quincas's spitting is not so much the action of a live person but more likely the post-mortem reaction of a dead body. Quincas does not appear to be doing anything in an active sense. The same is true when Quincas's friends prop him up in the coffin and he spits out the *cachaça* a second time. Immediately thereafter Cabo Martim and company begin to undress Quincas and trade their clothes for his, and

Quincas continues to show absolutely no visible sign of life. In fact, the signs he does show are clearly those of a corpse.

Quincas's comments in the company of his friends, concerning every-thing from his family's stinginess to his opinion of Tia Marocas, are, in most cases, faithfully rendered by the filmmakers, even to the point of being word for word in many instances. However, while Amado's text strongly suggests that Quincas actually speaks in the presence of Cabo Martim, Curió, Negro Pastinha and Pé-de-Vento, Quincas's comments in the film version are made by way of flashbacks to when he was alive and well with his friends in the streets of Bahia. His remarks are not something that he appears to be telling them now, but something that he has told them before. This is particularly evident in comments which clearly suggest true dialogue between Quincas and his friends in Amado's original, but which, in the film, have had any ele-ments that might suggest the same removed. At one point, in Amado's text, Quincas calls Marocas "um saco de peidos" (87) ["a sackful of shit"] (77), to which Negro Pastinha responds, "Não diga isso, paizinho. . ." (87) ["Now, Daddy, don't you talk that way."] (77), before going on to point out that he has seen worse. Negro Pastinha's response to essentially the same remark from Quincas in the film is virtually identical to his comments in the novella, except that he does not say "Não diga isso, paizinho," an omission which removes support for the notion of interactive communication between the two, and, given other aspects of the presentation of Quincas here and else-where in the film, it is almost certainly an intentional omission on the part of the filmmakers. While Amado deliberately leaves the door open for his reader to interpret Quincas's comments as being spoken in the presence of his friends, or at least in their *cachaça*-addled minds, the film makes it rather obvious that the comments do not come from a regenerated Quincas, but from his past life. Add in the visual cues available to the audience, and the story the film is telling is already beginning to be far different from the one, or more accurately, the *ones*, being offered to the reader at this point in the original.

Quincas's state as a corpse is even more obvious in the film when he and his friends move into the street. While Amado's use of language in the origi-nal, as previously demonstrated, does a wonderful job of suggesting, at least, an active Quincas in the events that unfold, the film is limited to showing a Quincas who looks and acts like a dead man, rather than someone who is merely "dead drunk." Amado, for example, brilliantly suggests that Quincas tries to trip his friends and deliberately sticks his tongue out as they move through the street, but the film's audience clearly sees a corpse being carried around by his drunken pals, his tongue involuntarily hanging out. The film also loses passive ambiguous acts on the part of Quincas such as when, in the original, the protagonist does not deny that it is his birthday. The film goes beyond this, however, and, perhaps surprisingly, even promotes Quincas as a corpse in scenes such as those in which his state as such seems deliberately emphasized. Amado's narrative, for example, states that Quincas lies silently on Quitéria's bed before she tells everyone that he has fallen asleep. In the film, however, she holds him up, her arm around him, as she talks to him. When she lets go, he flops, clearly corpse-like, on the bed, and there can be no doubt, if there ever has been in the film to this point, that Quincas is and remains dead.

The highly ambiguous bar fight scene from the original is, again, anything but ambiguous in the film. While the action, once again, follows the novella very closely indeed, and the dialogue is almost word for word throughout, there, again, is no question that Quincas is deceased. Even the scene's elongated, slow-motion presentation of Quincas spinning around, arms outstretched, in the middle of the melee, does not suggest a miraculously revived body, but a body thrown into involuntary action by the physical circumstances in which it finds itself. And once again, the filmmakers are forced to present the scene without the benefit of Amado's creative use of language (Quincas, we remember, "pretended not to hear" when the angry passer-by tells him to move his legs) which would lift the scene out of its one-dimensional presentation.

Quincas's arrival at Mestre Manuel's boat, hanging on the shoulders of his friends, is another scene in the film which accentuates his status as a corpse to the audience, and it is not included in Amado's narrative, suggesting, once again, that the filmmakers may, in fact, deliberately choose to present Quincas as dead, even to the point of emphasizing the fact so that there be no doubt (though certainly among those who only see the film and have not read the novella, there can indeed be no doubt). As in the original, Quincas lies in the stern of the boat with Quitéria, and once again, her words to him are essentially word for word those which she speaks in the narrative. Once again, however, the film does not benefit from Amado's double-jointed description which states that Quincas gave no answer, suggesting, at least, that he could have answered, but did not. In the film, the audience simply sees Quincas lying there, speechless, and clearly with good reason. How Quincas gets to his feet and stands against the aftersail in the film is as mysterious as it is in the narrative (and some might rightfully consider this gap of narration in the original, after such a carefully and masterfully worded text, a flaw, and perhaps the only one, in Amado's original text). There is ample and vivid presentation of a violent, boat-rocking storm, that, in fact better than Amado's narrative, presents a scenario which might explain how a dead Quincas could get in the position he does prior to diving or falling into the sea. At any rate, the audience sees Quincas, white-faced in the darkness, against the mast, before he is tossed overboard. The film carries a voice-over of Quincas's last words, but it is clear from the presentation of Quincas falling into the water, that he does not speak them, as suggested in the novella.

Clearly, the work presented by Avancini and company is Amado's *Quincas* in surface plot only, though quite faithfully, at that level. The theme identified by Chamberlain as the "relativity of truth," and the famously ambiguous context and language, the "defining characteristic," according to Fitz, which supports said theme, have been left out completely. The "blame" for this omission lies in part with the filmmakers, who have chosen not to present or in any way recognize the original's central ambiguity (though they have had to choose one of the novella's possible interpretations over the other, and they have chosen the more realistic one), but it also lies, again in part, with the limitations of their medium. Their audience can see, while Amado's reader cannot. Even more importantly, however, Amado's reader has the marked advantage of the author's ingenious use of language, and the film's audience misses out on that entirely, and it is this use of language, in particular, that makes the original such a skillfully crafted and thematic literary gem. This speaks less, however, to the limitations of the visual medium with which the filmmakers have to work and much more, once again, to Amado's creativity and, as Fitz calls it, his "finesse as a novelist" (228), underrated though it too often is.

All of the above is not to say that the film version of *Quincas* is without merit. In fact, quite the contrary is the case. As previously discussed, the film presents a very faithful rendering of the original's plot, as well as much of its dialogue. It also does a wonderful job of capturing the street world of *Quincas*, through, for example, location shooting, masterful casting throughout, and the music that permeates the film from start to finish (the use of two types of music, for example, one earthy and Brazilian, the other quite sophisticated and European, to portray the contrast between Quincas's friends and his family at the vigil is one of the highlights of the film). The decisions made in these and other areas by the filmmakers make the film entertaining indeed, and in some instances even more vivid in its portrayal of the story than the original, due in large part, this time, to the limitations of Amado's medium (Amado, for example, cannot use music in any way even approaching the way it is used for effect in the film).

The film version of *A morte e a morte de Quincas Berro Dágua* stands as vivid testimony to Jorge Amado's skill as a writer in general and, in particular, to his masterful use of ambiguity, via both action and language, in this memorable novella. The film may also demonstrate what many readers of *Quincas* already knew, that the story, to quote Giannetti again, had already "reached its fullest artistic expression" in the original. Still, in spite of its significant shortcomings in the critical area of ambiguity, the film deserves praise in other areas, and would almost certainly satisfy those who have not read the original *Quincas*. Amado's readers, however, might be hard pressed to say anything more complementary than, "Not bad, but the book was better."

**NOTES**

1. See Silverman for a discussion of Vanda's encounter with the deceased Quincas.
2. See Brower for a study of the role of alcohol in *Quincas*.

**BIBLIOGRAPHY**

Amado, Jorge. *A morte e a morte de Quincas Berro Dágua.* 56ª ed. Rio de Janeiro: Record, 1985.

————. *A morte e a morte de Quincas Berro Dágua.* Adapt. James Amado and Walter Avancini. Dir. Walter Avancini. Prod. Nilton Capello. Rede Globo, n.d.

————. *The Two Deaths of Quincas Wateryell.* Trans. Barbara Shelby. New York: Avon, 1980.

Brower, Keith H. "Alcohol as the Comedic Catalyst in Jorge Amado's *A morte e a morte de Quincas Berro Dágua.*" *Mester* 24:1 (1995): 185–196.

Chamberlain, Bobby J. *Jorge Amado.* Boston: Twayne, 1990.

Fitz, Earl E. "Structural Ambiguity in Jorge Amado's *A morte e a morte de Quincas Berro Dágua.*" *Hispania* 67 (1984): 221–228.

Giannetti, Louis. *Understanding Movies.* 8th ed. Upper Saddle River, NJ: Prentice Hall, 1999.

Silverman, Malcolm. "Duality in Jorge Amado's *The Two Deaths of Quincas Wateryell.*" *Studies in Short Fiction* 15 (1978): 96–199.

# Striking a Balance
## Amado and the Critics*

BOBBY J. CHAMBERLAIN

I. It has always seemed rather odd to me that among critics of Brazilian literature there is scant middle ground when it comes to appraising the fiction of
Jorge Amado. Brazilian and Brazilianist literary scholars, with few exceptions, have tended to divide neatly into one of two opposing camps—defend-
ers of the author and his detractors—as if the Manichaeanism so prominent in
the early characterization techniques of the analysand had somehow managed
to return and infect the analysts themselves. While it is not my intention here
to attempt to explain this phenomenon—my own research has moved on to
other areas—I should like in the following paragraphs to revisit what I regard
as the strengths and weaknesses of Amadian fiction in an effort to encourage
a more balanced assessment of the author's literary production. A brief,
diachronic review of the salient features of his works will provide a point of
departure.

II. On balance, it seems to me that Amado's oeuvre has changed considerably
over the last sixty-five years. This, despite a number of undeniable continu-
ities. The early novels and novelettes were marked by social consciousness
and often by strong political commitment. At first, they sought to document
and denounce societal injustices at the expense of "literary" concerns (*Cacau*
1933; *Suor*, 1934). In a preliminary note to *Cacau*, Amado explained: "Tentei
contar neste livro, com um mínimo de literatura para um máximo de honesti-
dade, a vida dos trabalhadores das fazendas de cacau do sul da Bahia. Será
um romance proletário?" ["I have attempted to recount in this book, with a
minimum of literature for a maximum of honesty, the lives of the workers on
the cacao plantations of southern Bahia state. Could this be a proletarian
novel?"][1] Moreover, characters were usually of a single piece; virtue and vice
were meted out according to a character's class affiliations. Protagonists were
styled as proletarian heroes who rebelled against their ruling-class oppres-

sors. Strikes and other popular uprisings were a fixture of such works (*Suor*; *Jubiabá*, 1935 [Eng. trans. 1984]; *Mar morto*, 1936 [*Sea of Death*, 1984]).

As the author matured, greater emphasis was placed on aesthetics. Popular culture and Afro-Bahian religious ritual were deftly woven into the novelistic text (*Jubiabá; Mar morto*), though many of the erstwhile narrative techniques were retained. Amado became known not only for the crudity of his scenes and dialogues but also for the lyricism of much of his prose (*Mar morto; Capitães da areia*, 1937 [*Captains of the Sands*, 1988]). Political sermonizing gave way to greater detachment; caricature replaced invective. Characters, both poor and rich, were shown to be victims of economic and historical forces beyond their control (*Terras do sem fim*, 1943 [*The Violent Land*, 1945]; *São Jorge dos Ilhéus*, 1944). But, still, many of the author's initial concerns and traits persisted, while a number of his earlier excesses continued to predominate from time to time (*São Jorge dos Ilhéus; Seara vermelha*, 1946; *Os subterrâneos da liberdade*, 1954).

Some saw in *Gabriela, cravo e canela* (1958) [*Gabriela, Clove and Cinnamon*, 1962] the appearance of a "new Amado,"[2] divorced from socialist realism and dedicated to the cultivation of a kind of picaresque humor. According to this view, the novelist had turned his back on Marxist ideology altogether, supplanting it with a commitment either to greater objectivity or to hedonism and bourgeois values. The particular assessment depended upon the critic's political leanings. Others, while conceding the transformation of Amado's "style," were not as convinced of his ideological metanoia. They acknowledged that the novelist seemed to have veered away from prescriptive socialist realism, but regarded *Gabriela* more as a switch of tactics than as a wholesale retreat from a leftist worldview. Whatever their opinions of the change, however, most scholars were in agreement that *Gabriela* represented a watershed in the author's literary development. With the publication of each subsequent work, this view seemed to gain increased currency. There was, to be sure, no shortage of social criticism in these novels. But, much of it could best be described as satire rather than polemic. Nor was there a dearth of lyricism, coarseness, violence, caricature, folk culture, or Afro-Bahian religious ritual. If anything, there was an intensification of such elements in all or some of the books. Yet, virtually everything was suffused with humor and irony, to the point that it was sometimes difficult to tell just where the author's sympathies lay.

But, if humor was the key to this new phase, it could not be regarded as being exclusive to it. Caricature had long been one of the mainstays of Amadian fiction. So too had other forms of comical overstatement, as well as such occasional phenomena as sarcasm, class humor, playful anecdotes, and ribaldry. What there was, then, was a proliferation of such techniques. To the comical overstatement of the earlier works was added ironic understatement. This was evident both in the author's greater use of verbal irony and in the increased incidence of incongruous juxtapositions. Among the other humorous and ironic devices that became hallmarks of the "new" Amado were wordplay, parody, pastiche, double perspective, the ironic narrator, the introduction of *roman à clef* characters, and the intervention of the supernatural.

The cultivation of satirical humor in *Gabriela* and subsequent Amadian novels reveals a strong preference for carnivalization of social injustice and struggle as opposed to the earlier denunciatory textual strategies. Lengthy, archaizing chapter and section titles punctuate many of the works. The title of section one of *Gabriela* reads:

> Aventuras e Desventuras de um Bom Brasileiro (Nascido na Síria) na Cidade de Ilhéus, em 1925, Quando Florescia o Cacau e Imperava o Progresso—Com Amores, Assassinatos, Banquetes, Presépios, Histórias Varias para Todos os Gostos, um Remoto Passado Glorioso de Nobres Soberbos e Salafrários, um Recente Passado de Fazendeiros Ricos e Afamados Jagunços, com Solidão e Suspiros, Desejo, Vingança, Ódio, com Chuvas e Sol e com Luar, Leis Inflexíveis, Manobras Políticas, o Apaixonante Caso da Barra, com Prestidigitador, Dançarina, Milagre e Outras Mágicas ou Um Brasileiro das Arábias"

> ["Adventures and Misadventures of a Good Brazilian (Born in Syria), All in the Town of Ilhéus in 1925, When Cacao Flourished and Progress Reigned, with Love Affairs, Murders, Banquets, Crèches, Divers Stories for All Tastes, a Remote and Glorious Past of Proud Seigneurs and Rogues, a More Recent Past of Rich Plantation Owners and Notorious Assassins, with Loneliness and Sighs, Desire, Hatred, Vengeance, with Rain and Sun and Moonlight, Inflexible Laws, Political Maneuvers, Controversy about a Sandbar, with Miracle Danceress, Prestidigitator, and Other Wonders or A Brazilian from the Arabies"]. (*Gabriela* 21)[3]

Typical of the equally parodic chapter titles of this phase are such captions as "De como Nacib contratou uma cozinheira ou dos complicados caminhos do amor" ["Of the intricate ways of love, or how Nacib hired a cook"] (*Gabriela* 152) and "Onde se trata de aposentados e retirados dos negócios, com mulheres na praia e na cama, donzelas em fuga, ruína e suicídio, e um cachimbo de espuma do mar" ["Which deals with retired government employees and businessmen, women on the beach and in bed, runaway damsels, ruin and suicide, and a meerschaum pipe"] (*Os velhos marinheiros* 85).[4]

Textual lists, reminiscent of catalogues, often appear in the body of these works. Employing incongruous juxtapositions, they tend to homogenize disparate elements as if to disrupt the normal hierarchies of the workaday world. One such piece of enumerative patchwork, appearing on the first page of chapter one of *Gabriela*, relates some of the sundry manifestations of the Bahian cacao-growing region's newfound wealth. From greater educational opportunities to larger houses, costlier furniture, better-stocked retail shops and burgeoning commerce, it quickly moves on to such telling growth indicators as booming nightclubs, increased drinking and gambling, and a mounting influx of females—"o progresso enfim, a tão falada civilização" [Progress at last, to such highly touted civilization] (p.25).[5] Another passage, commenting on the rapidity with which newcomers tend to assimilate the region's deep-rooted customs, facetiously opposes such actions as clearing wilderness, planting fields and cutting roads with gambling, frequenting bars and killing one's adversaries as if there were some kind of moral equivalency between the two modes of behavior (56).[6] Still another technique may be seen in *Gabriela* in the description of an elaborate Nativity scene (73–80).[7] Here, alongside the figures of Mary, Joseph, the Christ child, and others traditionally associated with this holiest of Christian scenes, there appear contemporary monarchs and statesmen from around the world, Brazilian inventors, Brazilian and European intellectuals, famous bandits and revolutionaries, matinee idols and scantily clad American movie actresses. Once again, an ironic leveling effect is produced by the pastiche.

Over the years, the novelist's increased use of irony, wordplay and incongruous juxtaposition, besides lending greater playfulness and irreverence to his fiction, has served to call into question the dogmatism of both political ideologies and religions. In particular, the various forms of irony have contributed to a relativization of novelistic truth as Amado has gone from a class-bound, black-or-white mode of characterization to one dominated by various shades of gray. In *A morte e a morte de Quincas Berro D'água* (1959) [*The Two Deaths of Quincas Wateryell*] (1965) and *Os velhos marinheiros ou o capitão de longo curso* (1961) [*Home Is the Sailor*] (1964), double perspective is used to fashion such a climate of uncertainty (Chamberlain 50–55). In *Tereza Batista cansada de guerra* (1972) [*Tereza Batista: Home from the Wars*] (1975), the author's utilization of multiple, unreliable narrators serves to achieve a similar effect. To the degree that such devices have become a commonplace feature of Amado's novels, the latter may be seen as having replaced an essentially monologic narrative discourse with greater dialogism, to use Bakhtinian terms.

Like irony, incongruous juxtaposition, and double perspective, the introduction of real-life characters and the intercession of Afro-Bahian divinities in *Dona Flor e seus dois maridos* (1966) [*Dona Flor and Her Two Husbands* (1969) and several of the other later novels have helped to variegate the fictional universe. Through a series of clever displacements, characters *à clef* have themselves been juxtaposed incongruously with fictional personages, thus producing a kind of homogenization of fact and fantasy, in which the boundaries of each are playfully expunged (Chamberlain 70–80). Much the same thing can be said of the anthropomorphic Yoruban gods, who are often reminiscent of their mischievous Graeco-Roman or Nordic counterparts. Their very presence in Amado's later novels, beside fictional and real-life figures, has resulted in an expansion of the narrow confines of the empirical world, which several critics have identified with "magic realism." By their roguishness, they are drawn ever more closely to the picaresque anti-heroes that Amado is wont to portray. Furthermore, insofar as they intervene in human affairs in the manner of *deus ex machina*, the author's supernatural characters, whose existence he regards as more metaphorical than real, perform a wish-fulfillment function, ironically reaffirming the necessity for the dispossessed themselves to redress social abuses, given the unlikelihood of religious or political relief (Chamberlain 80–84).

We might also mention the role of parody or pastiche in *Gabriela* (the chronicle), *Quincas* (the Gospels), *Tereza Batista* (literatura de cordel [popular chapbook verse]), and, to a lesser extent, *Dona Flor* (recipes and menus). It seems to me that Amado has used parody proper as well as pastiche and stylization of other genres and works in many of these novels. It appears, moreover, that his purposes in so doing have not always been the same, that they have varied from one book to another. To the degree that he has maintained a certain critical distance, Amado has engaged in parody as a means of satirizing a particular genre, such as the Renaissance crônica or the contemporary literatura de cordel (Chamberlain 33–37, 88–91; Curran). Besides mocking some of the most visible characteristics of these genres, he has sometimes used the technique to effect irreverent twists upon the plot formulas traditionally associated with them. The stylistic appropriation of the camp trappings of these literary forms has also allowed him to claim exemption from some of the criteria we normally use in reading novels. This, despite the fact that his facetious identification with the appropriated genres is never more than partial. There is likewise often an ironic dimension to such imitation insofar as the novel's everyday characters and actions may be seen to contrast markedly with the lofty, mock-heroic or mock-exotic trappings appropriated.

One might also cite the occasional metafictional and self-deprecatory roles of parody in *Tereza Batista*. In *Quincas*, however, the author's use of ironic pastiche would appear to be aimed not so much at the Gospels or the events therein recounted, although it does indeed have the effect of questioning religious dogmatism. *Quincas* is rather primarily a pre-figurative tale that makes use of a submerged Passion symbolism and carnivalization techniques as a means of irreverently satirizing contemporary class ethoi (Sant'Anna). But, in *Dona Flor*, the menus and culinary formulas would seem to function more as class indicators and enhancers of the overall sensuality of the narrative than as a vehicle for the lampooning of cookbooks.

III. In recent years, Amado has increasingly become the target of criticism by younger Brazilian and non-Brazilian literary scholars. The principal allegations involve such things as naïve populism and the consequent romanticization of poverty, sexual and racial stereotyping, inordinate prolixity and repetition of episodes and characters, pandering to the values of the marketplace, and failure to break away from timeworn nineteenth-century narrative models. Far from superseding earlier criticisms, such accusations have often been coupled with renewed charges of pornography and Manichaean characterization, albeit from different quarters. Several of these assertions would indeed seem to be borne out to one degree or another by my own reading of Amado. Others would not. A brief look at the issue would seem to be in order.

There is no denying the long-windedness of Amado's narrative style. Unamuno's well-known characterization of writers as being either oviparous or viviparous would undoubtedly include the Bahian novelist in the latter category. Part of his reputation as a storyteller has always been based on his reported habit of composing his novels on a typewriter without previous drafts and with little or no subsequent revision. Never at ease with the lean prose style of a Ramos or a Hemingway, Amado seems to have turned to parody of bygone and popular genres, starting with *Gabriela*, in a deliberate attempt to make a virtue of necessity. He appears indeed to have strengthened his traditional reliance on verbal excess in the process, at times fairly reveling in the discursiveness of his narrators as if to reaffirm his own affiliations with the Latin oratorical tradition or Bahian baroque aesthetics. Nor is there any doubt that the author has frequently appropriated earlier episodes and characters for use in subsequent novels. He has openly admitted to having reprised several strike scenes, for instance, simply to see how his previous treatment of them would be altered by greater infusions of humor and farce.

Whether such practices should be regarded as defects, however, is another matter. In his monograph on João Guimarães Rosa, Jon Vincent has labeled the various features of traditional regionalist fiction present in *Sagarana* (1946) as "deceptive simplicities," which, he feels, tend to obscure the underlying complexities of the work (Vincent 17). Notwithstanding the myriad differences between the fiction of Rosa and Amado, much the same thing can be said, I believe, of many of the latter's mature novels. The leisurely verbosity of the narrative style, the presence of chatty, bumbling narrators, the tongue-in-cheek imitation of older and popular literature, and, yes, the author's recourse to superannuated literary models often belie the fundamental sophistication of the works. Critics are wont to take the wordiness and trite formulas at face value without penetrating their inherent "double-voicedness." They see in Amado's imitation of popular genres an attempt at mystification, but fail to notice the demystifying subtext. The novelist's propensity to caricature and his neo-romantic identification with the Brazilian masses are cited as proof of his literary naïveté. But his desacralization of canonical discourses and the perspicacity of his social satire frequently escape detection.

This is not to say that all such criticisms are invalid, only that they have sometimes been shortsighted or overdone. Indeed, as we noted above, several of the most frequent allegations seem to be at least partially substantiated by a close reading of the works. Such is the case of sexual and racial stereotyping. For, despite the author's emphasis on women's emancipation in *Gabriela* and despite his portrayal of some strong female figures, such as Malvina and Ofenísia, the novel's protagonist is eminently stereotypical. Gabriela may not be the traditional passive female character. Nor can she be said to represent the only paradigm on which the novelist has fashioned his *mulata* figures. But, perhaps more than any other female personage in modern Brazilian literature, she incarnates the quintessential "exotic mulata," often touted as the sexual ideal of Brazilian white males (Queiroz Júnior, Brookshaw).[8] Not that strong-willed or unstereotyped women characters are in short supply in Amado's fiction. Many are to be found as early as *Mar morto* (Rosa Palmeirão) and *Terras do sem fim* (Don'Ana Badaró, Raimunda). But they are joined by a sizable number of golden-hearted prostitutes and mulata caricatures, who sometimes seem to be more a projection of the author's male ego than a reflection of the empirical world. Amado's record on racial and female characterization is thus a checkered one.

One can also point to the novelist's populism as something that leaves ample room for criticism. The increased use of irony for characterization purposes since *Gabriela* may have mitigated a strict class-line distribution of virtue, endowing the text with greater pluralism and discursive relativity. But it has not eliminated the author's identification with the poor altogether. On the contrary. Much of the irony employed is of the stable variety, in which the "author's meaning" is clearly discernible rather than concealed. One need only look at *Quincas, Dona Flor*, or *Tereza Batista* to confirm the novelist's partiality in this regard. On the other hand, to adduce what is clearly a sentimental and perhaps naïve neo-romantic populism as evidence of the novelist's justification of poverty, superstition, and underdevelopment strikes me as far-fetched and disingenuous (Galvão; Patai 11–40).

There is likewise something to be said for the notion that Amado's later fiction persists in the "closed," authoritarian molds of the nineteenth-century novel, often leaving little for the reader to supply.[9] Some critics have attributed this tendency, along with the novelist's continued insistence on sex and violence, to his catering to the values of the marketplace (e.g., Santiago). Implicit in them is the suggestion that by so doing he has compromised his literary integrity, preferring a quick profit over aesthetic quality. It seems to me that further examination of this topic, as it relates to Amado and others, is appropriate and might indeed yield valuable insights.

Such an in-depth inquiry is beyond the purview of the present essay. Suffice it to say here that Amado's case seems to me to be strikingly similar to those of several well-known Brazilian leftist playwrights who in recent years have forsaken the stage to write television soap operas.[10] There is no denying the fact that such mass-media productions are considerably more lucrative to the author. Yet, their audience impact is also vastly larger, thus investing the writer with greater potential to shape the opinions of a larger number of people, albeit within the inevitable ideological constraints imposed by the owners of the medium. There is no doubt that Amado, like these writers, must pay a price in order to gain access to such a mass audience. There are compromises to be made, both stylistic and ideological. The question is just how far one can go without compromising basic principles. To what degree is the writer using the "culture industry" rather than being used by it?

IV. Brazilian cultural critic and sociologist Roberto DaMatta has detected in *Dona Flor* and other latter-day Amadian novels a "triadic" structure, in which the writer's attempt to conciliate polar opposites leads to a third, synthetic position, one which itself assumes a positive value rather than being regarded as something "monstrous" or "grotesque" (DaMatta). Examples of this may be seen not only in Dona Flor's ultimate refusal to choose between her two husbands but also in the dénouements of such works as *Gabriela, Quincas* and *Os velhos marinheiros*. In DaMatta's opinion, it is this triadic structure that most differentiates the novelist's later works from those published prior to 1958, which he considers to be dualistic and ultimately monologic. He goes on to associate this tendency towards reconciliation with such traditional Brazilian institutions as the *jeitinho* (finding a solution), moderation, and the concession of personal favors, which are themselves grounded on a "relational" or integrational ethic. Unlike Anglo-Americans, with their passion for conflict, dichotomy, and separation, Brazilians have historically hybridized everything from their racial configuration to their culture and religious beliefs, he claims. And it is this basic precept that Amado has recognized by structuring his later novels so as to emphasize the relational element.

What this seems to imply, to my way of thinking, is that Amado has somehow hit upon the "hidden formula" on which much of Brazilian culture and civilization have been shaped, the weaving of thesis and antithesis into some sort of felicitous or harmonious synthetic blend. If, in fact, this is an accurate reading of DaMatta's assertion, I would agree with it only up to a point, however. Insofar as it acknowledges the signal importance of hybridization and relationality in both Brazilian society and the novelist's later fiction, it is an astute observation, one that most other critics have failed to detect. Imported hierarchies have, indeed, often been tampered with throughout Brazilian history through a process of "cannibalization," bricolage, or what Bakhtin referred to as "carnivalistic mésalliances" (Bakhtin 123). Whatever their provenance, racial, religious and other cultural categories have likewise tended to be relativized, nuanced or finessed rather than being expressed in discrete, air-tight terms. Moreover, Amado seems to have grasped these truths and incorporated them into the texture of his later narrative.

Yet, to the degree that both DaMatta and Amado may be read as failing to take into account the retention or creation of other, strict, often reinforced albeit unspoken hierarchies within this relational process—the inevitable contradictions and lack of finality inherent in any synthesis—their pronouncements may be questioned. All the more so if this relationalism is understood to constitute the only valid form of Brazilianness to the exclusion of all others (i.e., essentialism). That Brazilian culture has often made use of this triadic process, sometimes as a means of finessing what Roberto Schwarz has referred to as imported *idéias fora do lugar* ("misplaced ideas") (Schwarz 13–60), should not be interpreted as implying that the resulting syntheses have been peaceful or in any way democratic. To do so would be tantamount to conceding the validity of Freyre's well-known contention that Brazil has largely solved its racial problems through the process of miscegenation. Common as they are in Brazilian history, synthesis, syncretization and hybridization, whatever social, racial and aesthetic distinctions they may have disrupted, have never been free of the notion of hierarchy altogether. To be sure, the fusion of three "sad races" has always displayed a pronounced verticalism.

V. How, then, best to weigh the foregoing observations in order to arrive at a more equitable assessment of the the author's fiction, or at least one that will avoid the largely black-or-white evaluation that has heretofore prevailed? There is no easy answer. Of course, not every Brazilian literary scholar will agree with my initial observation regarding critical Manichaeanism or on the necessity to take another, fresh look at Amado's writings. Nor will all of them concur with the aforementioned analysis. Some may prefer to ignore the novelist's shortcomings or else to deny the literary value of his works (at least after *Terras do sem fim*) while perhaps conceding the importance of his role in opening up international literary markets to younger Brazilian authors. Such positions are probably comfortable to a segment of critics, but others may wish to reconsider their opinions. What is more, there is obviously no single, preferred formula for comparing an author's strengths and weaknesses in order to achieve an equitable appraisal. There is always, as there should be, a subjective element that is grounded in the critic's own aesthetic and ideological persuasions.

No doubt, there are other, perhaps better ways of attempting to account for the multiple dimensions of Amado's fiction. The preceding analysis should be viewed as but one among many potential methods of striking a critical balance, and, as such, it should be regarded as subjective and incomplete.

Amado's novels are, after all, frequently marked by irresolvable oxymorons and troubling perplexities. Attitudes and sympathies are sometimes seemingly contradictory, while the ideology of the text often appears to undercut itself. A reevaluation of his literary output is urgently needed, one that will cut through the lingering polemic that has long hampered a more complex appraisal.

## NOTES

\* The present essay is an adaptation and expansion of the final chapter of my *Jorge Amado*. Twayne World Authors Series 767. Boston: Twayne, 1990.

1. Translation and emphasis by the author.
2. The label is employed by Elizabeth Schlomann Lowe in a 1969 article published in the *Luso-Brazilian Review* (Lowe).
3. Jorge Amado, *Gabriela, Clove and Cinnamon*, trans. James L. Taylor and William L. Grossman. New York: Knopf, 1962, 3.
4. Amado, *Gabriela, Clove and Cinnamon* , 129. Amado, *Home Is the Sailor*, trans. Harriet de Onís. New York: Avon, 1979, 27.
5. *Gabriela, Clove and Cinnamon*, 5.
6. *Gabriela, Clove and Cinnamon*, 35.
7. *Gabriela, Clove and Cinnamon*, 53–59.
8. It should be noted that, despite her portrayal by Sônia Braga in the 1976 motion picture of the same name, the well-known protagonist of *Dona Flor e seus dois maridos,* unlike Gabriela, is nowhere described as a mulata, but rather as a brunette. This, of course, is not the only point on which critics of the novelist's fiction have sometimes been influenced more in their comments by the subsequent films than by the books on which they were based. Amado has often been criticized, too, for his alleged subscription to the outmoded Freyrian view of Brazil as a "racial democracy." In light of his denunciation of Brazilian racism in *Tenda dos milagres* (1969) and elsewhere, however, the notion would seem to be no more than an ideal to him, one to which all Brazilians should aspire.
9. Flora Süssekind carries the argument a step further, branding Amado's *Tocaia Grande* (1984) as essentialist, a "romance que se crê História" (a novel that fancies itself as History), a "romance de fundação" (foundational novel) of the type that argues for a cohesive, univocal, contradiction-free interpretation of what it means to be a Brazilian (Süssekind 82).
10. The most notable playwright to have done so is Alfredo Dias Gomes, a self-proclaimed Marxist, who has asserted that television has now become the theater of the masses.

# BIBLIOGRAPHY

Amado, Jorge. *Gabriela, cravo e canela: Crônica de uma cidade do interior.* 29th ed. São Paulo: Martins, 1966.

————. *Os velhos marinheiros: Duas histórias do cais da Bahia.* 17th ed. São Paulo: Martins, 1967.

Bakhtin, Mikhail. Problems of Dostoevsky's Poetics, trans. Caryl Emerson. Minneapolis: University of Minnesota Press, 1984.

Brookshaw, David. *Race and Color in Brazilian Literature.* Metuchen, N.J.: Scarecrow, 1986.

Chamberlain, Bobby J. *Jorge Amado.* Twayne World Authors Series 767. Boston: Twayne, 1990.

Curran, Mark J. *Jorge Amado e a literatura de cordel.* Salvador: Universidade Federal da Bahia, 1981.

DaMatta, Roberto. "Dona Flor e seus dois maridos: Um romance relacional," *Tempo Brasileiro* 74: Jorge Amado, KM 70 (July-September 1983): 3–33.

Galvão, Walnice Nogueira. "Amado: Respeitoso, respeitável," in *Saco de gatos: Ensaios críticos.* São Paulo: Duas Cidades, 1976. pp. 13–22.

Lowe, Elizabeth Schlomann. "The 'New' Jorge Amado," *Luso-Brazilian Review,* 6,2 (December 1969): 73–82.

Patai, Daphne. *Myth and Ideology in Contemporary Brazilian Literature.* Rutherford, N.J.: Fairleigh Dickinson University Press, 1983.

Queiroz Júnior, Teófilo de. *Preconceito de cor e a mulata brasileira.* São Paulo: Ática, 1975.

Sant'Anna, Affonso Romano de. "De como e porque Jorge Amado em *A morte e a morte de Quincas Berro D'água* é um autor carnavalizador, mesmo sem nunca ter-se preocupado com isso," *Tempo Brasileiro* 74: Jorge Amado, KM 70 (July-September 1983): 45–65.

Santiago, Silviano. "O teorema de Walnice e a sua recíproca," in *Vale quanto pesa.* Rio de Janeiro: Paz e Terra, 1982. pp. 69–88.

Schwarz, Roberto. *Ao vencedor as batatas.* São Paulo: Duas Cidades, 1977.

Süssekind, Flora. "Ficção 80: Dobradiças e vitrines," *Revista do Brasil* 2,5 (1986): 82–89.

Vincent, Jon S. *João Guimarães Rosa.* Twayne World Authors Series 506. Boston: Twayne, 1978.

# Gabriela, Clove and Cinnamon
## Rewriting the Discourse of the Native

JOANNA COURTEAU

Jorge Amado's novel, *Gabriela, cravo e canela* [*Gabriela, Clove and Cinnamon*] (1958), marks a new beginning in his creative production. It also seals Amado's falling out of favor with the communist party because it fails to denounce openly the evils of the capitalist system. Yet, Amado, who himself acknowledges a new direction in his literary production, vehemently denies that with this novel he has stopped caring about people. Amado's defense is summarized by Itazil Benício dos Santos in *Retrato incompleto* (1993),

> It shows in action . . . people of all classes—the rich and the poor, the good and the bad, colonels, cacau producers, exporters of cacau, political bosses. . . . in short, 'all elements of life' are contained herein, with the center of the narrative being occupied by the figure of Gabriela. (164)

In a passage on *Gabriela, Clove and Cinnamon* in the book *Jorge Amado* (1991), Bobby Chamberlain confirms Amado's continued preoccupation with people by characterizing *Gabriela* as a catalogue of "all elements of life." He ascribes the change that we perceive in this novel to Amado's use of humor and parody, which are especially evident in the ironic juxtaposition of incongruous elements. As a prime example of this juxtaposition Chamberlain cites the Nativity scene of the Dos Reis sisters, which, in addition to the traditional crèche characters, features such more recent secular celebrities as Zola and Dreyfus, Lenin and Dom Pedro II, Lillian Gish and Charlie Chaplin, etc. Chamberlain observes that, in addition to the socially levelling effect, this ironic juxtaposition "seems . . . to provide not only an index to sui generis tableau, but also, in microcosm, to Ilhéus, Bahía, Brazil and the world itself" (31). Other examples in this "enumerative patchwork," such as the continuous lively action and the cast of characters, which, in the wake of progress, have overtaken Ilhéus, have convinced Chamberlain that Amado not only cares about people but approves of all these manifestations of life and progress.

By mingling these incompatible elements under the irreproachable umbrella of progress, the novelist jokingly gives the impression that he is placing his stamp of approval on whatever changes may flow from the capitalistic cornucopia, irrespective of their possible deleterious social effects (32), which is paramount to saying that the book indeed lacks a scathing critique of the capitalist system.

In the conclusion to *Jorge Amado*, Chamberlain accepts the anthropologist Roberto DaMatta's explanation that it is Amado's ability to reconcile polar opposites by means of a synthetic third position which sets *Gabriela* and other post-1958 novels apart from the rest of his immense opus.

In DaMatta's opinion, it is this triadic structure that most differentiates the novelist's later works from those published prior to 1958, which he considers to be dualistic and ultimately monologic. He goes on to associate this tendency toward reconciliation with such traditional Brazilian institutions as the *jeitinho* (finding a solution), moderation, and the concessions of personal favors, which are themselves grounded on a "relational" or integrational ethic (102).

While I agree with critics' perception of *Gabriela* as a watershed novel, which through a complex parodic structure manages to reconcile polar opposites, to *dar um jeitinho* (to fix something or a situation somehow) where no conciliation seems possible, I do believe that the above perceptions of humor, variety and *jeitinho* may still lead to another, an altogether different reading. I would like to propose that by pursuing further Chamberlain's perception of the *presépio* (Nativity scene) as a microcosm of Brazil, if not the world, it is possible to show that what Amado achieves through this novel is a complete reframing of Brazilian national discourse. In such a reading the paragraph on the *presépio* functions as a structuring device for the whole novel, for it is capable of capturing the many voices present in the Brazilian discourse of nationality, where echoes of imperialism coexist with Leninism, Christianity with Islam, proletariat with aristocracy, cobblers with actors, etc. Where the novel as a whole leaves the *presépio* paradigm behind is in its ability to represent the fluid and dynamic manner in which the many voices of Ilhéus shift and change, and often exchange, their relative place and position within the many spheres of Ilhéus, this little Brazil in microcosm. In the world of the novel, much like in the *presépio*, the opposites learn to coexist peacefully, however, unlike in the *presépio*, their relative positions shift constantly from foreground to background and vice-versa. Whereas in the *presépio* accretion is the structuring trope, in the world of the novel change itself becomes the dominant trope.

Read as a structuring device the continuous construction of the *presépio* enables us to see in the novel such a reframing and redirection of the Brazilian discourse of nationality as to lead us to perceive *Gabriela, Clove and Cinnamon* as one of the seminal narratives of nationality within the theoretical context elaborated by theorists who range from Benedict Anderson (1991) to Doris Somner (1993).

In studies published or presented between 1992 and 1995 I have developed at length the theoretical context necessary to study the discursive practices of nationality as they have appeared in the texts of Lima Barreto, Graciliano Ramos and others. The brief summary which follows should be sufficient to lay the theoretical groundwork necessary to test the discursive practices of Jorge Amado in *Gabriela, cravo e canela.*

To develop a theoretical framework I have used the works of such thinkers as Benedict Anderson (1983, 1991), Saul Friedlander (1990), Richard Lehan (1990), John Tomlinson (1991), Eric Hobsbawn (1983) and others. Benedict Anderson develops the concept of a nation as an "imagined community," whose identity is defined in fictional narratives. Saul Friedlander explains the development of national consciousness through the mechanism of suppresion or retrieval of certain elements in history, and finally, Richard Lehan proposes that those works of literature which contribute to the formulation of national identity represent "flashpoints" in history.

The work of Tomlinson (1991) adds depth to this scenario by problematizing the difference between the concepts of national identity and political unity, which according to him rarely coincide in the same geographical territory. Although Tomlinson basically agrees with Benedict Anderson's constructivist view of nationality, he does give serious consideration to the theories of Giddens (1981, 1985) and Schlesinger (1987), who contend that the inexplicable involvement of profoundly psychological factors in the formulation of the concept of nationality is contrary to a purely constructivist process (72–80).

This purely constructivist process advanced by Benedict Anderson rests on two basic premises which are fundamental in the construction of national consciousness: one is, that although constructed this sense of identification among a people need not be false; and two, that in principle there is no real difference between various imagined representations of cultural solidarity, be they related to a *patria chica*, a region, or a nation.

> There is no reason to suppose that national imaginings always exclude other forms of identification, nor as we shall presently see, that they are always at the forefront of people's minds. And it is possible to argue that some of those elements of modernity which Anderson discusses in relation to national identity may also be relevant to an explanation of modern regional identity. A sense of belonging to a region like Andalucía surely requires the same 'distant imagining' as that involved in the sense of Spanish nationality, and probably derives from similar social developments (mass literacy, regional media, and so on). The contingent fact of the power of the capitalist

nation-state to police its cultural boundaries is enough to account for the
dominance of nationalism over regionalism, but it seems that quite similar
psychological processes are at work in both types of identification.

The attraction of Anderson's account, then, is its linking of national identity
with the processes of social modernity. National identity is a highly medi-
ated imaginary belonging which, in a sense, replaces earlier forms of cultural belonging. (83)

In spite of his reservations Tomlinson accepts Benedict Anderson's
premise that an imagined community exists when people search for identification with others beyond their immediate contact.

Having thus envisioned a nation as an imagined community, Benedict
Anderson attributes the rise of nationalism in the 19th century to the decadence and fall of the great royal dynasties and religious hegemonies. In a situation where there is an obvious lack of one king and one god, one way to
unite the inhabitants of a region is by seeking other, imaginary forms of identification. Anderson further proposes that in this search for new forms of
identification it is necessary to recognize the role played by the great works of
national fiction, which not only define, but also popularize, the contours of
the national conscience to the participant members of the target community.

Based on the writings of the above theorists it is possible to evolve a concept of nationality as a discursive construct which operates through the mechanisms of suppresion or retrieval, whose production may be appropriated
either by the state, or by its opposition, and whose dissemination is guaranteed by the "literary fictions" of national identity. The dynamics of supression
and retrieval explain, for example, the return to the myth of origins, with the
consequent glorification of the native population, in those moments when
national identity is uncertain or threatened. Such is the case of the Celtic
revival in the 19th century Galicia, where a return to the Celtic roots stirs a
desire for independence and national autonomy.

To better understand the glorification of the Indian in Brazilian literature
of the 19th century, we might compare it to the program of retrieval of Celtic
origins of Galicia as theorized by Manuel Murguía and inscribed in literary
texts by Rosalía de Castro. The program of Celticization of the Galician
region had a dual purpose: one was that those things identified as Celtic customs and practices would indeed be recognized as their own, not only by
Galician villagers, but also and especially by the literate Galicians, and
would thus unite them as members of the one Celtic community; and, more
importantly, it established Galicians as the descendants of the original inhabitants of these lands, as its primary native owners, a fact that would justify
their claim to both autonomy and independence. In summary, the poetry of
Rosalía stresses the value of the common Celtic origins, which, on uniting

all Galicians will help them fight off the power of the colonizing invader (Courteau, 1995).

The case of Galicia helps explain the emphasis on the Indian origins in the independence writing in Brazil, especially in the texts of José de Alencar and Gonçalves Dias, who, like Rosalía and Murguía, attempt to "Indianize" Brazilian origins in order to justify the struggle for independence, which becomes glorified as an effort to throw off the yoke of the tyrants. Simultaneously, the case of Galicia illustrates clearly that Brazilians were not Indians, and that laying claim to a native, Indian heritage in this case means something completely different than in Galicia. Yet it cannot be denied that the Indigenist ploy did work to unify the young nation, and that by 1889 the survival of the young nation was sufficiently guaranteed by the advent of the Republic, that the nativist recourse no longer played an important role except in the *ufanista* (boastful) discourse of the Republican State, which used the three myths of the Indian, the fertile land, and the docile people as a means of instilling national pride in all Brazilians.

The moment of the consolidation of the Brazilian state in the years between 89 and 92 is the focus of Lima Barreto's novel, *Triste fim de Policarpo Quaresma* (The sad end of Policarpo Quaresema; 1905), in which he shows beyond any doubt that the "Indigenist" ploy had outlived its usefulness, by showing that in fact almost no one in Brazil of that period identified with the Indian heritage, nor did anyone become moved or cry when precious Tupi customs were remembered.

The hero of the novel, Policarpo Quaresma, a self-taught civil servant, in his search for authentic Brazilian music embarks on a voyage of discovery for the *real* Brazil, only to learn that that which he thought was the *real* Brazil simply did not exist. Among the things that he believed were the ideas developed by José de Alencar and Gonçalves Dias, and promulgated by the independent state, that the Indian was a main component of Brazilian culture. Yet, when, on receiving relatives, he tried to use an Indian greeting, they were stunned and worried that it would bring Policarpo bad luck, which in fact it did, for on insisting with the Government that Tupi become the official language of Brazil, and after absent-mindedly writing a memo in Tupi, Policarpo is promptly shipped off to a mental asylum. At the end of the novel he admits that his desire to valorize the Indian element in Brazilian culture only met with ridicule (Courteau, 1992).

Having shown in the context of the independent republican state the suppression of the Indian contribution, Lima Barreto leads us to the logical conclusion that the wars of independence were not about liberating the native people from the yoke of a tyrant. Through this conclusion he problematizes the whole issue of American nationalisms. Clearly the impulse for independence of the American nations was unlike that of Galicia; it was not a desire for independence and autonomy by a native people. The wars represented a desire by a group of colonizers to be free of other colonizers, namely, the original colonial powers. To achieve freedom, they had to stress the difference that had since emerged between them and the central colonial power because of their absorption of the native people's culture, yet Lima Barreto shows that claim to be greatly exaggerated, if not totally fictitious.

Thus the confrontation of Rosalía and Lima Barreto's views on the importance of native people in the formulation of a national discourse gives us an insight into the dynamics of "inventing" nations, in which the purported native origins serve a very important function of unifying a nation, like a family, around a common ancestor, which unity in turn helps to build it, if it hasn't been formed yet, or preserve it, if its identity is threatened. We can thus see how in independent America the native is cannibalized in every sense of the word. Image is used to feed the drive for independence, while the independent state engulfs the native to such an extent that the Indian culture and being seem to be totally obliterated.

In *Policarpo Quaresma*, in addition to showing the marginalization of the nativist element in spite of the state claims to the contrary, Lima Barreto also shows that the other two features, the fertile land and the docile people, on which the state rested the *ufanista* discourse were equally fictitious. In demystifying the *ufanista* discourse Barreto also managed to design the necessary apparatus for the analysis of national discourse, which, parallel to the apparatus constructed by Benedict Anderson consists of three structuring emblematic elements: the Indian culture, the fertile land, and the docile character of the Brazilian people. These features glorified by the *ufanista* discourse can each unfold like a fan. For the Indian beckons to historical origins, the native, or the primordial customs and traditions. The land can have as its referent the whole issue of possession, conflicts of territorial claims, and modes of production for its utilization. Finally, the gentle people can refer to all the possible cultural, political, and social and economic manifestations which characterize Brazil.

While it is possible to see that *Gabriela, Clove and Cinnamon* gives a special contour to each of these structuring emblematic elements, I believe that it is primarily through its treatment and displacement of the element of the native that it succeeds in reframing and redirecting the Brazilian national discourse. Through a skillful weaving of the theme of love of Nacib and Gabriela and the themes of growth, progress and change of the city, Amado engineers a national discourse in which tradition coexists with change, being displaced by it without violence. Thus, in rewriting the paradigm of origins of Lima Barreto, Amado shows that the recourse of the native, rather than being marginalized, undergoes successive regenerations, as each generation legitimates its ownership of the land with successive privileging of the native's status. The claims of the aboriginal inhabitant are replaced with those of the conqueror, whose blood earned him the right to the land, to be replaced in turn by the farmer and ultimately by the trader, whose commercial skills assure us of the prosperity of the land through the building of communication links and markets for its products.

Furthermore, he shows that the very vitality and the economic health of the city, and by implication of Brazil, depend on its ability to displace the hold of these successive generations of natives and their control of tradition. Thus the love theme of Gabriela and Nacib becomes the paradigm for displacement of tradition while the confrontation of Colonel Bastos and Mundinho Correia represents the displacement of the claims of the native. The displacement of these two obstacles to change, both obstacles part of the same claim to origins, epitomized by the *barra* (the sandbar which blocks the seaport of Ilhéus) pave the way for a new city built on tradition, but open to progress. As a microcosm version of the immense enterprise of what is Brazil, Amado's discursive construct of Brazilian national entity is full of hope and optimism for the future. The city of the distant longing of migrant retirantes, which reminds us of the dream of Fabiano and Vitória in Graciliano Ramos' *Vidas Secas* (Barren Lives, 1948), becomes a reality for the immigrants Nacib and Gabriela, a reality which promises a better life for all.

The history of the city is retold through the eyes of its patron saint, Saint George, "who had seen the Indians kill the first colonizers to be in turn killed and enslaved by them; he had seen the rise of sugar gins and coffee plantations, some small, others mediocre. He had seen this land lie fallow without any future for centuries. Then he witnessed the arrival of the first seedlings of cocoa ... He had not imagined that with cocoa would arrive a new era of prosperity for this land under his care, and that horrible things would follow. Men killing men in cruel ambush for the possession of valleys and dales, rivers and hillsides, burning the woods and feverishly planting cocoa and more cocoa" (28). The ensuing growth and prosperity of the region brought in their wake other changes, such as, nightclubs and buses, an accredited school and an independent parish, newspapers and bookstores, etc., all beneficiaries of the cocoa boom.

Amado succeeds in reorienting national discourse and in displacing the importance of tradition by skillfully counterposing tradition and change throughout the novel and allowing the change to win. The very beginning of the novel, the preface, already stresses the confrontation between the two. "This story of love," says the narrator or the author himself, a distinction which is never made clear in this preface, "by a curious coincidence, as dona Arminda might say, begins on the very day ... that the landowner Jesuino Mendonça shot to death dona Sinhazinha Guedes Mendonça, his wife ... and Dr. Osmundo Pimentel, a dentist, recently arrived in Ilhéus, an elegant young man with poetic tendencies." (2) The juxtaposition of the announced, incipient love story of Gabriela and Nacib which becomes emblematic of modern

Ilhéus, and the violent end of the traditional marriage of D. Jesuino Mendonça and Dr. Sinhàzinha are echoed by similar confrontations throughout
the text. The year 1925, memorable for the love of Nacib and Gabriela, the
love which in itself becomes a harbinger of change, also becomes remembered for the duel between "Mundinho Falcão, the exporter of cocoa, and
Colonel Ramiro Bastos, the local old cacique," (30) a case which epitomizes
the displacement of the native.

What is remarkable about *Gabriela* is the negotiating nature of its discourse, with its ability to capture and emphasize the deals and commerce of
change. It replays again and again the old encounters between the original
dwellers and the Portuguese, in which the latter deal and trade beads and trin-
kets for information. Yet, although in those exchanges the native were ultimately the losers, in Amado's exchange every one who buys change comes
out a winner.

The three pivotal exchanges that mark the benefits of change are Coronel
Alfredo's adherence to Mundinho in exchange for the clearing of the sandbar,
which opens the way for free trade the world; Nacib's granting of divorce to
Gabriela in exchange for her right to free association; and finally Colonel
Bastos' realization that Mundinho will not accept the deal the Colonel offers
him, the joining of the old order and status quo by marrying one of his grand-
daughters in exchange for Colonel's support, but rather will insist on
exchanges on his own terms. Following a feeble attempt to enforce the old
order, Colonel Ramiro Bastos simply gives up and dies, a fact which in itself
becomes emblematic as well as prescriptive: there comes a time when the
*dominant* native and the established tradition must simply die. Ramiro Bastos' death, however, does not mark the end of *Coronelismo*, but it does signal
the inability in a world of change to survive of its most extreme intransigent
form. In this respect the colonel's death is paralleled by the removal of the
sandbar, which to be sure cannot be removed forever for sandbars do come
back, but not in the same intractable form nor in the same place. Through
these exchanges we can see how the continuing march of change is able to
displace its major obstacles, tradition and physical barriers.

In the first contact between the natives and the foreigners, when Mundinho first defies the political power of Colonel Bastos, the latter, recognizing
both his independence and his agressiveness, labels him *forasteiro* (stranger),
but then he admits that he too, like everyone else in Ilhéus, was a foreigner,

> As if Ilhéus itself were not a land of foreigners, people who had come from
> everywhere. But that was different. The others arrived quietly, yielding
> immediatly to the authority of the Bastos family. All they wanted was to
> make a living establishing themselves on the land. They did not attempt to
> monitor the "progress of the city or the region," they did not decide about
> the needs of Ilhéus. (90)

Yes, this stranger was indeed different; not only was he independent himself, but he helped establish democracy's greatest ally, and the Colonel's greatest enemy: the daily newspaper.

> That business about the newspaper was downright dangerous. If he did not satisfy a request of the editor, there would be the newspaper catering to the opposition, messing around with the city business, snooping around, destroying reputations. (91)

What was good for the colonel was good for Ilhéus.

> Do you need a daily paper? [he asked his son]. No. Neither do I. Therefore, Ilhéus does not need one and he moved on to another subject. (91)

Mundinho represented change in every way, in getting the state government to accredit the local school (91) in establishing the newspaper, in securing government support to remove the sandbar.

> Colonel Bastos tried to understand this new life, this birth of this new Ilhéus arising from the one that had been his . . . Why was it now slipping through his fingers?
> He would not give up without a fight. (94)

And fight he did. After Mundinho announced his candidacy he burned the papers that carried the story, he had one of his men attempt to kill the one colonel who openly supported Mundinho, in order to show that while "he was alive he was the Boss" (94). But that was exactly the point, he could not live forever, and when he died, change would replace him, and the tradition he stood for, peacefully.

The Captain, whose father had been defeated and replaced by the generation of colonels led by Ramiro Bastos, was the first to envision Mundinho's political candidacy. Quite aware of this world in flux, echoing Mundinho's words, "A civilization in process" (96), the Captain convinces Mundinho that he is the only person who can save Ilhéus, by painting a picture of a new Ilhéus, with banks and buses, beach avenues and daily papers, agricultural technicians and refined architects (96–97). Unaware of the paradigmatic role he plays in this continuous succession of natives, the Captain is very convincing as he announces the twilight of the colonels who have outlived their usefulness:

> The Captain's speech betrayed passion and desire to convince Mundinho, who concurred. The Captain was right, of course, the needs of the colonels no longer reflected those of the land, which was progressing so rapidly. (100)

The Captain knew that the battle that would ensue would be intense and only the removal of the sandbar might tip the scale in Mundinho's favor (101). Although the Captain's interest is seemingly personal, and Mundinho's involvement, in Amado's hands, acquires the significance not only of a simple transfer of power from one colonel to another, but of a paradigm for a peaceful shift. For the power of the family of Colonel Bastos was tied to the triumph of tradition, while that of Mundinho signified the triumph of change.

Similarly, the relation between Nacib and Gabriela marks the triumph of another pivotal exchange. Gabriela, a *retirante* (a migrant), the fruit of the *sertão* (hinterland of Brazil's N.E.), neither virgin, matron, nor prostitute, came to town looking for a job. As a purely natural being, she was not averse to pleasures offered by the senses: she loved to sing, dance, make love, cook spicy meals, and prepare visual displays. While she was free to pursue her own sensual goals in life, the relationship between her and Nacib flourished, but after she was bound by the restrictions and constrictions of married life, expectations of polite behavior and of marital fidelity, the relationship between them wilted on the vine. Only continued negotiation regarding the equality of their status, in which neither could impose manners and life style upon the other, resulted in a mutually profitable partnership, one which displaced completely the traditional arrangements of marriage of convenience, as exemplified by Colonel Melk, or concubinage, in which women were virtually bound to slavery, as was the case of Glória, until she escaped with a school teacher. The dissolution of Glória's concubinage in itself is an example of victory of change, for her colonel and master, on expelling her from his house after discovering her infidelity, foregoes the traditionally expected physical violence against both her and her lover.

Finally, Colonel Bastos' invitation of Gabriela to his dinner table in exchange for her saving the life of one of his *caboclos* (hired hands), marks the Colonel's final recognition of the power of change, and shows a further erosion of the traditional values, according to which a man of his stature and power would neither feel grateful nor obligated to a woman who was a servant and a concubine.

These examples show Amado's insistence on change which is hammered out through continuous negotiation, and not through force, retaliation, or violent confrontation. In fact, if we can see Amado as being prescriptive, it is in his insistence on the replacement of colonelist violence with the proper political processes of democracy, thus suggesting that negotiated change is far preferable to armed rebellion. One might even wonder if this insistence on the democractic processes is aimed at the communist rebellion of the Prestes' column, for 1925, the big year in the novel, is also remembered in the history of Brazil as the year in which Luis Carlos Prestes assumes the command of paulista forces, which under the name of "Prestes' column" wage war on the government in the backlands of Brazil (Jordan Young 27). Thus although the change framed in *Gabriela, Clove and Cinnamon* parallels the desire for change sought by the Prestes column, the degradation of colonelist system, the liberation of women, and the liberation of working people, the methods for achieving this change are dramatically different, for in *Gabriela* on every level negotiation displaces armed conflict.

While engineering the fictional displacement of the structures of tradition and power in Ilhéus, Amado does not fall into the pitfall of a topsy-turvy exchange, in which the old would simply yield to the new, thereby continuing the same old traditions, but rather he negotiates to leave the door open to future change. In this respect Amado resembles Paulo Freire, who acknowledges that there are no utopias, and the only means for preventing a dystopia is to leave the door open to continuous change.

In his book *Pearl Necklace*, Roberto Reis, synthesizing the thought of the Brazilian critics on the period of transition, with regard to political, social and economic phenomena such as the end of colonelism, the rise of the cities, the liberation of women, etc., claims that Brazilian intellectuals of the transition period (1850–1950) subscribed to fascism in their wholesale acceptance of elitism. I believe that it would be safe to say that the author of *Gabriela, Clove and Cinnamon* skillfully avoids privileging any group or any system, pleading at every possible opportunity for openness to change and to multicultural diversity. Thus he allows the old city of Ilhéus to coexist with the new, the agricultural mestizo field hand (caboclo) with the paid industrial or commercial clerk. He allows for a society in which class conflicts can work themselves out peacefully through negotiation as they have between Nacib and Gabriela. Through this microcosm of Brazil, recorded in *Gabriela, Clove and Cinnamon*, Amado reframes the discourse of Brazilian identity, which displaces both the "ufanista" creed and the Modernist exaltation. It is a discourse that proposes to dismantle everything that is fixed and rigid in Brazilian society, with an openness to constant change, and to the possibility of continuous hybridization.

However, change itself is not simple, for it may be problematized not only by the conflict and violence of those who oppose it, but also by the essentialist nature of those who support it. In this regard we may look at the mythical figure of Gabriela.

Although the figure of Gabriela described by Jean Roche (1987) as the incarnation of Jorge Amado himself, because of her unfettered and free nature, may epitomize change itself,

> The beautiful mulatta, a double symbol of purity and eroticism, designed as the incarnation of original purity which knows no sin . . . is the double negation of both religion and institution, and is the affirmation of sponteneity . . . and a revindication of freedom itself against social taboos. She is in effect Jorge Amado himself. (93)

It does problematize the whole concept of the construction of national consciousness through the mechanism of repression and retrieval, both of which are indispensable in bringing about change.

This destablizing quality of Gabriela is also perceived by Juarez da Gama Batista (1972) who in this refugee of the drought sees a person who transformed the story of Ilhéus into her own story (1987), thus suggesting that Gabriela may in fact function as a symbol of Ilhéus. Unlike the above authors, I prefer to read Gabriela not as a symbolic version of Jorge Amado or Ilhéus, but rather as a symbolization of Brazil, and it is in this symbolic configuration that the figure of Gabriela problematizes the constructivist view of nationality. Gabriela is a given; she is what she is. With her long history, which began with the loss of her original parents, her rape by the uncle who had been charged with her care, her indiscriminate choice of the best and the strongest to share her bed, regardless of their race or nationality, her life curiously parallels that of Brazil. Yet also curiously there is an essential quality in her, an alterity, that no amount of conscious manipulation can affect. We know that her inherent good nature can deal and negotiate with change all around her; what never does change is the essential nature of Gabriela. Thus with the figure of Gabriela, Jorge Amado problematizes change itself, while acknowledging all along its usefulness in the construction of a national discourse of the future. The essentialist nature of Gabriela leaves us then with an unsettling view of construction of nationality through the mechanisms of change. Through the imperviousness of the figure of Gabriela, Amado seems to be searching for that ineffable psychological dimension of the concept of nationality, which survives all changes, which all Brazilians with tears in their eyes recognize as uniquely Brazilian. Much like Tomlinson problematizes Anderson's constructivist view, so too Amado problematizes his own detached reframing through change of the national discourse, with this unchangeable primordial figure, which curiously enough echoes the theories of Giddens and Schlesinger. With Gabriela, Amado problematizes precisely that part of nationality-as-construct which leaves the theorists at odds, by considering the possibility that Brazil, like Gabriela, still is and always will be something that every Brazilian carries in his heart.

This problematization of change itself with the unexplainable, calm, essential immutability of Gabriela, serves to underscore continuing resistance in Brazilian literary discourse to constructivist views of nationality, which Amado resolves in his typical fashion by simply allowing change and Gabriela to coexist peacefully together. Amado's posture, far from conciliatory, is more like a shrug. It is as if he said, "What can I say? This, after all is Brazil, and in Brazil everything is possible."

In summary, then, I believe that the great contribution of Jorge Amado to the discourse of nationality is to show that although the concept of the native, the original inhabitant, is firmly rooted in the national pscyhe, it is a shifting concept which can be displaced by a series of negotiations, which negotiations, without destroying or marginalizing it altogether, move it to a background position, where it does not interfere with growth and change. As with the concept of the native, Jorge Amado shows the entire concept of nationality to consist of an unstable dynamic system, constantly in flux, constantly changing, in which change itself seems to be the most predictable trope. As in the *presépio*, new characters are added constantly, as others are moved or removed to make room for the new ones; unlike in the *presépio* this motion is continuous.

By foregrounding change as the dominant trope in *Gabriela,* Amado parallels Roberto Reis' critique of the nation as represented in the master discourse of the transitional elite, "the nation—term" (33). Having based his view on the writings of Marilena Chauí, Roberto Reis concurs with her claims that a "nation is not a permanent, immutable concept, it is rethought at every moment, starting from a concrete praxis." Thus, in his insistence on the heteroglossic utterance of the nationalist discourse, Jorge Amado not only continues the critique of the myth of the native of the *ufanista* discourse, already discredited by Lima Barreto in *Policarpo Quaresma,* but he also offers resistance to the monolithic view of the nation as identified with the state and the revolution of 1930.

## BIBLIOGRAPHY

Alexander, Robert J. "Brazilian Tenentismo." *A Century of Brazilian History since 1865.* Richard Graham, editor, New York: Alfred A. Knopf, 1969.

Amado, Jorge. *Ensaios sobre o escritor.* Bahia: Universidade Federal da Bahia, 1982.

———. *Gabriela, cravo e canela.* São Paulo: Livraria Martins Editora, 1963.

———. *Povo e terra,* edited by José de Barros Martins. São Paulo: Livraria Martins Editora, 1972.

Anderson, Benedict. *Imagined Communities.* London: Verso. 1983, 1991.

Bakhtin, M.H. *The Dialogic Imagination.* Austin, Texas: University of Texas Press, 1985.

Bhabha, Homi. *The Location of Culture.* London: Routledge. 1993.

Castro, Rosalía de. *Obras completas.* Madrid: Aguilar Publishers, 1972.

Chamberlain, Bobby. *Jorge Amado.* Boston: Twayne Publishers, 1990.

Courteau, Joanna. "A inscrição de nacionalidade na poesia de Rosalia de Castro, Antonio Machado e Fernando Pessoa." *Luso-Brazilian Review* XXX, No. 1, 1993: 181–196.

———. "The Demise of Myth in *Triste Fim de Policarpo Quaresma.*" *Brasil/ Brazil* no. 3, 1992.

———. "Language and Ethnicity: The Case of Rosalia de Castro." *Language & Ethnicity,* Vol. II. James R. Dow, editor. Amsterdam/Philadelphia: John Benjamins Press, 1991.

_____ *The Poetics of Rosalia de Castro's Negra Sombra.* Lewiston, Queenston, Lampeter: The Edwin Mellen Press, 1995.

De Certeau, Michel. *The Writing of History*. Trans. Thomas Conley. Minneapolis: University of Minnesota Press, 1992.

Dos Santos, Itazil Benício. *Jorge Amado: retrato incompleto*. Rio de Janeiro: Editora Accord, 1993.

Dow, James R. and Hannjost Lixfeld, editors and translators. *The Nazification of an Academic Discipline: Folklore in the Third Reich*. Bloomington, IN: University of Indiana Press, 1994.

Easthope, Anthony. *Literary into Cultural Studies*. London: Routledge, 1991.

Friedlander, Saul. "The End of Innovation? Contemporary Historical Consciousness and the End of History." *Substance XIX*. 2/3 (1990): 29–36.

Giddens, Anthony. *A Contemporary Critique of Historical Materialism, Vol. I: Power, Property and the State*. London: Macmillan, 1981.

Glauco, Carneiro. *História das revoluções brasileiras*. Rio de Janeiro: Cruzeiro, 1965.

Graham, Richard. *Brazilian Tenentismo. A Century of Brazilian History since 1865*. New York: Alfred A. Knopf, 1969.

Hobsbawm, Eric and Rauger, T. *The Invention of Tradition*. Cambridge: Cambridge University Press, 1983.

Lima, Barreto. *Triste fim de Policarpo Quaresma*. São Paulo: Editora Brasilianense, 1982.

Martin, John and van Bodegraven, Donna. "Amado's *Gabriela, Clove and Cinnamon* and Bruno Barreto's film Gabriela." *Film and Literature*. Lubbock, Texas: Texas Tech University Press, 1988.

Reis, Roberto. *The Pearl Necklace*. Translation by Aparecida de Godoy Johnson. Miami, Florida: University of Florida Press, 1992.

Roche, Jean. *Jorge Bem/Mal Amado*. São Paulo: Editora Cultrix, 1987.

Rodríguez, Francisco. *Análise sociolóxica da obra de Rosalía de Castro*. Vigo: A Nosa Terra Press, 1988.

Schlesinger, P. "On National Identity: Some Conceptions and Misconceptions Criticized." *Social Science Information*, Vol. 26 (2), 219–64, 1987.

Smith, A.D. *The Ethnic Revival in the Modern World*. Cambridge: Cambridge University Press, 1981.

Somner, Doris. *Foundational Fictions*. Berkeley: University of California Press, 1993.

Tomlinson, John. *Cultural Imperialism*. Baltimore, Maryland: Johns Hopkins University Press, 1991.

# *Malandro* Heaven

## Amado's Utopian Vision

PAUL B. DIXON

No discussion of Brazilian regionalism would be complete without including Jorge Amado. Few of the country's narrators, if any, have achieved a greater sense of place. Plentiful reference to the unique Afro-Brazilian realities of his native Bahia are, like *dendê* oil, coconut milk and *malagueta* pepper in a dish of *vatapá*, more than just incidental seasonings. To leave them out is all but unthinkable. Neither Amado himself nor his reading public seems at ease with settings other than those connected to the Bahian capital of Salvador or the cacao-growing region surrounding Ilhéus in the southern region of this state (Chamberlain, *Amado* 14).

However, as strong as these ties of local color may be, it should be acknowledged that Amado, like other writers of successful fiction, is no mere reproducer of geographical or ethnic information. He creates worlds that belong to the imagination as much as to reality. A strong lyrical disposition (Cândido, "Poesia") often prompts him to choose characters and situations that are poetically just, passionately true, but not empirically faithful. A satirical impulse (Chamberlain, *Amado* 29–30; Santos 167–71) relies on hyperbole and stereotype, for the purpose of entertainment and light-hearted social criticism. Perhaps because of his socialist affinities, he has also been moved to propose utopias—systematic social spaces that stand apart from and in contrast to existing circumstances. It is this utopian tendency that I wish to examine here.

Utopian writing is at its heart paradoxical. While by definition it purports to achieve an alternative, disconnected world (the term *utopia*, invented by Thomas More, comes from Greek roots meaning "nowhere"), in fact it is never far from current social reality. Utopia has an intimate relationship with satire, which is critically rooted in the real world. As Robert C. Elliott shows,

> Satire and utopia are not really separable, the one a critique of the real world
> in the name of something better, the other a hopeful construct of a world that
> might be. The hope feeds the criticism, the criticism the hope. Writers of
> utopia have always known this: the one unanswerable argument for the
> utopian vision is a hard satirical look at the way things are today. (24)

Jorge Amado's writing seems usually to participate in this dual relationship. When he satirizes real social conditions he tends to imply the existence of
"something better," proposing at least by imaginary compensation an alternative world. When he is more explicitly working within the domain of a fantasy
world, he nevertheless refers to and critiques real social conditions. As I will
try to show, Amado's utopian vision presents an interesting problematic from
the ideological standpoint. While it is presented as a kind of ideal world, many
readers will take issue with specific aspects of that world. The question that
arises is whether Amado's utopia is a flawed one, representing a near-sighted
or distorted vision of a better world, or whether it is a utopia that blurs the
boundaries between the alternative world and this one, allowing satirical criticism to touch part of its own supposedly immune space. In this essay, I will
focus primarily upon the novel *Os pastores da noite* (1964) *[Shepherds of the
Night]*, where I believe Amado's utopian tendencies can be seen most clearly.

## SHEPHERDS AND SHEEP

As its title suggests, the novel's utopian space has strong metaphoric associations with the arcadian tradition, in which shepherds, with rustic honor, over-
see their flocks in a setting of pleasant tranquility. Northrop Frye discusses
the pastoral as an alternative ideal that is less concerned with the critical
analysis of the writer's society than it is with the "dream of wish-fulfillment
fantasy" (41). With significant qualifications, Frye's characterization of the
pastoral world seems made to order for Amado's novel:

> The characteristics of this ideal were simplicity and equality: it was a soci-
> ety of shepherds without distinction of class, engaged in a life that permitted
> the maximum of peace and leisure. The arts appeared in this society sponta-
> neously, as these shepherds were assumed to have natural musical and
> poetic gifts.
>       . . . in the pastoral, though the Courtly Love theme of frustrated devotion
> is prominent, it is assumed that making love is a major occupation. . . . The
> pastoral, by simplifying human desires, throws more stress on the satisfac-
> tion of such desires as remain, especially, of course, sexual desire. (41)

One aspect of the pastoral that seems foreign to the novel is the fact that
Amado's text takes place in the city of Salvador, while the pastoral is an alternative to urban life. However, this discrepancy is mitigated through figurative

language, as we will see. Another is the pastoral's status as a space without class distinctions. As I will show, Amado does not eliminate class distinctions, but merely relativizes them. He creates in the novel a kind of *malandro* heaven, or rogue's paradise, which is typical of many of his urban novels (Chamberlain, "Rogue") and has the essential features of what Antônio Cândido has identified as the "dialectic of *malandragem*"—first, a comical mitigation of order and disorder; and second, a banishment of guilt ("Malandragem" 76–88).

If the *locus amoenus* is the idealized center stage of the pastoral tradition, then that same status is afforded to the "night" in Amado's text. This nocturnal space has numerous dimensions within the context of the novel. Most obviously, it has temporal reference—a good deal of the novel's action occurs after dark. But the derivational associations are more important. The primary characters are fixtures of the night-life of Salvador, involved in gambling, prostitution, carousing and other "shady" activities. They belong to the dark side of the city not only in the sense of traditional morality, but also in an economic sense. Like so many of the Brazilian poor, their gainful work is improvised, informal and outside the grasp of official accounting. These people get by, but in a real sense their productivity never sees the light of day. Night has a racial and ethnic aspect; the text gives particular emphasis to the African ancestry of many of its characters, and to the ethnic practices for which Salvador is renowned. The setting is also dark in the sense that it refers to poverty, disease, ignorance and other realities that constitute the side of social life often consigned to obscurity.

Although Amado's night is a utopian space, it is not one that entirely eliminates social infirmities. Rather, it displays them with the softness of moonlight. The light cast on his night appears as a tranquilizing shimmer, reassuring that in spite of everything, all is well. Amado's shepherds of the night, no less than their forerunners on the verdant pastures of idyllic Greece, exist in an idealized, imaginary "pleasant place."

The text's lyrical prologue establishes such an atmosphere, showing night to be "feita de prata e ouro, de brisa e calor, perfumada de pitanga e jasmineiro" (iii) ["made of silver and gold, of breeze and warmth, redolent of Brazilian cherry and jasmine"] (xi). Personifying the night, the narrator claims,

> Tomávamos da noite pela mão e lhe trazíamos presentes. Pente para seus cabelos pentear, colar par seus ombros enfeitar, pulseiras e balangandãs para ornamentar seus braços, e cada gargalhada, cada ai gemido, cada soluço, cada grito, cada praga, cada suspiro de amor. (iii–iv)

> [We took her by the hand, and we brought her gifts. A comb to dress her hair, a necklace to adorn her throat, bracelets and baubles for her arms, and laughter, moans, sobs, cries, curses, signs of love]. (xi–xii)

Here, then, night is a beautiful, passionate woman, worthy of the best gifts one can possibly give her. The figurative language above, while idealizing night, also sexualizes it. Elsewhere in the prologue it becomes abundantly clear that a sexual difference is at the heart of Amado's figuration of utopia. Night is female and like sheep in need of the guidance and ministration of shepherds. The shepherds are male and serve to protect, calm, direct and fulfill the night:

> Pastoreávamos a noite como se ela fosse um rebanho de moças e conduzíamos aos portos da aurora com nossos cajados de aguardente, nossos toscos bastões de gargalhadas.
> E, se não fôssemos nós, pontais ao crepúsculo, vagarosos caminhantes dos prados do luar, como iria a noite . . . perdida e solitária, acertar os caminhos tortuosos dessa cidade de becos e ladeiras? (i)

> [We shepherded the night as though she were a bevy of girls and we guided her to the ports of dawn with our staffs of rum, our rough rods of laughter.
> And if it were not for us, punctual with the twilight, lazy wanderers through the fields of moonlight, how would the night, . . . lost and alone find her way through the winding paths of this city and alleys?]. (ix)

Some of this bucolic evocation is reminiscent of biblical parables of the Good Shepherd: "Quantas vezes não tivemos de tomá-la nos braços para que ela não se afogasse nesse mar da Bahia e não ficasse o mundo sem noite para sempre" (iii) ["How many times did we not have to take her in our arms so she would not drown in the sea of Bahia and leave the world without night for ever and ever"] (x). Others, however, have a more troubling aspect as they conflate the desire for night to continue and the (perhaps) justifiably harsh remedy of the shepherd for the wayward sheep with a man's abusive correction of his female companion:

> Quantas vezes não tivemos de prendê-la pelas pernas e pelas mãos, de amarrá-la no portal dos botequins e ao pé da cama . . . , trancadas as portas e janelas, para que ela, amuada ou sonolenta, não partisse antes da hora, deixando um tempo vazio, nem de noite nem de dia, um tempo gelado de agonia e morte. (iii)

> [How many times did we have to hold her by the legs and hands, tie her to the doorpost of a tavern or to the foot of a bed . . . , barring doors and windows, so that she, sullen and sleepy, should not depart too soon, leaving behind an empty stretch of time, neither night nor day, a frozen space of agony and death?]. (xi)

Already in the prologue, the reader begins to perceive that, at least in its metaphoric dimension, the novel's utopia is centered upon a model of male domination. Mention of *machismo* in Amado should not surprise us in view of recent criticism (Galvão 16–22; Patai 131–40); however, the blatancy of certain passages in this text does give one pause:

> Quando ela chegava em seu berço de crepúsculo, no barco de uma lua antecipada, nas franjas derradeiras do horizonte, era uma pobre noite sem sentido, solitária, ignorante, analfabeta da vida ... Noite bronca, apenas de negrume e de ausência, inútil e grosseira.
>
> Em nosso apascentar sem limites, pastoreando-a pelas ânsias e ambições, pelas penas e alegrias, pelas amarguras e gargalhadas, pelos ciúmes, sonhos e solidões da cidade, nós lhe dávamos sentido e a educávamos, fazíamos daquela pequena noite vacilante, tímida e vazia, a noite do homem. Seus machos pastores, nós a engravidávamos de vida. (iii)

> [When she arrived in her cradle of dusk, on the ship of an early moon, on the outer fringes of the horizon, she was poor, meaningless night, lonely, ignorant, illiterate of life ... A dull night, nothing but darkness and absence, useless, and insip.
>
> As we grazed her in boundless pastures, shepherding her through desires and ambitions, through suffering and joys, through bitterness and laughter, jealousy, dreams, and the loneliness of the city, we gave her meaning and educated her, making of that small hesitant night, timid and vapid, the night of man. We, her shepherds, impregnated her with life]. (xi)

According to the prologue, then, Amado's utopian vision is figuratively represented as the night. It does not banish "penas" and "amarguras" but turns them, along with moments of joy, from something "inútil and grosseira" into something with "sentido." The agents in creating this ideal space, of course, are the shepherds. Amado's narrator states a boldly sexual prerogative, claiming for the "machos pastores" the role of educating and giving meaning to their nocturnal stewardship, and even of impregnating it with life. The novel's utopia, clearly, is "a noite do homem." What remains to be seen is what the specific aspects of this idealized vision are and how that vision may relate to the reader's reception.

Generally speaking, Amado envisions a mitigated, relational state of affairs that comes to terms with many of the basic polarities underlying Brazilian society. The anthropologist Roberto DaMatta identifies this desire for reconciling opposites and contradictions as one of the central cultural preoccupations of the nation (*Brasil* 119–20). He also claims that starting with *Gabriela, cravo e canela [Gabriela, Clove and Cinnamon]*, it is a primary concern of Amado's novels and provides a detailed discussion of *Dona Flor e seus dois maridos [Dona Flor and Her Two Husbands]* as a relational novel (*Casa* 92–111). Where in reality that quest for mediation often falls short, in the mature Amado's fictional world it normally succeeds.

## THE HOUSE AND THE STREET

DaMatta perceptively calls attention to the opposition of house and street as one of the basic underlying polarities of the culture. Although he allows some space for ambivalence (the house may contain oppressive family expectations and traditions, while the street shows the promise of diversion and entertainment), he seems unhesitant in assigning an essentially positive value to the house, and an essentially negative one to the street. The house is a space of nutrition, secure relationships, comfort and pleasure, while the street presents workaday struggles, uncertain relationships, inconvenience and struggle (*Brasil* 23–33). Reading Amado, on the other hand, tends to reinforce the ambivalent perception of house and street. His novels tend to emphasize the oppressive and confining aspects of the house. For example, the protagonist of *A morte e a morte de Quincas Berro d'Água [The Two Deaths of Quincas Wateryell]* throws away his bourgeois existence as an exemplary head of a respected household and becomes a celebrated bohemian. The heroine of *Dona Flor e seus dois maridos* becomes bored and impatient with her second husband's stolid respectfulness and his adherence to an orderly routine. Amado's street is a powerfully attractive space, really quite distant from the challenging, impersonal battlefield usually described by DaMatta. It seems to portray a kind of synthesis of house and street—a space for unfettered individual freedom, and at the same time one of secure interpersonal relationships. In *Os pastores da noite*, Amado infuses the traditional notions of the house with those of the street, and traditional notions of the street with those of the house.

Let us take, for example, the notion of the prostitute, or "woman of the streets." The profession involves all those negative associations DaMatta ascribes to the streets in Brazilian culture—impersonal, exploitive transaction, estrangement from family, struggle in the public space for financial sustenance, danger, violence, etc. Amado's prostitutes in *Os pastores da noite*, however, are quite at home. The best example is Otália, the young girl who arrives from out of town and is immediately "adopted" by Tibéria, the madam of a well-known house. The protection and affection Tibéria extends to the girl are nothing if not motherly. In fact, Otália is at once taken into a kind of secure, extended family. When Otália reports to Tibéria that her luggage has been stolen at the train station, the latter immediately calls upon close personal relations to resolve the situation. Since these friends, "pastores da noite," are themselves involved in such practices, they have little trouble finding the culprit and using the gentle persuasion of personal influence to achieve the return of her belongings. The street rogues behave as if they were Tibéria's nephews, providing her with loyalty and respect, making the house of ill-repute more like their favorite aunt's house.

The traditional family dwelling, on the other hand, tends to be characterized by deceitful relationships and lack of mutual respect. In the novel this space belongs to three families—Cabo Martim and his new bride, Marialva; Zico Cravo na Lapela, his wife, and their numerous children; and the chief of police, Doutor Albuquerque, and his spouse. Marialva, it turns out, is a long-standing devourer of men, who connives to betray the famous guitar-playing card shark Martim with his best friend. She hopes by this means to break his independent spirit and confine him to the house. Martim can only escape this emasculating trap by freely giving his wife to his friend, once he learns of their mutual attraction. Cravo na Lapela is the one who has stolen Otália's suitcase. Characterizing the incident as just another of his jokes, several friends turn up at his house to recover the goods. Unsuccessful in his attempt to escape through the back door, he agrees to return everything, much to the embarassment of his wife and daughters, who are already wearing Otália's clothing. The wife's lack of esteem for her husband is more than evident: "Tu não serve mesmo pra nada. . . Não tem jeito" (43) ["You are no good for anything . . . You don't have the knack"] (48). Albuquerque, whose high-minded attack on corruption and lawlessness in Salvador has gotten him in trouble with influential power brokers, is about to lose his job. His wife, tired of his "altissonância" (309) ("pompous folderol") (348) tells him to save face by resigning. An interior monologue reveals her low opinion of her spouse: ". . . ela sentiu pena, esse pobre marido, tão cheio de si e tão incapaz. Só ela e mais ninguém podia medir com precisão sua inutilidade, sua fatuidade" (310) [". . . She felt sorrow, that poor husband, so full of himself and yet a good for nothing. She and she alone could gauge the full extend of his incapacity, his fatuity."] (349). We see, in short, that Amado's homes tend to be spaces of distance rather than communion, disdain rather than respect, competitive strategy rather than enterprises of mutual support.

However, there is a modified domestic setting where such positive values thrive. This is represented in the novel by Mata Gato, the *favela* or shanty community whose spontaneous and invincible formation provides the central drama for the ending of the novel. As a collective domestic space, the *favela* contains the elements traditionally valued in the Brazilian home. It has a strong, respected, but unforbidding father in the figure of Jesuíno Galo Doido, the doyen of street rogues who, when the police raze the original shanties on the hill, cheerfully announces, "Minha gente, nada de desanimar. Eles derrubaram as casas, a gente faz de novo" (219) [My people, don't be discouraged. They tore down the houses; we'll build them again."] (247). Jesuíno is indeed a father figure, serving as source of wisdom, spiritual strength, and technical know-how in the construction, promotion and protection of the community, not through authoritarian imperative but through sympathy and loquacious charm.

The maternal figure at Mata Gato is Dona Filó. A never-married mother of numerous offspring by an assortment of fathers, she survives by numerous improvised means, including renting out her children for appearances to childless beggars. However, when the conflict over the shanty town begins to attract public attention she assumes the mantle of the self-sacrificing mother. A politician calls her "mãe de uma dúzia de filhos, matando-se dia e noite na tábua de lavar e na tábua de engomar para sustentar a familia . . . viúva e honrada, não saía por aí como outras . . . mãe amantíssima, . . . verdadeira santa" (268) [" mother of a dozen children, killing herself day and night over the washtub and ironing board to support her family . . . A widow and a decent woman, she did not do as others did, . . . This loving mother, this veritable saint"] (302). When thrust into the public eye, she in fact seems to become this saintly person, holding a child on each hip and speaking out for nurturing of life, childhood and humanity.

Supportive siblings are not lacking. The street urchins assume the role of the able and energetic younger brother. They act as soldiers in the *favela's* improvised army, pelting the police with stones when they attempt to take over the reconstructed shanties. They serve as sentinels and messengers, facilitating the interaction between this collective "home" and the outside world. The prostitutes play the role of a sympathetic sister, perhaps one who is away at school but who visits on weekends. As with the sister in a traditional family, they are not given such an active role in promoting the interests of the group, but provide much appreciated emotional support. This solidarity is especially apparent at crucial, "ceremonial" moments, such as births, baptisms, weddings, deaths and funerals. Amado's prostitutes in *Os pastores da noite* are a notable presence at such moments in the *favela,* but also provide general support and encouragement as the *favela* "family" strives to protect its values and interests.

Amado's *favela,* then, is a kind of middle ground between the house and the street. The fragile slats and cardboard of its walls stand in opposition to the fortress-like obsession with protection, privacy and exclusivity that tends to characterize Brazilian houses. The interactive space created is more inviting and open, but it does not cease to provide the uniting social structure traditionally associated with the family. Outlaws, beggars, homeless people, street children, poor unmarried mothers, prostitutes—those classes of people who in the real world tend to be most marginal and disconnected—these are the ones embraced and welcomed home. They impart to this utopian quasi-familial space all the raw vitality and resourceful tenacity that comes from the struggle for survival and receive in turn an unquestioning and unconditional acceptance.

## THE CHILD AND THE ADULT

Another significant dichotomy that Amado's writing seeks to mitigate is that which exists between the child and the adult. The contingent status of both conditions is well known. Childhood can involve a frustrating dependence and lack of power, but it is often fondly remembered for its simplicity, freedom from responsibility and playfulness. Adulthood usually brings empowerment and self-determination, but carries as well the burden of work and of responsibility for one's actions. As in the case of the house/street polarity, Amado's fascination with this dichotomy is a reflection of a predisposition in Brazilian culture. The numerous television programs, (perhaps the most notable being "Xou da Xuxa" and "Os Trapalhões") displaying adults who tend to act like children, or children who tend to act like adults; the general indulgence of children at moments such as birthday parties and "children's day"; the well-known affinity of Brazilians for the wonderful world of Walt Disney in all its manifestations; the precocious social maturity of many Brazilian young people; the popularity of cosmetic plastic surgery and probably even the centrality of Carnaval bely a mind-set where neither immaturity or maturity is satisfactory in and of itself. Rather, what is apparently sought for is the artful infusion of one condition into the other.

Perhaps the most outstanding example of this attempted synthesis is the protagonist of Amado's *Gabriela, cravo e canela*. Like so many of the author's female protagonists, Gabriela enjoys the adult prerogative of sexual activity, but seems exempt from the obvious consequences of such activity—particularly that of pregnancy. (Real-world solutions such as birth control usually seem unnecessary in Amado's fictional world.) Admired for her competence as a cook and for her willingness to risk personal danger to save a friend, she nevertheless tears off her shoes to join in a game of ring-around-the-rosey with children in the public square and cannot resist circuses.

In *Os pastores da noite*, characters show a similar equivocation between adulthood and childhood. Otália separates her affective life from her profession. When she acts as a prostitute she behaves and is treated as an adult—fully in control of her personal resources, fully competent to engage in the comercial exploitation of those resources. When not working, however, she behaves and is treated as an innocent girl: "Mulher só na vista, menina por dentro, mesmo no castelo queria era brincar de boneca e namorar como as moças donzelas" (290) ["But only outwardly a woman. Inwardly she was a child; even in the brothel what she wanted was to play with her doll and be courted like an innocent damsel"] (326). Much to the puzzlement of Martim, she frankly shows her affection for him but refuses to have sex. It is the girl who goes out with Martim, not the woman. She simply wants to "namorar com Martim para depois noivar, com aliança e tudo" (290) ["be courted by Martim and then become engaged to him, with ring and everything"] (326). When she sickens and dies, Tibéria and the other residents of the "castle" bury her in a wedding dress of the purest white.

Although perplexed by the behavior of Otália, Martim is not himself beyond uncertainty regarding his status as adult or child. He is clearly no

stranger to adult sexuality. But the people's reaction to the news of his marriage is generally one of shock and disapproval. Drinking companions are so
accustomed to viewing him as a playmate that they find it practically impossible to imagine him as a husband. If Martim is a child, his mother is the lady of
a house of ill-repute: "Para [Tibéria], Martim era como um filho, traquinas e
sem juízo, por isso mesmo mais mimado. E as mães não gostam de ver seus
filhos casados, amarrados a outra mulher" (51) ["To her, Martim was like a
son, naughty, impulsive, and for that very reason dearer to her. And mothers
do not like to see their sons married, bound to another woman"] (57). As
already mentioned, Martim decides to give away his wife upon learning that
his friend Curió is in love with her. Such a decision weighs the more juvenile
value of friendship against the more mature value of fidelity in marriage and
other contractual relationships, and opts for the former. After breaking with
Marialva, Martim remarries, but this time it is with Otália, just before she
dies. His vows are sincere expressions of loyalty, but significantly are offered
to a woman of public access. Cabo Martim assumes the mature sexual prerogative of "having and holding," but can't be held to the idea of exclusivity:
"Não era possível, a um homem só, dormir com todas as mulheres do mundo
mas devia-se fazer esforço para consegui-lo. Martim se esforçava ..." (124)
["It was not possible for one man alone to sleep with all the women in the
world, but he should try ... Martim did his best"] (139).

   Another character who negotiates the dubious space between youthful
comradeship and mature responsibility is Massu, the black deliverer of
parcels who adopts a light-skinned baby as his son (when the child's alco-
holic mother is about to die, she identifies Massu as the father, mainly
because he is the kindest of the many men with whom she has lately had sexual relations). Massu enthusiastically takes on his fatherly stewardship, but
soon finds that adult imperatives enter into conflict with more youthful ones.
He has no difficulty selecting Tibéria as the baby's godmother. However,
when all of his many male friends begin hinting that they would like to be the
godfather, he realizes that he cannot select one without denying the wishes of
the others. A big-hearted, naturally open individual, Massu agonizes at the
thought of having to exclude all but one of his friends from the coveted place
of honor. Actually, the question involves more than ceremonial distinctions;
according to the tradition, it is actually a kind of insurance policy for the
child, where someone outside the family assumes responsibility in case the
parents become incapacitated. Naming several godparents, it is understood,
would be like naming none since no one would have a definite assignment to
be responsible. Adults, alas, must often say no.

   The solution to the dilemma is a fine example of the famous Brazilian
"jeitinho" or artful dodge. Massu decides to consult a *candomblé* oracle
("mãe-de-santo") for guidance. After acquainting herself with the problem,
deliberating at length and consulting the spirits, she informs him that the god-

father is to be no mere mortal, but rather the African deity, Ogun. The ensuing tale of how a *candomblé* deity manages to stand as godfather at a Catholic baptism is not merely an amusing parable of Brazilian religious syncretism. On a parallel and isomorphic level, the story addresses the sometimes inevitable conflict between two types of interpersonal relationships—the classically adult relationship of parent to child, and the typically youthful relationship of friend to friend.

Jesuíno Galo Doido, the wisest of the shepherds of the night, is another figure exemplifying ambiguous maturation. Usually described in terms of his "cabeleira cor de prata" (33) ["silvery head"] (37), Jesuíno is always consulted by the other drunks, gamblers and flim flams when ethical or diplomatic questions arise. As already mentioned, he is the architect of the defense of the shanty town, Mata Gato. His demeanor during this defense, however, reveals that he is not all venerable seniority. Having just obliged the police to retreat, Jesuíno orchestrates a great manifestation of booing:

> No alto do morro, Jesuíno a ordenava, no final de seu comando, rindo-se contente: general dos esfarrapados, ... criança abandonada nas ruas da Bahia, com um chapéu de bico feito de lata e papelão, meio destruído pela chuva, a brincar de bandido de polícia. Nunca se divertira tanto. (255)

> [From the top of the hill, Jesuíno had ordered it as making the end of his command, laughing with contentment, the general of the tattered, ... A street waif of Bahia with a helmet made of tin and cardboard, soggy with rain, playing cops and robbers. He had never had so much fun]. (287)

Indeed, the entire atmosphere of Amado's "noite" is suffused with a sense of entertainment and calculated fun. As a general rule, characters go about their various enterprises with an intense concentration or seriousness. But the enterprises themselves gravitate around play. Characters engage in "o jogo" or various types of gambling—the animal lottery, card games, dice etc. They play army, play guitar, play robbers and play at building houses. Their rituals combine trickery and role playing. They have play weddings and make-believe families. The heart of all this play is really no different from that of other children—socialization. Conviviality is supreme in Amado's utopia (Portella 35). Lubricated by generous amounts of cheap liquor, play is Amado's mechanism for social communion.

## EXPLOITERS AND THE EXPLOITED

As a culture whose economic foundation rests on masters and slaves and whose gross social inequities are a continuing fact of life, the Brazilians attempt, imaginatively and otherwise, to mitigate such strong societal polarities. As DaMatta points out, one of the paradoxes of Brazilian culture is that it contains strong ideological mechanisms both for reinforcing and for breaking down social hierarchies. His treatment of the institution of Carnaval provides a good example, for while its interior structure inverts the hierarchy (placing members of the lower classes in the position of superior teachers, and members of the élite in the position of inferior students), its contextual situation as a sanctioned, temporary interruption of real life has the effect of reinforcing the traditional hierarchies (*Carnivals* 111–15).

Jorge Amado's mature writing is clearly involved in the imaginative mitigation of social inequities. Whether he is exploring the interaction of rich and poor in the productive environment, as in *As terras do sem fim [The Violent Land]*, or on the sexual frontier, as in *Teresa Batista, cansada de guerra [Tereza Batista: Home from the Wars]*, he usually arrives at some form of mutually satisfying relationship rather than a stand-off that defines but alienates the opposing interests. Novels such as *Cacau [Cacao]*, *Jubiabá* and *Capitães da areia [Captains of the Sands]*, which follow the more doctrinnaire Communist vision of an unrelenting class struggle, belong to his early career. It is the mutually satisfying aspect of Amado's hierarchical interactions that makes them part of a utopian vision. In the real world, such interactions tend to result in winners and losers; in Amado, the general rule is that everybody wins.

*Os pastores da noite* illustrates this tendency rather well. Because the construction of the shanty town takes place on private property belonging to a prominent citizen of Salvador, powerful people become involved in the question. The first manifestation of this power is a police invasion, destroying the huts and ordering evacuation of the property. But when the inhabitants refuse to leave, they begin to gain powerful allies. Journalists and politicians, primarily those allied with the opposition party, begin bombastically to champion the squatters. The boss of the illegal animal lottery lends his influence to the cause. Eventually even the governor declares his support, replacing the chief of police and mandating the state's purchase of the disputed land. On its most patent level, the squatters are the beneficiaries of this public contention, obtaining in the end a permanent dwelling place. In reality, however, everyone comes out ahead. The journalists sell more papers with their sensational reports. The politicians advance their campaigns for votes. The lottery boss gets the over-zealous police chief off his back, while the corrupt politicians he supports gain assurance of his continued funding. The governor steals his part of the show from the opposition legislators and is able to portray himself as a populist. The landowner makes a handsome profit on the deal and at the same time gains sentimental favor with his communist grandchildren. The police chief, though he loses his job, manages to come out ahead by becoming the darling of the powerful conservative element in the government. Even Jesuíno Galo Doido, who is shot and killed by the police in an aborted raid, is compensated by being transformed into *candomblé* deity, able to indulge his playful lusts *post mortem*: "... jamais se soube houvesse o Caboclo Galo Doido baixado em feita velha, em arruinado aparelho, em cavalo magro. Só descia nas mais belas filhas e não se importava se eram feitas de outros cabo-clos, sendo bonita lhe servia, nela varava a noite a dançar" (320)["... He was never known to descend into an old votary, a damaged instrument, a skinny horse. He descended only into the most beautiful, and he did not care if they were devotees of another deity. As long as they were pretty, that was all he asked; he spent the night in them, dancing"] (360). With satirical brilliance, Amado shows that each of the actors in this drama is motivated primarily out of self interest. Although the squatters actively cooperate with their more powerful allies, they are actually being used to enhance the positions of their "helpers." At the same time there is a suggestion that the squatters are not so naïve as to think that the assistance offered is purely altruistic; they may be using their counterparts as well.

The suggested model of interaction, then, is one of reciprocal exploita-tion. A mutual dependence holds between the privileged and the poor; each class manipulates the other in certain ways, and everyone gains something.

The clever manipulator is of course a consecrated Brazilian archetype known as the *malandro*. Born out of scarcity and propelled by need, the *malandro* searches about opportunistically for whatever resources might be available to provide satisfaction. Some of these resources inevitably belong to someone else and must be transferred. Relying always on wiley skills of per-sonal interaction, and often on deceit, the *malandro* obtains satisfaction "by hook or crook." DaMatta explains that *malandragem* in Brazil functions as a means for mediating the dichotomous tendencies of the culture (*Brasil* 104–05). Amado's novel demonstrates as a successful interaction what often falls short in reality. The novel is populated by malandros on all levels. Both the powerless and the influential are in some sense lacking in resources and driven by necessity. Each group finds what it desires in the other; convivial relations and "innocent" exploitation create a happy ending in Amado's para-ble of constructive social interaction.

The realm of sexual interactions is portrayed in terms of the same sym-metrical exploitation. Sexual abuse appears to have been banished from the imaginative world of *Os pastores da noite*, not because men refrain from beating women, but because the women appear to appreciate that kind of treatment. A case in point is when journalists descend on the shanty town and Dagmar poses for photographers in her bathing suit. This earns her a beating from her partner, Lindo Cabelo. The narration suggests that she has actually enjoyed this expression of jealous anger: "... constatemos, para somar à nossa experiência das mulheres e da vida em geral, ter ficado Dagmar não só mais discreta após os bofetes como também muito mais carinhosa" (224) ["We will merely state for the record, adding to our experience of women and of life in general, that after the slaps, Dagmar not only became more discreet but also much more affectionate"] (253). The relationship between the street barker, Curió, and the occultist, Madame Beatriz, vividly illustrates the same pattern. With promises of sexual intimacy, Beatriz has seduced Curió into promoting her "buried alive" act, which consists of her lying inanimate in a coffin for weeks, while the public pays to see her through the coffin's glass top. Curió diligently arranges for the coffin, the venue, and to the extent possible, the paying audience, without realizing that on the sly, Beatriz is coming to life to eat and take care of other necessities. When he finds out about the deception, he pulls her hair and slaps her until "ela agarrou-se a seu pescoço e, ao receber o terceiro tabefe, tomou-lhe da boca e o beijou enlouquecida. Curió quando parou de bater foi para sentir-se enleado por ela, num beijo infinito" (275) ["she threw her arms around his chest, and as he applied the third slap, she put her mouth to his and kissed him wildly. When Bullfinch finally stopped beating her, he felt himself her captive in a kiss that had not end"] (310). The couple brings its sexual fast to a close then and there, upon the smashed remains of the coffin. Thereafter they live together happily. Once again, what would in the real world probably be considered an abuse of power is cast here as a kind of mutually beneficial, bilateral exploitation. We are reminded of the pastoral metaphor introduced by the title and the prologue. It appears that in Amado's fantasy world, men are shepherds and women are sheep. For these provident pastors, having sex with women is to "lhes fazer o benefício" (313) ["generously service them"] (241). If the shepherds must use agression at times, it is for the good of the sheep, who eventually will be more happy than without it.

Mediation of society's hierarchical levels is at the heart of Amado's imagined universe. This relational middle ground involves money, social status, sexual relations and, of course race. According to DaMatta, *mulatismo* in Brazil is not merely the perfect crystalization of the cultural disposition to avoid absolute of exclusive racial categories, but is emblematic as well of the tendency to relativize nearly all polarities (*Brasil* 41). Idealization of the *mulato* (or to be more accurate, usually the *mulata*) is a significant feature of *Os pastores da noite*. The matter is fascinatingly elaborated in a friendly conversation between Pé-de-Vento, collector of mice and other animals for laboratory experiments, and his client, doutor Menandro:

> Uma vez, voltando de demorada viagem pelas estranjas, dera o doutor Menandro para elogiar as francesas, estalando a língua e movendo a grande cabeça de sábio. "Mulher igual a francesa não existe". Assim dizia e Pé-de-Vento, até então respeitosamente calado, não se conteve:
> —Doutor, vosmicê me adisculpe, vosmicê é homem sabido, inventa remédio para curar doença, ensina na Faculdade e tudo isso. Mas me disculpe a franqueza: eu nunca dormi com francesa mas lhe garanto que elas não ganham para mulata nenhuma. Seu doutor, não tem como natureza de

mulata para essas coisas ... Ah!, seu doutor, no dia que vosmicê pegar uma na cama, nunca mais quer saber de francesa nem pra lhe coçar as bretoejas ...

—De acordo, meu caro, sempre fui apreciador das mulatas. Sobretudo quando estudante e ainda hoje. Até me chamavam de "Barão das Amas". Mas quem lhe disse que na França não tem mulatas? Você sabe o valor de uma mulata francesa recém chegada do Senegal? (8–9)

[Once, on his return from long trip abroad, Doctor Menandro had lavished praises on French women, clicking his tongue and moving his ponderous, wise head. "There are no women like the French."

Wing-foot, who up to that point had been respectfully silent, was unable to restrain himself: " Doctor, you will be good enough to excuse me. You are a learned man who invents cures for ailments, teaches in the Medical School and all that. But you must excuse my speaking out this way: I never slept with any French women, but I can guarantee you that no mulatta has to take a back seat for them. Doctor, sir, they just don't have a mulatta's nature for such a thing ... Ah, Doctor, sir, the day you lay one of them, you'll never want to hear about a French woman again, not even to scratch an itch ..."

"I agree with you, my dear fellow. I have always had a high opinion of mulatto women. Especially when I was a student. I was even known as the 'Baron of the House of Maids.' But who told you that there are not mulattas in France? Do you know what a jewel a French mulatta fresh from Senegal is?"]. (9–10)

Aside from the context of the conversation, the matter of *mulatismo* has its own logic of cultural mediation. It is emblematic of the relativization of the basic social hierarchy of masters and servants. It may be a product of the abuse of power, pure and simple. Treatment of the *mulata* in Brazilian literature in general, and in Amado in particular (Hunsaker) has normally been discussed in those terms. But who can deny that consensual intercourse, the mutual and voluntary exchange, the equivocal circle of using and being used, is not also involved in the phenomenon? Depending on how one chooses to view it, miscegenation can serve as a reminder of one group's exploiting another, or as a sign of living together and ending such exploitation. The novel clearly treats it as the latter, and the function of *mulatismo* within the conversation is interesting. Pé-de-Vento and Menandro represent opposite ends of the social hierarchy, and yet they are freely engaging in amicable conversation. Discursive markers, such as Pé-de-Vento's frequent use of apologies, expressions of reluctance at offering an opinion and formal pronouns serve to mediate the class difference between him and the doctor. Menandro, on the other hand, uses unpretentious and informal language (including the "kitchen error" of using the verb "ter" in stead of "haver" to express the idea "there are"), which can also be taken as a desire to bridge the distance in their respective social stations. The common ground of that conversation is, of course, the praise of women as sexual partners. But within that common ground, there arises a difference of opinion. The doctor, who has traveled widely, especially appreciates French women, while the mouse-catcher is a great fan of *mulatas*. Menandro's desire to maintain the common ground, to preserve the agreeability of the interchange, is shown in a fine artful dodge, a bit of conversational *malandragem*. He points out, as if he had been thinking in such terms all along, that he's really talking about French *mulatas*! The form of the dialogue, with its facilitating formulas, cooperative style, and clever compromise, demonstrates effectively Amado's ideal of mediating differences through resourceful and loquatious social interaction. Whether coincidentally or not, the subject of the dialogue—*mulatas*—seems to confirm all the more strongly the ideal, by serving in itself as a metonymic signifier of that very interaction.

The figure of the *mulata*, emblem of relativity and mediatiation, is ultimately what serves to relativize the utopian discourse of the novel. As Pé-de-Vento walks from his meeting with Menandro to be with other friends at a bar, he imaginatively contemplates an ideal world, filled with these beautiful creatures:

> A Ladeira do Pelourinho, em sua frente, enchia-se de mulatas . . . Um mar de seios e coxas, de ancas ondulantes, de perfumados cangotes. Desembarcavam às dúzias das nuvens agoras negras no céu, povoavam as ruas, um mar de mulatas e, nesse agitado mar, Pé-de-Vento a navegar. Mulatas subiam a ladeira correndo, outras vinham voando, uma encontrava-se parada sobre a cabeça de Pé-de-Vento, um seio crescia e se alçava no céu, o passeio repleto de bundas, pequenas e grandes, roliças todas, a escolher. (10)

> [The slope of Pelourinho, which lay ahead of him, was full of mulatto women. A sea of breasts and thighs, swaying haunches, perfumed napes. They had disembarked by the dozen from the clouds of heaven, which were now black, filling the streets, a sea of mulattas, and on this heaving sea, Wing-Foot set sail. Mulattas were running up the hillside; others came flying; one was standing above Wing-Foot's head; a breast grew until it touched the sky; the path was full of rumps, large and small, all well fleshed; you had only to choose]. (10)

This paradisiacal vision literally defies the laws of gravity, with its flying women and its moon in the shape of a breast. It is also an obvious defiance of whatever gravity may reside in the reader; the clearly hyperbolic nature of the representation marks it as a man's unmitigated sexual fantasy. Peeking in on the private thoughts of one of the "shepherds of the night," the novel begins to expose such thinking as nothing but playful macho meanderings. Such mental kite-flying invites a distanced, ironic response from a typical reader. The ironic situation grows as Pé-de-Vento arrives at Alonso's bar and finds friends engaged in a lively argument about whether the gunshots, fisticuffs and other adventures depicted in the movies are "de mentira" (13) ["all lies"] (14) or whether they really happen. Readers, at least those who no longer believe in the tooth fairy, will experience ironic detachment at the thought that there could be a serious argument over such a question. Since they are unable to resolve the movie question (Jesuíno being unavailable for consultation), the group turns to other preferred topics of conversation. Pé-de-Vento, returning to his favorite theme, announces "Mandei buscar na França um navio com quatrocentas mulatas. Vai chegar na quarta-feira." (15) [" I ordered a shipload of four hundred mulatto girls from France. They will be arriving on Wednesday"] (17). Here then is a concrete test to determine whether or not the character has bona fide status as a "shepherd of the night"—a giver of protection, direction, correction meaning, and life to the female "sheep." As has been shown, the narrative is cast as an alternative, utopian world rather than a real one. That being the case, the fulfillment of the promise is at least a theoretical possibility. For Pé-de-Vento to remain unproblematic as a macho benefactor, he should deliver on his promise to bring the French *mulatas*, or at least make a serious effort to do so. But since he does not make the slightest move either to import the girls or even to find out if it might be possible, he is revealed to be an idle fabricator of male fantasies. The novel's pleasant space, then, where men are men and know what is best for their women, is not entirely devoid of the corrosive bite of satire. In general, the narrator's attitude seems consistent with the macho bravado of the characters. But the occasional treatment of characters from a distant, ironic perspective causes us to wonder how far this conflated perspective can be carried.

The depiction of a *malandro* utopia, where people shun adult responsibilities, where felicitous social opportunism solves immediate problems without creating structural change, and where women are figuratively represented as dumb animals, probably met with some objection in the 1960s when *Os pastores da noite* appeared; there can be no doubt about such objections today. But the status of this utopian vision is not particularly clear, since the novel raises the possibility that the "pastores da noite," the prime inhabitants of that utopian space, can be satirically unmasked as naïve children, seduced by their own male fantasies. Does the novel present us with a utopia, pure and simple, elements of which seem unpalatable to enlightened tastes? Or does it present us with a curious hybrid between utopia and distopia, a space where the results belong to a better world, but the means for obtaining those results raise real questions, imply real criticism, and suggest another vision of a modified world that is better still?

## BIBLIOGRAPHY

Amado, Jorge. *Os pastores da noite*. São Paulo: Martins, n.d.

————. *Shepherds of the Night*. Trans. Harriet de Onís. New York: Knopf, 1967.

Bandeira, Manuel. *This Earth, That Sky: Poems by Manuel Bandeira*. Trans. Candace Slater. Berkeley: U of California P, 1989.

Cândido, Antônio. "Dialética da malandragem (caracterização das *Memórias de um sargento de milícias*.)" *Revista do Instituto de Estudos Brasileiros* 8 (1970): 67–89.

————. "Poesia, documento e história." *Jorge Amado, povo e terra* (São Paulo: Martins, 1972). 114–17.

Chamberlain, Bobby J. *Jorge Amado*. Boston: Twayne, 1990.

————. "The *Malandro*, or Rogue Figure, in the Fiction of Jorge Amado." *Mester* 6 (1976): 7–10.

DaMatta, Roberto. *Carnivals, Rogues, and Heroes: An Interpretation of the Brazilian Dilemma*. Trans. John Drury. Notre Dame: University of Notre Dame Press, 1991.

————. *A casa e a rua: espaço, cidadania, mulher e morte no Brasil*. São Paulo: Brasiliense, 1985.

————. *O que faz o brasil, Brasil?* Rio de Janeiro: Rocco, 1991.

Elliott, Robert C. *The Shape of Utopia: Studies in a Literary Genre*. Chicago: University of Chicago Press, 1970.

Frye, Northrop. "Varieties of Literary Utopias." Frank E. Manuel, ed. *Utopias and Utopian Thought*. Boston: Houghton, 1966. 25–49.

Galvão, Walnice Nogueira. *Saco de gatos: ensaios críticos*. São Paulo: Duas Cidades, 1976.

Hunsaker, Steven V. "Representing the *mulata*: *El amor en los tiempos del cólera* and *Tenda dos milagres*." *Hispania* 77 (1994): 225–34.

Patai, Daphne. *Myth and Ideology in Contemporary Brazilian Fiction*. Rutherford, N.J.: Fairleigh Dickinson University Press, 1983.

Portella, Eduardo. "La Terre sans terreur." *Europe* 67.724–25 (1989): 32–36.

Santos, Itazil Benício dos. *Jorge Amado: retrato incompleto*. Rio de Janeiro: Record, 1993.

# Bitter Harvest
## Violent Oppression in *Cacau* and *Terras do sem fim*

SANDRA L. DIXON

Jorge Amado has said that he sells Brazil. For many readers, the country vividly portrayed in his fictional works is filled with lush vegetation, samba music, and carefree people. It appears as a tropical paradise where all citizens live harmoniously. Through a select reading of Brazilian history, it can be postulated that the nation's relative political stability has been achieved by the yearly tradition of *carnaval*. This celebration may serve as a release for volatile emotions. When the general population has permission to don costumes and dance uninhibitedly through the streets, it may be less likely to resort to violence as a protest against unpleasant social reality.

Generally speaking, Brazil has not been perceived by other countries as a violent land until recently. In 1889, the Republic was formed with relatively little bloodshed. When viewed within a greater South American context, Brazil appears to have been a peaceful nation.[1] However, violent impulses cannot be suppressed solely by unbridled revelry. Throughout Brazil's history there have been violent clashes between the landowning elite and a largely disenfranchised population.

In his earlier works, Jorge Amado depicts conflicts which were constantly played out in the country's northeastern region. Two novels which address the problematic relationships between cacao growers and workers are *Cacau* [*Cacao*] (1953) and *Terras do sem fim* [*The Violent Land*] (1942). Written nearly a decade apart, these works reflect a political and artistic maturity in the author. Nonetheless, they are similar in that violence appears as a constant. The characters in each novel move within a violent environment as either perpetrators or victims.

Two types of violence proposed by Ariel Dorfman are present in *Cacau* and *Terras do sem fim*: vertical, or that which is directed toward the oppressors; and horizontal, which an individual perpetrates upon friends and family members.[2] The former arises from political unrest: the "have-nots" against the "haves," while the latter primarily comes from frustration with certain circumstances. Horizontal violence also originates with exclusively personal differences among individuals.

Amado wrote *Cacau* to expose the social injustice which existed during the first decades of the twentieth century in Bahia's cacao region. As part of his politically committed literary phase, the book presents simplistic characterizations of the cruel cacao planter and his hard-working, long-suffering workers. However, the depiction of violence and its role in that social system take the novel beyond the realm of a simple exposé about exploitation in cacao country.

In the first few pages, the figure of the planter's hired killer predominates. Described as "preto, forte, alto, brigão" [Black, strong, tall, quarrelsome],[3] Honório is said to have killed some people on the orders of his boss Mané Frajelo. In spite of his dubious claim to fame, Honório is considered the best buddy in the world. His name suggests an honorable and trustworthy nature, which may seem ironic to the outsider, but upon further examination, he indeed appears to be a hero . . . a great guy.

The chapter entitled "Heroi da Tocaia e do Cangaço" ["The Hero of the Ambush and of Banditry"] contains his method of murdering a marked man:

> É a tocaia. Pela noite sem lua o viajante vem do povoado. A goiabeira solitaria no caminho esconde o homem e a repetição. É um tiro so. O corpo cai. O que atirou vai dizer ao que mandou que o serviço está feito e receber os cem mil-réis prometidos. No outro dia o corpo é encontrado e enterrado ali mesmo. E tudo continua sem novidade [It's the ambush. On the moonless night a traveller comes from the town. The solitary guava tree on the road hides a man and a repeating rifle. It's only one shot. The body falls. The one who did the shooting is going to tell the one who ordered it that the job is done and then he receives the one hundred "mil-reis" promised to him. On the following day the body is found and buried right there. And everything continues as always]. (*Obras* 150)

The unemotional description of the hired killer's *modus operandi* reflects the nonchalance with which the populace views violence in this area. A sniper's stealth and marksmanship are admired while a victim's suffering is ignored. Only the boss's will matters in this social system. Within the typology of violence put forth by Dorfman, there exists an implied hierarchy. The chain of command originates with Mané Franjelo ("the one who ordered the job") and terminates with Honório, the assassin. His position as trusted employee to the planter and as amiable comrade to the workers is paradoxical. If his job is to kill his employer's enemies, he may be called upon to murder the very people with whom he socializes: the workers who resent their exploitation by Mané Frajelo and may consider harming him.

The narrator, José Cordeiro, thinks of Honório as a friend and something of a mentor: "Honório me ensinou o serviço. Ficamos bons camaradas naquelas sombras carinhosas dos cacaucais . . ." [Honório taught me the job. We became good buddies in the caressing shades of the cacao trees . . . ] (*Obras* 148). José also echoes the sentiments of the general community when he expresses admiration for his friend's talent for killing.

> Honório era técnico em tocaia e o coronel Misael tinha inúmeros inimigos . . . Não sei se o coronel sentia remorsos, Honório, não. Tinha a consciência limpa e clara como a água da fonte Era bom camarada e nós o estimávamos muito [Honório was a technician in the ambush and Colonel Misael (Mané Franjelo's real name) had countless enemies . . . I don't know if the colonel felt remorse, Honório didn't. He had a clean and clear conscience like water from the spring. He was a good buddy and we held him in high esteem]. (*Obras* 150)

It seems unimportant to the narrator, an advocate of the proletariat, that his friend murders on behalf of their employer. Honório serves as a symbol of Mané Frajelo's power. No worker dares to challenge the authority of either man. In this way, everyone is kept in his place within the social hierarchy.

The status quo is upset when a worker slashes the face of Mané Frajelo's son, Osório. This member of the landholding class is attacked by a social "inferior." However, Osório was caught in bed with the fiancée of his attacker, Colodino. Such behavior is an affront to the man's honor, and must therefore be avenged. In this instance, violence comes "from below" rather than "from above" as in the preceding case. In an effort to maintain his personal integrity, Colodino seeks his satisfaction in blood, which, according to the code of honor, is acceptable.

Despite whatever justification he may have, the desperate man's act must be met with violence. Mané Franjelo summons Honório to his house and offers him fifteen hundred mil-réis to kill Colodino. However, he does not choose to do so. The narrator askes him why and later offers his own opinion concerning his friend's motivation.

> —Por que você não matou Colodino? Por que queria bem a êle?
> —Eu gostava de Colodino . . . Mas eu não quemei o bruto porque ele era alugado como a gente. Matá coroné é bom, mas trabaiado não mato. Não sou traidô . . .
> Só muito tempo depois soube que o gesto de Honório não se chamava genero-sidade. Tinha um nome muito mais bonito: Consciência de Classe
> ["Why didn't you kill Colodino? Why were you fond of him?"
> "I liked Colodino . . . But I didn't burn the brute because he was a hired man like us. Killing the Colonel is okay, but I don't kill a worker. I'm not a traitor . . ."

Only a long time afterward I found out that Honório's gesture was not
called generosity. It had a much lovelier name: Class Consciousness].
(*Obras* 208)

Honório's refusal to kill a comrade, clearly upsets the well-structured
social order which he previously helped maintain. In keeping with Amado's
political agenda, this character, once the enforcer for the oppressor, comes to
realize the error of his ways.

The optimistic conclusion reflects the author's concern with the
deplorable conditions associated with cacao cultivation in northeastern Brazil
during the nineteen twenties and thirties. The ending also lays bare the truly
violent nature of the struggle between growers and their exploited hired help.
In *Cacau*, there is a clear emphasis on the vertical or social violence used to
maintain the status quo specifically so that cacao production can be increased
to support and enrich a landowning elite.

The specter of violence also pervades *Terras do sem fim*, but Amado presents another aspect of Dorfman's typology: that of horizontal violence or
violence perpetrated upon family members and friends. In *Terras do sem fim*,
the principal instigators of violent acts are rivals within the same land-owning
class. Colonel Horácio and the Badaró brothers wage battles over land by
using their political influence as well as hired killers. They create a sphere of
terror which affects their own families and the members of their community.

Unlike their counterpart, Mané Frajelo in *Cacau*, the planters of *Terras
do sem fim* are portrayed as noble patriarchs. The author has commented upon
the predominance of death in the novel:

La muerte, . . . , y también el amor, están muy presentes, pero la muerte es
casi lo que domina. Hay tantas matanzas, todo es una batalla [Death. . . and
also love are very much present, but death is that which most predominates.
There are so many murders; everything is a battle].[4]

The grand purpose of the battle waged in *Terras do sem fim* is that of
acquiring land; but the unanswered question remains: At what cost? The
planters create an atmosphere of fear, causing tension in every aspect of their
personal lives. Relatives and friends are forced to perform according to the
accepted social standards of the day.

As in *Cacau*, Amado presents the hired assassin as a principal means by
which the planters secure their power. At times, the Badarós and Horácio participate in the violence which they instigate, but more often than not, they uti-
lize the services of gunmen. Negro Damião, an employee of Juca Badaró,
seems the ideal killer. His description differs from that of Honório in *Cacau*.
He is first presented lying in ambush; that is to say, on the job. His talent and
his faithfulness are his outstanding character traits. Invariably identified with

his employer, he has become an agent of violence whose fame has spread to the capital.

Quem não conhece nessas redondezas ao negro Damião, o jagunço de confiança de Sinho Badaró? Sua fama corre terra, há muito que está além de Palestina, de Ferradas e de Tabocas. Dos botequins de Ilhéus onde comentavam seus feitos, ela viajara nos pequenos navios até a capital e um jornal da Bahia já publicara seu nome em letra redonda [Who in the vicinity did not know Negro Damião, Sinho Badaró's trustedhired gunman? His fame spread throughout the land, farther than Palestina, Ferradas and Tabocas. From the taverns of Ilhéus, where they remarked about his deeds, it traveled on small boats to the capital and a Bahian newspaper had already published his name in round letters].[5]

In the sixth chapter of "A Mata" ["The Forest"] in *Terras do sem fim*, Damião undergoes a transformation. As he waits in ambush for Firmo, one of Horácio's enemies, questions once put to him echo through his mind: "—Tu acha bom matar gente? Tu não sente nada? Nada por dentro?" [Do you think it's good to kill people? Don't you feel anything? Nothing inside?] (*Obras: Terras 78*). Upon reflection, he realizes that he has affected more lives than those of his victims. His violent actions have destroyed familes and caused irreparable suffering. The images which plague him while he waits to take yet another life drive him mad. In realizing that he has harmed individuals not directly connected with the planters' land feuds, he feels true remorse.

This is the only chapter of the novel in which the consequences of violence are graphically depicted. Damião's mental anguish reflects the guilt caused by a social system which is maintained by means of assassination and terror. Novelistically, it seems appropriate that the agent of terror, the wild beast or "a fera," as Horácio calls him, should be depicted wandering through the forest. Only in this state of agitation, can he understand the seriousness of his actions.

Through Damião, the planters maintain a power base. The oppressive atmosphere assures the cooperation of the entire community in producing ever greater yields of cacao. However, not only the lower classes suffer from the threat of violence to themselves and their property. The colonels' families also live under a rigid patriarch-centered social order which is supported by the constant threat of violence.

The characterization of Ester, Colonel Horácio's beautiful young wife, reveals the personal toll of the violent environment created by the planters. She harbors contempt for the savage land and the savage behavior of her husband. Considered a fine prize by her spouse and longing for cordial company, she takes the lawyer Virgílio as a lover—an action which defies the strict social code of the period.

The extent of her contempt for her circumstances is seen during a dinner

party with her husband and the young, attractive lawyer. Horácio asks her to
play the piano for their guest. His condescending attitude triggers a reaction
in Ester which seems uncharacteristic of her genteel nature.

> Ester ouvia muda, um ódio ia subindo dentro dela. Maior ainda que que sen-
> tira na noite do seu casamento, quando Horácio rasgou seus vestidos e se
> lançou sobre seu corpo. Estava ligeiramente tomada pelo vinho, embria-
> gada também pelas palavras de Virgílio, e seus olhos era novamente os
> trêfegos e sonhadores olhos da normalista dos anos passados. E viram um
> Horácio transformado num grande porco sujo, igual a um que havia na
> fazenda e habitava os lamaçais próximos a estrada. E Virgílio surgia como
> um cavalheiro andante, um mosqueteiro, un conde francês, mistura de per-
> sonagens de romances lidos no colégio, todas nobres, audazes e belas. Ape-
> sar de tudo, apesar do ódio—o mesmo por causa do ódio?—era delicioso
> aquêle jantar [Ester silently listened, a hatred rising within her. It was
> greater than that which she felt on her wedding night when Horácio tore off
> her clothes and threw himself onto her body. She was a little bit under the
> influence of the wine, (and) also intoxicated by Virgílio's words, and her
> eyes were once again the restless and dreamy ones of the schoolgirl of years
> past. And they saw Horácio transformed into a big, dirty pig, like the one
> that was on the plantation and lived in the mudholes near the road. And
> Virgílio appeared as a wandering knight, a musketeer, a French count, a
> mixture of characters from the novels read in school, all noble, daring, and
> handsome. In spite of everything, in spite of the hatred—or really because
> of the hatred?—that was a delicious dinner]. (*Obras: Terras* 89–90)

The sexual violence endured by Ester is seen throughout Brazilian history, and, unfortunately, often as a normal characteristic of the traditional
Brazilian plantation society. Ester's hatred is never openly expressed. However, while appearing passive and accepting of her condition, she visualizes
another reality. Her affair with Virgílio can be considered as a defiant act—a
response to the violence under which she suffers. The fact that she betrays her
husband puts her at odds with the class to which she belongs, but her rebellion goes unnoticed by her husband and society at large since she dies without
revealing the affair. It appears, then, that her only escape from the sexual and
mental abuse heaped upon her by Horácio and his violent society is death.

In these two earlier works by Jorge Amado, violence appears as a back-
drop to all action. If characters are not planning violent acts to further political or personal ends, they are seeking to defend themselves from bodily
injury or to retaliate for suffering that others may have caused them. The violent acts described in *Cacau* and *Terras do sem fim* serve to impose a strict
social order. Seldom is an attack depicted as an emotional release but rather it
is portrayed as a calculated aggression. Ambushes and gunfights are regarded
as necessary to maintain the *status quo*.

What stands out in the two novels are the portrayals of the hired assassins. In *Cacau*, Honório is perceived by other characters as honorable. His acceptance in society, among workers and landholders alike, distinguishes him as a heroic figure. Since the novel ends with him giving up his profession and joining the proletariat cause, his participation in the violent hierarchy can be seen as a temporary aberration. The character no longer engenders violence horizontally, but vertically.

The tortured image of Negro Damião reflects the destructive force of violence. Never completely accepted like his counterpart in *Cacau*, the killer understands the despicable nature of his crimes. During his "mad scene" in the section entitled "A Mata," Damião relives his life, and realizes that he is an outcast. He even contemplates the concept of hell for a time, remembering the words of a friar who once said that merely killing one person would result in fiery condemnation. However, the feeling of remorse for the numerous murders he committed overwhelms him and ultimately drives him insane. He becomes a pathetic character who no longer has the respect of anyone. The system for which and in which he worked throws him away. Damião becomes a ghost, insanely haunting the forest.

Despite popular images to the contrary, violence has been a consistent presence in the historical development of Brazil. Although not necessarily explosive and completely disruptive as in the cases of other South American countries, institutionalized violence has kept a powerful landholding class in power in rural areas such as those portrayed in *Cacau* and *Terras do sem fim*.

Inside Brazil's beauteous tropical tranquilty there exist man-made conflicts. Greed and guns are as much a part of Jorge Amado's Brazil as rhythmic music and *carnaval*. His depictions of the rougher north-eastern lifestyle sharply contrast with the image of a peaceful land inhabited by friendly people. The success of these novels lies in his ability to aid the reader in glimpsing the violence which he witnessed in his childhood years. It was uncontainable, leading to easy death.[6] Sadly, this violence is also characteristic of the country which Amado has sold to the world.

## NOTES

1. Joseph A. Page, *The Brazilians*. Reading, Massachussets: Addison-Wesley Publishing Company, 1995, 229–135.
2. Ariel Dorfman, *Imaginación y violencia en América*. Santiago de Chile: Editorial Universitaria, S.A., 1970 (17–32).
3. Jorge Amado, *Obras de Jorge Amado*. São Paulo: Livraria Martins Editora, 1970 (125).
4. Jorge Amado, *Jorge Amado: Conversaciones con Alice Raillard*. Trans. Rosa S. Corgatelli. Buenos Aires: Emecée Editores, S.A., 1992, 165.
5. Jorge Amado, *Obras de Jorge Amado: Terras do sem fim*. São Paulo: Livraria Martins, 1942, 71.

6. In *Jorge Amado,* Amado states that his childhood was marked by violence: "Toda mi infancia marcada por esa violencia incontenible, esas luchas, la muerte fácil" [all my childhood was marked by an unstoppable violence, those fights, the easy death] (190).

## BIBLIOGRAPHY

Amado, Jorge. *Conversaciones con Alice Raillard.* Trans. Rosa S. Corgatelli. Buenos Aires: Emecée Editores, S.A., 1992.

———. *Obras de Jorge Amado.* São Paulo: Livraria Martins Editora, 1970.

———. *Obras de Jorge Amado: Terras do sem fim.* São Paulo: Livraria Martins, 1942.

———. *O país do carnaval (romance); Cacau (romance); Suor (romance).* Obras Series, 10. São Paulo: Martins, 1974.

———. *Terras do sem fim (romance).* Obras Series, 7. São Paulo: Martins, 1974.

———. *The Violent Land.* Trans. Samuel Putman. New York: Knopf, 1945.

Chamberlain, Bobby J. *Jorge Amado.* Boston: Twayne, 1990.

Dorfman, Ariel. *Imaginación y violencia en América.* Santiago de Chile: Editorial Universitaria, S.A., 1970.

Foster, David William and Roberto Reis, comp. *A Dictionary of Contemporary Brazilian Authors.* Tempe: Center for Latin American Studies, Arizona State University, 1981.

Menezes, Raimundo de. *Dicionário literário brasileiro ilustrado.* São Paulo: Edição Saraiva, 1969.

Page, Joseph. *The Brazilians.* Reading: Addison-Wesley, 1995.

Scott, Nina. " Humor and Society in the Frontier Novels of the Americas: Wister, Güiraldes, and Amado." *Proceedings of the Xth Congress of the International Comparative Literature Association. New York 1982. Ed M.J. Valdés.* New York: Garland, 1985.

# "Dressing Down" the Warrior Maiden
## Plot, Perspective, and Gender Ideology in *Tereza Batista cansada de guerra*

ELLEN H. DOUGLASS

In a special subsection of an issue of *Colóquio-Letras* dedicated to Jorge Amado on his eightieth birthday, the Brazilian novelist received the following high praise for his representation of women: "O escritor Jorge Amado é, em suas páginas, o amante e o amigo de todas as mulheres" ["The writer Jorge Amado is, in his pages, the lover and friend of all women"][1] (Rodrigues 259). In light of feminist critiques of Amado's works which have been provided by scholars as influential as Walnice Nogueira Galvão and Daphne Patai, this identification of Jorge Amado as the "friend and lover" of "all women" cannot but strike us as naive. Yet it can also serve to remind us that, regardless of the existence of a strong feminist identification and critique of "machismo" as it operates in the writing of Jorge Amado, the matter of this author's record on the representation of women is far from resolved. On the one hand, the idea that Amado's female characters are often based in gender stereotypes more flattering to masculine egos than to flesh-and-blood women has been advanced often and widely enough that it can now be cited as a "critical commonplace"(Hunsaker 225). On the other hand, however, Amado has been cited by several critics, women as well as men among them, as "feminist" in his championship of the greater freedom of Brazilian women. Some of these favorable analyses, to be sure, resemble the birthday tribute cited above in terms of their failure to take into account the complexities of the feminist critique. Linda Hall's reading of Amado as a novelist who stands up for women by "elevat[ing] the heroines in his stories to goddesslike status while maintaining their warm humanity" (67), for example, glosses over the fact that idealization is, all too often, only the flip side of objectification. Other critics, however, Maria Luisa Nunes among them, present more sophisticated analyses of the ways in which the texts of Jorge Amado may be viewed as sites in which "the concerns of feminism and [of] patriarchal narrative intersect" ("Narratives by and about Women" 8). Jorge Amado's record on female characterization is, in short, and as one of the Brazilian author's longest-standing and most sympathetic critics has put it, "a checkered one" (Chamberlain 101).

In the context of this "checkered record," the 1972 *Tereza Batista cansada de guerra [Tereza Batista: Home from the Wars]* presents a particularly compelling set of questions. The third of Amado's novels to feature a female protagonist, *Tereza Batista* comprises, according to the author himself, an intentional statement on "Brazilian womanhood." In an interview published the same year as the novel, Amado compared his newest heroine with the female protagonists of his 1958 *Gabriela, cravo and canela [Gabriela, Clove and Cinnamon]* and 1966 *Dona Flor e seus dois maridos: [Dona Flor and her Two Husbands]*. "Gabriela and Dona Flor are characters with whom readers easily identify; hence their popularity. With Teresa Batista I tried to create a third image of the Brazilian woman—sensual, romantic, courageous, long-suffering, decent" (qtd. in Patai 111). As Daphne Patai has observed, the precise extent and meaning of the "difference" between Tereza and her predecessors is open to debate. The faces of patriarchally defined "Woman" are many, and Tereza partakes, to be sure, of at least one of them: the "prostitute with the heart of gold" (Patai 124).

Yet even as Tereza resembles the stereotype of the beautiful and benevolent prostitute, she also recalls another, less conventional, image of womanhood: the "warrior maiden" figure defined by her refusal to remain within the perimeters of activity and identity prescribed for persons of her sex. Perhaps most widely known in her Franco-Christian manifestation as Joan of Arc, the warrior maiden also turns up in two cultural systems more pertinent to the story of Tereza Batista: the Brazilian folk literature known as *literatura de cordel* and the Afro-Brazilian religious system *candomblé*. In his reading of *Tereza Batista* as a novelistic rendition of themes and structures common to the *literatura de cordel*,[2] Mark Curran points out the similarity between Amado's protagonist and the *donzela guerreira*[3] of popular literature: "O conceito da mulher valente mais do que o homem, boa de briga, lutadora, tem seu modelo na tradição oral e escrita" ["The figure of the woman who is more courageous than a man, good in combat, a fighter, has its model in oral and written tradition"] (59). Thanks especially to the work of Candace Slater, this identification of Tereza with the *cordel* warrior maiden is by now firmly established.

What remains to be emphasized, however, is that the novel itself directs us to compare Tereza with yet another "manly woman," namely, the *candomblé* diety or *orixá* Yansã. Despite the fact that Tereza is attended, as we learn through the mouth of a character identified as a *candomblé* priestess, by an astonishing array of *orixas*, her primary spiritual guide and guardian is the goddess Yansã (Amado, *Tereza Batista cansada de guerra,* 316). Often known simply as the *candomblé* goddess of rivers, winds and storm, Yansã is also a "gender-crossing" figure in so far as she embodies the conventionally masculine activities and attributes of war and bravery.[4] Within the text of *Tereza Batista*, in fact, it is the warrior aspect of Yansã which assumes primary importance. When Januário Gereba, the novelistic character who serves as an authority on Bahian religion in addition to as Tereza's primary love interest, identifies Tereza as a "daughter" of Yansã, he focuses on the "coragem" and war-like "disposição" of the *orixá*: "Apesar de mulher, Yansã e santo valente, ao lado de seu marido Xango empunhou as armas de guerra" ("Yansã was a woman, but she was the bravest spirit of them all, just the same; she fought in battle beside her husband Xangó").[5] (39). In so far as Amado's protagonist can thus be seen to participate in *candomblé* as well as *cordel* traditions of biological females who assume the clothing, qualities and occupations of men, she, like her sisters in figurative as well as literal transvestitism, can be read as a challenge to the patriarchal premise that biological sex is the equivalent of socially constructed sexual identity.

To pose a challenge is not, of course, to realize a victory, and Jorge Amado's image of "female heroism" is rife with equivocation. While the dynamics of this equivocation are, as we shall see, highly complex, we have only to consider the resolution of this novel to catch a relatively unambiguous glimpse of Jorge Amado's final position on the figure of the warrior maiden. The fact that the protagonist assumes the mantle of masculine valor in the first place is, as Slater has pointed out, represented as a consequence of necessity rather than choice. When male characters renege on their responsibility to protect women, Tereza Batista steps in to fill the void. But when a "real man" comes along, at last, in the figure of Januário Gereba, the pretense of female heroism gives way to an underlying current of female dependence. Reunited with Januário on page 418 of this 421-page novel, Tereza Batista bursts into tears, throws herself into her lover's arms and, within a few short paragraphs, lies down in his boat and asks him to "make [her] a baby." Observing that the story of the *donzela guerreira* of *cordel* literature also ends, more often than not, with a similar renunciation of the protagonist's unconventional "warrior ways," Slater points to the ideological significance of such a denouemont:

> ... the protagonist has the courage to do battle but renounces her warrior ways when conditions permit. Not surprisingly, Tereza eventually meets a man who is a genuine fighter and whose promise of a child symbolizes a restoration of traditional male/female roles. (152)

The message, both clear and conventional, goes something like this: in the best of all possible worlds males can, and do, act like men, thereby allowing females to act, per their truest nature, as women.

By mobilizing the figure of the warrior maiden in *Tereza Batista*, Amado does, in fact, raise feminist concerns and expectations. Yet by quashing this figure according to the requirements of patriarchal gender constructs, Amado manages to quash the same expectations he raises. As we chart the course and dynamics of this ideological double dealing, we will attend to two distinct if interrelated levels of the novel. The first of these, plot, concerns the story according to which Tereza Batista moves from a 12-year-old girl sold into sexual slavery to the evil Capitão, to the 26-year-old woman making love with her sailor on the deck of his boat. The second narrative perspective, concerns the meanderings of the voice of the authorial narrator figure to whom it is given to tell the bulk of the story of Tereza Batista. Especially in view of the fact that the authorial narrator is a dramatized figure, a character in his own right, these two levels of analysis are neither easily, nor completely, distinguishable. On the one hand, it is important to keep in mind that the plot line is constructed and delivered through the perspective of a personalized and fallible, rather than impersonal and omniscient, narrator. On the other hand, it is also important to recognize that this narrator character, portrayed as a man who has traveled throughout Northern Brazil in search of the truth about the enigmatic figure of Tereza Batista, is the protagonist of a plot of his own. *Tereza Batista* comprises, in short, a "frame tale." Framing the "inner" story of Tereza Batista is the "outer" story of the process by which the inner tale has been constructed. As we trace the process according to which the warrior maiden figure is at once deployed and destroyed in the course of this complex novel, we will attend to the plot of the inner tale, the tale of Tereza Batista, as well as to the variations in narrative perspective which are a function of the outer tale, the tale of the authorial narrator.

## PART I: PLOT AND THE WARRIOR MAIDEN

Any analysis of the relationship between plot and ideology must attend, in particular, to the question of narrative resolution. Observing that "narrative structures and subjects are like working apparatuses of ideology, factories for the 'natural' and 'fantastic' meanings by which we live," the North American feminist critic Rachel Blau DuPlessis identifies narrative outcome as "one place where transindividual assumptions and values are most clearly visible" (3). Though DuPlessis herself studies literature written by women, her insight into the particular ideological punch carried by narrative endings is highly pertinent to our analysis of Jorge Amado's *Tereza Batista*. In Candace Slater's discussion of the relationship between this novel and the *donzela guerreira* of *cordel* fame, the ending of the story is, as we have seen, regarded as ideologically decisive: between the return of Januário and the promise of a baby, the novel represents and recommends a "restoration of traditional male/female roles." Even more forcefully, Daphne Patai, in her analysis of *Tereza Batista* as a textual transmitter of "the ideology of machismo," views the protagonist's final union with Januário as a clear denunciation of her previous "heroic status":

> In *Tereza Batista* we see a heroic figure who is nonetheless assimilated into
> a peculiarly male vision of femininity . . . Tereza's heroic status (created by
> the use of epithets as well as by her feats against various evils) makes all the
> more striking her complete submission to Janu, for it affirms how much of a
> man he must be to dominate such a woman. (136)

Faring somewhat better than her Franco-Christian sister Joan of Arc, Tereza
Batista is not herself burned in the flames of her society's wrath. Nevertheless, her pretensions to masculinity do "go up in flames" as she assumes a
feminine role vis-a-vis a masculine man, thereby reinforcing the ideology
according to which females normally and *ideally* act like women and males
normally and *ideally* act like men.

If the warrior maiden figure is not ousted completely until the story of
Tereza gives way to closure, this final denunciation is by no means unexpected. To the contrary, the representation of the protagonist in terms of the
warrior maiden paradigm is characterized by instability throughout the narrative. At various points throughout the five books and 421 pages of this novel,
Tereza is represented as thinking and acting like a full-blooded warrior
maiden. Like the *donzela guerreira* of *cordel* literature, she displays courage
and fighting prowess in a series of battles. Like the Yansã of *candomblé*, her
fearlessness and valor are so great that she stands as firm in the presence of
evil spirits as she does in the presence of evil men. Yet there is also another
side to Tereza, a side that emerges whenever, and as just as soon as, the threat
of danger is diffused. In this aspect, Tereza is not only so beautiful and sensual that she inspires the universal desire of men, but she is also, for her own
part, desirous of nothing so much as the love of a "real man." If this more conventionally feminine aspect of Tereza definitively displaces the warrior-
maiden aspect at the end of the novel, it also competes for attention
throughout the length of the text. Or, to put it another way, as Tereza Batista
traces her trajectory from 12-year-old rape victim to 26-year-old aspiring
mother, she displays a continuous oscillation between her aspect as warrior
maiden on the one hand and her aspect as conventionally feminine woman on
the other. As the feminine aspect of Tereza oscillates in this way with the warrior-maiden aspect, the relationship between the two sides of the protagonist
gradually emerges as one of competition rather than complementarity.

Let us begin by considering the episode from the first book or *folheto*[6] of
the novel in which the warrior maiden aspect of Tereza first appears in full
dress. When a bully threatens to hit a woman in the Paris Alegre cabaret,
Tereza acts in a manner which establishes her courage and physical prowess.
In direct contrast to a number of male onlookers who hold back from inter-
vening, Tereza marches over to the fighting couple, declares that "homem que
bate em mulher não é homem" ["A man who hits a woman isn't a man at
all"][7], spits in the bully's face, and engages him in hand-to-hand combat

(18–19). Especially as some of the bully's friends step in along the way to assist in subduing the raging figure of Tereza, the protagonist's persistence and eventual victory might reasonably be interpreted as "courageous." Though the authorial narrator never draws such a conclusion himself, neither does he leave interpretation in the hands of the reader. Instead, he mobilizes another, non-narrator character, the sailor Januário Gereba, to put a name to the heroism of Tereza Batista. Arriving on the scene as the fight is in progress, Januário is initially taken aback by the sight of such fighting prowess in a woman: "'Virgem Nossa Senhora',," he comments from the sidelines, "mulher mais boa de briga do que essa ai não vi ate hoje'" ["Holy Virgin, I never saw a better woman in a fight in all my days"][8] (20). After this moment of hesitation, however, Januário makes a move which serves to consolidate the identification of Tereza as a figure of the warrior maiden: as he steps into the fray to lend his assistance, he issues the war cry "'La vou eu, Yansã!'" ["Yansã! here I come!"][9] (11). While there is some confusion, expressed through the perspective of the authorial narrator, as to just how to understand this "grito de guerra" ["war cry"]—is Januário identifying Tereza as Yansã, or is he identifying himself as Yansã's devotee?—both interpretations reinforce the identification of Tereza with the *candomblé* goddess of war. If Tereza is to be viewed, as Januário later asserts more explicitly, as a "filha" of Yansã, it is only fitting that Januário, her lover, is an *ogan* or devotee of this same *orixá*.

Yet almost as soon as Tereza assumes the mantle of the warrior maiden, the more feminine aspect of the protagonist comes decisively into play. First, Tereza's success in the bar brawl is not attributed to Tereza herself but, rather, to Januário. As Tereza reflects, in a later chapter, back on the night of the fight, she thinks about how Januário "sozinho tinha posto fim ao bafafa, rindo e falando alto . . ." ["He had put an end to the fight single-handed, laughing and shouting . . ."][10] (26). Given that Tereza was bleeding at the mouth and about to be attacked by a pair of hostile police officers when Januário arrived on the scene, it would make sense for her to think of him as a partner in her eventual victory over the bully and his friends. Instead, however, she regards Januário as having accomplished this victory "sozinho." Furthermore, when Januário, also reflecting back on the fight, refers aloud to Tereza as "mulherzinha valente de se tirar o chapeu" ["The sort of brave little gal a man takes his hat off to"][11] (20). Tereza is quick to contradict him: "Sou valente nada . . . Mais bem medrosa, so que não posso ver homem bater em mulher" ["I'm not brave at all . . . Really, I'm timid. It's just that I can't stand to see a man hit a woman"] (27). Tereza Batista's heroism, far from being an essential quality, is simply a response to an extreme circumstance: she cannot bear, as she states, to see a man hit a woman. In the absence of such extremity, however, she is "medrosa" or "faint-hearted" as a "real woman" should be.

This conversation in which Tereza objects to being labeled a "mulher valente" occurs at the beginning of a *folheto* composed of three interlocking plot lines: the story of Tereza's debut as a professional dancer at the Paris Alegre cabaret, the story of Tereza's role in assisting an elderly widow to defeat a usurer in court, and the story of Tereza's love affair with Januário. While all three of these plot lines evoke the heroic as well as womanly sides of Tereza, all serve, in the final analysis, to distance the protagonist from her warrior maiden persona.

Tereza's relationship with Januário begins when the sailor first encounters the protagonist engaged in the bar brawl. Despite the fact that this opening serves to establish Tereza's potential for heroism, the story of the protagonist's relationship with the sailor is rapidly transformed into a conventional love story involving a manly man and a womanly woman. In contrast to the cowardly men who held back when the bully hit the woman in the bar, Januário Gereba is, as Tereza herself perceives him, "a inteireza de homem" ["a real man"] (29). Even Januário's hesitation to act on his love for Tereza, to approach her sexually, forms part of this representation of him as a "real man." Learning that Januário intends to return to his wife, an invalid who has nothing to live for but her marriage, Tereza interprets his honorableness as yet another sign of his manliness: "Tu é direito, Januário Gereba, falou como um homen deve falar" ["You've treated me straight, Januário Gereba. You're the way a man ought to be; you tell the truth like a man"][12] (47). At the side of this manly man, Tereza Batista is able, for her part, to put aside her warrior-like defenses and blossom into a womanly woman. In the full knowledge that Januário will leave her eventually, Tereza chooses to put aside any hope for her own future happiness, and to live, however briefly, for his love and his touch. In keeping with the patriarchal notion that men are born to act but women are born to love, Tereza Batista makes of the sailor her "homem, . . . marido, . . . amor, . . . vida, . . . [e] morte" ["man, . . . husband, . . . love, . . . life, . . . (and) death"][13] (62), the very center of her life and identity.

The only things which serve to distract Tereza from the intensity of her love affair with Januário are her impending debut at the Paris Alegre and her participation in the legal struggle of Joana das Folhas. Learning that her lawyer admirer Lulu Santos is representing the widow Joana against a usurer who aims to swindle away her farm, Tereza helps to concoct and carry out a defense which requires that the illiterate old woman learn to write her own name. In so far as the usurer, Libório, is the same man who hit the woman in the bar brawl, Tereza's participation in this legal struggle serves to present her in renewed combat with the bully she has already once defeated. If Tereza goes up for a second time against the very same bully, however, she does not go up against him in the very same way. Cast as the friend and helpmeet of Lulu Santos, Tereza works behind the scenes, never even putting in an appearance in court, as she teaches the old Joana the rudiments of writing. Even as this role serves to remind us of Tereza's hatred of injustice in general and bullies in particular, it presents her in a way which emphasizes her "womanly" qualities of kindness, patience and modesty. Furthermore, it suggests her willingness, even eagerness, to accept direction from those men deemed to be "good." Evoking the memory of Tereza in the bar brawl, the story of her renewed opposition to the bully Libório also serves, paradoxically, to soften and diffuse this image of female heroism.

Though the warrior-maiden and feminine aspects of Tereza compete throughout the first *folheto*, it is the latter—the "womanly" side of Tereza—which emerges as victorious. The third and final plot line—the story of Tereza's debut at the Paris Alegre cabaret—illustrates this conclusion in a particularly vivid way. At this point, it is important to point out that Tereza's presence in the Paris Alegre cabaret on the night of the fight is attributed to the fact that she is about to make her debut as a samba star. Whereas Tereza in her guise as warrior maiden is associated with masculine qualities, Tereza-as-*sambista*[14] is feminine to the hilt. Beautiful, sensual and adorned for the consumption of masculine glances, Tereza-as-*sambista* is modeled on a specific, and highly sexualized, stereotype of femininity: the stereotype of the Brazilian *mulata*. Thus, when the protagonist finally steps onto the stage of the Paris Alegre, the narrator announces her as a "*mulata* nacional de dengue e requebro" ["national *mulata* in all her sensual pride"][15] (64). On one hand, this debut of Tereza-as-*sambista*, of Tereza as "womanly" woman, has been delayed by the need for her to "put in an appearance" as the warrior maiden. When a man defied gender etiquette by raising his hand to a woman in public, Tereza had to put aside her womanly qualities long enough to set things right. Once the proper relations of men and women have been reestablished, however, the way is clear for Tereza to restage her dancing debut. In the final chapter of the first *folheto*, the protagonist steps onto the stage of the Paris Alegre and "solta . . . a bunda como (Januário) lhe ensinou" ["(Lets) her ass fly the way (Januário) had taught her"][16] (66). From Yansã to *mulata*, from warrior maiden to womanly spectacle, Tereza Batista settles into a role more appropriate to her sex.

The oscillation between the warrior-maiden and feminine aspects of Tereza Batista which begins in the first *folheto* is, as we have established, resolved definitively in the conventional ending of the novel. Along the way, however, the contest between warrior maiden and womanly woman continues unabated, with each apparent "resolution" giving way to renewed tension and competition. The more closely we look at the novel, the more rapid the oscillation between the warrior-maiden and feminine sides of Tereza Batista. Within the context of a *folheto* or even a scene dominated by the warrior-maiden aspect, that is, the feminine side may appear as a momentary "blip" on the textual screen, or, by the same token, vice versa. In the episode depicting Tereza Batista's long-delayed debut as a samba star, for example, the final image of her "shaking her buns" is preceded by a brief scene in which yet another bully threatens to hit yet another woman. This time, however, Tereza has only to flare into verbal indignation for the man to remember his manners. The protagonist's potential to become a figure of the warrior maiden, though invoked, is not realized. Instead, the womanly or, in this case, *mulata* aspect of the protagonist is maintained, and the samba show can go on.

Since it would be neither possible nor desirable to conduct such a close reading of a novel the length of *Tereza Batista*, let us step back and survey the oscillation between the warrior-maiden and womanly aspects of Tereza in a more general and schematic way. Although the five *folhetos* of the novel are arranged in a non-linear fashion, we will, given our present focus on plot, proceed chronologically. At age 12 and in the context of her resistance to the cruel Capitão, Tereza Batista may be identified as a figure of the warrior maiden. As she opposes the rapist with more courage and success than any of his previous victims, she steels herself with the gender-crossing refrain: "Guerreiro não chora nem na hora da morte" ["Fighting men don't cry, not even when they're dying"][17] (109). When the Captain brings out the branding iron, however, Tereza is finally reduced to complete submission. Depicted primarily in terms of sexual humiliation—"Tereza por fim obediente. Chupa, ela chupou" ["Tereza had learned obedience at last. Suck! and she sucked"][18] (116)—this erasure of the warrior maiden and her courage prepares the way for Tereza to be reborn, in her sexual relationship with Daniel, as a patriarchally defined woman: "Abrem-se as pernas de Tereza, as coxas da menina enfim mulher" ["Tereza opened her legs, the thighs of a girl who was a woman at last"][19] (167). When Tereza rises up to kill the Captain with a jerky knife, this incarnation of the protagonist as a conventionally receptive and love-hungry "woman" cedes, for one brief episode, to a renewed appearance of Tereza-as-warrior-maiden or, as she is referred to at this moment in the text, "Tereza Medo Acabou" ["Tereza Ain't-Afraid-No-More"][20] (183). It is not long, however, before "Tereza Medo Acabou" is subsumed into yet another incarnation as conventional "woman": sweeping her up onto the croup of his horse, Emiliano Guedes, Tereza's first "true" Prince Charming, installs her in his house in the country where she "flourishes," under his "knowing and patient hands," into an "incomparable woman" (228). It is after Emiliano dies that Tereza goes to the city where she first meets Januário, and where, as we have seen, she reassumes the identity of the warrior maiden during the fight in the bar, but then drops it again to become a samba-dancing *mulata*. Following the re-ascendance of Tereza-as-conventional-woman in the figure of the *sambista*, the protagonist goes on to engage in two of her most unambiguously heroic episodes: in the first, she leads a group of prostitutes in battle against an epidemic of smallpox; in the second, she plays a leading role in the "closed basket" strike of prostitutes in Bahia. Yet these "heroic" episodes give way, in turn, to her final reunion with Januário, and to her definitive resumption of womanliness in favor of warrior-maidenness at the end of the novel.

As Tereza Batista, "cansada de guerra," lays down with Januário Gereba in the final chapter of the novel which bears her name, the figure of the warrior maiden can be seen to "lay down" her arms. In the secure presence of Januário, "a inteireza de homem," Tereza Batista can at last settle comfortably into her own preferred and preferable identity as "a inteireza de mulher" ["a real woman"].

If this is the last time we will witness the defeat of the warrior-maiden figure, however, it is by no means the first. Launched in the first *folheto* of the novel, the representation of Tereza Batista as a figure of the warrior maiden is characterized by equivocation from the moment of its inception. At the level of plot, this equivocation is expressed in the protagonist's oscillation between two distinct, and mutually exclusive, identities. Whenever and wherever Tereza appears in her warrior maiden persona, the more womanly Tereza soon comes along to steal the show.

## PART II: NARRATIVE PERSPECTIVE
## AND THE WARRIOR MAIDEN

Like a disobedient schoolchild called to the front of a classroom, the gender-crossing figure of the warrior maiden is only deployed in the text of *Tereza Batista* in order to be roundly denounced. Although this denunciation occurs, as we have seen, in the oscillations and resolution of the plot, it is not a matter of plot alone. Instead, the processes by which this novel undermines and, ultimately, repudiates the figure of the warrior maiden, are also matters of narrative structure and, in particular, of narrative perspective.

Much has been written about the innovative and apparently "popular" narrative structure of *Tereza Batista*. As various critics have observed in detail, the similarities between *Tereza Batista* and the *literatura de cordel* are not restricted to Amado's adaptation of the popular figure of the warrior maiden, but include structural parallels as well.[21] For the purposes of the present discussion, the most important structural parallel between Tereza Batista and the *literatura de cordel* concerns what Mark Curran has called the *modus operandi* of the poet behind the literary work. The method of the popular Brazilian poet is, as Curran points out, more akin to that of the journalist than of the twentieth-century Western novelist: the *cordel* poet works by traveling throughout the North of Brazil, by soliciting testimony with regard to a specific theme or themes, and by synthesizing this testimony into stories in verse. Similarly, the primary narrator of *Tereza Batista* is represented, by his author, as a man who travels throughout Northern Brazil in quest of the truth about the legendary figure of Tereza Batista, and who, to this end, gathers and synthesizes the testimonies of twelve distinct secondary narrators. Furthermore, the representation of the authorial narrator as a man who collects and presents his material after the manner of the *cordel* poets is reflected in the structure of the novel itself. Following the brief introductory segment in which the authorial narrator announces that he is about to tell us the story of Tereza Batista, we encounter, in each of the five subsequent books, two or more secondary narrators. The testimony of these various secondary narrators, indicated in the novel by the use of italicized print, is always structured in the form of a "talking to," an interlocutor clearly identifiable as the authorial narrator. While the authorial narrator does not, at any time, speak directly "back" to these secondary narrators, he does, nevertheless, weave the information they give him into his own account of the story of Tereza Batista, the non-italicized narrative that, even as it is punctuated by the voices of the secondary narrators, comprises the bulk of the 421-page narrative.

Within the context of this multivocal narrative structure, the question of narrative perspective becomes complex indeed. First, since the authorial narrator as well as each of the twelve secondary narrators speak in his (or, in two cases, her) own voice, this means that we encounter as readers no less than thirteen distinct first-person points-of-view. Second, and what is more important to the present argument, the authorial narrator increases the quantity of points-of-view even further by exercising, in those portions of the story which he narrates himself, the privileges of free-indirect discourse. Despite his status as a character in his own right, that is, the authorial narrator enjoys and exercises the ability to dip in and out of the perspectives of minor as well as major non-narrator characters.[22] Thus even when the narrative is presented, as it is for the bulk of the novel, as emanating from the voice of this authorial narrator figure, the point-of-view is multiple.

As we consider the role of narrative perspective in the representation of Tereza Batista, we will focus on the central and determining voice of the authorial narrator. To some extent, this choice is pragmatic: it would be impossible to do justice, in an essay of this length, to thirteen different first-person voices. There is also, however, a more substantive reason for paying particular attention to what goes on in the perspective of the authorial narrator. In so far as it both synthesizes and surpasses in length the testimonies of the secondary narrators, the story constructed by the authorial narrator is represented as the fullest and most accurate account available to us about the life of Tereza Batista. No one person can ever, as the authorial narrator himself cautions us, know "toda a verdade" ["the full truth"] about the life of Tereza Batista (11). But the account presented through the voice of the authorial narrator, an account which is itself represented as the product of a sustained journey and copious set of interviews, is about as close to the "full truth" about Tereza Batista as we are going to get.

Confining ourselves, then, to the voice of the authorial narrator, we can see that this voice undermines the representation of Tereza Batista as warrior maiden from three distinct angles. First, the authorial narrator speaks about Tereza from a point-of-view which is represented as his own. Second, the authorial narrator portrays the thoughts and feelings of Tereza Batista "herself" in order to represent her, ostensibly, from her "own" point-of-view. Third, the authorial narrator also portrays the inner visions of other story characters, both major and minor, in order to show us what they think and feel about Tereza Batista. In the authorial narrator's over-all representation of Tereza Batista, each of these perspective angles or points-of-view contributes, in its own way, to the erasure and denunciation of Tereza-as-warrior-maiden in favor of the representation of Tereza as a figure of conventional femininity.

Let us return to the series of episodes treated in Part I of this essay, the episodes which begin with Tereza's fight in the Paris Alegre cabaret. Since this is the point in the novel at which Tereza is most specifically identified with the *candomblé* goddess of war Yansã, it is a promising point-of-departure for any discussion of the relationship between Tereza Batista and local as well as cross-cultural figures of the warrior maiden. At the level of plot, as we have seen, the representation of Tereza as Yansã is eventually displaced by a competing representation of the protagonist as an embodiment of conventional femininity: while this displacement begins in the protagonist's attempts to play the "little woman" to Januário, it culminates, after his departure, in her assumption of the flamboyant femininity of the dancing *mulata*. Even as the displacement of the warrior maiden is being accomplished through the machinations of plot, however, it is also being furthered through the meanderings of narrative perspective.

The first point to be made concerns the ends to which the authorial narrator puts the perspectives of non-narrator characters other than Tereza. As the protagonist makes her way through the oscillating plot of the first *folheto*, the authorial narrator is not the only one following her movements. Instead, she is the object of any number of gazes, almost all of them masculine. Tereza's primary love interest as it emerges in the first *folheto* is, of course, the sailor Januário. Yet so great are the beauty and grace of Tereza Batista that she also accumulates, without meaning or wanting to, a trail of unrequited lovers. The poet, the dentist, the painter, the lawyer, the judge, the nightclub owner: all of them are watching Tereza with longing. We know this not only because the authorial narrator *tells* us it is so, but also because he shares the narrative perspective with this "corte dos apaixonados" ["court of lovers"] (64). Thus, for example, when Tereza first appears in full *sambista* dress at the Paris Alegre cabaret, the authorial narrator reinforces his statement that "a formosura de Tereza não passou despercebida" ["Tereza's attractiveness did not go unnoticed"][23] by allowing Tereza's lawyer admirer to alert her to the fact that her poet admirer "não tira os olhos [dela]" ["can't take his eyes off (her)"][24] (16). Or, even more directly, we get a glimpse of Tereza dancing, as well as of her "court" of onlookers, through the jealous eye of the nightclub owner:

> Tereza ensaiou e dançou vestida com trajes ainda da companhia: turbante, saiote, bata. Boa parte do corpo à mostra, mas para quê? No piano, melancólico, Flori renega a corte lítero-artística, por vezes jurídica, quase sempre odontólgica, aos pés de Tereza Batista ... [Tereza rehearsed and danced in a costume that had once been part of the company wardrobe: turban, short skirt, and lace overblouse. A considerable part of her was bare, but what of that? Melancholy Flori, seated at his piano, cursed the never-failing literary, artistic, occasionally juridical, almost always odonto-logical court at Tereza Batista's feet . . .].[25] (22)

By mobilizing so many points-of-view as he tells the story of Tereza Batista, the authorial narrator communicates, first of all, that this is a protagonist worth watching. Yet he also lets us know just *how* Tereza is viewed, not only by himself, but also by others. Along these lines, it is highly significant that of all of these non-narrator characters, only one, Januário, sees Tereza as a figure of the warrior maiden. The others perceive her, instead, as an embodiment of conventional femininity.

As we established in Part I of this essay, the identification of Tereza with Yansã during and after the bar fight is placed in the mouth of a single character, Januário Gereba. Although it is not entirely clear what Januário means when he invokes Yansã in the midst of the brawl, he later explains, in conversation with Tereza, that the protagonist reminds him of the *candomblé* goddess of war. Revealing himself as an *ogan* or devotee of Yansã, Januário offers his opinion that Tereza herself "deve ser filha de Yansã sendo as duas iguais na coragem, na disposição" ["must be a daughter of Yansã; they had the same courage, the same fearless temperament"][26] (39).

In opposition to this single view of Tereza as Yansã, stand the opinions of a whole multitude of non-narrator characters who view her, instead, as the apex of femininity. Most of the characters associated with this opposing point-of-view form part of Tereza's "court" of admirers, and most of them both love and perceive her in her role and dress as a *sambista*. Let us take, for example, the minor character of the judge. Although this character is portrayed as officiating at the trial in which Joana das Folhas defeats the usurer thanks to writing lessons provided by Tereza, he is not represented in any direct interaction with the protagonist until the night of her long-postponed debut as a professional dancer. As soon as he sees Tereza in her *sambista* costume, any "admiration" he may have felt for her as a result of the court case gives way to a much stronger impression of the protagonist as a potential mistress:

> Os olhos do admiração do doutor juiz cresceram de imediato em olhos de devoção e desejo: ah! fosse ele desembargador no Tribunal de Justiça do Estado e lhe ofereceria lar e carinho, mas com os estupêndios de juiz de

direito mal chegando para a família legalmente constituída, ... como pensar em amásia, em amante, em amiga, casa militar? [The eyes of the judge, (initially full of admiration,) were soon brimming with (devotion) and desire. Ah, if only he were a judge on the State Court of Appeals, he could offer her a home and heart; but the stipend of a lower-court judge was barely enough to feed his legally wedded wife and his children ... ; there was no use in thinking of a 'military home' with a friend, mistress or concubine in it].[27](65)

While there can be no mistaking the note of irony in the depiction of this inner vision, this irony is not directed against the judge's perception of Tereza but, instead, against his pecuniary world view.

The judge's perception of Tereza as a person defined more by her womanly wiles than her heroic actions is shared by so many characters, including a number of relatively "bohemian" ones, that it can only be viewed as dominant. In particular, the poet and the painter, characters for whom the authorial narrator expresses outright sympathy, lead the way in defining Tereza in terms of her feminine rather than heroic qualities. Upon first meeting Tereza, the poet perceives her essence as follows: "sua obrigação e ser bela, somente" ["Your only obligation is just to be beautiful"][28] (17). Similarly, the painter's repeated attempts to capture Tereza on canvas will culminate in an image which reveals her womanly beauty rather than her warrior-like heroism:

... muitos [retratos de Tereza Batista] pintou, de memória quase todos, se bem vários anos depois ... houvesse ela consentido em posar ... para aquele quadro premiado onde Tereza se alça em ouro e cobre, mulher completa, na força da idade e da beleza, vestida porém com os mesmos trajes do tempo do Paris Alegre: turbante de baiana, curta bata de cambraia sobre os seios soltos, o colorido saiote de barbados, as pernas nuas, o reluzente coxame. [He was to paint many [portraits of Tereza], mostly from memory, though some years later she did consent to pose for him ... for the prizewinning picture he did of her, standing all copper and gold, a glorious woman in the full flower of her years and beauty, and wearing the costume of the old (Paris Alegre) days: the Bahian turban, gaily colored flounced short skirt, bare legs and gleaming thighs].[29] (23).

Especially given that the authorial narrator himself has credited the painter with "olhos penetrantes" [penetrating eyes] (23), this depiction of Tereza as a "mulher completa" down to her "reluzente coxame" is certainly to be understood by us as trustworthy.

Yet even as the number of non-narrator characters who fail to perceive Tereza as a warrior maiden begins to add up, we are left with an unanswered question. Given that the character of Januário Gereba, the man who knows Tereza best, recognizes the protagonist as a figure of Yansã, what does it matter if all these other men, all these unrequited lovers, see her as a conventional woman instead? Isn't the perception of Januário Gereba, when all is said and done, the most important perception of all? On one hand, the answer to this question is yes: in light of his status as Tereza's true love, Januário is, with the possible exception of Tereza herself, the non-narrator character best positioned to discern the "true" nature of the protagonist. Yet the fact of the matter is that Januário's perception of Tereza as a daughter of Yansã is presented as ephemeral rather than enduring. As noted in the first part of this essay, Tereza and Januário engage in a post-brawl conversation in which the protagonist vigorously objects to being called "mulher valente." Even as Tereza and Januário carry on this conversation, Januário observes that the woman at his side no longer resembles the "exalted girl" of the fight: ". . . a seu lado na rua, [Tereza] não se assemelha a moça exaltada da briga, num acanhamento modesto, ouvindo-o contar . . ." ["Beside him in the street, (Tereza) didn't look like the exalted girl of the fight; she had a modest timidity about her as she listened to him speak"] (27). Januário's perception of Tereza is changing, now that the bar fight is over, from a view of the protagonist as heroic to a view of her as "modest" and "timid."

This shift in Januário's perception of Tereza is confirmed when the pair return to the subject of *candomblé orixás*. Having become sweethearts since Januário first identified Tereza as a daughter of Yansã, the two are making love in the sea when the sailor decides to revise his previous opinion. " 'Agora tu não e Yansã'," he pronounces. " 'Tu só é Yansã na hora da briga. Agora tu é Janaína, rainha do mar' " [" 'You're not Yansã any longer; you're only Yansã when it's time to fight. Now you're Janaína, the queen of the sea' "][30] (55). In contrast to Yansã, female warrior *orixá*, Janaína, "queen of the sea," personifies the construction of femininity in terms of sensuality, mystery and, even death. Janaína is about as close as one gets, in the *candomblé* pantheon, to the concept most commonly known in the West as the "Eternal Feminine." As Januário re-names Tereza as a figure of Janaína, his perception of the protagonist merges with the perception of the poet, the painter, and all the rest. In the absence of strife, in a world made right, Tereza appears to the sailor as the most feminine of goddesses.

As he constructs his representation of Tereza Batista as more womanly than heroic, the authorial narrator makes frequent recourse to the points-of-view of a host of non-narrator characters. Yet he also makes use, at moments quite heavily, of observations made from his own point-of-view. At times, the authorial narrator exercises his own point-of-view in editorial commentary which reminds us of his status as a character in the same fictional world he purports to represent. Most often, however, the authorial narrator speaks through his own point-of-view in a way which more closely resembles the voice of a non-dramatized, even omniscient, narrator: he adopts a tone which is seemingly neutral and uninvolved, and which seems to emanate at once from nowhere and everywhere. In both of these modes—self-consciously involved on the one hand, ostensibly uninvolved on the other—the authorial narrator makes use of his own point-of-view to construct Tereza Batista as the quintessence of a patriarchally defined femininity.

Earlier, I suggested that the authorial narrator expresses strong sympathy for the masculine characters who make up Tereza Batista's "court" of unrequited lovers. On the one hand, this sympathy functions to validate this particular group's perception of Tereza as a figure defined by femininity rather than by heroism. On the other hand, however, it also serves to establish that the authorial narrator "himself" views Tereza in much the same way. Having informed us that Tereza Batista has reached a point in her life when she will only have sex out of love, the authorial narrator pauses to consider the plight of her many admirers. In the process of expressing sympathy for what are ostensibly *their* hurt feelings, however, he manages to convey these feelings as if they were his own:

> Ai! nenhum lhe toca o coração, nenhum lhe desperta o desejo dormido, acende a recôndida centelha! Para amigo, sim, qualquer deles: o rábula, o poeta, o pintor, o dentista, o *cabaretier*; para amante, não. Quem se conforma com a doce amizade de mulher bonita? Coisas de coração, quem as pode entender e explicar? ["Alas! No man can touch her heart, none can awaken the dormant desire nor kindle the hidden spark! As friends she gladly accepts them all—lawyer, poet, painter, dentist, nightclub owner— but as lover none. But what man can be satisfied with a beautiful woman's friendship? Who is there who understands the ways of the heart? Who can explain them?"].[31] (25)

Especially in light of the fact that the opening "Ai!" is the first word of a new chapter, we can be quite sure that we are in the point-of-view of the authorial narrator. The sigh of longing is his, as is the rhetorical question: "Who can be content with the sweet friendship of a beautiful woman?" Across a distance of time and space, the authorial narrator is imagining himself into a seat on Tereza Batista's "court." As he does so, he indicates that he too feels, albeit vicariously, love and longing for this legendary woman. And he also indicates that he, like Tereza's many admirers, views her, first and foremost, as a "beautiful woman."

Here we have a clear example of how the authorial narrator, speaking through his own point-of-view and in a self-consciously *involved* way, contributes to the construction of Tereza as more feminine than heroic. What happens when the authorial narrator speaks through his own point-of-view, but in an ostensibly *uninvolved* way, is somewhat more complex. Speaking in a tone of neutrality, objectivity, even omniscience, the authorial narrator manages, at the same time, to further steer the representation of Tereza Batista in the direction of conventional femininity. In illustration of this point, we will consider the way in which the authorial narrator uses this seemingly "neutral" point-of-view in the construction of two diametrically opposed representations of Tereza: the representation of Tereza-as-Yansã, and the representation of Tereza-as-*sambista*.

Across the seventeen chapters of the first *folheto*, there are two distinct moments in which Tereza is explicitly perceived as a figure of Yansã. The first of these is the episode of the bar fight; the second is the post-brawl conversation in which Januário recognizes Tereza as a daughter of the warrior *orixá*. Since the second identification between Tereza and Yansã is filtered entirely through the perspectives of the protagonist and Januário, it does not concern us here. In the case of the bar brawl episode, however, the authorial narrator does operate in his own apparently "neutral" point-of-view much if not all of the time. For the most part, the authorial narrator's descriptions of Tereza-as-Yansã are economical, even terse: relying on verbs to describe her actions rather than on adjectives to describe her appearance, the authorial narrator also steers all but entirely clear of editorial commentary. Thus, at the sound of "a mão do homem na face da mulher" ["a man's hand striking a woman's face"],[32] Tereza marches over to the fighting couple, declares that "homem que bate em mulher não e homem" ["A man who hits a woman isn't a man at all"],[33] spits in the bully's face, and dares him to hit her instead. Then, when she sees he intends to take her up on her suggestion, she kicks him in the shin, pulls his hair, spits in his face some more, and, after a protracted struggle, ends the thing by kicking him in the testicles (18–20). Beyond informing us that Tereza had learned to spit "na infância em brinquedos de cangaço e de guerra com petulantes moleques" ["in infancy in games of cowboy and Indian and in fighting fleet-footed boys"][34](19), the authorial narrator neither elaborates on, nor draws any conclusions about, the actions he describes. Instead, as we have seen, it is given to Januário to suggest the comparison between Tereza Batista and Yansã by crying out, as he enters the fray, " 'Lá vou eu, Yansã!' " [" 'Yansã! Here I come!' "].[35]

In comparison with his single and laconic description of Tereza-as-Yansã, the authorial narrator's representation of Tereza-as-*sambista* presents a marked and highly significant contrast. Even limiting ourselves to those portrayals which emanate from the point-of-view of the authorial narrator, descriptions of Tereza as a samba star multiply so rapidly during the course of the first *folheto* that they defy enumeration. Suffice it to say that repeatedly, even excessively, the authorial narrator pauses to describe Tereza in her samba clothing. Furthermore, whereas the authorial narrator's single account of Tereza's appearance as warrior maiden is comprised of verbs which convey the specific actions of the protagonist, his various accounts of Tereza-as-*sambista* dwell more on what she looks like than on what she does. In fact, at times these descriptions of Tereza-as-*sambista* become so chockfull of detail

that they have the effect of stopping the narrative (not to mention the protagonist) dead in its tracks. When the protagonist finally steps, for example, onto
the stage of the Paris Alegre, the authorial narrator actually dispenses with
verbs altogether in order to give us a good long view of Tereza-as-*sambista*:

> As luzes então se apagaram, eram onze horas da noite, a bateria do *jazz*
> irrompeu e o pistom abriu alas para ela passar, a estrela candente do samba.
> A luz vermelha de um refletor caiu sobre a pista de baile: Tereza Batista,
> vestida de saiote e bata, torso de baiana, sandálias, colares, pulseiras, saldo
> ainda da Companhia de Variedades Jota Porto & Alma Castro, beleza muçu-
> rumim ou cigana, cabo-verde ou trigueira, *mulata* nacional de dengue e
> requebro [At eleven sharp the lights were dimmed, the drums rolled a fan-
> fare, and trumpets heralded the incandescent Star of the Samba. The red
> glow of a spotlight fell on the dance floor, lighting up Tereza Batista. She
> was dressed in a short skirt and a Bahian's chemise, sandals, necklaces, and
> bracelets left over from the Jota Porto & Alma Castro Variety Show, all of
> which set off the dusky, gypsy-Indian-African beauty of the national *mulata*
> in all her sensual pride].[36] (64).

Narrating an episode about Tereza-as-Yansã, the authorial narrator tells us
only that she "spoke, spit and kicked" before he hands the baton of interpretation over to the character of Januário. Narrating an episode about Tereza-as-
*sambista*, however, the authorial narrator becomes much more involved. Not
only does he linger over every detail of the protagonist's appearance, but he
himself carries out the act of interpretation to its very end. The protagonist
is—the authorial narrator himself has said it—"*mulata* nacional de dengue e
requebro."

Furthermore, even as the authorial narrator looks upon Tereza in this
unmediated way, he adopts a tone which also serves to mask his own presence as mediator. The tone of the "*mulata* nacional" passage is not that of a
dramatized and involved narrator-character, the kind of a narrator-character
who might tell us in an aside just how much he wishes he had "been there."
The tone of this passage is, instead, that of a neutral and omniscient third-per-
son narrator, a narrator who wants us to believe he can see across time and
space in order to tell us *precisely* what Tereza was wearing and *precisely* how
she looked.

Is Tereza a warrior woman, is Tereza a conventionally feminine woman,
or is Tereza, perhaps, some combination of the two? Speaking in his own
voice, and with all his pretensions to omniscience, the authorial narrator himself comes down on the side of Tereza's essential femininity.

The final point-of-view through which the authorial narrator undermines
the warrior-like aspect of Tereza is that of the protagonist herself. Already we
have seen how Tereza, in conversation with Januário, directly denies his
perception of her as "mulher valente": "'sou valente nada ... mais bem

medrosa'" [" 'I'm not brave at all. Really, I'm timid'"] (27). This objection, far from a matter of passing modesty, accurately suggests the way in which Tereza thinks about herself throughout the course of the first *folheto*. In almost all of the passages in which the authorial narrator treats us to a view of the inner vision of his protagonist, she is preoccupied in an obsessive and powerless way with the figure of her lover Januário Gereba. As she recalls, repeatedly, her lover's "peito de quilha" and "grandes mãos calosas,"[37] Tereza is inspired to compare him with mythical figures of enormity and power: "Januário Gereba—Gereba não vem de Yereba, o gigante? Gereba, não e o urubu-rei, o grande voador? Assim Tereza o conheceu e soube. Foi quanto bastou para saber" ["Januário Gereba—doesn't the name Gereba come from Yereba, the giant? Isn't Gereba the condor, the grandest high-flyer of them all? That was how Tereza knew him, and that was all she had to know"][38] (26). Perceiving in Januário Gereba "a inteireza de homen," the essence of masculinity, Tereza Batista also perceives in him the totality of her own fate as a woman. Though she watches still as a statue when he leaves her at last, she is crying out inside: "Ai, Janu, meu homem, meu marido, meu amor, minha vida, minha morte" ["O Janu, my man, my husband, my love, my life, my death"][39] (62). More than her man, her husband, her love, he is, as well, her life and her death. And she is, per the evidence of her own thoughts and feelings, "ela que tão-somente deseja na vida ser feliz junto ao seu homem no mar" ["She who wanted nothing from life but to be happy with her man at sea"][40] (65).

Though Tereza may *look*, at some moments and to some people, like a figure of the warrior maiden, she certainly does not *think* like a warrior. A particularly vivid illustration of this point is to be found in the story of Joana das Folhas' legal victory over the usurer. In Part I of this essay I argued that this story evokes the image of Tereza-as-warrior only to erode it. While that argument was based solely on plot considerations, at this time we can see how an analysis of narrative perspective serves to reinforce it. Especially since the usurer is the same man who hit the woman in the bar brawl, this story serves to remind us of Tereza's hatred of bullies and capacity for heroic action. Yet even as Tereza renews her fight against injustice by agreeing to help Joana das Folhas, she is represented as hard-pressed to think about anything but Januário. Wondering why the sailor has failed to keep an appointment with her, Tereza's attention veers from a conversation in which the lawyer Lulu Santos is providing background information crucial to the case: "A brisa da noite vinha do porto, Lulu Santos a falar ... , o pensamento de Tereza em Januário Gereba: onde andara?" ["The night breeze swept in from the harbor. Lulu Santos talked ... ; and all the time Tereza was thinking about Januário Gereba and wondering where he could be"][41] (35). Only after Lulu Santos stops speaking nearly two full pages of text later, do we receive an indication, and an equivocal one at that, that Tereza has turned her attention to the matter at hand: "Os olhos de Tereza se perdem na distãncia mas ela não pensa em mestre Januário Gereba, dito Janu por bem-querer, nem nas areias do mar. Pensa na negra Joana das Folhas. . . ." ["Tereza was looking off into the distance, but now she was not thinking of Captain Januário Gereba, known to his friends as Janu, nor was she thinking of the sea breaking on the sand. She was thinking only of black Joana das Folhas . . ."][42] (36). Within a few short paragraphs, however, Tereza has already forgotten poor Joana all over again: "Tereza na varanda esquece Lulu Santos, Joana das Folhas . . . Onde andara o malvado? Prometera vir com o cachimbo de barro, a pele curtida ao vento, o peito de quilha, as grandes mãos que a suspenderam no ar. Não viera, por que?" ["Tereza stayed out on the porch. She had forgotten Lulu Santos, Joana das Folhas . . . Where could he be, confound him? He had promised to come, with his claypipe and his windburned skin and his chest like a keel and his hands that lifted her into the air. Why didn't he come?"][43] (37). Tereza Batista does have a hatred of bullies: in the story of Joana das Folhas, her actions, at least, prove it. But we have only to consider the inner vision of the protagonist to confirm that, as much as she may detest injustice, she loves Januário more.

By explicitly linking Tereza Batista to the *orixá* Yansã, the first *folheto* serves to launch a novel-wide presentation of the protagonist as a figure of the cross-cultural warrior woman. By undermining the very same link between Tereza and Yansã which it serves to establish, the first *folheto* also sets in motion the textual strategies by which the figure of the warrior maiden will be repudiated as a unsatisfactory and undesirable model of womanhood. The repudiation of the warrior maiden in favor of a more conventional, patriarchally defined woman is not simply a matter of plot but also, as we have seen in Part II of this essay, of narrative perspective. Whether speaking through the voices of non-narrator characters or through his own point-of-view, the authorial narrator consistently uses narrative perspective itself as a tool for diffusing and even attacking the association between Tereza Batista and the cross-cultural figure of the warrior maiden.

On the basis of a close reading of the entire text of *Tereza Batista*, it is possible to confirm that the narrative strategies and effects which we have identified in the first *folheto* are operative throughout. At times the authorial narrator filters his account of the story of Tereza Batista through the points-of-view of non-narrator characters represented in interaction with the protagonist. At times he speaks, whether as a self-conscious character or in a tone which suggests omniscience, in his own unmediated voice. At times, he filters his narrative through the inner vision of Tereza Batista herself. Whatever the strategy, however, the effect is always and everywhere the same. Tereza Batista is perceived, and thereby constructed, as a figure more feminine than warrior-like, as a protagonist who, although she may have acted the part of the hero in a tight situation or two, is at heart the most womanly of women.

Though it is infeasible to reproduce a close reading of a novel of this length in a chapter-long essay, the work of other feminist critics who have conducted readings of *Tereza Batista* may be cited in support of the assertion I am making here. Since *Tereza Batista* was published in 1972, it has drawn the close, and scathing, attention of two distinguished feminist critics: the Brazilian Walnice Nogueira Galvão and the North American Daphne Patai. While neither of these critics deal in any length with Amado's use of the warrior maiden motif, both make arguments related to the one I have been making in so far as they stress the ideological implications of narrative perspective. Galvão, in what is certainly the most powerful portion of her 1976 "Amado: respeitoso, respeitavel," focuses on what she called the "irresponsible" manipulation of free-indirect narration in the extensive rape scenes which dominate the second *folheto* of the novel. Observing that the *folheto* which contains the story of the pre-pubescent Tereza's repeated violation and torture at the hands the much older Capitão occupies a disproportionate one-third of the 421-page novel, Galvão accuses Amado of constructing the rape episodes in such a way as to "titillate" the reader with scenes of sadism and pedophilia. In particular, Galvão zeroes in on the way in which the authorial narrator appears, at moments, to express admiration for the sexual prowess of the rapist. Similarly, Patai, in her analysis of Amado's representation of sexual violence in terms of what Frederic Jameson has called the "ideological double standard," finds that a number of narrative strategies converge to place the reader in a duplicitous position vis-à-vis the rape scenes. On one hand, the reader is called upon to condemn the acts of violence which are being represented, ostensibly, "only" for the purpose of critiquing them. On the other hand, the reader is invited to perpetrate and enjoy, albeit vicariously, these very same acts of violence. Among the narrative sleights of hand by which such duplicity is accomplished, Patai focuses on the manipulation of free-indirect narration: by concentrating on Justiniano's "thoughts, reactions, pleasure and anger," the narrative "urges a kind of complicity on the reader" (132).

Thanks to the analyses of Galvão and Patai, there can be no mistaking two things: first, that the rape scenes in the second *folheto* of *Tereza Batista* serve to approve sexual violence; and second, that the manipulation of narrative perspective is crucial in producing this ideologically reprehensible effect.[44] Building on these valid and important conclusions, I would suggest that it is also significant that the twelve-year-old girl who is the object of so much violence in the second *folheto* is a protagonist with ties, as we have seen, to the figure of the warrior maiden. Though it is true, as Patai observes, that the authorial narrator spends the bulk of the rape scenes in the point-of-view of the rapist, it is also true that he gives us a couple of brief glimpses into the mind of the victim. And what she is usually thinking, albeit in a pathetically silent and circumscribed voice, is that she must not cry because "guerreiro não chora nem na hora da morte" ["Fighting men don't cry, not even when they're dying"][45] (109). As this twelve-year-old "guerreiro" learns fear and submission through the increasingly violent interventions of Justiniano—as she learns, thanks to the application of a branding iron, and as the authorial narrator so explicitly tells us, to "suck" when the Captain says "suck"—we are also witness to another, more figurative, rape. We are witness to the "dressing down" of the warrior maiden herself, to the violation and denigration of a symbol of female heroism. Furthermore, since the authorial narrator overwhelming adopts and approves the point-of-view of the rapist, we are presented with the distinct possibility that this rape of the warrior maiden is not such a bad thing.

In the first *folheto* of *Tereza Batista*, as we have seen in this essay, the authorial narrator uses point-of-view in a way unfriendly to the figure of the warrior maiden. In the second *folheto*, I am suggesting, and per the analyses of Galvão and Patai, the relationship between the authorial narrator and the warrior maiden gets downright sadistic.

*       *       *

At the outset of this essay I cited a statement published as recently as 1993, and in a major journal of literary scholarship: "O escritor Jorge Amado é, em suas páginas, o amante e o amigo de todas as mulheres" ["The writer Jorge Amado is, in his pages, the lover and friend of all women"] (Rodrigues 259). In the face of this extraordinary assertion, I have only two things to say: Not these pages, and not this woman.

More suggestive, to be sure, is Maria Luisa Nunes' view of Amado as a writer in whose works "the concerns of feminism and [of] patriarchal narrative intersect" ("Narratives by and about Women," 8). In so far as it puts into play the figure of the warrior maiden, the text of *Tereza Batista* evokes feminist concerns. As the feminist archetypal scholar Carol Rupprecht among others has noted, the figure of the warrior maiden is often perceived by women as a figure of empowerment and hope.[46] Most obviously, the figure of the warrior maiden suggests that women can and do exercise qualities, such as bravery and the ability to protect themselves from physical harm, which have been reserved in many cultures for men. More subtly, the figure of the warrior maiden may be interpreted as a challenge to the notion that human beings come in two genders alone, thereby paving the way, not for women to become like men, but for men and women alike to conceive of entirely new forms of identity.[47] Yet the story of Tereza Batista is also, as we have seen in the course of this essay, profoundly patriarchal. By means of narrative strategies related to point-of-view as well as plot, this novel not only manages to renounce the warrior maiden but also, I would suggest, the feminist possibilities she embodies.

Yet what does it mean to say that the concerns of feminism "intersect" with those of patriarchal narrative? Perhaps the word "intersect" is adequate to describe the relationship between "feminist concerns" and "patriarchal narrative" in the novel Nunes analyzes, Amado's 1958 *Gabriela, cravo e canela*. But in so far as it fails to capture the difference between peaceful coexistence, mutual cooperation, and outright conflict, the word "intersect" is entirely inadequate to describe the relationship between feminist concerns and patriarchal narrative in the text of *Tereza Batista*. When Jorge Amado deploys the figure of the warrior maiden, he enters the terrain of feminist hopes and visions. When he repudiates the figure of the warrior maiden, he repudiates, as well, the possibilities she represents. In the case of *Tereza Batista cansada de guerra*, the concerns of feminism on the one hand, and of patriarchal narrative on the other, are not placed in "intersection" but, instead, in opposition. By means of five books and 421 pages of patriarchal plot twists and point-of-view strategies, Amado wears down the warrior maiden figure until, at last, "cansada de guerra," she surrenders her feminist potential altogether.

## NOTES

1. Unless otherwise noted, all translations will be my own.
2. The Brazilian *literatura de cordel*, or "literature on a string," is a popular genre which takes the form of pamphlets called *folhetos*. It gets its name from the fact that the *folhetos* are literally strung up for sale on clothesline-like cords or strings.
3. "Donzela guerreira" is most commonly translated into English as "warrior maiden."
4. Among those who overlook the warrior attributes of Yansã are Nunes ("The Preservation of African Culture"), Walker and Bastide. Galvão, by contrast, includes Yansã right alongside Joan of Arc in her cross-cultural listing of warrior maiden figures ("Frequentação da donzela-guerreira").
5. Trans. Barbara Shelby, *Tereza Batista: Home from the Wars*, 36.
6. In a manner reminiscent of the way in which the *folhetos* of the *cordel* tradition are grouped and strung up for display by vendors, *Tereza Batista* consists of five self-contained but interrelated books which, by virtue of their inclusion between the covers of a single novel, are "strung together" to form a multipartite but unified text.
7. Shelby, *Tereza* 10.
8. Shelby, *Tereza* 1.
9. Shelby, *Tereza* 11.
10. Shelby, *Tereza* 19.
11. Shelby, *Tereza* 20.
12. Shelby, *Tereza* 47.
13. Shelby, *Tereza* 67.
14. A *sambista* is a professional samba dancer.

15. Shelby, *Tereza* 71.
16. Shelby, *Tereza* 72.
17. Shelby, *Tereza* 133.
18. Shelby, *Tereza* 142.
19. Shelby, *Tereza* 210.
20. Shelby, *Tereza* 232.
21. For detailed discussions of the relationships between *Tereza Batista* and the *literatura de cordel*, see Slater, Chamberlain and, especially, Curran.
22. Since this aspect of narrative perspective in *Tereza Batista* has received little if any critical attention, it is worth pausing to underscore the way in which it departs from conventional textual practice. In his well-known "tabulation of the forms an author's voice can take," Wayne Booth has this to say about free-indirect discourse: "This method is omniscience with teeth in it: the implied author demands our absolute faith in his powers of divination. We must never for a moment doubt that he knows everything about each of [the minds he illumines], or that he has chosen correctly how much to show of each" (102–3). In direct contradiction to this literary "rule of thumb," the authorial narrator who assumes the privilege of free-indirect discourse in *Tereza Batista* does not and cannot inspire in his reader anything approaching "absolute faith." In the first place, the authorial narrator's status as a character in the action is structurally at odds with the exercise of "omniscience with teeth in it." It is not feasible that this character, no matter how far and how wide his travels, no matter how many and how perspicacious his witnesses, could have ascertained the precise thoughts and feelings of so many different characters in so many different moments. Furthermore, one of the conceits at the heart of the *cordel*-like narrative structure of this novel, one of the reasons given for why the authorial narrator has had to travel so far and solicit the testimony of so many witnesses, is that it is impossible for any one person to know the "full truth" about the legendary figure of Tereza Batista. In the introductory segment which precedes the first of the five *folhetos*, in fact, the authorial narrator himself pauses to warn us that "[não] existe no mundo quem saiba toda a verdade de Tereza Batista" (11) [there isn't a soul "in the world who knows the whole truth about Tereza Batista" (xiv)]. How, then, is it given to the authorial narrator to know not only what so many characters have thought and felt in the presence of Tereza, but also so many of the thoughts and feelings of Tereza herself? The text in which this authorial narrator is embedded refuses to yield an answer to this question.
23. Shelby, *Tereza* 7.
24. Shelby, *Tereza* 7.
25. Shelby, *Tereza* 15.
26. Shelby, *Tereza* 36.
27. Shelby, *Tereza* 72.
28. Shelby, *Tereza* 8.
29. Shelby, *Tereza* 15.
30. Shelby, *Tereza* 59.
31. Shelby, *Tereza* 18–19.
32. Shelby, *Tereza* 10.

33. Shelby, *Tereza* 10.
34. Shelby, *Tereza* 10.
35. Shelby, *Tereza* 11.
36. Shelby, *Tereza* 71.
37. "Keel-like chest" and "great callused hands." These descriptors occur a number of times throughout the first *folheto*; see, for example, page 26 in the original, and page 20 in the translation.
38. Shelby, *Tereza* 19.
39. Shelby, *Tereza* 67.
40. Shelby, *Tereza* 67.
41. Shelby, *Tereza* 31.
42. Shelby, *Tereza* 33.
43. Shelby, *Tereza* 34–5.
44. Although Jon Vincent has taken issue with Galvão's reading of *Tereza Batista*, his objection concerns another aspect of her analysis, namely, her assertion that Amado's representation of Tereza as a prostitute is an unrealistic "producão imaginária de machismo latino-americana" (Galvão, 21). In my opinion, this is neither the central nor the most interesting component of Galvão's critique of *Tereza Batista*; instead, Galvão is at her best when she is elaborating the argument I have referred to here, the argument concerning Amado's ideologically charged manipulation of narrative perspective in the rape episodes. Having said this, however, I would also note that I cannot agree with Vincent's assertion that Galvao's critique of Amado's depiction of prostitution is beside the point because "these are characters in novels and therefore necessarily included in the suspension of disbelief required for other lies" (16). The point is not that Amado fails to represent prostitutes realistically but, instead, that he represents them in a way which reinforces patriarchal constructions of femininity and feminine sexuality. As Hunsaker states in his discussion of the representation of the *mulata* in another novel by Amado, "Literature accumulates and intensifies social power and control, and thus participates in the formation of the culture and consciousness of the consumer of literature" (232). Furthermore, Amado himself has stated repeatedly his intention to wield the power of literature in a politically responsible and even revolutionary way. In a 1984 interview with Berta Sichel, for example, Amado asserted the following: "Every writer is political, even those who think they have nothing to do with politics, since the mere act of writing is a political act—the writer exerts influence on the readers, and this is a political action" (18).
45. Trans. Barbara Shelby, *Tereza*, 133.
46. For another discussion of the warrior maiden as a symbol of female power and resistance, see Carolyn Heilbrun's reading of George Bernard Shaw's St. Joan in *Toward a Recognition of Androgyny* (110–111).
47. Even as we recognize the feminist potential of the warrior maiden, it is important to remember that this figure cannot be taken to imply, in and of herself, a subversion of patriarchal gender constructs. Depending upon the story and interpretive context in which she finds herself, in fact, the warrior maiden may also have far less liberating implications. Focusing on the fact that the warrior maiden is typi-

cally motivated by unshakeable loyalty to a father or father figure, Galvão suggests that "a donzela-guerreira, antes de ser uma aspiração feminina, e mais uma fantasia masculina" ("Frequentação da donzela-guerreira," 20). Marina Warner, in her book-length study of Joan of Arc, points out yet another way in which the figure of the "masculine woman" can serve to bolster the egos and power of patriarchally defined men: "Joan's life, probably one of the most heroic a woman has ever led, is a tribute to the male principle, a homage to the masculine sphere of action" (155). And finally, there is always, as the work of Candace Slater suggests, the question of denouemont: the story of the *donzela-guerreira* of Iberian ballad inevitably ends in the revelation of the protagonist's hidden femaleness, a revelation which prepares the way for the restoration of traditional gender roles. The story of *Tereza Batista* is not, in short, the first warrior-maiden narrative which ultimately serves to reinforce the same patriarchal social order which it would initially appear to subvert.

## BIBLIOGRAPHY

Amado, Jorge. Interview. With Berta Sichel. *Americas* 36.3 (May-June 1984): 16–19.
———. *Tereza Batista cansada de guerra.* 23rd ed. Rio de Janeiro: Record, 1986.
———. *Tereza Batista Home from the Wars.* Trans. Barbara Shelby. New York: Avon, 1975.
Bastide, Roger. *The African Religions of Brazil.* Trans. Helen Sebba. Baltimore: Johns Hopkins University Press, 1978.
Booth, Wayne C. *The Rhetoric of Fiction.* Chicago: University of Chicago Press, 1961.
Chamberlain, Bobby J. *Jorge Amado.* Ed. David W. Foster. Twayne World Author Series 767. Boston: G.K. Hall, 1990.
Curran, Mark J. *Jorge Amado e a literatura de cordel.* Salvador: Fundacão Cultural do Estado da Bahia, 1981.
DuPlessis, Rachel Blau. *Writing Beyond the Ending, Narrative Strategies of Twentieth-Century Women Writers.* Bloomington: Indiana University Press, 1985.
Galvão,Walnice Nogueira. "Amado: respeitoso, respeitavel." In *Saco de gatos: ensaios críticos*, 13–22. São Paulo: Duas Cidades, 1976.
———. "Frequentação da donzela-guerreira." In *Gatos deoutros sacos*, 8–59. São Paulo: Brasiliense, 1981.
Hall, Linda B. "Jorge Amado: Women, Love and Possession." *Southwest Review* 68.1 (Winter 1983): 67–77.
Heilbrun, Carolyn. *Toward a Recognition of Androgyny.* New York: Norton, 1982.
Hunsaker, Steven. "Representing the *mulata: El amor en los tiempos del cólera* and *Tenda dos milagres.*" *Hispania* 17.2 (May 1994): 225–34.
Nunes, Maria Luisa. "Narratives By and About Women in the Third World." *Brasil/Brazil* 2 (1989): 5–27.
———. "The Preservation of African Culture in Brazilian Literature: The Novels of Jorge Amado. "*The Luso-Brazilian Review* 10.1 (June 1973): 86–101.
Patai, Daphne. *Myth and Ideology in Contemporary Brazilian Fiction.* Rutherford, NJ: Fairleigh Dickinson University Press, 1983.

Rodrigues, Urbano Tavares. "A mulher de prazer entre as personagens populares de Jorge Amado." *Coloquio-letras* 127–128 (Jan.-June1993): 257–259.

Rupprecht, Carol. "The Martial Maid and the Challenge of Androgyny." *Spring* 1974, 269–293.

Slater, Candace. *Stories on a String: The Brazilian Literatura de Cordel.* Berkeley: University of California Press, 1982.

Vincent, Jon S. "Jorge Amado, Jorge Desprezado." *The Luso-Brazilian Review* 15, Supplementary Issue (Summer 1978): 11–17.

Walker, Sheila S. "Everyday and Esoteric Reality in the Afro-Brazilian Candomblé." *History of Religions* 30.2 (Nov. 1990): 103–128.

Warner, Marina. *Joan of Arc: The Image of Female Heroism.* New York: Knopf, 1981.

# The Vox Populi in the Novels of Jorge Amado and John Steinbeck

EARL E. FITZ

Although there are many strong parallels between the fiction written by John Steinbeck (1902–1968) and that by Jorge Amado (1912– ), none is more revealing of the numerous affinities between these two writers than the nature of the voice, or ethos, that emanates from their narratives. Apropos of this, both writers rely heavily upon their characters to put into action the liberal and humanitarian social reforms they so ardently advocate and it is by means of what their men and (more rare in Steinbeck's case) women reveal about themselves and their societies that Amado and Steinbeck are able to transform what could easily be empty political posturing into impassioned cries for freedom and justice. The enduring popularity of Steinbeck and Amado derives primarily from this same tendency, from the singular ability of each author to create vivid (if too often stereotypical or sentimentalized) characters who, speaking for the common people, impart a powerfully human dimension to the political, economic and social issues with which these two authors were and are concerned. And while a sharp and, in the case of the early Amado, overtly communistic social consciousness[1] may thus be said to provide the ideological ground of their best work, it is the special ability of Amado and Steinbeck to express the "voice of the people," the "vox populi," that constitutes their greatest similarity.

We know that Amado, who has been writing novels about the "have-nots" and marginals of Brazil since he was nineteen, is appreciative of Steinbeck's work.[2] An important and closely related question, though, is two-fold in nature: when did Amado begin to read Steinbeck, and to what degree, if indeed at all, was he influenced by him? In reading and comparing the works written by and about each author, it seems clear that we are not dealing here with a problem of literary influence as much as with a case of similar response to similar stimuli, the latter being the social and political problems that developed in Brazil and the United States as a result of the world-wide depression of the 1930s. The methodology selected for this essay, therefore, is that of "rapprochement" rather than that of a more orthodox influence study. My intention is to show how two socially aware writers, working in different places but at the same time, responded to the tensions of their age and place by framing their most successful novels not in the crudely jingoistic phraseology of the so-called "proletarian novel"[3] but in what was for them the revivifying and almost mythically empowered voice of the people. The enduring appeal of their characters, the freshness of the language they speak, and the power of their convictions all combine to save the novels of Jorge Amado and John Steinbeck from being mere propaganda pieces for the political attitudes implied and, as in the case of the early Amado, advocated through the texts themselves. Inseparably linked, as we shall see, to their modes of characterization and to their thematics, the singular ability of Amado and Steinbeck to express the spirit of their people stands out as the most salient artistic feature uniting them.

# I

Two early novels, *Capitães da areia* [*Captains of the Sands*] (1937) and *Tortilla Flat* (1935), bear this out. These works not only reflect the sharp social consciences of their authors, they show how each writer was beginning to experiment with a new kind of character, one through whom, through whose speech habits, the authors hoped to heighten the impact their social commentary would have on the reader. In *Tortilla Flat,* which is less of a novel than a loosely connected series of sketches centering on the free-living but marginalized Mexican-Americans of California's Salinas Valley, Steinbeck sought to protest the spurious values of an excessively materialistic society. Living hedonistic, picturesque lives, his characters, always sympathetically portrayed, represent a simpler, less competitive and more idealistic way of life. To achieve his goal, Steinbeck, as many critics have pointed out, availed himself of the Arthurian legend and, turning those fanciful romances on their heads, transformed Danny, Pilon, the Pirate and their cohorts into modern day Knights of the Round Table. More loveable than believable, these characters eventually find themselves in quest of a kind of Holy Grail, one which, in the context of their story, turns out to be the simple, carefree life lived by the "paisanos" themselves. Their romaniticized poverty, however, is very different from the grinding and darkly malevolent type endured by the characters of Amado's 1937 novel.[4]

While the spirit of *Tortilla Flat* is basically gay and slightly unreal, as in a fable, the spirit of *Capitães da areia,* published in the throes of not only an economic depression but of violent political turmoil as well, is depressing and grimly realistic. Indeed, the tone of the Amado work tends to be essentially tragic, not because Amado is any less sympathetic to common people and their problems than is Steinbeck but because of the way *Capitães da areia* is structured. The last third of the novel is permeated by pathetic, often excessively naturalistic scenes of failure, death and destruction, a feature of the book that stands in sharp contrast to the more whimsical spirit of *Tortilla Flat*. Overall, the world of the homeless urchins of *Capitães da areia* is much more brutal, violent and uncompromising than is the world of the amoral and romantically naive young people in *Tortilla Flat*. But in both cases, it is the very disinctive style employed that determines the different tones involved, the starkly contrasting attitude about the futures that these superficially similar but really very different characters face.

Although the tone of these two works may be in contrast, the attitude of the authors toward their characters is not. Both Amado and Steinbeck believe deeply not only in the inherent goodness of their characters but in their ability to see what is of real value in life, this being a quality that is more discernable in Steinbeck's works than Amado's, where overt socio-political conflicts too often tend to dominate. Politically, Steinbeck and Amado both endorse the rightness of their characters' outlooks and, in so doing, tacitly challenge the moral validity of the exploitative and materialistic society that engulfs them. This is particularly true of Amado, who in his crude early novels like *Cacau [Cacao]* (1933) and *Suor [Sweat]* (1934), expressed his own political views in such a way that it mars the artistic quality of his fiction. At this stage in their respective careers, Steinbeck, dealing with similar issues, is the more sophisticated of the two writers, though in time this difference will virtually disappear. It is through an effective, if not always subtle, use of dialogue that Steinbeck and Amado both manage to animate their characters with a kind of simplistic but too often awkwardly articulated political consciousness, one which, in *Capitães da areia* (and in other of Amado's early works), comes alive for the reader by producing a distinctly naturalistic sense of the harsh environment in which these abandoned children live. Moreover, they are repeatedly shown to be in a more or less constant state of open and aggressive conflict with the controlling classes of their society, the clubs of the police and the uncaring attitudes of the bourgeoisie in particular. In the more idyllic and less realistically portrayed world of Monterey, Danny, for example— although (like the other characters) often depicted in terms of animal images[5]—is not so much in direct physical conflict with the authorities, as is typically the case in *Capitães da areia*, but with the ethics and morals of the philistine society to which he stands in opposition, the society whose value systems he neither shares in nor accepts. Danny's underlying innocence, pre-Fall and Eden-like in nature, is what the characters of *Capitães da areia* and *Tortilla Flat* have in common, however. The primary difference, then—and it is a major one—is the degree to which the characters of *Tortilla Flat* and

*Capitães da areia* are affected by the society that surrounds them. This sense of an innocence unjustly violated by an abusive socio-political structure is more starkly presented in the Amado novel than in the Steinbeck work, where the violence visited on the characters is more ethical than physical. In the Brazilian's novel, the violation reflects a relentless day to day struggle for existence, while in the American's text it takes the form of a more speculative, theoretical concern about what kind of value systems should inform a just society.

There is, on the other hand, a greater thematic and structural unity to *Capitães da areia* than *Tortilla Flat*, and this signals another important distinction between them. In *Capitães da areia*, Amado plays out the lives of his characters, showing, primarily through his pessimistic conclusion, the empty future that awaits them, the futility and rejection that, because of the inherently and unalterably exploitative nature of Brazil's feudalistic northeast, are in store for them as they grow to maturity. In *Tortilla Flat*, by way of contrast, there is no such sense of the characters developing through time; Danny, for example, the linchpin of the story, accidentally dies in a bacchanalian orgy and his shack is ritualistically burned down. While Steinbeck's world in this book is primarily static and resigned in terms of the characters who inhabit it, Amado's is both more dynamic and vitriolic. Amado, moreover, is unrelenting in his portrayal of how force can be brutally brought to bear against those who stand outside of the prevailing system and who, in their poverty and pride, will not conform to its codes of behavior. In both books, however, the characters are presented as being essentially "pure" in their primitiveness, and, in their simplicity, represent an antidote to the suffocating and destructive socio-economic structure that constantly threatens them.

Two related works, also from the tumultuous depression era, are *Jubiabá* (1935) and *In Dubious Battle* (1936), the "strike" novels, respectively, of Amado and Steinbeck. Both books are politically charged, particularly in regard to their main characters, and both deal openly (as do, in Amado's case, *Seara vermelha* [Red Harvest] and *São Jorge dos Ilhéus*) with the issue of Marxian class conflict, an issue that was much in the air during the 1930s in both Brazil and the United States. In addition, however, Amado links the then inchoate issue of African racial awareness and pride to the larger, more sociological issues of racism and economic exploitation in Brazil. The result is a complex and largely satisfying work that binds together several politically sensitive social themes into a single, lyrically affective narrative. Both novels end in large scale general strikes, and in each case the outcome is rather "dubious." For Amado, this is because of the way he develops the protagonist, a black vagabond turned social rebel named Antônio Balduíno who develops as more of a symbolic figure—a physical and psychological champion of his race and class—than a "realistically" portrayed character. For

Steinbeck, too, the outcome of the strike is in doubt, but in his text it is because of what we learn from the lips of his protagonist, the much more mimetically depicted Doc Burton. Refusing to join the Communist party in fomenting the strike, Burton declares, at a crucial point, that he believes "in men" and not in "the cause."[6] Seeming to speak for Steinbeck himself, Burton then abruptly disappears from the story, the implication being that in the "dubious" ideological struggles of our time the voice of the human spirit is at best ignored and often consumed by the great theoretical systems that are at odds. In both novels, then, a conspiratory, repressive and rapacious socio-economic system seems to win out, yet in each case the real "victory," uncertain though it may be, is that the characters, typified in the figures of Doc Burton and Antônio Balduíno, have, in their basic humanity, called attention to what is wrong. Speaking in the true voice of the people, these protagonists identify the cancerous problems that are destroying their respective societies and, through their words and conduct, suggest what reforms must be forthcoming if internecine civil war (and, in Antônio's case, racial war) is to be avoided. Each of these two books, which, in spite of their numerous technical flaws, can be justifiably ranked among their author's best overall efforts, are unabashedly political in theme and tone. The language employed tends to be supple and colorful, and, generating the very real sense of drama that permeates these texts, only occasionally wooden or doctrinaire, as was often the case in much of the "social realism" of the time. Indeed, it is largely because of this artistically compelling (and, for Amado, often lyrical) language that the reader's response to these novels is sympathetic, a direct result of the ways the two protagonists and their situations are portrayed.

Two other well-known populist works, *The Grapes of Wrath* (1939) and *Seara vermelha* (1946), can be termed the "hegira novels" of Steinbeck and Amado. The American book, a powerful depiction of the Oklahoma farmers' desperate flight from their homes to find work in the "promised land" of California, caused a national furor when it was first published in the United States, a nation that, even by the late 1930s, still had not come to grips with the countless human tragedies that gave real meaning to the devastating social and economic effects of the Depression experience. Like the Pulitzer Prize winning American novel, *Seara vermelha*, which both chronicles the flight of a family clan from its home and develops into a story of individual human beings struggling against mighty odds, also proves to be a story in which a popular ethos, expressed through the "vox populi" of the characters, plays a major role. Just as the Joad family, forced off its land by drought, dust storms, bank failures, personal poverty and the foreclosure of their mortgage, desperately seeks a better life to the West, in California, so, too, is the family of the old "sertanejo" farmer, Jerónimo, driven off his land in Brazil's poor, drought-stricken northeast and forced to migrate more than a thousand miles to the "promised land" of São Paulo, in the South. Old Jerónimo and Grandpa Joad are subsistence farmers, politically impotent, poorly educated men whose lifetimes of struggle to eke out a living from the harsh lands of their respective parts of the world are cruelly rewarded by economic ruination and social ostracism. And just as the "Okies" flee the ravaged "dust bowl" of 1930s Oklahoma, so, too, do the "sertanejos" flee the devastated "sertão," their own climactically and economically stricken region. In contrast, however, to what happens to the comparatively more successful Joad family, Jerónimo's family, unable to maintain its strength and unity in the face of an onslaught of social, economic, and personal crises, is gradually destroyed. In *Seara vermelha* the latifundiary system of the Northeast is pinpointed as being the main cause of the human suffering (Ellison, 100), whereas in *The Grapes of Wrath,* the basic problem is more nebulous. In one sense, Steinbeck suggests, it is capitalism in general because the land, which plays a key role in both works, may never be possessed by one man (or institution) to the exclusion of all others; no one ever really owns the land. We are its caretakers, and, as Faulkner reminds us in *The Bear,* and as much Native American literature shows, it is a sacred gift to the human race. We desecrate the land by trying to buy and sell it, to hoard it as private property and to exploit it to exhaustion. The land, both novels imply, exists for the good of all mankind and should not be taken away from true farmers, the Grandpa Joads and the Jerónimos of the world, the people who honor and love it, merely because of a downturn in the business cycle. That this very thing is permitted to happen, then, emerges as the real crime in both *The Grapes of Wrath* and *Seara vermelha,* and the fact that it can happen on such a large scale reflects the abiding concern of both Steinbeck and Amado that an unchecked capitalistic system will eventually begin to commit crimes against its own, innocent people, the very people it should most protect.

The conclusions of these two novels also highlight their striking similarity; just as the Steinbeck work, an odyssey of dispossessed sharecroppers, is, finally, a story of individual and collective growth—of the need for human solidarity—so, too, does the Amado novel end with a strong, unambiguously expressed political message, one that is both public and private in its impact. In each work, the conclusion concerns not so much the resolution of the conflicts already developed in the narrative itself, but the promise of what the real political future could be like for the poor, powerless and sorely afflicted people depicted in it. There is a strong suggestion in each work, especially in the Amado novel, that the people must stop fighting among themselves and organize so as to combat the vast array of socio-economic forces that keep them chained to a life of penury and political impotence. This essay-like conclusion mars the Amado work even more than the quasi political mysticism of *The Grapes of Wrath* gives it an air of unreality, of an ideal sought after but, the reader feels, not likely attained.

## II

An additional point of comparison between these two writers involves books written considerably later in their respective careers. *Sweet Thursday* (1954) and *Gabriela cravo e canela* [*Gabriela, Clove and Cinnamon*] (1958), for example, are novels which mark a significant change in the kind of fiction each author was writing at the time. Steinbeck, who had spent the war years experimenting with non-fiction and the post-war years struggling rather unsuccessfully with several new themes, returns perhaps more hopefully than confidently, in 1954 and *Sweet Thursday*, to the carefree world of his beloved Monterey "paisanos." Although he has little new to say here, Steinbeck's writing once again takes on the energy, warmth, and enthusiasm for life that had made him so popular during the depths of the Depression. But in the glow of the post-war boom, the United States began to change dramatically and rapidly, more rapidly, it seems, than Steinbeck was able to comprehend. What was thematically notable in *Sweet Thursday* was an elaboration and intensification of the argument that the world of "big business" and material acquisition was contrary to the best interests and better instincts of the human being, a theme which had been hinted at but not substantially developed in *Tortilla Flat* and *Cannery Row*. Steinbeck, the idealist lost in a sea of avaricious and crass money-makers, found himself increasingly dismissed by the critics as "quaint" but "irrelevant," an anachronistic voice championing values that were now out of step with America's new-found power, prestige and material prosperity. This dilemma would eventually anger and confuse Steinbeck about where the true strength and beauty of America lay and would ultimately estrange him from the very people—the outcasts and misfits, the forgotten and dispossessed—who had, during the desperate and frightening 1930s, been the source of his truth and power as a writer.

But if Steinbeck's fate during the fifties was to gradually lose touch with the people, his Brazilian counterpart, Jorge Amado, also experiencing a period of growth and change, was able to establish a new and increasingly sophisticated fusion with his people, who, in ever more satisfying ways, would continue to be the source of his inspiration and appeal. We can say, then, that in 1958, with *Gabriela, cravo e canela,* Amado did not "return to his roots" as much as he perfected his artistic relationship with them, intitiating, in the process, a new and very fecund phase of development.[7] Ever since *Jubiabá* (1935), *Mar morto* [*Sea of Death*] (1936), and *Terras do sem fim* [*The Violent Land*] (1944), Amado's work had clearly shown that he did his best writing when he could concentrate on the creation of clearly delineated and vibrant characters (including, in sharp contrast to Steinbeck, numerous strong, if arguably stereotypical, female creations) and contextualize them in a politically volatile environment. As Amado became more adept at the process of characterization, and as he gained control over the other sundry technical demands of his craft, his style became increasingly fluid, subtle and poetically expressive. While never a sophisticated novelist, in the technical sense of the term, Amado became a great storyteller, a writer whose special genius lies in his ability to create characters who are both engaging and representative of their respective culture groups. In short, Amado's texts became mirrors in which the Brazilian people could view themselves. So while Steinbeck, frustrated by what his society had become as well as by what he himself now wanted to say about it, began, after *Sweet Thursday*, to move away from his "paisanos" and toward hesitant, unsure stories involving America's newly affluent urban middle-class, Amado, since *Gabriela, cravo e canela*, has focused ever more sharply on the always charming (some would say one-dimensional), often larger-than-life characters of his native region, Bahia, on that area's sensual and colorful folklore and on its social and political history.[8] In Steinbeck's case, however, unlike Amado's, this attempt to deal with characters and themes that were essentially alien to him met with little success.

An elaborate allegory of the Cain and Abel theme, *East of Eden* (1952), perhaps Steinbeck's most ambitious undertaking after *The Grapes of Wrath*, had a mixed reception, with many critics objecting to its structural looseness, its lack of cohesion and its blurry focus. Undaunted, Steinbeck tried again, in *The Winter of Our Discontent* (1961), to fathom the tangled skein of ethical contradictions and moral and political corruption that had come to characterize the "establishment" in American society. Attempting here to revive and refit some of the primitive goodness of his *Cannery Row* characters, Steinbeck tries, unconvincingly, to tell the story of a man who attempts to maintain a sense of personal integrity while laboring to "make it" in the world of "big business." Failing in this final attempt at fiction, Steinbeck turned, for the remainder of his career, to journalism and chronicles in an attempt to understand what had become of him and his country in the years between the end of World War II and the early 1960s. Given the social background of the majority of American soldiers who fought in the Vietnam war, it seems likely that Steinbeck, had he lived long enough, would, in spite of his early "hawkishness" on the subject, have come to realize that that singularly alienating and brutal war was being fought too extensively by his "paisanos," by the very people whom he had championed so ardently years before. It seems a certainty that the Vietnam experience, especially in terms of its social implications about who suffers and who doesn't in American society, would have inspired Steinbeck to return to writing about the characters and social issues he understood best.

On the other hand, the many novels produced by Jorge Amado since *Gabriela, cravo e canela, Os velhos marinheiros* [*Home is the Sailor*] (1961), which contains Amado's masterpiece, the short novel *A morte e a morte de Quincas Berro Dágua* [*The Two Deaths of Quincas Wateryell*], *Os Pastores da noite* [*Shepherds of the Night*] (1964), *Dona Flor e seus dois maridos*

[*Dona Flor and Her Two Husbands*] (1966), *Tenda dos milagres* [*Tent of Miracles*] (1969), *Tereza Batista, cansada de guerra* [*Tereza Batista: Home from the Wars*] (1973), *Tieta do Agreste* [*Tieta the Goat Girl*] (1978) and *Farda fardão* [*Pen, Sword, Camisole*] (1979), to cite only a few, show how resolutely Amado has continued to create stories about the down-and-outs, the "malandros" and riff-raff of Brazilian, and especially Bahian, society. And although, as in the case of Steinbeck, Amado idealizes these characters whenever necessary, he has proven to be, as Steinbeck at his best was, a master story-teller, a writer working in the grand oral tradition who, as we see in *Terras do sem fim* or *Tenda dos milagres*, has a knack for reproducing the speech patterns of the people and for bringing disparate social issues into the purvue of his intensely regionalistic, even local characters and types. Unlike Steinbeck, who, in *East of Eden* and *The Winter of Our Discontent*, felt he had to create both new character types and a new language for them in order to deal with new social questions, Amado has managed, as in *Tenda dos milagres* (racism in Brazil), *Tereza Batista* (feminism in Brazil)[9] and *Tietá* (the problems of industrialization and pollution in Brazil), to couch problems of contemporary political, social or economic significance in terms of the common folk of Bahia. Realizing that his characters constitute the essential appeal of his work, Amado, in contrast to the post-1939 (*Grapes of Wrath*) Steinbeck, advances these themes primarily through the voice of his people, and not, as Steinbeck had fallen prey to, in the artificial voice of someone new, a stranger to the writer's sensibilities. This crucial point about the integration of theme, speech and character explains why one writer, Amado, has been able to grow in both popularity and technical skill while the other, Steinbeck, began to lose his way, to see his creative powers, his popularity and his relevancy slip away, never to be regained.

Stylistically speaking, Amado, like Steinbeck, utilizes two very distinct ways of recreating reality: one is both starkly mimetic, even naturalistic, but intensely humanitarian, while the other is poetic, powerfully scenic, and, particularly in the case of the later Steinbeck, abstract and mythic, perhaps excessively so. In their early work, both writers concentrated on dealing with characters, situations and themes which were based on the local scene, on definitively regional realities. Amado would recognize this orientation as the taproot of his creativity as a writer and would move ever closer to it, distilling and refining his narrative techniques as he went along. Steinbeck, as we have seen, would move away from the source of his strength—his characters, his linguistic inventiveness and his narrative appeal—and then try, after both he and his society had changed, to return to it. Hence, on this key issue of how a writer perceives his own strengths and weaknesses, we see how Amado and Steinbeck effectively reversed positions in terms of who was the superior craftsman. Early in their careers, Steinbeck was writing the more artistically successful fiction (most critics feel he did his best work in the years between

1935–41), but later on, in the 1950s and beyond, when Steinbeck was becoming lost as regards who and what he would write about, Amado, slowly gaining an ever more accurate critical perception of his own work, began to emerge as both the more aesthetically successful writer and as the more popular writer.

But through it all, both Amado and Steinbeck show themselves, in their best moments, to have been in love with life and to have been committed to social and economic justice. It is this constant and passionate commitment to life and to the preservation of simple human dignity that gives their best work its power and its enduring appeal. Both writers, moreover, believe fervently in the collective future of mankind, and this is the point at which their always progressive and humanitarian political ideals come into play in their fiction. Amado, like Steinbeck, succeeds best when he is dealing with certain kinds of people in certain kinds of situations, and it must be said that both writers fail when they attempt, as the young Amado and the post-1939 Steinbeck did, to discourse woodenly on the manners, morals, and politics of modern life, to abstract their stories and characters from the real and valid points they wished to make, to stray from the power of their narratives and to mount basically political or moral disquisitions at the expense of artistic integrity. The early Amado, more egregiously than even the later Steinbeck, had a destructive tendency to allow his always vivid language to lapse (as in *O país do carnaval* [The land of carnival], *Cacau,* and *Suor*) into diatribe and raillery. But in works like *Tortilla Flat, Cannery Row, The Grapes of Wrath, In Dubious Battle, Jubiabá, Tenda dos milagres* and *Mar morto,* to cite some of these writers' more successful efforts, Amado and Steinbeck both take pains to immerse their stories in a very identifiable human perspective, one uniquely theirs. Only then do they allow their social and political criticisms to come into play. The result, in these novels, at least, is a felicitous kind of fiction, one that so merges the human with the political that it ceases to be doctrinaire and becomes affective, inspiring and truly universal in significance—the voice of common people everywhere. And while we must note that a consistent flaw in both Amado and Steinbeck's work is their penchant for sentimentality, we must also note Amado's ever-present tendency to politicize virtually all aspects of his art and, on occasion, to romanticize poverty. So while both Amado and Steinbeck share many positive artistic features, they also share some recurrent flaws.

## III

Before concluding this essay, a few observations should be made about what many critics have termed the "proletarian" aspects of the fiction produced by these two Depression-Era writers. The basic critical problem here is one of definition. What do we mean, critically speaking, when we use the term "proletarian?" If we wish to have it refer to a literary work that is directed at the lumpenproletariat and that would incite these people to violent overthrow of the existing social and economic system, then the novels of neither Amado nor Steinbeck can be said to be truly "proletarian" in spirit. The early Amado, however, comes much closer to fitting this definition of the term than does Steinbeck, who was, in addition to being more of an individualist, or populist, than he was a radical leftist, ever more the social reformer than revolutionary. But if by the term "proletarian" we mean to refer to a book that focuses attention on the problems of the poor and the disadvantaged, then both Amado and Steinbeck, at least in their early work, could easily be termed "proletarian novelists."

But they are much more than this as well, and here we confront the basic point of comparison. More than anything else, Jorge Amado and John Steinbeck are the "people's novelists," the two writers who, at their best, find their strength, truth and inspiration in the little people, the outcasts, the abused and the powerless, an approach to fiction writing that had a special poignancy for readers during the Great Depression of the 1930s. Speaking for these people, Jorge Amado and John Steinbeck become the consciences of their societies and, playing this vital role, they remind the rest of us, in visceral and sometimes crudely inelegant ways, that in our respective cultures all is not as it should be, that the "American dream," like the "Brazilian dream," is still a cruelly unattainable myth for many people. Both Steinbeck and Amado have, in their best work, become the articulate and moving voice of the people, the writers of their time and place who sought to speak of the broken dreams and shattered lives of the dispossessed and the marginalized. As long as there are people who wish to improve the standard of living for all members of their society, the novels of Jorge Amado and John Steinbeck will be read and loved. And this is as it should be because these novels represent the "vox populi," the cries of an outraged populace rising up to oppose the stubbornly resistent evils of exploitation, repression and ignorance. The result is that works like *The Grapes of Wrath, Cannery Row, Jubiabá* and *Gabriela, cravo e canela* are a joy to read in spite of their artistic shortcomings. The most successful novels of Jorge Amado and John Steinbeck are brimming with an irrepressible zest for life; more than that, they are a paean to it.

## NOTES

1. As Jay Parini notes, Steinbeck's best work epitomizes the socially committed literature of the 1930s, although he was suspicious and even disdainful of Communism. This point signals a significant difference between the two authors.
2. Selden Rodman, *South America of the Poets* (New York: Hawthorn Books, 1970), p. 122. Amado notes here that he likes the "young Steinbeck" and that he "especially" liked Erskine Caldwell, that latter observation being interesting in regard to Caldwell's somewhat cruder, more sensationalistic style.

3. Amado's three earliest novels, *O país do carnaval* (1932), *Cacau* (1933), and *Suor* (1934), are marred by their stylistic clumsiness, a defect that Amado began to correct in his post-1935 works, beginning with *Jubiabá*, which Fred Ellison terms ". . . a minor masterpiece of the literature of the 'thirties'" (Ellison, 94). Álvaro Lins, in fact, sees *Jubiabá* as inititiating a new phase in Amado's work, one characterized by a greater concern over aesthetic issues (Lins, 1947).

4. It is interesting to note that the post-1958 Amado was often criticized for allegedly "romanticizing" poverty, a charge that might also be leveled at the early Steinbeck.

5. An interesting comparative study could be made by contrasting Steinbeck's utilization of animal imagery in *Tortilla Flat* and that employed by Amado's great contemporary, Graciliano Ramos, in *Vidas sêcas* (1938).

6. John Steinbeck, *In Dubious Battle* (New York: The Viking Press, 1963), p. 141.

7. Elizabeth Lowe, "The 'New' Jorge Amado." *Luso-Brazilian Review*, 2 (1969): 73–82.

8. See M. L. Nunes, "The Preservation of African Culture in Brazilian Literature: The Novels of Jorge Amado," *Luso-Brazilian Review* 10 (1973): 86–101.

9. Amado, whose political stock, like that of Steinbeck, tends to go up and down, has also been attacked as a sexist and, because of his arguably stereotypical presentation of women (Ana Mercedes, of *Tenda dos milagres*, for example), an exploiter of women.

## BIBLIOGRAPHY

Barros Martins, José de, ed. *Jorge Amado, povo e terra*. São Paulo: Livraria Martins Editôra, 1972.

Benson, Jackson J.*The True Adventures of John Steinbeck, Writer: A Biography*. New York: Viking Press, 1984.

———. *The Short Novels of John Steinbeck*. Durham: Duke University Press, 1990.

Chamberlain, Bobby J. *Jorge Amado*. Boston: Twayne, 1990.

Ditsky, John. *John Steinbeck, Life, Work and Criticism*. Fredericton, N. B.: York Press, 1985.

Ellison, Fred P. *Brazil's New Novel: Four Northeastern Masters*. Berkeley: University of California Press, 1954.

Fitz, Earl E. "The Problem of the Unreliable Narrator in Jorge Amado's *Tenda dos milagres.*" *Kentucky Romance Quarterly,* Vol.XXX, No. 3 (1983): 311–321.

———. "Structural Ambiguity in Jorge Amado's *A morte e a morte de Quincas Berro Dágua.*" *Hispania* 67 (May 1984): 293–304.

French, Warren. *John Steinbeck*, 2nd ed. Boston: Twayne, 1975.

Kiernan, T. *The Intricate Music: A Biography of John Steinbeck*. Boston: Little, Brown and Company, 1979.

Lins, Álvaro. *Jornal de Crítica*. Rio de Janeiro: José Olimpio, 1947.

Lisca, Peter. *The Art of John Steinbeck: An Analysis and Interpretation of its Development*. Ph.D. thesis, the University of Wisconsin, 1955.

Lowe, Elizabeth. "The 'New' Jorge Amado." *Luso-Brazilian Review* 2 (1969): 73–82.

Milliet, Sérgio. *Diário Crítico*, IV. São Paulo: Editora Brasiliense, 1944.

Montenegro, Olívio. *O Romance brasileiro*. Rio de Janeiro: José Olympio, 1938.

Nunes, Maria Luisa. "The Preservation of African Culture in Brazilian Literature: The Novels of Jorge Amado." *Luso-Brazilian Review* 10 (1973): 86–101.

Parini, Jay. *John Steinbeck: A Biography.* New York: Henry Holt and Company, 1995.

Silverman, M. N. "Allegory in Two Works [*Jubiabá* and Os *pastores da noite*] of Jorge Amado." *Romance Notes* 13 (1971): 67–70.

Tati, Miecio. *Jorge Amado: vida e obra*. Belo Horizonte: Editora Itatiaia, 1961.

# A Character in Spite of Her Author
## Dona Flor Liberates Herself from Jorge Amado

ELIZABETH LOWE

Jorge Amado's strength as a novelist lies in part in his skill at character development. His busy, folkloric canvasses of life in Brazil's northeastern cacau belt portray a vast array of cultural and socioeconomic types which are contemporary and historical, real and fictional. Some are mere caricatures, others are fully drawn to support complex social themes. Paulo Tavares catalogued the characters of Amadian fiction (which as of 1979 numbered over 4,000) and Bobby Chamberlain offers a typology of the juxtaposition of real-life with fictional, mythical and supernatural figures in the later novels, showing how this "displacement of character" explains much of the humor and subtlety in the Amadian oeuvre.[1]

The female protagonists of the later novels, Gabriela, Dona Flor and Tereza Batista have attracted a wide following of readers around the world. All three women symbolize a particularly Brazilian reality and at the same time are extremely appealing to a global audience. Amado is in fact one of the most widely translated authors in the world, a phenomenon which in itself bears closer examination since the author's fictional universe is really best understood by the inner circle of Amado's contemporaries, the artists and intellectuals of Bahia and Brazil.

Here we will focus on the broad crosscultural significance of the novel *Dona Flor e seus dois maridos* [*Dona Flor and her Two Husbands*], considering how the main character symbolizes key aspects of Brazilian society and then "translates" those from Amado's Salvador to a global level. I will then refer to some techniques of character development that contributed to the transformation of Flor from "uma pequena burguesa cheia de preconceitos" [a little bourgeoise full of prejudices][2] into a character who offers "an alternative vision of gender, narrative voice and identity."[3]

To examine Amado's process of character building may shed some light on the controversy over his "sexist" portrayal of women and gender relations.

*125*

Flor personifies the victory of ambiguity, in contrast to Fuentes's "tragedy of ambiguity" as cited by Fitz and Payne.[4] The tradition of ambiguity in the Brazilian novel is analyzed by Fitz and Payne, who trace the "alternative vision of such issues as gender, narrative voice and identity" to Machado de Assis. The "new novel" which grows out of the "gender-bending tradition of Machado de Assis" reveals the contradictory and complex nature of reality. It also depicts male/female relations and attributes as fluid and complementary, not binary and exclusive.[5] Flor's "contrasexuality" (her male *animus*) emerges in the course of her development as a character and empowers her to take the dominant, decision making role in defining her relationship with her two husbands. Jorge Amado's writings and characters like Flor illustrate Roberto DaMatta's theories of Brazilian culture, which he insists does not operate on the "either-or/ two Brazils" model imposed by traditional "Brazilianist" scholarship driven by northern, western models. Rather, he stresses, Brazilian culture is best understood by the "both-and" model, a dynamic, holistic approach to culture which looks at multiple tendencies operative in the society as a whole. Through a case study approach, DaMatta illustrates how "both hierarchical/personalistic and egalitarian/individualistic codes operate simultaneously" in Brazilian society. This "personalism" is very evident in Amado's fiction. Indeed, Amado claims that "as mulheres dos meus livros são como elas são na realidade ... não posso virar de costas e falisficá-las" [women in my books are the way they are in real life ... I can't turn my back to this reality or falsify it].[6] What first limits and imprisons Flor, her gender, her social class and her mixed race, is ultimately what liberates her for it enables her to see beyond a "stable" and "binary" reality[7] to find stability in compromise. Flor opts not to choose between her living husband and the dead one, and in so doing she achieves balance and growth.

It is interesting and paradoxical that what makes Amado so delightful to read, so "accessible," is in fact the very key to his complexity as an author. His characters and situations are, on the surface, exactly "what they are"—yet they can be read as icons for a complex, Brazilian, reality. Amado typically allows his characters to take over control of their "destinies" from the author at some point in each of the novels. Once this happens the character finds a voice which is expresssive of the personalism of Brazilian society as well as of a very personal, individualistic identity. Amado is on record that he had planned a different ending for *Dona Flor*.[8] In the first, contemplated ending, Amado had Flor despairing over giving herself back to Vadinho and then vanishing with him under the *candomblé* spell which she had initiated. "Eu penso uma coisa assim meio poética, os dois desaparecendo, o outro marido entrando e vendo ela morte na cama" [I am thinking about something somewhat poetic, the two of them disappearing, the other husband coming into the bedroom and finding her dead on the bed]. According to the author, however, Flor "rebelled" and took over, calling Vadinho back and thus creating the richly symbolic tale that has seduced readers all over the world. "No dia seguinte, revi a cena e fui continuar. O que aconteceu então? Depois que o Vadinho fez amor com ela e foi embora, o marido entra no quarto, possui Dona Flor e ela acha ótimo! Então ela, e não eu, resolveu ficar com os dois. Eu não esperava que dona Flor fosse capaz de romper com aqueles preconceitos todos . . . Dona Flor impôs o fim do livro. Toda vez que o personagem está conduzindo o livro, você sabe que o livro está andando e toda vez que o personagem reage contra qualquer coisa, é você que está errado" [The next day I reviewed the scene and continued. What happened then? After Vadinho made love to her and went away, the husband enters the bedroom, makes love to Dona Flor and she thinks it is wonderful! So she, not I, decides that she will stay with both of them. I did not think Flor was capable of breaking with those prejudices . . . Dona Flor decried the ending of the book. Every time a character is leading the story, you know the book is going well and every time the character reacts against something it's you who are wrong] (44).

It is this complexity that often escapes a first reading, and, interestingly, it is what made the American film version of *Dona Flor* fail. For all the apparent simplicity of Amado's novels, he requires a sophisticated and culturally connected readership that can pick up on the "tragedies and victories" of ambiguity that distinguish his characters and the choices they make. This crosscultural paradox is artfully explicated in Catarina Edinger's essay, "*Dona Flor* in Two Cultures." Edinger demonstrates how the 1982 American film *Kiss Me Goodbye* turns *Dona Flor* into a situation comedy for a homogeneous American "mass" audience which completely misses the theme of choice and ambiguity that makes Dona Flor an interesting character in a significant novel.

We might thus conclude that the very elements that make Amado so "translatable" lead to some interesting misinterpretations. First, the duality and personalism of Brazilian life which Amado's characters portray are difficult to translate cross-culturally. Secondly, the way women are portrayed by Amado within this cultural framework makes it seem that the treatment is crass and sexist. While it would be a stretch to place Amado in the same category of "new" novelists as Lispector, Piñon et al., he does demonstrate some of the reality-bending traits of the Machadian tradition.

Edinger's comparison of the American film and the Brazilian novel brings out a number of points that explain why the Amado novel did not translate into a successful American film. The essay illustrates the complexity of the Amado novel by looking at the crosscultural implications of the themes of choice and ambiguity and the nature of the "woman's dilemma," points that are relevant to a better understanding of Dona Flor's strength as a character.

The theme of choice and ambiguity is central to *Dona Flor* and consistent with the expression of Brazilian cultural and national identity which marks Amado and his generation.[9] While the moral universe of the United

States is, from the perspective of our neighbors in the southern hemisphere, "polarized," in Brazil moral distinctions are not as clear. Moral decisions, such as those involving adultery, are not only dealt with compassionately but with considerable humor in the fictive worlds of Amado and his literary compatriots. This subtlety is difficult to translate into the North American ethical code. While the genre of the "Comedy of Remarriage" ("separation, divorce and the process of reuniting") is universal, Flor's way of dealing with remarriage after the first husband's death is drastically different than Kay's in "Kiss Me Goodbye."[10] While the film, in Edinger's analysis, focuses "on the woman's dilemma as perceived primarily by herself," success in dealing with her dilemma is in large part socially and culturally determined. Amado's world is that of popular Salvador, its middle and lower classes, where the spiritist belief system of African Brazilian *candomblé* is part of everyday life and where behavior is ruled by personalist principles. Flor derives her identity and her strength from her interaction with this milieu and the complex rules that drive it. Kay, on the other hand, lives in "colorless" New York City and the movie plot calls for "little interaction between leads and secondary characters, and practically no influence from the social context at large."[11]

Thus the resolution of the love triangles, in which the protagonist is torn in her affections between a creative, sexy, but deceased spouse and a serious, dependable, living husband, is diametrically opposite in the Brazilian novel and the American film. Edinger shows how Flor, like Hedda Gabler, realizes that an "either or choice" is not satisfactory. (Flor, however, gets the best of both worlds, while Hedda is sentenced to a less satisfying end). Kay's problem is different than Flor's and it is not "mutually exclusive. Jolly never threatens to make love to her again . . . so that there's nothing emotionally at stake."[12] Obedient to the Protestant tradition, which demands forthrightness and transparency, Kay confronts Rupert with the situation and demands that he help rid her of the past relationship. In her case, Rupert is the sensible choice as well as the only one available.

Flor, however, concludes that she cannot and does not wish to make a choice, thus reaffirming the value of unresolved confusion. Ambivalence and sensuality are paired here and endorsed as positive values. The American version supports "rationalization, verbalization and openness of conflict" which ultimately ends in a resolution that eliminates the source of conflict. Also suppressed is sensuality and, by association, personal choice and freedom. Kay is portrayed as restricted and ultimately defeated by her rule-bound world and her professionalism; Flor, on the other hand, moves beyond her sex-object status and claims the victory of the chooser over the chosen.

Flor's growth as a character and her development from caricature to full blown character supports the major thematic elements of the Brazilian novel. Amado poses the provocative rhetorical question, "Qual a verdadeira Dona

Flor?" [Who is the real Dona Flor?] and he works a great deal at her characterization, relying on physical description and symbolic tropes, probes into her psychic life, and association with a series of opposing emblems that characterize her social roles. Chamberlain notes that Flor's story is based on "the formula of thesis, antithesis and synthesis. She moves from a position of dependence on one rather unidimensional man to one of dependence on another, in every way his opposite." Chamberlain concludes from this that the "Hegelian dialectic serves as the work's primary principle" and that the novel illustrates the need for a "hybrid solution, one that will reconcile the best of two competing forces while rejecting the worst."[13] While my conclusion is the same, I propose that Flor does more than move between opposite positions of dependence. Her choice not to choose is a step beyond dependence on two men. It is a compromise that empowers her in the psychological, sexual, economic and social arenas.

Amado weaves back and forth between Flor's physical and emotional states which mirror each other in sensuous culinary imagery. This intertextual mimetism is the principal technique used to develop the symbolic aspect of Flor's character. The signature description of Flor is the "morena reconcuda, servida de carnes" with the delicate round face, color of mate, eyes of oil. She thinks of herself as the hot spicy dish that she is serving up to her husband. Later, her silent eulogies to Vadinho are woven into her cooking lectures, and the pressure of her needs becomes so great they boil over into action. This action becomes directed by the power of the African Brazilian *candomblé* rituals. Interestingly, Vadinho is a devoté of Exú, the god of confusion. For Flor, this becomes a blessing, and the confusion turns out to be creative.

As a social icon, Flor (Florípedes Paiva Guimarães) is both "food" (sex object) and cooking teacher (producing member of society). The food-sex metaphors of the novel are analyzed in detail by Chamberlain, who links them as "effective means of spoofing the respective social classes" normally contrasted but here comically coupled through the terms of dietary and sexual preferences. Flor's sexuality evolves in the novel as she makes the transition from Vadinho's wife to widow, to wife of Teodoro, and, then finally, to the status of woman with two husbands. She first fears then accepts her sexual needs and, finally, actively seeks to satisfy them.

Flor performs comfortably within and crosses the boundaries of both "home" and "street" in DaMatta's dichotomy of Brazilian social life. Thus the vitality and sense of progress in this character who moves from a passive/object role to an aggressive/subject role and then, with a new found sense of identity, is able to comfortably negotiate back and forth between the two states of being. In a sense, this is symbolic of Brazilian cultural and national identity writ large. It is worth noting that it is characteristic of literature by and about women in Brazil to identify the main character with the theme of national identity. This has occurred since José de Alencar's *A escrava Isaura* and continues today in the works of Clarice Lispector (*A hora da estrela*) and Nélida Piñon, most recently in *The Republic of Dreams*. Chamberlain suggests that *Dona Flor* can be read as a political allegory of the Getúlio Vargas dictatorship. Vadinho would be "equated . . . with the traditional liberal populist politicians, Teodoro with Mareshal Humberto Castelo Branco and his clique of hard-line generals and technocrats, and Flor with Brazil, the Brazilian government and the Brazilian people."[14] Brazil, like Dona Flor, must define its future through the compromise and alliance of its populist and elitist elements. Flor is destined to wage the "terrible battle between matter and spirit" which, the author implies, the country must take on if it is to achieve the social equity, "order and progress" of a modern nation.

If one compares Flor to her predecessor, Gabriela, and her successor, Tereza Batista, it is possible to note an evolution of the female character as symbol for a country in transition as well as a gauge of Amado's attitudes towards the Brazilian "puzzle." Basic to Gabriela's character is the possession of freedom to pursue the enjoyment of the sensual life. Flor, in redefining her relationship with her two husbands, achieves personal satisfaction, economic and political autonomy (a freedom from dependence.) Tereza Batista, is as Chamberlain observes, a "legendary heroine" who does not experience any of the growth expected of a modern character.[15] Her story is an allegory of survival, and her heroic feats after a lifetime of sexual abuse consist of leading armies of prostitutes to fight against disease and social injustice. Tereza's story is told within the conventions of cordel poetry and a strong overlay of Amadian parody of his own novelistic techniques. As a character, she can be seen as a parody of her predecessors, Flor and Gabriela, and as such her happy ending is less powerful and significant than theirs yet it emphasizes the theme of survival rendered in a serious fashion in the previous novels. The fact that Amado would resort to parody in this last novel of the womens' "trilogy" could be interpreted as a shift of authorial perspective on the Brazilian situation, a lightening or jading of point of view about the national dilemma.

It is not clear that Amado set out to achieve these outcomes for his female protagonists any more than he intended to write for a world audience. The viability and symbolic depth of his later heroines and the "translatability" of his novels are due in large part not so much to doctrinaire intent as to his skill as a novelist. Amado is skilled in the arts of character development and is able to paint detailed portraits of people from the streets of Bahia that are so convincing as to seem "real" while at the same time investing them with symbolic content. His long experience with crafting novels allowed him the freedom in the later works to "release" his characters from too tight authorial control to take on a life of their own. It is understandable that an

American filmmaker would think that the Brazilian novel *Dona Flor* might translate into a film for a mass American audience due to the touristic appeal of the characters and situations of the Brazilian work. It is also possible for the same reason to understand why Amado is viewed as sexist. The surface elements of his later works encourage superficial interpretations of the texts. Yet, really to translate Amado and to achieve a full understanding of his treatment of character, he must be read in full context, that is the broad historical, social and spiritual environment of twentieth century Brazil, a country in transition.

## NOTES

1. Bobby J. Chamberlain, *Jorge Amado* (Boston: Twayne, 1990), 70 ff.
2. Alvaro Cardoso Gomes and Regina Rodrigues Neves, *Amado,* (São Paulo: Editora Nova Cultura), p. 44.
3. Judith A. Payne and Earl E. Fitz, *Ambiguity and Gender in the New Novel of Brazil and Spanish America.* University of Iowa Press, 1993, p. 2.
4. Ibid., p. 7.
5. Ibid., p. 3.
6. Cardoso Gomes and Rodrigues Neves, p. 52.
7. David J. Hess and Roberto DaMatta. *The Brazilian Puzzle.* New York: Columbia University Press, 1995. p. 8.
8. Ibid., p. 44.
9. Cf. The theories of Brazilian culture in the works of Darcy Ribeiro, particularly in his most recent publication, *O povo brasileiro.*
10. Catarina Edinger, " Dona Flor in Two Cultures," *Literature and Film Quarterly.* 19 (4), 236–237.
11. Ibid., p. 237.
12. Ibid., p. 238.
13. Chamberlain, p. 63.
14. Ibid., p. 64.
15. Ibid., p. 85.

## BIBLIOGRAPHY

Cardoso Gomes, Alvaro and Sonia Regina Rodrigues Neves. *Jorge Amado.* São Paulo: Nova Cultural, 1990.
Chamberlain, Bobby. *Jorge Amado.* Boston: Twayne, 1990.
Edinger, Catarina. "Dona Flor in Two Cultures." *Literature and Film Quarterly*, v. 19, no. 4 (October 1991), pp. 235–241.
Hess, David J. and Roberto DaMatta. *The Brazilian Puzzle: Culture on the Borderlands of the Western World.* New York: Columbia University Press, 1995.
Payne, Judith A. and Earl E. Fitz. *Ambiguity and Gender in the New Novel of Brazil and Spanish America.* Iowa City: University of Iowa Press, 1993.
Tavares, Paulo. *Criaturas de Jorge Amado.* Rio de Janeiro: Editora Record, 1985.

# Jorge Amado
# and the Classical Tradition
## Aristophanes in Bahia

ENRIQUE MARTÍNEZ-VIDAL

With very rare exceptions Jorge Amado's novels take place in the Northeastern Brazilian state of Bahia. All of his narratives reflect the rich multiracial mixture of this region and his characters come from all walks of life. For this reason the action in his novels moves through all the different social levels which characterize this fascinating region. Because Amado focuses on Bahian history and society, critics have qualified him as a regionalist writer whose stories do not seem to transcend the local tales and folklore of his native land. Yet the merits of his works, especially those published after *Dona Flor e seus dois maridos* [*Dona Flor and her Two Husbands*], must be appreciated for having structures and themes which transcend their regional background.

There is no doubt that the complexity of Bahian customs as well as society are reflected in Amado's works. This is due to the fact that the historical and ethnic background of this area of Brazil are explored by the writer from different perspectives. The common people, *o povo,* fill the pages with their daily struggle in search of identity and a better way of life. Seldom is the novel of this author's second epoch not filled with Afro-Brazilian religious elements. Amado loves the gastronomy of his native land and even speaks of food, to the point of incorporating recipes in his novels. All these customs and cultural values, including the most minute nuances, are interwoven in the sociological patterns which become essential to his narrative art. The strong African presence in Bahia, in particular, and in the "nordeste," in general, is well portrayed. The fusion of races and beliefs becomes part and parcel of the literary production of a writer who seems determined to be the voice and conscience of this unique culture that created him, and, which in turn, becomes grist for the mills of the mythopoetic process.

In the same manner that the Bahian culture represents many and diverse cultural currents that have through generations merged and have formed its own and unique form, Jorge Amado's intellectual and literary baggage also

*133*

will represent many different and distinct sources and origins. This study will attempt to focus upon and analyze some classical archetypes and myths of the Western tradition, and how Jorge Amado will incorporate them in the narrative process. Although the general idea could be used to analyze many, if not all of Amado's novels, this study will be limited primarily to one particular work, *Tereza Batista cansada de guerra* [*Tereza Batista: Home from the Wars*].

*Tereza Batista cansada de guerra* is the saga of Tereza, an orphan raised by an aunt, and whose relatively carefree and happy childhood comes to an end when this aunt sells her to a local merchant. Capitão Justo is the wealthy merchant whose money and power have allowed him to indulge in his hobby, which is to rape young adolescent girls. While in the hands of this depraved character, Terreza falls in love with a young man who comes from a well-to-do family. The faint hope of finding a way out of her situation comes to an abrupt end when Capitão Justo discovers the affair. Having caught them in the act, he humiliates the young lovers in his own brutal and peculiar way. With a cry of desperation, "Medo acabou! Medo acabou, capitão!" [My fear is over! My fear is over, Captain!],[1] Tereza plunges a knife into her sexual abuser and tormenter, thus bringing his life to an end. He dies in the very room where he had killed the child's innocence by the spilling of her blood, and now it is her turn to take away his miserable life with a knife and the spilling of his blood. The very poignant symbolism of this final action does not escape us.

The consequences of his death will bring Tereza to jail, ending the first part of her ordeal and travails. Actually, it is the end of the first part of three, for the novel can easily be divided into three parts. So the second part of this literary tryptic begins when she comes out of jail and needs to find a means of surviving in an environment that is quite hostile to a woman of her class without a family. In the society depicted by Amado few are the options left for a young woman like Tereza. One of them is a life of prostitution.

Amado treats the prostitutes in his novels with a great degree of understanding and even compassion. For Emile Zola, the high priest of Naturalism, Zola's Nana is but a character in his parable to moralize against the capitalist decadence of the French second Empire.[2] This moralization is very evident in the last page of the novel. Yet for Amado his prostitutes are human beings made of flesh and bone who are victims of a traditional exploitative society.

In Western literature the figure of the prostitute has been used to reflect either certain personal or collective evils, or at times even virtues. There is what has been archetypically called the "bitch-witch" who embodies the evil traits in a woman and who will use her sexual powers to seduce and destroy men. Again in reference of Zola, Nana was portrayed as a conduit through which she destroyed the very men who ironically had sustained a socio-economic system which had led her to that position. On the other hand, we have the prostitute with the heart of gold whose patron saint is none other than the

Christ-forgiven Mary Magdalene. This archetype can be traced in modern time to Victor Hugo's play *Marion de Lorme* (1831).[3] From Hugo's time to the present many are the novels and plays that incorporate the figure of the harlot viewed with compassion and understanding.

Amado seems to cast the prostitute in a very real and amoral mold, and for this reason there is not any particular model in his works. But in general, a detailed analysis of these different characters seems to reveal that Amado's prostitutes fall into the category of the good "bad girl"—somewhat akin to the character that we find in Jean-Paul Sartre's play *La Putain respétueuse*. This sense of abnegation on the part of a woman who is viewed as placed in the lowest rung of the social ladder is made patent in an event which happens at the beginning of the second part of Amado's novel.

Between the first part of the story, the one narrating her misfortunes with the merchant, and the second adventure with Dr. Guedes, Amado inserts a short story about Tereza which has the subtitle: "ABC da peleja entre Tereza Batista e a bexiga negra" [The battle between Tereza Batista and the small-pox]. The three distinctive parts of the novel are divided by number, yet this story's division is done by the letters of the alphabet, from A to Z. It tells of Tereza who, while wandering in the backlands of Northeastern Brazil, comes to know a young physician with a promising career. Dr. Oto Espinheira is appointed medical chief of a rural district in the State of Bahia, and it is at this point that he takes Tereza in as his concubine or mistress, *rapariga*. This young doctor seems to have the proper ambitions and the right connections, the latter being most important in a Latin society. However, he has a flaw, which is his lack of courage. His cowardice stems from such a strong sense of self-preservation that it overrides his duties to the medical hippocratic oath. The town of Buquim as well as the general area comes under the terrible whip of a smallpox epidemic. People begin to fall prey to this plague and many die after a horrible ordeal. Everyone is tested under these circumstances including those dedicated to curing and succoring their fellow human beings. Dr. Oto, along with his nurse, is unable to cope with the situation, and, at the thought of dying at an early age, promptly takes the first train bound for the capital, Salvador. Tereza, however, does not go away, and she assumes the responsibility for creating a system that will alleviate this dreadful situation. She gathers all the vaccines and other medicines which were sent to Dr. Oto by the State government and goes on recruiting a body of prostitutes to help her administer to the sick. These harlots, now turned "Florence Nightingales" of the Backlands, toil without ceasing and with a great deal of abnegation. Later on in his work, Amado will repeat a similar situation, as can be read in one of his most recent novels, *Tocaia Grande [Showdown]*.[4]

The familiarity that Tereza shows with the world of small town prostitution was not acquired in Buquim. As it has already been mentioned, she is jailed for stabbing to death the "Capitão," the fiendish merchant who had abused her sexually; she is beaten by policemen who had been friends of the murdered "Capitão" and spends time in jail and in a convent where the nuns try to reform her. Once free, the only option for her to make a living is to work in a local brothel. She knew that these women had great courage and possessed a great capacity for compassion. What they accomplished during the plague became part of the lore in those parts of the interior of Bahia. Amado ends this chapter addressing the readers and reminding them of Tereza's role and importance in this event ". . . repito e acreditem se quiser: quem deu jeito à bexiga negra solta nas ruas de Buquim foram as putas de Muricapeba com Tereza à frente" [. . . I repeat and let anyone who wish to believe, know that it was the whores of Muricapeba who with Tereza leading them fought the plague that was loose in the streets of Buquim] (224).

Like the hero or heroine in the Picaresque tradition, Tereza moves on not only geographically but also through different social classes. In that second part of the novel, we have the story of her relationship with Dr. Emiliano Guedes, a very wealthy and important man in that region and one of its powerful political bosses. He sees her at the house of the merchant, and now that she is free Dr. Guedes invites her to share his house. For a time they live what appears to be a blissful life.

Amado depicts Dr. Guedes as a very learned and refined member of this rural society. His tastes are those shared by the Brazilian upper class country squire. We find out that although his roots are Bahian, he has travelled to Europe and this has given him very cosmopolitan tastes. It is during this period of Tereza's life and with the guidance of this older man that she begins to learn about a more sophisticated way of life. Tereza is a very attractive young women and endowed with a sharp mind and an inborn ability to absorb new ways and life styles. Dr. Guedes sees in her a diamond in the rough, sheer raw material that can be molded into a more refined and, to his understanding, superior woman.

Tereza becomes a very adept pupil and, like a sponge, she absorbs everything that her mentor teaches her. The reader is invited to observe how through the social amenities of these times, Emiliano Guedes educates his eager pupil. He introduces her to a different level of gastronomy, that is to say, the culinary arts and a certain knowledge of fine wines and spirits all as part and parcel of her educational process. Rare is the novel of Amado which does not include a presentation of the Bahian cuisine, a cuisine that he will underscore as one of the best in the world. One could say that in these chapters of the novel, in the process of educating Tereza to the diversity of the cuisine of their region, Amado is also educating the reader on the gastronomic wonders that the region has to offer. We also learn that eating well prepared dishes is not enough, because a well presented table is only but the center piece conducive to civilized conversation. The dining room of Dr. Guedes becomes a gathering place for people who will share excellently prepared dishes as well as conversation on a multitude of pertinent subjects. He always makes sure to invite those who in the hinterlands of the region are considered professionals with a certain amount of intellectual discernment. In addition, they have the highly cherished virtue of being very loyal to him.

These banquets which take place in Dr. Guedes' home remind us of the classical banquets of ancient Athens: guests concentrated on the food; the sparkling conversations were an important feature of the symposium, and drinking sessions would follow. At this time, the most important man was the symposiarch. Dr. Guedes, because of his importance both politically and intellectually, did not have to have the roll of the dice to take charge. No wives were allowed in these symposia of classical times, yet there was always the presence of at least one female, the flute-girl. This young woman, most of the time a slave, was also the center of attention when there was too much strong wine flowing freely and it was not unusual to have an old man chasing after her. On other occasions she was auctioned off to a guest, thus becoming his property for the remainder of the evening. One does not need to belabor the obvious to see a parallel between the functions of Tereza at these Bahian banquets and those of the humble but beautiful and gifted female slave of Antiquity.

Besides this parallel that has been pointed out between the banquets held at Dr. Guedes' home and the symposia of ancient Greece, another classical theme seems to emerge from the reading of this segment of the novel. Dr. Guedes loves Tereza very deeply, and his desire is to take this young uneducated woman and mold her by educating her in the refined ways of his times. Tereza is an avid and fast learner, and we see her taking the shape of a more sophisticated lady. Here we can appreciate shades of the ancient myth Pygmalion. This man who had fallen in love with an exquisite statue he had molded sees his dream becoming true thanks to the intervention of Aphrodite, when the goddess breathed life into it. Aphrodite is the goddess of love, and it is also love which seems to drive old Dr. Guedes to raise to higher levels the woman whom he has taken under his care. The contrast between the ways in which the "capitão" and Dr. Guedes treated Tereza are worthy of notice. One is moved by brutish lust and the other by love. The hatred and the psychological harm that was brought by the merchant stand in stark contrast with the tenderness and concern showed by Dr. Guedes towards the young woman whom he has taken as his mistress.

All seems to indicate a pleasant and idyllic end to the story with Dr. Guedes who as the mythological Pygmalion would possibly marry his ward. But Amado's sense of irony strikes again, and the relationship between Tereza and her mentor comes crashing down in the most peculiar of circumstances. Emiliano Guedes is an old man, and eventually his age catches up with him for his heart gives up in a moment of blissful sexual enjoyment with this mistress. Of course one could expect that upon Dom Emiliano's death

Tereza would have received some material reward for all the time spent with him, yet the opposite is true. Guedes' heirs descend like vultures upon the spoils and because he has not made any specific will which would include Tereza, she is left destitute, and once again she has to move. She moves downward from a sociological standpoint, and, triggered by necessity, she feels that she has to move geographically. Her wandering will lead her eventually to Salvador, the capital of the Bahia.

## A BAHIAN LYSISTRATA

The last section of our literary tryptic takes us to the capital where Tereza encounters a more complex world, and where all she has learned in her wandering in the interior is put to practice and tested. "A greve do balaio fechado na Bahia" [The Closed Box Strike of Bahia] is one of the three subtitles in the last section of the novel. It refers to an important event in our story, and it happens while Tereza is trying to make a living in Salvador. She has eventualy arrived at the capital searching for the sailor whom she had met while making a meager living as a cabaret dancer in a small coastal town.

When she arrives she discovers that Januário, her lover, has sailed away in a cargo ship bound for far away places. Tereza settles down trying to lead as much of a normal life as possible while waiting for the return of her sailor. Normalcy is within the experience that she has had in her stormy past—which obviously left her with very limited options regarding the possibility of employment. At least Dr. Guedes had developed some of her artistic talents, and in the process he gave Tereza a sense that she could aspire to be more than a prostitute. Her ambition was to be a dancer, and, with the little experience that she had dancing in a cabaret in a small town, she tries to find this line of work in the capital. A Brazilian reality is that in the social subculture in which she moves, the line between cabaret singers or dancers and the world of prostitution is tenuous at best and nonexistent at worst. For a classical Greek, Tereza has therefore passed from being a *pornai* to being a *hetairai*.

The subculture that Amado depicts in this segment of the novel is the one generally found in the urban cabarets, bars, and brothels. Whenever we find these marginal elements in society, we also find a police force which comes into play with its harassments, briberies, and abuse of the prostitutes. The latter are the real victims, not only abused by the police, but also exploited by the pimps who take their money and abuse them physically. The potential for venereal disease, like the proverbial Damocles' sword, is ever present and hanging over their heads. This "corrupt" and "corrupting" world has traditionally scandalized the upper classes in general and the women of this social class in particular. The women of Salvador are obviously no exception, and in the story they apply a sort of pressure to see whether the officials and officers in charge of the city law and order will do something to eliminate or at least curb the prostitutes. It is at this particular junction that the high- ranking police chief in charge of "morality" in the city is pressured to do something drastic towards the elimination of what is called a social blight by both these morally high-minded members of the upper class and obsequious politicians. Of course, soon they all discover that it is close to impossible to eliminate such a well established business in Salvador de Bahia. Therefore, the police chief, Labão Oliveira, and his police force come upon a "brilliant" plan, forcing all the prostitutes take their trade to an abandoned area at the edge of the city.

The prostitutes do not agree with the new police regulations. They are fully aware that while their traditional neighborhood where they were plying their trade was not the best, at least it was superior to the miserable new site to which they were compelled to move. As they begin to complain and drag their feet, the police resort to physically harassing, sometimes brutally, these poor, disenfranchised women so as to make them obey the orders given. It is at this point of the story that they cannot stand it any longer, yet they are fully aware that force must be met with force. It is clear in their mind that a group of help-less women cannot fight against a police force that has declared an all-out war against them. Therefore they come up with a strategy that hopefully will bring an end to that war, and this they do by collectively deciding to declare a strike. The first tactic of this strategy is to close shop or rather, as they say, close the box or basket (*o balaio fechado*). No longer will any man in that city, regardless of his social class, do commerce with them, for, as far as they are concerned, the men can take their sexual appetites to their wives ... assuming that they have them.

It is Nilia Cabaré, a well-liked prostitute, who proclaims in one of the local bars what eventually becomes the slogan of the strike: "Fique sabendo todo mundo que enquanto elas não voltarem pra Barroquinha, estou de balaio fechado, não recebo homem. Por nenhum dinheiro. Quem for mulher direita que me siga, tranque o xibiu, faça conta que é Semana Santa!" [Let everyone know that until they [the prostitutes] do not return to Barroquinha, I will have my purse closed, I will not receive any man for any man in the world. Let any true woman follow me by shutting close her pussy, and make believe that it is Holy Week] (363).

Tereza and all these poor women are tired of the war that society wages against them, and the situation that arises in Salvador takes us back to another place and another time. In Athens in the fifth century before the Common Era, a woman of the city, Lysistrata, is also tired of the war that is tearing apart all the Greek city-states. Athens had spent the flower of her youth in an absurd war in Syracuse (Sicily), as well as against Sparta and her allies. The cost in lives and money has been staggering. Lysistrata rallies not only the women of Athens but those of the other city-states to strike against this madness brought upon them by men. It is in what we could call the first international women's conference that closing the "man-purses" has to be the only way that will

bring men to an understanding that they must be prompt in declaring peace
. . . or else.

This parallel between these events transpiring in Salvador and those
which are found in one of Aristophanes' comedies is pointed out by Amado in
his narrative. One of his characters will allude to it. When the governor of the
state gets involved in the situation, which is worsening daily, he fears that it
may take on national and even international proportions. After all, he says,
the American fleet is in the waters of the Bahia de Todos os Santos, and what
is going to happen with so many sailors in the city of Salvador while all the
prostitutes are on strike? He calls a trusted councilman or alderman, Reginaldo Pavão, to see what he has to say about the matter: "Patético, a voz
encharcada em lágrimas, Regilnaldo Pavão fala en tragédia grega. Por que
grega? O vereador leu Aristófanes?—Desejou perguntar o Excelentíssimo,
mas a hora não é própia para gozação" [How pathetic and in his tearful voice,
Reginaldo Pavão speaks as in a Greek tragedy. Why Greek? Has the alderman
read Aristophanes?, asked his Excellency the governor to himself, yet these
were no times for rejoicing] (398).

As we begin to compare Aristophanes' *Lysistrata* with the very humorous tale that Amado weaves in this last part of the novel we become aware of
the similarities as well as the differences which are to be found. In Aristophanes' comedy there is a need to bring all the women together for that common cause which is the cessation of all Pelloponesian hostility and also to
avoid the potential problems caused by backsliding women. Lysistrata, aware
of this need, engages everyone involved in a religious ceremony. It is also significant that the women take over the Acropolis as the headquarters for her
"campaign" because in this epoch everyone in the city was aware of the religious significance of this place. Some critics of Aristophanic comedy believe
that the significance of such ceremony is nothing more than a parody. But
parody or not the dimension of the sacred in Aristophanes is emulated in
Amado's novel where similarly we encounter a religious ceremony. To bind
all the striking women together there is an appeal to the Afro-Bahian deities.
It is Pai Natividade, a Candomble priest, who calls upon Exú to help the strik-
ers and to cast a curse upon any prostitute who would break the covenant. The
"Pai de Santo" warns: "A rapariga ficará podre, carregada de doença, comida
de sífilis, cega, paralítica, leprosa. O cafetão ou a cafetina morrerá antes de
completar um mês. De morte feia, curtindo dores" [Any transgressing whore
will contract a rotten illness, will be eaten by syphilis, blind, cripple, and a
leper. Any pimp or panderer, male or female, will die before a month is over
of an ugly and painful death] (368).

The strike was having great success in Salvador, but just as in the Greek
comedy, there was confrontation and violence. Aristophanes had two levels
of confrontation, one on a personal plane such as Lysistrata versus the chief
elder or *proboulos,* and the other, more communal in nature and stylized with

the confrontation of the two choruses, one made up by the old man and the other fashioned by the old women. Amado also introduces his *proboulos* in the figure of the Assistant Chief, Labão Oliveira, who is the epitome of a coarse, ambitious, corrupt, violent, sadistic representative of Salvador's finest. As is to be expected, at the end he receives his just deserts as he is struck down violently. There are many other similarities but to continue pointing them out would not add too much the main thesis as proposed in this study. As we continue in the analysis of the text it is worth noting that there are differences. These differences will be just as important as the similarities as we examine Amado's craft in the making of this literary work.

As already mentioned, the central idea in Aristophanes' comedy was to present a group of women representatives of the different warring Pellopone-sian city-states who want to bring the men of their respective city-states to the conference table and bring this fratricidal war to an end. Eventually there is a happy ending. Amado, however has a different problem, even though it also involves a kind of war. He presents the struggle as being between the rich and the poor, the powerful and the powerless, those with high society mores pitted against those lacking in morals, corrupters of good social behavior. The author presents us the plight of those whom society considers its dregs: the prostitutes of Salvador. Therefore, behind all the banter and humor, the comi-cal situations, outrageous characters, and the clever and spicy language used to describe it all, we find that the author has a very serious concern and a very clear vision of a society that he perceives as callous and unjust towards the disenfranchised. In this second literary epoch of the author, when he moves to a higher artistic plateau, the political and social ideas which we find almost pamphleteering in nature in his early works do not disappear, but they rather become interwoven with the plots and characters in a far more subtle man-ner.[5] We must remember that the comedy of Aristophanes has very strong political and social underpinnings. His views on the politics of his time, the treatment of women and his sense of *communitas* form an intrinsical part of his theatrical production.[6]

The usage of striking prostitutes in Amado's novels stands in clear con-trast with the women in *Lysistrata*. K. J. Dover, a classical critic, refers to this matter in the following manner:

> A curious feature of the plot of the play, commonly unnoticed in modern discussion of it, is that the strike is not in fact of all women but the strike of the wives of citizens. Slave-prostitutes, slave-concubines, hetairai, all the women who made extra-marital sex easily accessible at Athens, are never mentioned in the play.[7]

Obviously the opposite is true in *Tereza Batista cansada de guerra.* Aristophanes presents us with a sisterhood of wives from different Greek city-states and Amado has a sisterhood or "brothelhood" composed of prostitutes and other women that are close to that profession, such as cabaret singers and dancers. On the other hand, the wives depicted in Amado are those very prudish ladies of the upper classes who are trying to persuade their wealthy and politically influential husbands to do everything possible to eliminate the blight which is prostitution. Within the spirit of Aristophanic humorous use of puns both visual as well as verbal, Amado also presents the reader with very comical characters and situations.

In *Tereza Batista cansada de guerra* Jorge Amado depicts the society of his time and region. The rich literary influences which are detected in his literary craftsmanship serve him well, and he uses them very cleverly as he narrates the life and struggle of a woman of the poor class. Tereza wanders from one place to another, from one situation to another, always trying to make a niche for herself in a society which tends to be unjust and very class oriented. Amado will use Aristophanic plots and elements in his novel, yet in his process of incorporation and assimilation, he will make any changes that will suit his narrative purpose. But beyond similarities and differences one cannot help but detect that Amado and Aristophanes are kindred spirits. This can be appreciated in the humor of the situations depicted as well as in the portrayal of the characters. The humorous, bawdy use of the language is very similar. Amado, like Aristophanes, will use the sexual imagery in a very comical manner. But behind all this, each author has a view and strong opinion of the politics and the social structures of their respective times and countries. Amado's knowledge of Western thought and literary tradition are evident and his ability to weave them together in a clever and artistic manner serves his purpose very well.

## NOTES

1. *Tereza Batista cansada de guerra.* Rio de Janeiro: Editora Record, 183. All quotations from this novel will be from the same edition. Translations from the Portuguese are by the author of the essay.

2. Zola's view of prostitution is far more complex than just a metaphor for his political and social views. It seems apparent to the careful reader as well as the student of the literary movement which he represents, that prostitution was the result of a corrupt social system. Yet, Jill Warren in her study, "Zola's View of Prostitution in *Nana*," besides analyzing the many different possibilities of metaphorical interpretations, very keenly observes that there are strong evidences of Zola's attitude towards sexuality.

3. Pierre L. Horn and Mary Beth Pringle in their "Introduction" to the work that they co-edited, *The Image of the Prostitute in Modern Literature,* have come up with nine archetypal figures of the prostitutes as protrayed by male writers in the last two centuries. It seems that some categories are but subcategories or variations of some already well established ones. Nonetheless their study, although

relatively short, is extremely useful for those interested in this particular literary theme.

4. In *Tocaia Grande* (Rio de Janeiro: Editora Record. 1984), Amado writes about this unwelcomed guest, the death bearing plague, as if it were a being with its own identity, its own ontology. The language that he uses to describe it follows an allegorical anthropomorphic imagery: "Chegava de repente, sem se fazer anunciar. Derrubava, pelava e escaldava, esvaziava as tripas e o juízo o homem mais forte a um molambo, antes de matá-lo ... Morte dolorosa, suja e fedorenta, atroz" [Suddenly, it arrived, without any introduction or preamble. Knocking down, flaying and scalding, emptying guts as well as wits, reducing the strongest man before killing him to a mere weakling ... A painful, dirty and malodorous, dreadful death] (392–393).

5. There are critics of Amado's works who assert that the novels of his latter period do not have the same ideological thrust as those belonging to an earlier phase. Along this line of thinking, the Brazilian critic, Alfredo Bosi, in his *Historia concisa de la literatura brasileira* (São Paulo: Cultrix, 1982) states: "Na última fase abandonam-se os esquemas de literatura ideológica que nortearam os romances de 30 e 40; e tudo se dissolve no pitoresco, no "sabroso," no apimentado do regional" [In the last phase any schemes of literary ideology which guided his novels in the '30s and '40s are left behind; and all is reduced to the picturesque, the "luscious," the spicy regional elements] (459). This seems a rather superficial view of Amado's literary works from a latter period. There is no doubt that the novels from this period are more complex and more humorous than those from his earlier times. Does this complexity and richer fictional craftmanship mean that the socio-political ideology has been lost? A careful intertextual analysis will uncover the fact that Amado never loses his multidimensional vision of Brazilian society, including his insights on the many political and social injustices. Jon S. Vincent in the summary of his doctoral dissertation, *Jorge Amado: Politics and the Novels,* points out that the socio-political views of this author are reflected in his earlier as well as later novels.

6. An excellent study on this subject matter can be found in Vol.I (chapter 5.27) of Kenneth J. Reckford's, *Aristophanes' Old-and new Comedy* (Chapel Hill/London: The University of North Carolina Press, 1987).

7. *Aristophanic Comedy* (Berkeley and Los Angeles: University of California Press, 1972), 160.

## BIBLIOGRAPHY

Amado, Jorge. *Tereza Batista cansada de guerra.* Rio de Janeiro: Editora Record, 1987.

———. *Tocaia grande.* Rio de Janeiro: Editora Record, 1984.

Aristophanes. *Lysistrata* in *Five Comedies of Aristophanes.* Garden City, New York: Doubleday and Company, Inc., 1955.

Bosi, Alfredo. *História concisa da literatura brasileira.* São Paulo: Cultrix, 1982.

Cartledge, Paul. *Aristophanes and his Theater of the Absurd.* Bristol: Bristol Classical Press, 1990.

Dover, K.J. *Aristophanic Comedy.* Berkeley and Los Angeles: University of California Press, 1972.

Horn, Pierre and Mary Beth Pringle, eds.*The Image of the Prostitute in Modern Literature.* New York: Frederick Ungar Publishing Company, 1984.

Reckford, Kenneth J. *Aristophanes' Old-and-New Comedy.* Chapel Hill and London: The University of North Carolina Press, 1987.

Vincent, Jon S. *Jorge Amado: Politics and the Novel.* Ph.d. Thesis. Albuquerque, New Mexico: The University of New Mexico, 1970.

Warren, Jill. "Zola's View of Prostitution in *Nana.*" *The Image of the Prostitute in Modern Literature.* Eds., Pierre L. Horn and Mary Beth Pringle. New York: Frederick Ungar Publishing Company, 1984.

# Jorge and Zélia Amado's Long Visit to Pennsylvania State University in 1971

## Surprise and Success

GERALD MOSER

### PREPARATIONS FOR A FORAY INTO ACADEMIA USA

Who had the brilliant idea in 1970 of luring no less a writer of international celebrity than Jorge Amado to a Cinderella among the centers of Luso-Brazilian studies, struggling to grow at a state university in the United States? Penn State was at that time little known in Brazil, except among educators who were taking advanced courses in its Department of Education.

Whoever it was, Dr. Martin Stabb, my department head at Penn State, was aware of my plan to spend a sabbatical leave traveling through Brazil, from Pará to Rio Grande do Sul. He therefore charged me with looking up Amado at his house in the city of Bahia and bringing him an invitation from Stanley Weintraub, Director of the Institute for the Arts and Humanities, to give a series of lectures at Pennsylvania State University. The Institute would sponsor the visit and the department would co-sponsor it. I was to ask Amado if he would be interested in coming in the fall of 1971 and staying at the University during the entire fall semester as a visiting lecturer.

To prepare myself before stopping in Bahia I had read Amado's *Tenda dos milagres* [*Tent of Miracles*], just published then, about the *candomblé* and other African traditions of Bahia, knowing Amado's affection for them. I also went to Olga de Alaketu's *candomblé* sanctuary on the opening night when Amado was to be present.

Two days later, on Monday, May 18, at eleven in the morning, I rang the bell of the Amados' blue house in the Rio Vermelho section of the city. Two maids opened the door and challenged the stranger. I presented my visiting card. After consultation with the masters I was admitted. Jorge Amado himself came and welcomed me with a smile and a friendly handshake. Immediately he led me to the veranda; we sat down and were served a *sorvete de graviola* together with a glass of water. At that point the lady of the house, Dona Zélia, made her appearance. Although she, too, was meeting me for the first time, she was equally friendly and unassuming.

In the course of our conversation I remarked that I was surprised that in *Tenda dos milagres*, Professor Levenson, the only American character to appear in all of Amado's prose fiction, had been given such an appealing personality. Amado explained that Levenson had to be made *simpático* because he alone recognized the importance of the Bahian mulatto scholar Pedro Archanjo's findings. In that connection Amado mentioned two actual American Brazilianists, Herskovits and Pierson. It was pure coincidence, according to Dona Zélia, that several months later, after the novel had been written, another American professor, Bradford Burns, like Levenson teaching at Columbia, visited the couple in Bahia.

More drinks were served, among them *caninha*, the Brazilian rum with lemon, accompanied by candied fruit from Sergipe. At last I managed to suggest the idea of a trip to Pennsylvania to lecture there. Amado protested that he was no professional lecturer and had already declined an invitation to lecture at Columbia. His unassuming, natural way of conducting the conversation bore out the truth of what he told me. Besides, he said that he was planning a trip to Europe in 1971.

They insisted that I stay for dinner, meeting Jorge's brother James, the painter Jenner Augusto, who had illustrated *Tenda dos milagres*, and other guests. When I left the hospitable Amado household I had the distinct feeling that the Brazilian writer was going to decline Penn State's invitation, since he had not commited himself.

It came as a pleasant surprise to be proved wrong. Many months later, on January 4, 1971, Professor Weintraub received a letter from Bahia, written on December 22, 1970, in which Amado wrote, after having consulted his American publisher Alfred Knopf: "I confirm my agreement to your kind invitation" (2). During the same month of January Knopf wrote to Jorge Amado: "Thank goodness you have at last written the Pennsylvania State University confirming your acceptance of their offer. They were beginning to be very worried indeed" (3). On February 20, Amado wrote another letter to Dr. Weintraub, in which he specified what he would be able and willing to do instead of giving formal lectures:

> I will be very glad to come and talk to the students, also being available to talk to them about my works and at the utmost (*sic*) about Brazilian literature, but please remember, always as a writer and not as a Professor.
>
> As for the theme "Occultism in Western Literature" I must tell you the following: My knowledge on the subject has been acquired through my life experience and it is very limited and only on *Candomblé* from Bahia. The same goes for Latin-American Literature, History and Sociology. (4)

His objection to air travel could have prevented his coming as well. It was overcome when, unable to find passage on one of the by then rare passenger ships plying the Atlantic, his Brazilian travel agent discovered a Japanese ship that would land in the harbor of Los Angeles. Amado could therefore report to Weintraub: "I have already bought our fare on the Japanese ship 'Brazil Maru', leaving Santos on July 1st for Los Angeles and we will be [there] on the 22nd of the same month. I tour the States up to the time for the opening of the term at the University" (5).

At a time earlier than 1970 his arrival would have caused another serious problem because of the anti-red hysteria whipped up by Senator Joseph McCarthy, although Amado had resigned from membership in the Communist Party of Brazil several years earlier. It is true that a precedent was in his favor. He had been able to visit seven of our states in 1937, taking the opportunity to visit John Dos Passos and Michael Gold, as he told a Penn State student, Linda Joyce Simpson, in an interview he gave her in November 1971, and recorded by her on tape. He had not used that first American trip for any political activity, and it was unlikely that he would in 1971. The only visits he intended to make, beside to Penn State, were to Brazilian friends in Hollywood and to the Knopfs in New York City.

He asked the Knopfs to suggest the best itinerary for crossing the United States, once he and his wife would have left Los Angeles. Knopf obliged, suggesting Hollywood, San Francisco and the Brazilianists at Berkeley, as well as the Grand Canyon, Chicago, New York City, Boston and Washington, D.C. (6). He also urged Amado not to buy a secondhand car for the cross-country trip, as Amado had planned, but to use busses, "unless Zélia loves to drive" (7). The Amados followed the suggested route, but added a detour through Canada, visiting Ottawa, Montreal and Québec, leaving out Washington as a result. They ended up by purchasing an American car, once they reached the east coast.

Since April, Zélia Amado had been excited by the prospect of the trip. "I have a great desire to know your country," she wrote to Knopf, "and above all to see you again" (8). In September, coming from New York City, where they had visited Alfred Knopf and his wife, the Amados arrived in State College, Pennsylvania. This was shortly after the beginning of the Fall semester at Penn State and not long after the publication of the American edition of *The Tent of Miracles*. His first letter written there to the Knopfs was very upbeat: " [ . . . ] Both Zélia and myself are very happy with living accommodations and arrangements here; it is a beautiful place, we have a very comfortable apartment, the University is both imposing and impressive, and the people—pupils and professors—are very kind and thoughtful. I think the whole experience of my visit here will be both useful and pleasant to me [ . . . ]" (9).

## AT PENN STATE: NO LECTURES BUT INFORMAL TALKS
## AND AN EVENING OF READINGS

Taking into account Jorge Amado's aversion to giving lectures, his own preferences and the interest of the University, as interpreted by its Department of Spanish, Italian and Portuguese, a calendar of events was drawn up. They were to begin on the last day of September 1971 and to end on November 29. Six weekly "round table talks" by the Brazilian author were to be supplemented by "An Evening with Jorge Amado," during which he would read passages of his own choosing from his novels. With the exception of the first talk, offering a background introduction to Brazil, the next five were to deal with specific novels. Open to the public at large, though aimed at the students of Brazilian literature and the Portuguese language, the talks and readings would be delivered by Amado in Portuguese. Interpreters were to translate his words into English, not simultaneously, but immediately after convenient pauses. Consequently the poor author had to interrupt his train of thought constantly while the translators, none of whom was a professional, had to rapidly come up with faithful renderings.

Those seven "performances" were,

1. Brazilian Society and the Brazilian Writer. The experience of an Author and Editor. October 7.

2. The Frontier: "The Violent Land" [*Terras do sem fim*, 1943] October 14.

3. Plantation Economy and Plantation Culture: *Gabriela, Clove and Cinnamon* [*Gabriela, cravo e canela*, 1958] October 21.

4. The Occult: *Dona Flor and Her Two Husbands* [*Dona Flor e seus dois maridos*, 1966.] November 14. (Originally scheduled for October 28, it was postponed in order to allow the Amados a weeklong visit of New York City and Philadelphia).

5. Jorge Amado Reads from his Novels. With Comments and Translations into English. November 10.

6. African Culture, Its Survival and Transformation: *Shepherds of the Night* [*Os pastores da noite*, 1964]. November 18.

7. Miscegenation—Another Melting Pot?: *Tent of Miracles* [*Tenda dos milagres*, 1969]. November 23.

Tape recordings of all seven were made. Those tapes remain available to any interested person willing to climb to the Rare Books Room of the Pattee Library at Penn State. Regretfully, the question and answer periods were not recorded completely.

1. Thanks to the recordings we know that at the first session Jorge Amado was introduced by Dr. Stanley Weintraub, whose Institute underwrote the writer's visit. Weintraub pointed out that Jorge Amado was the most distin-

guished foreign writer to stay at Penn State for an extended length of time. Other illustrious Brazilian intellectuals, Érico Veríssimo as early as 1954, had only made one-day stands. Without further ado, Amado delved into his subject for the evening, the nature of Brazilian society, thus providing a background for the fictional yet realistic treatment of various social aspects in his novels.

*"Sou um escritor da Geração de 1930"* [I am a writer of the 1930s generation], was his self-definition, offered at the outset, an allusion to the bloodless revolution led by Getúlio Vargas. That revolution ushered in the industrialization of southern Brazil, broke the power of the big feudal landholding families and received great support from the common people and the intellectuals.

Amado stressed that he was only one of a number of writers, mostly novelists, who through literary works drew attention to the problems created by poverty and backwardness in the countryside, as well as in the cities. They did so, as he added, in a language that broke with the "academic" literary style which clung to the classics of European Portuguese. It was, he said, a violent action, to adopt the spoken idiom of Brazil enriched through the mixture of peoples and cultures. *"Não somos latinos, senão em parte "* [we are not Latins, only in part], he reminded his listeners. *"Em parte somos Africanos"* [In part we are Africans]. He recognized that this linguistic revolution had been pioneered eight years earlier, in 1922, by other young men and women who called themselves *modernistas* (Modernists), influenced in their turn by European "vanguards." In his own generation of writers dealing with Northeastern Brazil, the "Hump" of the country, Amado paid homage to "the incomparable master of us all, Graciliano Ramos," author of *Vidas sêcas [Barren Lives]*.

Turning then to the general character of Brazil and that nation's history, Amado first mentioned what it had in common with the other countries of Latin America: massive misery, feudalism, widespread illiteracy, frequent dictatorships. He noted next what distinguished Brazil from the rest, in his opinion. Beside the obvious differences, such as language, "perhaps the most important one," he considered the different composition of the population more fundamental, i.e. European + African Black in contrast to European + Amerindian in most of the others, seeing it reflected in the Brazilian people's joy of living, versus the sadness of the Mexicans, for example.

Concluding this part of the talk, he recounted the historic episode of Palmares, the runaway slaves' republic. He insisted on Brazil having a *mestiço* culture from the outset: "There is no way [in Brazil] *not* to mix."

About the position of the writer in Brazilian society he said little in the short time that remained. To live as a writer or as any creative artist, he maintained, is difficult in his country. "Basically, writing is still a hobby of *amadores* [amateurs], not an occupation of *profissionais* [professionals], since the reading public is so limited." And yet, was he not an exception to the rule, appealing also to large numbers of readers beyond his region, his country, his continent? Another important matter, relating to the position of the writer, went unmentioned: political commitment. In the nineteen thirties, that period of social conflict, he and two other leading writers, Monteiro Lobato and Graciliano Ramos, became public figures when they took a radical political stand and joined the Communist Party of Brazil. He became so popular that he was elected a member of Parliament. No doubt, he had mellowed since, and prudence advised him not to touch on that part of his career, although it was to his credit that throughout his life he had been acting in accord with the social conscience that gave meaning to his writing.

One of his listeners, Professor Terry J. Peavler of Penn State, when asked years later to recollect his impressions, wrote that Amado "made no particularly memorable comments on politics. He seemed to be, as both Mart [Martin Stabb] and I recall, an old-time, mellow leftist" (10).

At the end of the session Amado had been eager to answer comments and questions from the audience. "I came here to learn and to listen," he assured us. One questioner asked him: "Have you thought of writing a novel about Palmares?" To which he replied: "It tempts all of us. I haven't had the courage."

2. The way in which the Brazilian author conveyed the social meaning of his novels to his readers was like offering a bitter pill wrapped inside the sweet cover of entertaining story-telling artistry. This technique became quite clear in the second talk he gave. It centered on *Terras do sem fim* [*The Violent Land*], an early novel about life in the countryside of the southern part of his native state when cocoa had been king there. Reacting to the prevailing manner of romanticizing the patriarchal planters, picturing them as kind, their wives as glamorous, and their laborers as happy darkies, he told us that, as a member of the Generation of 1930, he had covertly criticized the exploitation of labor, the bloody ferocity of the struggle for virgin land, and the moral decay of the planter family, drawing on personal experience since he himself came from a cocoa planter's family of the region. He stressed the importance of another Northeastern writer José Lins do Rêgo, for Rêgo's novel *Menino de engenho,* about life on a sugar cane plantation in neighboring Pernambuco, pointed the way. It preceded by one year Amado's novel, one of four the later published on the rise and fall of the cocoa economy.

The revealing part of Amado's second talk was what he said on that occasion about his evolution as a writer. We learned that he considered his first three books on the cocoa planters, including *Terras do sem fim,* as "*apenas cadernos de anotação para romance*" [" hardly notebooks for a novel"]. For him, his first novel in the true sense of the word, was *Jubiabá,* with its black protagonist. Moreover, he described how these works of fiction were taking years to form in his head, usually starting with facts, events that had happened to real persons, and an idea they gave him. As an example he cited the idea of developing a novel around Dona Flor, inspired by a real person, an idea which *"me acompanhou durante mais de vinte anos"* ["(This idea) was my companion for more than twenty years"].

3. Before entering on comments about a second novel, *Gabriela, cravo e canela*, Amado paid homage to another writer, an homage to his friend, the Chilean poet Pablo Neruda, because he had just received a telegram informing him that Neruda had been awarded the Nobel Prize for literature.

Only then did Amado tackle the subject at hand, by pondering the reasons why his *Gabriela* had enjoyed so great a success in Brazil and elsewhere. He guessed that it became popular because of the confidence it expressed in humanity's progress. He had personified the successful struggle for greater tolerance of diversity in Gabriela's lover, the *turco* Nacib, a Lebanese immigrant, who married Gabriela, his Brazilian barmaid. While the message was universal, the locale was the state of Bahia, more precisely Amado's hometown, the port city of Ilhéus. The introduction of a Lebanese character, the author added, coincided with a historical circumstance, the inclusion of no fewer than three men of Lebanese origin in one of the Brazilian government cabinets during the presidency of Juscelino Kubitchek, himself the scion of Czech immigrants. An anecdote relates that Kubitchek had ordered the enlargement of the port of Ilhéus upon reading the novel.

Amado must have been encouraged by the success of *Gabriela*, for he revealed that here, at Penn State, he was thinking of the plot of a novel that would have a girl similar to Gabriela as its heroine. Indeed, one year later, back in Brazil, he wrote and published the novel *Tereza Batista, cansada de guerra*. There was a difference, though. Tereza was conceived as a *"mulher de muito mais fibra, muito mais determinação"* [A woman with more fiber (character) and greater determination] (11).

The session ended with Amado doing something different. He read a passage from the book he had discussed. It was the passage about the *pastorinhas* [Shepherdesses], the *filhas de santo* [daughters of the saint], the female acolytes who perform the sacred dance in a *candomblé* sanctuary culminating in a trance as they are being "possessed" by one of the African deities.

4. The most fascinating talk turned out to be Amado's fourth. At least I think so. It dealt with *Dona Flor e seus dois maridos,* a novel combining three apparently unrelated and disparate themes, or to use Amado's term, "levels." All three were out of the ordinary. They even could be considered weird. The first was the predicament of an ordinary housewife of the lower middle class in Bahia, called Dona Flor. She found herself having two husbands simultaneously, an unexpected situation disturbing her so greatly that Amado told us, "I expected her to kill herself in a romantic fashion. But no, she did not." The second theme was the bohemian life of a certain Vadinho, an impish fellow, originally a member of the same lower middle class. However, he had

become an incarnation of Exú, the devilish mischiefmaker in the *candomblé* pantheon. And the third was the magic world of the *candomblé* cults.

Amado set the stage by playing a record of Brazilian music, among whose instruments was a *berimbau*, the single string mounted on a stick. We were to hear how the *berimbau* accompaniment of the *candomblé* songs and dances sounds. Then he reviewed the actual events which led him to write the novel. Finally he read a passage in which Amado's real-life friend and *compadre*, the Portuguese banker Celestino, supposedly recollects Vadinho's life soon after the latter's demise.

Amado entered into a detailed description of the *candomblé* centers, six hundred and eleven of which were registered in Bahia, an indication of the important function the occult and the supernatural fulfill in the thinking of Bahians. He did not fail to add that most devotees of the *candomblé* belong at the same time to the Catholic Church. "Rare are those who, like myself, are only adherents of *candomblé*."

During the question period only questions about *candomblé* were asked. One listener wanted to know what was the attitude of the Church toward those African cults. "Nowadays," Amado replied, "the Church tolerates them, whereas neither the Church nor the faithful of the *candomblé* show any tolerance of protestantism." He was to return to the subject of the African side of Bahian religiosity in another session.

A different interpreter assisted Amado during this session. She was Linda Joyce Simpson, a bright young graduate student, who had been in Brazil. Every now and then she was helped by Amado's wife Zélia, who had a good command of English.

5. "An Evening with Jorge Amado" was the title of the fifth session. Different from the others, it consisted exclusively of readings by the author of passages in the original Portuguese he had selected from his novels. He claimed that he had never before read from his works in public. This surprised me, as he had done precisely that during the previous two sessions, as if in preparation for this evening. At any rate, we were made to feel privileged to attend something like a première. He dedicated the event to a friend who was present, Mrs. Ellen Knopf, the wife of his American publisher. The couple had come from New York City to visit the Amados. They were among an audience of about a hundred people who had come from as far as New York City, the West Point Academy, Philadelphia, Pittsburgh, Carbondale (Illinois) and Washington, D.C., to our remote town between the many ridges of the Appalachian Mountains. To take care of the crowd, the session was held in an auditorium. It had been widely publicized as the seventh lecture of a series sponsored by the Department of Spanish, Italian and Portuguese.

What the author selected from among the many different facets of his fiction provides a clue to his preferences. He picked passages from the five novels he was to discuss in the other sessions. They spanned roughly a quarter of a century. From each he took one or two passages. From the earliest, *Terras do sem fim*, he had intended to read three: the beginning of the early chapter *"Gestação das cidades," "Era uma vez três irmãs"* [Once upon a time there were three sisters], like a fairy tale, to be followed by a long reading from the chapter *"A mata"* ["The Forest"], which begins lyrically with the words *"A mata dormia o seu sono"* [The forest was sleeping its dream] and the third from the chapter "O mar" ["The Sea"], beginning *"O homem do colete azul não respondeu"* [The man with the blue vest did not answer]. But he left out the third, perhaps because it did not fit the epic mood of the novel.

From *Gabriela, cravo e canela* he chose the short *"Lamento de Glória"* [Glória's Lament], in the second chapter, followed by a longer reading, *"Noite de Gabriela"* [Gabriela's Night], where Nacib enters the front room of his house and takes off his shoes. From *Dona Flor e seus dois maridos*, Amado read *"Apêlo de Dona Flor em aula e em devaneio"* [Dona Flor's entreaty in her cooking class and her reverie], which in the translation begins "Why don't they leave me alone with my mourning and my loneliness?" He also read its twenty-eighth chapter, *"A guerra dos santos"* ["The War of the Saints"].

The novel *Os pastores da noite* was represented by its lyrical introduction, which has nothing to do with the main paradoxical plot, the temporary conversion of Cabo Martim, rake and cardshark, to a devoted, love-smitten husband of a prostitute, who then goes through the farce of a make-believe marriage to another to make her happy on her deathbed, or the equally paradoxical subplot of the unforeseeable victory of the poor dwellers of a hillside slum, an *invasão* [invasion], won over the police, sent out to expel them. Instead, Amado chose the introduction, in which the rake and his gang, as "shepherds of the night," whose "lambs" were the girls in the brothels of Bahia, appear transformed into devotees of Bahia at night, deified as divine Might, whom Amado at one point calls *Putona*, the Great Whore.

Evidently, the Brazilian author gave preference to the erotic element, to heroines such as Gabriela, Dona Flor and Might as the symbol of Bahian love life. On the other hand, combined with it, he seemed to enjoy lyrical *devaneios*. A third element, farce, he also seemed to relish, as shown by his selections from *Os pastores da noite* and especially his last selection, *"Do território mágico e real"* ["From the Magical and Real Territory"], the carnivalesque final page of *Tenda dos milagres*, a playful satire disguised as the parade of a *escola de samba* glorifying the mulatto scholar, Pedro Archanjo, and mocking the intelligentsia that had disregarded him. Copies of this final reading in translation were the only ones distributed among the audience during the seven sessions.

6. The session dealing with *Os pastores da noite* was announced as a talk about "the survival and transformation of African culture," although this theme appears only in a subplot, the christening of a black child in a Catholic

church of Bahia, attended by a crowd of worshippers all dressed in white because it is also the day sacred to Ogun, so much so that the priest, a mulatto, goes into a trance because he is temporarily possessed by that pagan African deity.

For good measure, Amado added remarks about two other works of his, the novellas *Os velhos marinheiros* [*Home is the Sailor*] (1961) and *A Morte e a morte de Quincas Berro d'água* [*The Two Deaths of Quincas Wateryell*] (1959). He took pains to show that all of these works had the same message in common, a faith in humanity, i.e. that human beings are capable of changing their destiny. As an afterthought he added that those writings presented the defense of what he called most sacred, "the right to dream," exemplified in the dream childlike Otália has kept alive throughout her short life of prostitution in *Os pastores da noite*, the dream of being courted as if she had remained a virgin, with the courtship ending in a real wedding with all pomp and circumstance.

Returning briefly to the Afro-Brazilian topic, Amado repeated that "the African influence is the strongest and the deepest, the one received with the most love." He did refer to the folk arts of Bahia, such as the painted ex-voto tablets to thank Our Lord of Bomfim for his *milagres* or intercessions. He mentioned several individual artists by name, for example the young sculptor Aguinaldo. Turning to Bahian literature he referred to the "touch of African traditions" in the works of Xavier Marques and Adonias Filho.

7. A theme bound to appeal to an American university audience concluded the series of talks: How an American university professor, an outsider, was to discover the merits of a humble black-skinned Bahian scholar, Pedro Archanjo, who had studied the survival of African traditions and had published several booklets on the subject. The official academies and other authorities had ignored him, and he had ended as a pauper, though highly regarded by the black populace among whom he spent his life. Archanjo's misfortunes and posthumous vindication were the theme of this last session, as they were narrated in what was then Jorge Amado's latest novel. It so happened that it remained the only work in which the author introduced a character hailing from the United States, and this in an unexpectedly favorable light.

Always amiable, Amado did not omit during the concluding session to pay final compliments publicly to the Pennsylvania State University and its community, saying:

> Foi uma experiência muito importante para mim. Aprendi muita coisa. Vi muita coisa: vi uma grande universidade americana funcionando. Encontrei e fiz alguns excelentes amigos—amigos que fazem agora parte da minha família [For me it has been a very important experience. I have learned many things: I have seen how a great American university works. I found and made some excellent friends—friends who are now part of my family].

In short, it had been a good experience for him and for us.

The Amados had indeed experienced much more than the seven public sessions offered by the Brazilian writer. Not counting the excursions they had taken to Philadelphia and New York City during their stay at Penn State, a series of other events made their residence among us pleasant. The opener, preceding the public sessions, was a reception given for the couple by the faculty and students to inaugurate an exposition of Amado's books and memorabilia at the University Library, arranged by Charles Mann, the curator of its large collection of manuscripts and rare books. They were invited to evening meals at private homes and to outings in the surrounding region. Visits to several classes followed, among them one on Spanish American literature before 1880, to which Jorge Amado contributed remarks about the early Bahian poet Gregório de Matos, known as *Bôca de Inferno* ["Hell's Mouth"], and about early Brazilian letters in general. He also attended Prof. Roberto Lima's popular comparative literature class of over a hundred students on the literature of the occult, giving it an excellent talk on "the Magic Afro-Brazilian Religions of Bahia." He illustrated it with photos taken by his friend, Pierre Verger, with pictures in books and recorded music. There, too, was time for questions. In reply to one of them, Amado stated that he had been familiar with those religions *"desde menino"* ["since childhood"] but had been associated with one only since 1934, the *terreiro* (locale where Afro-Brazilian cults worship) of Procópio (Xavier de Sousa). " Did Procópio cast evil spells?" the same questioner wanted to know. "No doubt against the police," was the roguish answer he received.

Both Amados were present at meetings of the Círculo Ibérico, where the husband submitted to be interrogated about "Brazil Today" in Spanish, and of the Portuguese student group where their friend, the young Bahian poet Ildázio Tavares, was also present. This group adopted the name *Clube do Bate-Papo* [The Chatting Club], at the suggestion of Dona Zélia.

Two dinners completed the social program at the end of November, an intimate one at the same private home where an early reception had taken place. They reciprocated with a typical Brazilian dinner at their apartment. The other was the *jantar de despedida* [farewell banquet] at a downtown restaurant, at which the Amados once more met the friends they had made.

## SOME EFFECTS OF THE VISIT: HOW LONG WOULD THEY LAST?

The prolonged visit of a renowned foreign author to a great educational institution is bound to have some effects. The question is whether they will last for a long time or be as fleeting as the echoes of the words he or she spoke while present. Jorge Amado's visit led to quite a few initiatives. Several, probably

most, remained confined to the academic world. At one of the subsequent
annual conventions of the Modern Language Association of America, held in
Chicago in 1977, an entire panel, moderated by Regina Igel of the University
of Maryland, was composed of three papers on Jorge Amado. The second,
presented by Terry J. Peavler of Pennsylvania State University, dealt with
"Jorge Amado at Penn State."

The success of Amado's visit encouraged the University's Institute for
the Arts and the Humanities, together with the Department of Spanish, Italian
and Portuguese, to invite other prominent Latin American authors, notably
the Argentinian Jorge Luis Borges, who came for only one lecture, however.
More to the point, they brought a second Brazilian, the playwright Alfredo
Dias Gomes and his wife Jeanette Clair, author of popular *telenovelas*
(Brazilian "soap operas"), to the campus, once more for an entire semester.
During their stay, his play *O berço do herói* [The Cradle of the Hero], in the
translation by Leon F. Lyday, of our department was performed by the University's Theater Department company, directed by Manuel Duque. After-
wards, the translation was published in the *Modern International Drama
Review* (vol.xi, no. 2, 1978.) Unfortunately, no other Brazilian author came
after Dias Gomes.

Among the students who were among Amado's audiences, he was to
have a tangible influence on Mrs. Linda Joyce Simpson, who had served as
one of the interpreters and to whom he had given an interview. He helped
her to obtain a fellowship that enabled her to spend some time in Portugal.
One thing the Amados' visit did not bring about, contrary to expectations,
was a marked increase the enrollment in courses of Brazilian and Portuguese literature. However, the *Clube do Bate-Papo* has continued to meet
to this day, attracting especially Brazilian post-graduate students and their
families.

In the world outside academia, the downtown bookstores and newsstands
stocked several of Amado's novels. It may be that the showing of a Brazilian
film based on *Dona Flor and Her Two Husbands* early in 1978 owes something to the Amados' visit of Hollywood in 1971, followed a year later by the
production of *Saravá* in New York City, a musical comedy based on the same
novel. In this connection, another result may have been a Brazilian film festival organized for several years at Penn State by Catherine Egan.

Personally, my wife and I, like several other Pennsylvanians, are proud to
count the Amados among our friends since their visit. The friendship led to a
long and cordial correspondence and many gifts: Jorge and Zélia Gattai
Amado's works, inscribed with dedications to us, and various Brazilian
objects, such as a leather vest like those worn by northeastern *vaqueiros*
(cowboys). Their generosity was boundless. It left a lasting memory. One
could imagine that they took to heart what a Portuguese diplomat recom-

mended to his country as as a policy: *Ganhar amigos, muitos amigos!* [To win friends, many friends!].

Did the Amados' stay at an American university leave a profound impression on them? In his autobiographical notes gathered years later as *Navegação de cabotagem, apontamentos para um livro de memórias que jamais escreverei* [Coastal Navigation, Notes for a Book of Memoirs that I'll Never Write] (1992), the novelist mentioned the cities of Bahia, Rio de Janeiro, São Paulo and Paris innumerable times. Hundreds of others also figure there, but Penn State and its town of State College occur only once and then perfunctorily. However, one piece of information subsists which records some of Jorge Amado's impressions of Penn State, with acute observations on its students and the "generation gap." They are contained in an interview given to Zora Seljan, a Brazilian journalist, printed in the illustrated weekly *Manchete* (Rio de Janeiro) of January 15, 1972, that is, at a time when his impressions were fresh. About American life in general at that time he was quoted as saying:

> Duas coisas me chamaram particularmente a atenção nos Estados Unidos: O alto nível de confôrto do homem comum e a liberdade de crítica que todos têm [Particularly, two things called my attention in the United States: The high level of comfortable living for the common man and everybody's liberty to criticize].

About the young Americans he saw at Penn State, he observed:

> A juventude americana está promovendo uma revolução de cuja profundidade ainda não nos damos exata conta ... A distinção entre a juventude actual e as gerações anteriores é enorme, chegando a adquirir aspectos intensamente dramáticos ... Creio que grande parte dessa revolução começa dentro das universidades, nas quais o estudante cada vez mais aprende a firmar seus pontos de vista e a exigir soluções rápidas e eficientes para os problemas [American young people are promoting a revolution whose depth we have yet to fully fathom ... The difference between today's youth and past generations is enormous and it has been acquiring dramatic aspects ... I believe that a large part of this revolution begins within the universities, where the students are learning more and more to consolidate their points of view and demand quick and effective solutions to problems].

In retrospect, it seems to me that the visit to Penn State formed a pleasant and even instructive episode without major consequences among the three visits Jorge Amado paid to the United States. Afterwards, he and Dona Zélia felt *saudades* of the carefree months spent among us at Penn State. His initial doubts were dispelled, which had dictated lines in a letter written to me in Los Angeles on July 24, 1971:

Também eu desejo que essa estada na Universidade—tão fora de minhas habituais ocupações—resulte em algo útil. Sou o auth-professor, o anti-didático, e por isso mesmo vacilei muito em aceitar o convite [I also wish that my stay at the University—so far from my usual occupations—may have useful results. I am not professorial and basically anti-didactic, and for this very reason I hesitated a long time to accept this invitation].

## NOTES

1. Amado, Zélia Gattai, typescript of "Intimate Picture of Jorge Amado," trans. Edgar Miller, c. 1970, p. 11.
2. Amado, Jorge, to S. Weintraub, Salvador, Bahia, December 22, 1970 (Amado Papers, The Pennsylvania State University, Institute for the Arts and Humanities).
3. Knopf, Alfred, to Jorge Amado, January 11, 1971 (Amado Papers, The University of Texas at Austin, Harry Ransom Humanities Research Center).
4. Amado, Jorge, to S. Weintraub, Salvador, February 20, 1971 (Amado Papers, P.S.U.).
5. Amado, Jorge, to S. Weintraub, Salvador, March 16, 1971 (Amado Papers, P.S.U.).
6. Knopf, Alfred, to Jorge Amado, Tucson, March 20, 1971 (Amado Papers, Univ. of Texas).
7. Knopf, Alfred, to Jorge Amado, April 14, 1971 (Amado Papers, Univ. of Texas).
8. Amado, Zélia Gattai, to Helen and Alfred Knopf, on board the S.S. Giulio Cesare bound for Genoa, April 11, trans. of her letter written in French (Amado Papers, Univ. of Texas).
9. Amado, Jorge, to Alfred Knopf, State College, Pa., September 30, 1971 (Amado Papers, Univ. of Texas).
10. Terry J. Peavler, inter-office note to S. Weintraub, January 28, 1975 (Amado Papers, P.S.U.)
11. Amado, Jorge, declaration quoted in an unsigned article, *O Estado de São Paulo*, Suplemento Literário, 10 December 1972, p. 2.

## ACKNOWLEDGMENTS

I owe thanks for permission to use the collections of Amado Papers belonging to the Institute for the Arts and Humanities at Penn State and the Harry Ransom Humanities Research Center at the University of Texas-Austin, the tape recordings of Jorge Amado's talks kept in the Pattee Library of Penn State and of the interview he granted to Linda Joyce (Simpson), which she lent to me.

# The Early Jorge Amado

CELSO LEMOS DE OLIVEIRA

Jorge Amado is by far the most popular writer from Brazil in this century. His literary career spans more than six decades, if we date it from the publication of his first novel, *O País do carnaval [The land of carnival]* in 1931. At this point one could take a single decade of his production and make it the subject of a lengthy critical commentary. Like most writers with a wide readership, he has been taken up by a number of critics with diverse opinions, but there seems to be a general agreement that his work is somewhat uneven. This is characteristic of most Latin American novelists during the last half of the century, as it was true of the best North American novelists—Dreiser, Hemingway, Faulkner, Fitzgerald, Dos Passos—during their heyday at an earlier stage. It may be that novelists in the Americas have been so intent on discovering and exploiting a new subject that they have not had the patience of Joyce and Thomas Mann (to say nothing of Flaubert and Henry James) when they built up their *oeuvres*. Nevertheless, Jorge Amado has sustained his career remarkably well, and he deserves to be judged by his best.

A new critical book from Brazil draws attention to his early work again. This is called *Jorge Amado: Romance em tempo de utopia [The Novel in a Time of Utopia]*; its author is Eduardo de Assis Duarte. He published it in Natal in 1995. The author discusses almost everything that Jorge Amado wrote through the mid-1940s, and that was half a century ago. The novels of this early period are very much concerned with politics and the excitement over the communist revolution which had spread from Europe to South America and other parts of the world. Perhaps the most typical novelist of the period was André Malraux. Many young writers followed his example in their intellectual and literary productions if not in their lives. It was indeed a *Tempo de utopia*. As the title of this essay indicates, I shall limit my discussion to Jorge Amado's early phase and the seven novels that he published between 1931 and 1943, culminating in *Terras do sem fim [The Violent Land]*.

This period coincides with some fairly drastic changes in Brazilian politics, which will be of interest insofar as they affect this writer's work.

His first novel, *O País do carnaval*, was written in 1930 when he was only eighteen. This was of course at the moment when Getúlio Vargas took power. Amado was in Rio de Janeiro at the time, but chiefly to finish his preparatory course for law school, which he entered in 1931 but didn't finish until 1935. By that time he had published four novels; it is a wonder that he managed to keep up his studies as long as he did. He was also gradually involved in left-wing political activities, and in 1936 he was briefly jailed by the Vargas government for his alleged part in an uprising in the Northeast. Before long he was traveling outside Brazil and meeting communist intellectuals in Mexico and the United States—such figures as Diego Rivera and David Siqueiros, the Mexican painters, Michael Gold, a novelist, and the actor Paul Robeson. About the time that Vargas established the Estado Novo dictatorship in 1937, Amado was arrested in Manaus, taken to Rio and not released till the following year. One might note here how his career parallels that of Graciliano Ramos, another *nordestino* who was arrested and taken to Rio about the time that his novel *Angústia* [*Anguish*] was published in 1936. Indeed there was already a literary relationship between these two writers, who had met in 1933. Early in 1935 Graciliano published a review of Amado's third novel, *Suor* [*Sweat*]; this will be taken up later. The difference between these two, who seem to have much in common at this point, is that Graciliano was twenty years older, a slow starter whose first novel, *Caetés* (an Indian tribe), wasn't published until 1933, two years after Amado's first. It is interesting to learn that *Caetés* was published by the businessman-poet Augusto Frederico Schmidt, who two years earlier had published *O País do carnaval*. Schmidt, who still has some fame as a poet, may not necessarily have been recognized as one who promoted the early careers of these more famous *nordestino* novelists.

*O País do carnaval* is the work of a very young man who still has much to learn about fictional technique, but it tells a story that to some extent is the story of the author. The central figure is Paulo Rigger, the son of a cacao planter, like Jorge Amado. Paulo has been educated in Europe. Back in Bahia, he joins an intellectual group who represent different points of view, political, philosophical, and religious. Although the leader of the group is a sympathetic older man, Pedro Ticiano, Paulo eventually finds the young communist, José Lopes, to be the most articulate, and Ticiano has to be rejected. At the end Paulo also rejects Bahia itself, the Land of Carnaval. In retrospect this novel seems to anticipate much in Jorge Amado's career. Although he wasn't educated in Europe as his fictional counterpart was, he would eventually spend much time there in a kind of self-exile, but this was after World War II. Indeed he didn't settle permanently in Salvador, his present home, until 1963.

At any rate, although *O País do carnaval* is a novel of slight fictional interest, it represents an important moment in the career of its author.

Its early publication encouraged him to write a novel almost every year during the 1930s. He wrote too quickly, at least at this early stage, but he was finding his subject. *Cacau [Cacao]* and *Suor [Sweat]*, the novels that he brought out in 1933 and 1934, are probably no better written than *O país do carnaval*, but they are closely involved with the life of Bahia, and they laid the groundwork for the novels that he would write later. *Cacau*, for example, is the first of his novels about plantation life and especially the appalling conditions in which the migrant workers existed. His method is straightforward reportage for the most part, and there is a genuine if crude authenticity about what he conveys. We learn a great deal about the class divisions in this rural society; the poor whites are hardly better off than the blacks and mulattoes, but now and then they try to rise out their class. One of them, a *Sergipano* (native of the northeastern state of Sergipe), is romantically involved with the daughter of a planter, but in the end he turns to his own people. Here, as in *O País do carnaval*, we see the theme of a search for an identity. The *Sergipano*, uncertain of his bearings, like Paulo Rigger in the earlier novel, finally takes up the cause of the working class, rural and urban. Although this is a rather simplistic conclusion, one has to grant Jorge Amado a considerable sincerity in these early novels. Another thing that he already has at this stage is a sense of humor. Like his American counterpart, Erskine Caldwell, who dealt with a similar world of poor white and black sharecroppers in *Tobacco Road* (1932) and *God's Little Acre* (1933), he enlivened his fiction with a raucous humor that made them more than sociological tracts. William Faulkner, a greater novelist than Caldwell and Amado, had already made fictional art out of such a world in *As I Lay Dying* (1930), and humor is an important part of this. Eventually Amado would make humor a major constituent of his fictional scene in such novels as *Gabriela, cravo e canela [Gabriela, Clove and Cinnamon]* and *Dona Flor e seus dois maridos [Dona Flor and Her Two Husbands]*.

The very title of *Suor* suggests the naturalistic mode in which Amado was writing in those days. This is the first of his many novels that he would write about the "city of Bahia," in this case viewed from the perspective of the underdog. The Bahia of the 1930s had slums that were no worse than those of Rio and São Paulo, but the scale was smaller, the poor lived in closer proximity to the well-to-do. The author describes in great detail a tenement where he actually stayed in 1928, when he was only sixteen. The opening paragraph sets the tone: "Os ratos passaram, sem nenhum sinal de medo, entre os homens que estavam parados ao pé da escada escura" [The rats went by, without any sign of fear, beside the men who were standing at the foot of the dark stairs].[1] Much of the action takes place here, A note at the end of the novel indicates that Amado began writing *Suor* at that time, in

1928, in this place that is called Ladeira do Pelourinho [Hill of the Pillory]. He evidently laid the manuscript aside until 1934, when he quickly finished it; it is one the shortest of his novels. One has to give him credit for fulfilling an adolescent literary ambition, even if this book has less fictional interest than his others.

All the more remarkable, then, that Graciliano Ramos chose it as the subject of a review-essay early in 1935. He had recently published his fine second novel, *São Bernardo* [*Saint Bernard*], and had quickly attained his top level as a writer. In the review he both praises and criticizes his young Bahian friend (they had met in 1933). In general he approves of the way in which Amado and other new writers approached the fictional subject that they had derived from their own experiences:

> É natural que a literatura nova que por ai andam construindo se ocupe com ele. Sempre vale mais que descrever os lares felizes, que não existem, ou contar histórias sem pé nem cabeça coisas bonitas, arrumadas em conformidade com as regras, como há tempo, quando um subjeito, sem nunca sair do Rio de Janeiro, imitava a algaravia de Lisboa e procurava assunto para obra de ficcão do Egito e da India [It is natural that the new literature, that is being created now would deal with him. It is always easier to describe happy homes that do not exist, or to tell wild stories or write about beautiful things, set forth according to rules, as in the case when a fellow without even leaving the city of Rio de Janeiro imitates the way of speaking in Lisbon and looks for fictional sources in Egypt and India].[2]

But he also pointed out that *Suor [Sweat]* was not properly a novel; it was hardly more than a series of sketches set in the sprawling tenement. We could put it another way and say that the novel simply doesn't have a completed action, and no amount of authentic detail can compensate for that. But it did introduce something important that Amado would take up before long in other works: his extensive knowledge of the pervasive African culture in Bahia. Eventually the music and religious rituals, the cookery and domestic customs of this colorful city would become an important part of his fiction.

After these two short novels (*Cacau*, 128 pages, and *Suor*, 155 pages in recent editions) Jorge Amado, still very young, wrote *Jubiabá*, his most ambitious work of the 1930s. It is surely admirable that a twenty-three year old managed to do this at the same time that he was finishing his law degree in Rio. He had his family responsibilities now, because he had married in 1933, and his first daughter was born in 1935. His earliest novels were being translated into Russian and Spanish. It must have been an *annus mirabilis* for him.

*Jubiabá* represents a change in Amado's fictional procedures. He abandoned the fragmentary method used in *Suor* for a conventional plot which centers on the formation of a hero. He continued to use dialect and the language of the common people, but he expanded his stylistic resources in various ways. As Eduardo de Assis Duarte has recently pointed out,

> Em *Jubiabá*, vemos materializar-se esse encontro com o popular não apenas en quanto matéria ficcional, mas igualmente na direção oral, os folhetos de cordel, os ABC dos heróis sertanejos. A estrutura do romance assimila e combina essas formas, de sorte que é possível discernir elementos seus no enredo cheio de façanhas, no ritmo marcado pelas repetições, no tom de estória contada. A própria concepção do romance, fundada na narração dos feitos de um herói, inspira-se no cordel e, mesmo, na mais longínqua herança narrativa [In *Jubiabá*, we see the fictional subject of the common people brought together with the oral tendency, the *cordel* literature, the ABC of the northeastern heroes. The structure of the novel assimilates and combines these two forms in such a way that it is possible to distinguish their elements in the plot filled with adventures, in a rhythm marked by repetition, in the tone of an oral narrative. The conception of the novel itself, based on the narration of the deeds of a hero, comes from *cordel* literature and from an even more remote narrative].[3]

The hero is Balduíno, who, a minor character in *Suor*, now becomes the central figure in *Jubiabá*. Jorge Amado has also put another character, this one from real life, in the novel. In 1992 he published a sizable collection of memoirs, fragmentary and out of chronological order, in a book called *Navegação de cabotagem [Coastal navigation]*. Here he records the following incident from Maceió in 1933:

> Cicerone nas ruas e graças da cidade, Aurélio Buarque de Holanda leva-me ao puteiro na noite morna de Maceió. O futuro dicionarista, novel literato, popular entre e mulherio, que o trata pelo apelido com intimidade, é disputado: *contigo vou de graça, belo corpo.*
> Apaixono-me por Lindinalva, filha de usineiro arruinado, abandonada pelo noivo. Estendidos na cama conversamos no intervalo, no quarto o olor de alfazema, o toco de vela ilumina Santo Antônio. Lindinalva é loira de trigais maduros (a imagem é velha e gasta, eu sei, mas é porreta), eu iria colocá-la inteira no *Jubiabá*, a Aurélio a devo, aproveito para de público agradecer a prenda [A guide through the streets and to what the city has to offer, Aurélio Buarque de Holanda, takes me to the whorehouse on a warm night in Maceió. The future dictionary writer, new man of letters, is popular among the women, who call him by his nickname; he is very familiar and coveted: *With you I'll go for free, Handsome Body.* I fall in love with Lindinalva, the daughter of a ruined sugar cane refinery owner, abandoned by her fiancé. Lying down in bed, we talk during a break; in the bedroom there is a smell of lavender, the candle stub illuminates Saint Anthony. Lindinalva is blond, hair like ripe wheat (the image is old and worn out, I know, but it is good). I will place her in *Jubiabá*, I owe this to Aurélio and take advantage to thank him publicly for the present].[4]

So this little incident becomes part of the novel with scarcely any change. *Jubiabá* begins *in media res*, and only later does the reader become aware of the identity of the young black who twice knocks down his opponent in a boxing match. The audience of students, soldiers, and workers cheer him when he has the upper hand and boo when he appears to be losing. His victory at the beginning of the novel already points toward the potential racial situation, because his defeated opponent is a white man, a German in fact. In 1935 it was still bold to have a black from the slums as the chief character in a novel. The course of *Jubiabá* has Balduíno, an orphan, brought up by a well-to-do family. He is infatuated by Lindinalva, the daughter of the family that takes him in, but he leaves while he is still an adolescent. Later he finds her living in a degrading fashion after being seduced by the lawyer Barreira. Balduíno sees her die and adopts her son.

The central intention of the novel, then, is to show the development of a hero with an enlightened political consciousness through a character who starts out with the odds against him. What about Jubiabá? He is a very old man, almost a hundred, a *pai-de-santo* who protects Balduíno. This *candomblé* priest is a mentor to the hero, and his presence allows the author to widen the perspective of the scene by describing the religious ceremonies and other African customs that make Bahia the extraordinary place that it is. One of the finest episodes in the novel, a kind of set piece of description, is "Macumba" (Chapter 7), where the author actually introduces lines of incantation in Nagô, an African language (then he gives the Portuguese equivalent). This is more than local color. It would not be too much to say that Jubiabá instills a great pride in their common heritage in his protégé, and this certainly complicates the motives of a character who is something more than the hero of a "socially conscious" novel of the 1930s.

The last part of the novel, running through four chapters, concerns a general strike in the city. Jorge Amado has well orchestrated this big episode. We move in and out of the crowds along the docks. Barreira, the lawyer who has seduced Lindinalva, is introduced as one who betrays the workers. The violence escalates, but finally the workers' demands are met by the utility company. Balduíno has returned as a labor agitator and becomes a leader in the strike, indeed its hero, who will be celebrated in a samba that is sung all over the city. Now he goes to the old man: "E Jubiabá o feiticeiro, se inclina diante dele como se ele Oxolufã, Oxalá velho, o maior dos santos" [Then Jubiabá, the magic man, bows before Antônio Balduíno as if he were Oxolufã, the old Oxalá, greatest of spirits].[5]

This brings us virtually to the end of the novel, whose somewhat idealized hero has triumphed over adverse circumstances. *Jubiabá,* of course, resembles many novels of the period, for instance John Steinbeck's *In Dubious Battle* (1936), in having a strike, successful or otherwise, as a climactic episode. But Jorge Amado's use of the special character of Bahia, and especially its racial situation, makes *Jubiabá* endure better than most of the so-called proletarian novels of the period. It marks a decided advance over his earlier fiction. When it was translated into French, it was reluctantly accepted by André Gide, who thought its presentation had a certain vulgarity about it. But in the same year, 1939, Albert Camus called it a magnificent and astonishing book. Camus (1913–1960) was a contemporary of Amado, and his enthusiasm was perhaps accounted for by his youthful experience in Algeria, so different from Gide's but somewhat like Amado's in Bahia. At any rate, by the time that literary figures of this caliber were taking up his work, Jorge Amado had begun to move into the international scene. *Jubiabá* was not translated into English, however, until much later. In 1984, following the popularity of *Gabriela, Clove and Cinnamon* and *Dona Flor and Her Two Husbands* in the United States, Avon Books brought out paperback versions of *Jubiabá* and *Mar morto* [*Sea of Death*], Amado's next novel. But most of the early work discussed here is still unavailable in English.

In one respect *Mar morto* picks up where *Jubiabá* ended. Published in 1936, this is another novel of Bahia confronting the sea. At the end of *Jubiabá*, Balduíno, now a hero after the successful strike, goes down to the docks and looks out at the waves. He longs for the time when he can go to sea; the experience he has gained in the strike has made him confident in his strength. He imagines himself leading strikes in other ports and making his farewell. And now he is caught up in a kind of universal surge of love for all who are seeking release from their slavery. The political implications of this scene are obvious. Amado has it taking place in the night, and the docks are silvery in the moonlight. The lyricism diffuses the political theme; public and private destinies blend for Balduíno, now alone.

*Mar morto* opens with the same setting along the waterfront of Bahia. This time there is a storm at night. The shifting point of view gives us a panorama of men and women anxiously trying to save themselves or looking out to sea in the hope that their lovers will return. The lights in the city go off and on. In this theatrical setting we gradually move to Lívia, who in some ways is the chief character of the novel. She is the sweetheart, later the wife, of Guma, a mulatto sailor who drowns during a heroic rescue at sea. Jorge Amado tries to set up a certain tone, that of the traditional story teller, in a brief prose-poem that he prints in italics; this comes just before the novel proper gets underway:

> Vinde ouvir essas histórias e essas canções. Vinde ouvir a história de Guma e Lívia que é a história da vida e do amor no mar. E se ela não vos parecer bela a culpa não é dos homens rudes que a narram. É que a ouvistes da boca de um homen da terra, e, dificilmente, um homen da terra entende o coração dos marinheiros [Come listen to these stories and these songs. Come hear the story of Guma and Lívia, which is the story of life and love on the sea. And if you don't find it beautiful, the fault won't lie

with the rough men who tell it, because you're hearing it from the mouth of
a man of the land, and only with great difficulty can a man of the land
understand the heart of sailors].[6]

In *Jubiabá* Jorge Amado sometimes gives another dimension to the
action by introducing the African god Oxalá. In the brief scene, already
quoted, where Jubiabá sees Balduíno for the last time, he bows before the
young hero as if he were Oxalá. In *Mar morto*, where the perspectives tend to
be feminine, the African deity who figures in the action is Yemanjá, the sea
goddess. In a sense the two novels complement each other. Lívia fears
Yemanjá, and indeed she looks upon her as a rival in love. After Guma
drowns, Lívia goes to sea in her husband's *saveiro* (a small sailing boat typical of the coast along Bahia) to confront the force of nature. She often accompanied Guma in his voyages, but she isn't a woman of the waterfront; she
wasn't born there. Nor can she be as indifferent about death as are some of the
other women, who almost expect their husbands to be doomed.

The story is a fairly simple one, as Jorge Amado already suggested in his
prefatory prose-poem. Guma loses his boat, the "Valente," and, reduced to
poverty, he becomes a smuggler for an Arab who deals in silk. At the climax
of the novel he is trying to bring a sloop overloaded with silk into a harbor
during a storm. The sloop overturns; Guma manages to save two Arab boys
but loses his own life to the sharks that surround the capsized boat. This is
good narrative from "um homen da terra," as Amado calls himself in the preface. After that, Lívia insists that Guma's body be sought; finally only she is
left to continue the search:

> Olharam e viram. Dona Dulce olhou também da janela da escola. Viu uma
> mulher forte que lutava. A luta era seu milagre. Começava a se realizar. No
> cais os marítimos viam Yemanjá, a dos cinco nomes. O velho Francisco gri-
> tava, era a segunda vez que ele via. Assim contam na beira do cais [They
> looked and they saw. Dona Dulce saw too as she looked from the window of
> the school. She saw a strong woman who was fighting on. The fight was her
> miracle. It was beginning to take place. On the waterfront the sailors saw
> Yemanjá, she of the five names. Old Francisco was shouting, it was the sec-
> ond time he had seen her].[7]

And so the story teller's voice brings the novel to a close. Jorge Amado has
introduced a minor character, Francisco, an old sailor, as a kind of commenta-
tor on the action; his presence often conveys a quiet continuity in life.
Reduced to mending nets on the beach, he represents a persistence in human
existence, a bottom level of activity perhaps, but one that carries its own dignity. As for Yemanjá, anyone who has lived in Brazil is aware of the power
that a cult of the African deities can exercise on its worshipers. Yemanjá is not

a literary invention at all; Lívia's obsession with the goddess is absolutely typical, and not just in Bahia.

This novel has had an unusual reception over the sixty years since it was first published. By 1994 it had gone through sixty-eight editions in Brazil; its popularity seems guaranteed. It has been translated into at least twelve languages aside from English (the translator here being Gregory Rabassa). But some critics who admire Jorge Amado do not always care for the "lyricism" that runs through parts of the novel, the frequent mention of "os gemidos de amor" and the moonlight that emerges rather too often. The very real poverty of the people along the seafront may be romanticized in this fashion, they think. Eduardo de Assis Duarte, in what is probably the best critical study of Amado's work in this period, rather curiously omits any mention of *Mar morto*; perhaps he thinks it unworthy of detailed commentary. But it should be considered as a simple story in a long tradition of romance that goes back to the *Daphnis and Chloe* of Longus, a late Greek writer, except that it lacks the traditional happy ending. Set in a world in which Yemanjá is still worshipped, it has something authentic about it sixty years after its first publication. The social criticism that may be implied is fairly slight in this case.

In the following year, 1937, right on schedule as it were, Jorge Amado brought out his next novel, *Capitães de areia* [*Captains of the Sand*]. The social criticism here is very obvious. The situation concerns the life of a group of abandoned adolescents who live in a warehouse on the waterfront of Bahia. The narrative gives us a realistic picture of this gang and their fight for survival in search for food and money. The author, in his sometimes crude but lyrical fashion, tries to show the gap between the social classes and the crimes that are generated because of this situation. These youths are to be considered as the victims of an insensitive society. Capitães de areia is the name of the gang that the author clearly wants the reader to sympathize with. By comparison with members of rival gangs, this group is composed of relatively sincere, kind, and even noble youths.

One could say that the novel starts out from *Jubiabá*. We have the same kind of growing up process in the main character that we saw in the boyhood of Balduíno in the earlier novel, and, again, a character who becomes a leader and fights against the system that created him. Both *Jubiabá* and *Capitães de areia* have something of the Bildungsroman about them in this respect. At the same time *Capitães* is the last of what might be called Jorge Amado's proletarian cycle. The thematic relationship between *Suor, Jubiabá, Cacáu*, and *Capitães* is quite evident. A minor character in one novel becomes the main character of another; Baldo in *Suor* becomes Balduíno in *Jubiabá*, and his childhood is in effect a major part of *Capitães de areia*. The intention of *Capitães de areia* was to draw attention to the neglected adolescents and not necessarily to call for a proletarian revolution. Nevertheless this novel was censored by the government in 1937, and hundreds of copies were burned in public by the Bahian militia.

The main character, a youth named Pedro Bala, has a counterpart in a novel by Mario Vargas Llosa, *La ciudad y los perros* [*The Time of the Hero*]. Here the society in a military academy is also pictured as violent, and the hardships endured by the young cadets are quite similar to what the Capitães de Areia gang goes through. It is also interesting to know that Vargas Llosa in his turn had his novel burned by the militia of Lima. The Colegio Leoncio Prado is not that much different from the old harbor warehouse where the boys in *Capitães de areia* live.

Eduardo de Assis Duarte in his chapter on the novel summarizes very well its essence when he says: "*Capitães de areia* concentra a força de seus méritos mais na denúncia candente da condição dos meninos de rua, única em toda literatura dos anos 30, do que na construção cuidadosa das estapas ascensionais do Bildungsroman proletário" [*Capitães de areia* concentrates the strength of its merits more on a strong denunciation of the condition of the street kids, unique in 1930s literature, than on the careful construction of the different phases of a proletarian Bildungsroman].[8]

After his continuous run of novel writing in the 1930s (six novels published between 1931 and 1937), Jorge Amado withdrew from fiction for six years. He came back to the scene with *Terras do sem fim* [*The Violent Land*], arguably his finest work, in 1943. There were understandable reasons for this absence. In 1937, about the same time that *Capitães de areia* was published and his books were burned in Salvador, he was jailed in Manaus, taken to Rio and held in prison till the following year. He did manage to publish a book of poems in 1938; presumably poetry was not subject to government censorship. In 1941 he went into exile in Argentina, and during the next two years he published two "safe" books: *ABC de Castro Alves* (a lyrical biography of the romantic poet) and *Vida de Luíz Carlos Prestes, el caballero de la esperanza* [*The life of Luis Prestes, the knight of hope*] (published in Buenos Aires; later issued in Brazil in Portuguese). Jorge Amado has always been a very professional writer who can turn his talent to various literary projects as the occasion demands.

So it may have always been fortunate that he had this vacation from novel writing for several years, because *Terras do sem fim* is decidedly superior to his earlier novels. The political issues that gave him so much trouble are implied in this work, but he has put them into an historical setting that perhaps was remote enough from the political situation of 1943 to make it immune from censorship. The landscape of *Terras do sem fim* is southern Bahia during the boom in cacao around 1912. This was of course the year of Amado's birth. The novel, among other things, tries to document the rapid and violent changes that took place in this area of Bahia that was being exploited by the greed of the adventurers who descended upon it. They came from a variety of backgrounds, women as well as men, all of them after easy money and fertile land.

The story is built up around the conflict between Coronel Horácio Silveira and the Badaró brothers, Sinhô and Juca. These rival plantation owners are trying to extend their vast properties by invading the Sequeiro Grande, a great tract that promises to be the most fertile part of the area when it is planted with cacao trees. The winner in this ruthless conflict will be the richest man in southern Bahia. Jorge Amado's father was involved in this situation in 1917, and the boy, then only five years old, actually took part in a little episode that he later put in this novel. The story is complicated by several other characters, especially the women. The author here has a much larger social range than he used in his earlier novels. Sinhô, the older Badaró brother, has a daughter, Don'Ana, who eventually becomes the survivor of her family. Horácio has a wife, Ester, who is rather more refined than her husband with his plebeian origins. She takes a lover, the young lawyer Virgílio, whom Horácio hires to substantiate his claims on the Sequeiro Grande. After Ester's death Horácio discovers her letters to Virgílio and has the lawyer killed. Then there is the prostitute Margot (not the only prostitute in the novel) who has an affair with Virgílio but later becomes the mistress of Juca Badaró. And there is a gambler, João Magalhães, introduced in the first pages of the novel, who marries Don'Ana after promising old Sinhô to adopt the Badaró name. Although the Badarós are aristocratic (at least by local standards), Juca is almost completely lacking in noblesse oblige, and the only man whom he respects is his older brother. Aside from these characters, the author has included many servants, plantation workers, even a would-be assassin, at considerable length.

Many critics, including Fred P. Ellison, have spoken of the "epic grandeur" of the novel. Although it isn't much longer than *Jubiabá*, it has a larger subject, and what at first might seem to be a local affair in the southern part of Bahia is representative of much in Brazilian history. The locale may have shifted to Amazonas or Mato Grosso, but the issues of exploitation, greed, and violent rivalry are the same today. In this respect, the novel has a continuing interest. With a larger group of characters to work with, Jorge Amado has orchestrated the action superbly. He brings us much closer to relatively minor figures who turn out to have considerable importance. For instance, the novel opens on the deck of a liner leaving Bahia for Ilhéus, a port city down the coast and the gateway to the "violent land" of cacao plantations. The ship is filled with adventurers of both sexes. The focus is on João Magalhães, a gambler who tries to pass himself off as an army engineer. After the first chapter we don't see him again for much of the novel. But eventually he turns up in the middle of the action and marries Don'Ana. Also on board is the pretty Margot, no doubt already a woman of experience. Long before the novel is over she becomes the mistress of Virgílio, Coronel Horácio's lawyer, and then Juca Badaró; indeed, she is a kind of intermediary between the rival forces. Another passenger is Coronel Maneca Dantas, who mentions his plantation, Auricidia, named after his wife to whom we are presently introduced. Auricidia in fact was the name of the *fazenda* where Jorge Amado was born in 1912. In the following year his father was wounded by an assassin's bullet there, and in 1914 it was destroyed by a flood.

Jorge Amado's kind of humor, admittedly coarse at times, was never used to better advantage. It is, for example, amusing as well as ironic that João Magalhães, the gambler who has come to Ilhéus to seek his fortune, should be chosen by Juca Badaró to make a quick survey of the Sequeiro Grande, because he is completely fraudulent. Very serious issues are involved. In another episode that certainly has serious dimensions, Dr. Jessé, a physician who is a close friend of Coronel Horácio, is presiding over a tree planting ceremony in the middle of a *praça*. School children and their teachers are in attendance, verses are recited, and the national anthem is sung. Just as Dr. Jessé is about to plant a cacao tree, a gang of thugs from a plantation friendly to the Badarós ride into the little town, causing widespread panic. Dr. Jessé, a pompous sycophant of a man, is humiliated as he plants the tree. The leader of the armed band, Coronel Teodoro das Baraúnas, then urinates on the tree and Dr. Jessé before inciting his gang to burn the town registry office. On a more domestic level there is a scene in which two laborers, carrying the corpse of a man who has just died from typhus, bring their burden in a hammock to the great house where Dona Auricidia lives. One of her children runs out to the veranda and reports the news: "Mama, there is two men with a dead man—a skinny dead man." And Dona Auricidia, a former schoolteacher, replies, "Don't say: 'There is two,' Ruy. 'There are two,' is what you should say."[9] Jorge Amado now writes of the upper class with a certain wit even when his characters are at their most ruthless. He *dramatizes* his scenes and his social issues instead of setting them up as vehicles of propaganda. He has arrived at his top level as a novelist.

Indeed, he would not perform so well again for fifteen years. In 1954 Fred P. Ellison, in his pioneering critical book, *Brazil's New Novel*, wrote: "Only in *The Violent Land*, where they are unadulterated by ideological considerations, do we fully perceive the imagination, enthusiasm, and lyrical feeling for reality that distinguishes Amado's writing."[10] This was his judgement more than a decade after *Terras do sem fim* appeared. It is true that during much of the 1940s and 1950s Amado was busy in politics, or he was living abroad, or writing occasional travel books. When he came back to fiction in 1958 with *Gabriela, cravo e canela*, he may have seemed a different writer, but *Terras do sem fim* meanwhile did a lot for his reputation. It had the good fortune to be translated into English by the famous Samuel Putnam in 1945. Putnam had recently translated Euclides da Cunha's *Os Sertões* for the University of Chicago Press, and this undoubtedly gave him a background for

*Terras do sem fim*, which he translated as *The Violent Land*. This was the first Amado in English. The publisher was Alfred Knopf in New York. Knopf had become very friendly to certain Latin American novelists, and especially Brazilians. When Jorge Amado returned to fiction in 1958, it was Knopf who published and promoted him thereafter in the United States. It was a profitable arrangement for everyone concerned since Amado would become almost as successful in English as he was in Portuguese.

## NOTES

All translations are by Celso de Oliveira, unless otherwise indicated.

1. Translated from Jorge Amado, *Suor*. Rio de Janeiro: Editora Record, 1986. p. 9.
2. Translated from Graciliano Ramos, *Linhas tortas*. São Paulo: Martins, 1962. p. 94.
3. Translated from Eduardo de Assis Duarte, *Jorge Amado: romance em tempo de utopia*. Natal: Editora UFRN, 1995. p. 91.
4. Translated from Jorge Amado, *Navegação de cabotagem*. Rio de Janeiro: Editora Record, 1992. p. 379.
5. Jorge Amado, *Jubiabá*, translated by Margaret A. Neves. New York: Avon Books, 1984. p. 286.
6. Jorge Amado, *Sea of Death*, translated by Gregory Rabassa. New York: Avon Books, 1984.
7. *Sea of Death*, translated by Gregory Rabassa. p. 273.
8. Translated from *Jorge Amado: romance em tempo de utopia*. p. 145.
9. Jorge Amado, *The Violent Land*, translated by Samuel Putnam. New York: Alfred A. Knopf, 1945. p. 97.
10. Fred P. Ellison, *Brazil's New Novel: Four Northeastern Masters*. Berkeley and Los Angeles: University of California Press, 1954. p. 164.

## BIBLIOGRAPHY

Amado, Jorge. *Jubiabá*. Translated by Margaret A. Neves. New York: Avon Books, 1984.
———. *Navegação de cabotagem*. Rio de Janeiro: Editora Record, 1992.
———. *Suor*. Rio de Janeiro: Editora Record, 1986.
———. *The Violent Land*. Translated by Samuel Putnam. New York: Alfred A. Knopf, 1945.
Duarte, Eduardo de Assis. *Jorge Amado: romance em tempo de utopia*. Natal: Editora UFRN, 1995.
Ellison, Fred P. *Brazil's New Novel: Four Northeastern Masters*. Berkeley and Los Angeles: University of California Press, 1954.
Ramos, Graciliano. *Linhas tortas*. São Paulo: Martins, 1962.

# From *Lundu* and *Modinha* to *Samba de Enredo* and *MPB*
## Popular Music and the Fiction of Jorge Amado[1]

CHARLES A. PERRONE

Novelists of the second generation of Brazilian Modernism were often preoccupied with depicting regional traits in pursuit of *brasilidade*, or Brazilianness, the stuff of national character. Authors associated with the novel of the
Northeast utilized folk, traditional, and popular culture, following, as romantic and realist writers had, what a leading chronicler of Brazilian literature
called a "legítimo pressuposto, o de que essas manifestações da alma popular
servem de base à literatura, ao mesmo tempo que são um veículo de apri-
moramento de caráter brasileiro pela especialização particularista que pro-
movem."[2] More than one analyst of the work of Jorge Amado has underlined
the fundamental role of folk repertories and narrative-song cycles in his fiction. Critic and fellow novelist Adonias Filho writes that in ". . . todos os
romances baianos de Jorge Amado—o que se continua é um cancioneiro. Cir-
culando na oralidade narrativa, a seguir no abecedário, para converter-se
finalmente em ficção erudita, o cancioneiro preservar-se-ia nas raízes fol-
clóricas através de constantes literárias."[3] While this account refers to preservation, balladry and other forms of music in Amado's fiction operate well
beyond the folk dimension; they exhibit dynamism, evolution, and transition
to modern spheres.

The significational potential of folk and popular music was clear to Jorge
Amado from the outset of his literary career. He understood well the promi-
nence of music in the cultural complex of Bahia, and musical situations comprise a consequential aspect of his production, from the early fiction of the
1930s to related works of the 1980s. All of his novels use music to some
degree, from isolated mentions in a few titles to more fully developed internal
systems in others. As a whole, the narrative world of Jorge Amado is
estimable as a source, or literary point of reference, of local and national cultural, and specifically musical, information. The fictional world of the leading
novelist of Bahia offers, as a compatriot suggested decades ago, the perspec-

tive of a non-academic social science: "a antropologia de Jorge Amado ...
não é a dos compêndios para universidades." The trajectory of his fiction is
traced by the consciousness of problems that people face to overcome the
obstacles to being themselves.[4] Music plays a part in tracing that curve, as
such awareness is often manifested and realized in song and performance.

Amado views music as a key and "indispensable" element of popular life
and, therefore, of his fiction. He regards song as an instrument of emphasis:
"O canto na minha narrativa é como um fundo musical para sublinhar o tra-
balho, a alegria, a desventura, a luta e o amor do povo."[5] His source is usually
"a boca do povo" [word of mouth], but he has also written original verse for
musical situations in his novels and for real-life settings. He also draws on
actual compositions and musical figures to create atmosphere and to compli-
cate narrative circumstances. Amado himself has been the object of suggestive homages in popular music.

In fictional situations concerned with the expressive behaviors of given
cultures, musical phenomena can be particularly revealing. They may
involve, beyond sound production itself, varied song texts, solo and group
performance, the corporeal dimension of dance, and diverse types of social
occasions or interaction. In Amado's novels, the presence, symbolism, and
functions of music vary considerably. Sound events can be passing mentions, auditory background, or the attention-generating fulcrum, or focus, of
an entire scene. Citations of a song text can be relatively perfunctory or
woven into the fabric of narrative schemes, as leitmotifs or bearers of information. In addition to specific functions in the narration, these instances
may serve as active ingredients of setting or narrative space, as illustrations
of folk life or popular culture, or as markers, of ethnicity, regional identity,
gendered attitudes, or class. Amado's use of music has been consistent with
his evolving literary orientation, more socially purposeful or critical in his
first committed phase, and more broadly appealing in the stage that begins
with *Gabriela, cravo e canela* [*Gabriela, Clove and Cinnamon*], which Paes
(58) aptly characterizes as "populismo entre sentimental e folclórico."
Music is, to be sure, a constant vehicle of the sentimentalism and folklore
that occupy the author.

The greater portion of Amado's treatment of musical themes indeed
involves folk culture, which has been been the object of some investigation.[6]
The present study—with explicit recognition that the spectrum of musical
experiences in the author's novels ranges from strictly rural oral traditions to
instances of concert (art, classical) music—will primarily concern urban
popular music in the fiction of Jorge Amado.[7] In half of the author's works of
long fiction, popular music figures to some degree, and in some cases it has
a noteworthy place. It will be fruitful to see how Amado portrays, and to
what ends he utilizes, samba and other popular genres, as well as musical
allusions. The most pertinent contexts of popular music in his fiction will

prove to be scenes of urbanization, circumstances of social strife, and, of course, carnival.

Amado's first novel, *O País do carnaval [The land of carnival]* is unique in his output, for it ultimately has more of an existential than an exploratory nationalist thrust in the dominant vein of 1930s' fiction. The title, in addition, would suggest a more substantial role for music than the relatively limited one it does play in overall perspective. Still, one of the novel's most intense and significant moments is prepared by a musical motif. Popular music, moreover, is intimately linked to an impulse of discovery and self-identification, especially in the protagonist, both as an individual and as a citizen. Well into the novel, Paulo Rigger, in an unusually nationally self-conscious moment, proclaims: "Só me senti brasileiro duas vezes. Uma, no carnaval, quando sambei na rua. Outra, quando surrei Julie, depois que ela me traiu."[8] Roberto DaMatta found this phrase to be pregnant with meaning, "prenhe de significado" (*Carnavais* 69), and employed it to initiate a semiotic analysis of Brazilian social space. The noted anthropologist, recalling that literature of the period was being driven by the search for the essence of what is truly Brazilian, characterizes the phrase not only as revealing and provocative but also as tragic. If in other countries a search for identity might pose problems of civics—involving flags, hymns, crowns, or heroic struggles—to be Brazilian, for the paradigmatic character, is to melt into the undifferentiated crowd dancing samba in the street and to adopt a typically authoritarian (and crude) patriarchal behavior, physically abusing the European lover who had betrayed him. Thus, in the case of Brazil, the most encompassing process of identification must bring into play carnival and the control of female sexual favors. While one can note here how DaMatta does not get beyond the strictly masculine point of view of the novel, that very restriction fits well his own assignment of importance to the above cited phrase: it sums up, like a true sociological model, some basic elements of the ritual world of carnival and of the ingredients of the carnivalesque world, as it plays out in modern Brazil. The carnival scene of the novel introduces a structural category—interior (home)-exterior (street)—that opposes authority and control to lack of control and massification (*Carnavais* 69–70).

As far as the fictional logic of the protagonist's "pregnant" words is concerned, DaMatta fails to note a rather straightforward and significant connection with music. Song, in fact, is instrumental in creating one of the prime tensions of the novel. When the protagonist returns to Brazil after a stay in Europe, the declared site of "civilization," he confronts music as an index of the soul of the people. A musical citation introduces, early in the novel, the context of search for identity, and the representativity of music, as well as the issue of abuse. This occurs when the protagonist visits Rio de Janeiro (capital and symbolic center of the nation) for the first time:

Paulo Rigger parou em frente de uma casa de discos. Uma marcha bem can-
tada enchia o espaço com uma música estranha, nostálgica, cheia de senti-
mento que Paulo não compreendia.
A marcha rugia:
*Essa mulher há muito tempo me provoca...*
    *Dá nela...*
    *Dá nela...*
—Isso deve ser a música brasileira—pensou Rigger. A grande música do
Brasil.
E ficou a escutar enlevado pela barbaria do ritmo. A alma do povo devia
estar ali. E como era diferente da sua... Ele não bateria nunca numa mulher.
A música bradava:
    *Dá nela...*
    *Dá nela...* (26)

[Paulo Rigger stopped in front of a record store. A wellsung march filled the
air with a strange music, nostalgic and full of feeling, that Paulo didn't
understand. The march roared: "That woman has been provoking me for a
long time... Let her have it, let her have it." "That must be Brazilian music,"
Rigger thought. "The grand music of Brazil." And he stopped to listen, let-
ting himself be carried away by the barbarity of the rhythm. The soul of the
people must be there. And how different it was from his own... He would
never strike a woman. The song howled: Let her have it, let her have it.]

The impressionable young visitor soon initiates a sexual relationship with the
sensual French woman Julie. When the topic of jealousy comes up, he plays a
pertinent recording he likes— "... numa casa de cabôclo/ um é pouco/ dois é
bom, três é demais ..."—and explains to her "o que queria dizer aquela
música brasileira" (30) [what that Brazilian song meant]. The cited refrain
says: "In a backlander's home / one is little / two are good / three are too
many." Amado here cites the conclusion to the narrative song of rural tragedy
"Casa de caboclo" (Hekel Tavares-Luiz Peixoto), a successful recording in
the late 1920s in the voice of Gastão Formenti. Readers of the early 1930s
were not unlikely to recognize the allusion to the song, which illustrates a
classic male melancholy, recourse to (mortal) violence, and a unilateral masculine point of view (cf. Beltrão, 121–122). While implying like topicality,
the lyrico-narrative radio song also sets up a comparison with loud live music
of revelry, as the protagonist, soon afterward, mingles with the crowd in seasonal celebration:

Quando Paulo Rigger saiu, um grupo de mulatas sambava na rua. Côr de
canela, seios quase à mostra, requebravam-se voluptuosamente, num
delírio. Paulo viu ali todo o sentimento da raça. Viu-se integrado no seu
povo. Caiu no samba, a berrar:
    *Dá nela...*
    *Dá nela...* (31).

[When Paulo Rigger went out, a group of mulatto women were dancing
samba in the street. The color of cinnamon, nearly revealing their breasts,
they were moving voluptuously, in a delirium. There Paulo saw all the senti-
ment of the race. He saw himself integrated with his people. He jumped into
the samba, shouting "Let her have it, let her have it."]

Given the linear scheme of Amado's debut novel, it is no surprise that the
refrain of the carnival march should echo once again, precisely in the after-
math of Rigger's battering of his unfaithful lover, which is represented as a
loss of moral sense. At this point, the Dionysian urge has become an impulse
of male-dominant violence of control and punishment. In the person of a protagonist who fancies himself a thinker, a cerebral-carnal dialectic has resolved
itself, at least temporarily, in favor of the latter. In this sequence, songs have
functioned as a developing motif, as carriers of tension, and, cumulatively, as
markers—of ignorance, search, knowledge, contrast, emotion, and psychological profile. This preparation needs to be taken into account to understand
DaMatta's insight into the protagonist's charged words.

As for additional musical history, the primary lyric from which Amado
quotes is that of "Dá nela" by Ary Barroso, a seasonal hit in 1930 which, for
the benefit of future readers of the novel, would become a standard of the
Brazilian carnival repertory. The march heard on the street contrasts stylistically with the song that Rigger himself chose to play on the victorola inside,
which is a song in the *sertanejo* (backlands) style popularized among middle-
and upper-class listeners in the 1910s and 1920s by renowned poet-singer Cat-
ulo da Paixão Cearense. While this song type is more appropriate to the character's bourgeois status, it is curious that Rigger can "explain" to Julie what
the song means, since he has been depicted as a less-than-fully-informed
youth in the process of (re-)learning his own culture. While there is no further
elaboration in the brief passage itself, one might take the liberty to speculate
and wonder what is involved in "explaining" the music. Does Rigger tell the
complete tragic story of the song (that some readers of the time are familiar
with)? Or does he simply interpret the surface level of the cited words (i.e.,
three's a crowd, let's be alone together)? Or, from a wider socio-musical angle,
does conveying meaning include telling the nature of the (by implication) less
barbarous genre and its contexts? Does Rigger not only like but know the
social implications of preferring this type of music? Whatever inferences may
be drawn, such questioning can only add to the scene's rich dissonance.

In his committed novels, Amado's narrators are much more likely to
interpret such scenes, as seen in the first work the author thought of as a "proletarian novel," *Suor [Sweat]*. A conflict therein between different sub-sec-
tors of the emergent working class in Salvador—long-term resident blacks
and recent rural immigrants—achieves resolution through music-making. A
defiant song with colonial overtones, a folk air Amado observed as a youth, is

performed at a gathering where the verse of backland bards and *batuque*-type dance music mix:

> Apareceram violões. Cantaram côcos da terra distante e desafios de canta-
> dores célebres. As lavadeiras esqueceram a zanga e se aproximaram.
>> ... *e fiz tanta estrepolia*
>> *que os reis mandou me chamá*
>> *pra casá com sua fia.*
>> *O dote qu'ele me dava*
>> *Oropa, França e Bahia ...*
>
> Uma moça dançava o passo miudinho do côco. Os homens batiam com as
> mãos. A voz do cearense continuava:
>> ... e eu disse que não queria (346).

> [Guitars appeared. They sang *cocos* from a faraway land and duels of cele-
> brated bards. The washerwomen forgot their anger and came near. "... and I
> made such a fuss / that the kings called for me / to marry their daughter / the
> dowry I'd get / Europe France and Bahia ..." A young woman was dancing
> the little steps of the *coco*. Men were clapping their hands. The voice of the
> man from Ceara state continued "... and I said I didn't want it"]. (346)

In this musical diversion, antagonisms are dissolved and harsh historical realities are put on hold. In the passage, the prolific social historian of popular
music José Ramos Tinhorão (vol. 2, 421) admires the strength of rural
migrants in a new urban context and the solidarity they achieve in a musical
occasion, which illustrates, in addition, music in transition from rural origins
to a new urban environment. Authorial intention in the scene is abundantly
evident, as the participants continue "[e]squecidos da escravidão de que vin-
ham, sem pensar na escravidão para que marchavam" [forgetting about the
slavery from which they came, without thinking about the slavery toward
which they were marching], which alludes to a new bondage of employment
and recalls unavoidably the legacy of slavery. This condition connects to the
other prominent musical moment of the novel, when an inebriated black man
sings, during a process of growth of consciousness, an old slave song—
"Xiquexique é pau de espinho/ umburana é pau de abeia/ Gravata de boi é
canga/ paletó de negro é peia ... " [that cactus is full of thorns / that tree is
full of bees / the yoke is an ox's tie / shackles are a black man's jacket] (280)
that offers evidence of continued oppression as well.

Memory of historical suffering is also revitalized in song in the "musicalized" novel *Jubiabá*. In this work, many forms of musical practice—from folk
narrative (e.g. *abecê* or *ABC*) and the chants of Afro-Bahian religious cults
(*cânticos de macumba*) to *modinhas* [sentimental parlor songs] and recurring
contemporary sambas—figure both as social occasions and as textual
instances. In a global appreciation of Amado's early work, Roger Bastide crafts

an interesting (if not absolutely reliable ethnomusicologically) analogy between a prominent feature of traditional music in Bahia, the call-and-response structure, and the shape of his fiction. Therein, the epic impulse is understood to be complemented by "o movimento lírico [que] se dá pela repetição rítmica dos mesmos temas, segundo a lei do diálogo entre o solista e um côro, assim como, nas festas populares, acontece com os criadores de samba, de jongo ou os acompanhadores de capoeira" [the lyrical movement that is given by the rhythmic repetition of the same themes, according to the law of dialogue between a solo singer and a chorus, just as it occurs, in popular fests, with the creators of samba, *jongo*, or those who accompany *capoeira*]" (60).

The protagonist of *Jubiabá*, Antônio Balduíno, is markedly versatile, playing the martial art-dance *capoeira*, singing, playing guitar, and drawing on traditional and urban sources alike in composing material of his own. Bastide asserts that this novel owes some of its excellence precisely to the form it follows: "a própria técnica da literatura oral negra, onde um improvisador canta e um coro responde ao solista" [the very technique of black oral literature, where one sings improvising and a chorus responds to the solo singer] (45).

Balduíno, in this transpositional view, "faz o papel de solista e a seu canto responde o coro das personagens secundárias, os soldados, os carregadores, os operários" [plays the role of solo singer; to his song responds the chorus of secondary characters, the soldiers, the warehousemen, the workers] (60). Clearly, the concept of oral literature employed here must be a broad one encompassing, beyond spoken narrations, both folk and popular song repertories.

In terms of musical history, there are two particularly valuable passages in *Jubiabá*. The first noteworthy episode, part of the build-up to a musicalized conclusion, involves the exploitation of a typical urban figure. At one juncture, Balduíno becomes a casually inventive popular composer in the manner of the *malandro* usually associated with Rio de Janeiro of the 1930s.[9] The character's behavior and lyrics stereotype a life style of the slick big-city hustler:

Muitas vezes, quando ele andava pelas ruas da cidade nos seus passeios malandros, ele começava a bater no chapeu de palha uma música que inventava e ia cantando uma letra, tudo tirado de sua cabeça. Depois cantava o samba novo para os amigos do morro:
  "Vida de negro é bem boa, mulata . . .
  tem festa todos os dias
  baticum lá no terreiro
  morena para a folia . . ."
  Fazia sucesso nas festas:
  "Senhor do Bonfim é meu santo
  ele faz feitiço forte,
  eu sou é malandro, mulata
  e você é minha desgraça. . . ." (88)

[Often, as he bummed through the streets of the city, he would start to drum his fingers on his straw hat, singing a verse of a song he had made up out of his own head ("A black man's life is really fine/ Parties every night/ Lots of rhythm, lots of rhyme,/ Black girls to hold you tight." He was always a great success at parties. "The Lord of Bonfim protects me, / He's powerful and strong/ I was a carefree playboy / Until you came along.")][10]

What proves to be of most interest here is not the hero's expression of values or his talent but how that skill is taken advantage of. When Balduíno's reputation gets beyond the neighborhood, a gentleman appears offering to buy sambas. Once purchased from the naive popular composer, these tunes are recorded by others, played on the radio, and sold as sheet music. Credit and profit go to the purchasing agent not the original maker, whose lack of familiarity with the media allows for his continued exploitation. While, within the dominant perspective of the novel, this episode unfolds in service of Amado's thesis of sociopolitical criticism, it further delineates common problems in the early commercialization of urban popular music: the lack of information on the part of marginal composer-musicians and the virtual theft of authorial rights and royalties.

By the final sequence of the novel, Balduíno has found fulfillment in a successful labor struggle. He loudly sings "A Vitória da greve" (lyric by Permínio Lírio), a samba composed at the end of a 1934 work stoppage at the Bahia Light and Power company.[11] This borrowing documents local history and lends powerful authenticity to the conclusion, when the hero realizes that his *ABC*, or symbolic primer, should not be the discourse of *malandragem* [hustling] but rather the strike itself. Balduíno's bardic role continues in the novelistic realm of Amado's Bahia as his deep voice is heard singing a verse of denunciation in the first part of *Os subterrâneos da liberdade: Os Asperos tempos [The freedom underground: harsh times]*. He later composes an anti-imperialist *ABC* in honor of a persecuted party leader rumored to be dead in *Á luzuz no túnel [The light in the tunnel]*.

> "Os gringos americanos,
> que vivem aqui como donos,
> explorando o brasileiro,
> roubando o nosso dinheiro
> pra levar pro estrangeiro,
> esses gringos desgraçados,
> com a polícia amigados,
> de noite, na escuridão,
> mataram Zé Gonçalão
>
> . . . . . . . . . . . . . . . . .
>
> —Viva o povo brasileiro
> livre do jugo estrangeiro!,
> morreu assim a gritar." (324)

[The American gringos, / who live here like owners, / exploiting Brazilians, / stealing our money / to take abroad, / those disgraceful gringos, / friends with the police, / at night, in the dark, / killed Zé Gonçalão ... "Long live the Brazilian people / free of the foreign yoke" / he died shouting thus].

In his post-engagé phase, Amado constructs another kind of multi-work *Comédia baiana [Bahian Comedy]* in which forms of popular culture, while not associated with militancy or social protest per se, may comprise expressions of resistance, and most certainly of self-affirmation. Tinhorão—within his concern for social history, as well as for the quality of literary portraits of musical phenomena—asserts that the return to carnival scenes in *Dona Flor e seus dois maridos [Dona Flor and Her Two Husbands]* situates Amado "entre os bons fixadores de cenas da vida popular ligadas à produção de música popular." Of particular interest is the opening of the novel, the death of the first husband Vadinho during carnival, which shows "uma participação direta da gente das camadas médias da cidade na brincadeira do povo na Bahia" [among those who portrayed well scenes of popular life linked to the production of popular music ... a direct participation of people from middle sectors of the city in the diversions of the people of Bahia].[12] Within the amatory dimension of the novel, the most notable musical practice is a *serenata*, or serenade. In an extended street scene, Vadinho and his cohorts sing what is identified as a *modinha* with a known composer. This choice is most appropriate both because the ultra-romantic lyric cited refers to the serenade itself, "Canto ... e a mulher que eu amo tanto / não me escuta, está dormindo. ..." [I sing ... and the woman whom I so love / hears me not, she sleeps] (125), and because the song has historical resonances. Composed by Cândido das Neves, nicknamed "Indio" (1889–1934), the title in question is "Noite Cheia de Estrelas." It was a hit in 1928 in the recording of famed vocalist Vicente Celestino, who registered it as a (Brazilian) *tango*. Several other recordings followed, increasing public familiarity with the tune over the decades. When referring to this composition as a *modinha*, Amado may have been employing the term in a generic sense of romantic song, or thinking of a particular style of interpretation. Further direct association of fiction and reality in this scene is made with the naming of Vadinho's partner in song as a young talent, Dorival Caymmi (b. 1914). This is the revered songsmith and senior statesman of popular music in Bahia known for his compositions based on such varied aspects of local culture as fishermen, tropical cuisine, *baianas* [local food vendors in typical dress], traditional round samba, Afro-Bahian cults, and serenade.

The relationship between the two acclaimed artists of Salvador and environs, novelist Amado and singer-songwriter Caymmi, constitutes not only an interesting, and necessary, aspect of the theme of music in the former's fiction, but a window onto the nature and interpretation of local cultural relations as well. Both have long recognized the virtually familial links of their

works, Amado noting that when he first heard Caymmi sing he was reminded
of his own literary creation, Antônio Balduíno in *Jubiabá* ("Moço," 9–10).
For his part, Caymmi notes having explained as early as 1940, in *Anuário
brasileiro de literatura,* the kinship of their respective works (5th ed. *Cancioneiro,* 138). Beginning in the 1930s, when both were novices in Rio, their
relationship has never lacked in continuity. They have worked together on
theatre pieces, cinematic adaptations, and publications, notably Amado's
prefaces to his friend's songbooks and sound-recording compilations. Before
*Dona Flor,* the composer and his well known song of internal migration (re-
popularized by Bahian vocalist Gal Costa) appeared in a chapter heading of
*Os velhos marinheiros [Home is the Sailor]*: "Do ita navegando ao sol, capí-
tulo quase folclórico a ler-se com o acompanhamento musical de 'Peguei um
Ita no Norte' de Dorival Caymmi'" [Of the little boat navigating in the sun-
shine, an almost folkloric chapter to be read with the musical accompaniment
of 'Peguei um Ita no Norte' by Dorival Caymmi] (235), whose lyric is cited in
the story. There are numerous concrete connections between Amado's fiction
and Caymmi's music. The latter has written several compositions based on
the former's works, and the writer has written some half dozen lyrics for the
composer's related tunes. Among these songs are "É doce morrer no mar"
(from *Mar morto [Sea of Death]*), "Cantiga de cego" and "Retirantes" (from
*Terras do sem-fim [The Violent Land]*), "Modinha de Gabriela" (sound track
for the television soap-opera version, also popularized by Costa), and the
song-epigraph "Modinha de Dorival Caymmi para Teresa Batista." The
epigraphs of the four sections of *Gabriela cravo e canela* are musico-poetic
crystallizations of narrative information, and the pair also collaborated on a
declamation with musical accompaniment of these lines.[13] With so many
such connections, it has been almost commonplace to state that the two are
ambassadors of Bahian culture, and that Amado is to literature what Caymmi
is to popular music. This may be true in terms of formative years, the national
and international projection of fundamental images and themes (characteristic peoples of Bahia, local cultural practices, etc.), perception of representativity, and popular reception of the artists. But there is room to question the
ultimate validity of such comparisons, as Risério has intelligently, and sympathetically, suggested.[14] In any case, it is clear that allusions to, and alliance
with, such a revered figure as Caymmi, helps the author establish familiarity
and appeal to a broad readership.

Amado's most extensive representation of Afro-Bahian expressions is
*Tenda dos milagres [Tent of Miracles]*. From the perspective of Tinhorão, this
work is "o melhor elogio já feito à instituição cultural do povo brasileiro, em
oposição ao alienado e academizante saber oficial das elites" [the best praise
ever paid to the cultural institution of the Brazilian people, in opposition to
the alienated and academicized official knowledge of the elites]" (Vol. 2,
422). Utilizing much historical documentation, Amado here captures the

struggles of early twentieth-century Afro-Bahian religious and secular, largely carnival, groups against rejection by official society and police repression. Where music is concerned, there is even a reference, in the context of a seasonal dramatic dance, to *lundu*, the African-derived dance that had given rise to one of the first forms of national popular music in the eighteenth century. In terms of number of quotations, the dominant form in *Tenda dos milagres* is the traditional *cantiga de capoeira*, but a more emotionally powerful account is the depiction of *afoxé*, the African-embassy procession with links to the cult houses of *candomblé*. This type of ensemble, with its adoption and promotion of African heritage, frightened authorities and was a particularly important manifestation of carnival in Salvador in the early decades of the century. It is, however, with the contemporary phenomenon of samba schools (which emerged in Salvador in imitation of Rio), that, foreshadowing Amado's own enshrinement, final homage is paid to the hero, who is adopted as an annual theme:

> No carnaval de 1969, a Escola de Samba Filhos do Tororó levou às ruas o enredo "Pedro Arcanjo em Quatro Tempos," obteve grande sucesso e alguns prêmios. Ao som do samba-enredo de Valdir Lima, vitorioso sobre cinco ótimos concorrentes da ala dos compositores, a Escola desfilou pela cidade a cantar:
>> "Escritor emocionante
>> Realista sensacional
>> Deslumbrou o mundo
>> Oh! Pedro Arcanjo genial
>> Sua vida em quatro tempos
>> Apresentamos neste carnaval." (371)

> ["In the Carnival of 1969, the Sons of Tororó took to the streets with a theme of "Pedro Archanjo in Four Movements" which was highly successful and won several prizes. The samba school paraded through the city singing the theme song by Waldir Lima, who won the composer's award by defeating five strong competitors: 'Thrilling author / Sensational realist / He dazzled the world / Oh! Pedro Archanjo the genius / Whose life in four movements / We'll show you in this carnival"]. (371)[15]

The hero of the *Tenda dos milagres*, ingenious writer and agitator for the education and appreciation of the Afro-Bahian population, had been recognized in earlier episodes in *folhetos* (chapbooks) and sung verse. One of the cited tributes was the work of "o jovem Caetano Gil, desatento às regras estabelecidas, bravo e rebelde trovador, tirando verso e música na viola, sambas e modinhas que cantavam o amor, a vida e a esperança" (168) [a brave rebel of a balladeer ... paid little attention to established rules but drew verses and music out of his guitar itself, sambas and modinhas that sang of love, life, and hope, trans. 158]." The effectiveness of this characterization is enhanced to the degree that it recalls, in terms of stance and mode, the celebrated local poet of satire of colonial times, Gregório de Matos, the "Bôca do Inferno" or "Mouth from Hell," as well as two leading figures of pointedly rule-breaking youth culture, Caetano Veloso and Gilberto Gil, on whose names, clearly, Amado based the name of his minor character. The author again utilizes these two icons of *MPB* (*Música Popular Brasileira*, hybrid post–Bossa Nova popular music) in *O sumiço da santa* [*The War of the Saints*], where dozens of real-life personages are mixed freely into an "updated" narrative of celebration of local events and culture. In the appearance, on Gregório de Matos street, of "os *afoxés* e os blocos afros . . . cada qual com sua música poderosa e sua negritude radical, produto da mestiçagem brasileira, inconfundível (368) [. . . the *afoxés* and Afro groups . . . each with its own powerful music and its radical negritude, the product of Brazilian miscegenation, unmistakable]," (368) there is a quotation of "Filhos de Gandhi," an epoch-marking song of Gilberto Gil's. [16]

As for Veloso and what he represents, the opening salvo of a landmark lyric of his is cited in the novel in the actions of a maritime congregation, which appears in the midst of profane and religious songs, carnival sambas, church hymns, and protest songs, several said to have been banned by the military regime. While the song cited, "Alegria Alegria" (1967), was not in fact censored, it was indeed contestatory and a vehicle of non-conformism, and it did mark, in the context of military dictatorship, the beginnings of a "Bahian explosion" in MPB (see Perrone, *Masters*). Finally, in a moment of light quasi-magic realism, Amado represents the movement of two African-Brazilian deities toward African destinations, as they are singing a well-known *frevo* by Caetano. What is pertinent here is not the musical form invoked, for the cited song, "Atrás do Trio Elétrico," celebrates, with essentially no connection to African-derived music or religion, the magnetism of the electrified march music of carnival ensembles in Salvador playing atop moving trucks. The link is textual, as a part of the lyric embodies the scene's suggestion of the two sides of the Atlantic and origins: *"Quem já botou pra rachar/ aprendeu/ que é do outro lado/ do lado/ que é do lado/ que é lá/ do lado de lá . . . "* (389) [If you've split it in two, / you've learned / that it comes from the other side / of the side / that's beyond the side / that's beyond / the side that's beyond . . . trans. p. 309]." Thus, re-direction of the successful pop song becomes an additional point of reference to affirm, as Amado repeatedly has, the dominant Afro-Bahian cultural world.

In numerous cases, Amado honors singer-songwriters of local origin who are established nationally and internationally when he avails himself of recognized lyrics. These echoes of popular music, whether poeticized or prosaic, lead into a not infrequent area of discussion surrounding Amado's literary work, especially the later output, involving the relative complexity of his fiction, the level of analytical depth, problematizations of local culture, and commercial appeal of the author's work. Whatever literary judgement is adduced, and all suggestions of potential for stereotyping aside, there is no questioning Amado's respect for popular music, his assignment of importance to it in the domain of Brazilian expressive culture, and the evidence of the diverse musicality of Brazilian people in the fiction. As for Amado's at-large reception, he stands as an icon of contemporary culture of Bahia, and has achieved, in effect, in the popular culture of Brazil at large, canonization, or apotheosis—the apex, a crowning moment of glory and recognition—as a motif of samba would have it. No less is indicated in his selection as the theme of a leading samba school in Rio de Janeiro in the late 1980s. Their lyric alludes to representative characters and works that have been treated here, and many more manifestations that would be considered in a global appreciation of the symbolic and functional uses of music in the fiction of the author honored.

> Sob os olhos graciosos de Oxalá
> Desce a Serrinha
> Esquenta o País do Carnaval
> É muita pimenta, dendê e cacau
> Você sabe que tem festa, meu amor
> Lá na Tenda dos Milagres
> Vem que eu vou, eu vou
> Jubiabá tá no portão
> E as Iaôs jogam pitangas pelo chão
> Com os pastores da noite
> Vem gente lá das Terras do Sem-Fim
> Oriundo lá das matas de Oxossi e Ossain
> O famoso Valentim
> E ao som dos atabaques
> Rola o suor dos Ogans
> Olha que papo maneiro
> Entre os velhos marinheiros
> E os novos capitães
> Vem gente que sofreu demais
> Lá do sertão e da beira do cais
> É doce morrer no mar
> Nos braços de Iemanjá
> Teresa Batista cansada de guerra
> No samba de roda esquece as mágoas
> Tiêta se beber faz graça
> Quincas Berro D'água agitando a massa
> Põe tempero na panela Gabriela
> Mexe, mexe com amor, cozinha com o teucalor
> Bota logo o vatapá na tigela

Quem mandou foi Dona Flor
É gente que chega e tem gente para chegar
Ekchêupa ba ba ê ekchêupa ba ba
Axé Brasil, pai Amado saravá, saravá.[17]

[Under the graceful eyes of Oshala / Serrinha school comes down / heats up the Land of Carnival / It's a lot of pepper, palm oil and cocoa / You know there's a party my love / In the Tent of Miracles / Come on, I'm heading off / Jubiaba is at the gate / and the priests toss cherries on the ground / With the Shepherds of the Night / People come from the Violent Land / Hailing from the forests of Oshossi and Ossain / The famous Valentim / And to the sound of drums / the sweat of Ogans drips / Hey cool talking / between the Old Mariners / and the new captains / People who suffered a lot are coming / From the backlands and the docks / It's sweet to die at sea / In the arms of Yemaya / Teresa Batista home from the wars / Forgets her troubles in round sambas / Tieta is funny if she drinks / Quincas Wateryell shaking up the crowd / season the pans Gabriela / Stir with love, cook with your heat / Put the stew in the pot now / Dona Flor said so / People coming and people to come / Ekcheupa ba ba e ekcheupa ba ba / Peace, father Amado, greetings].

## NOTES

1. The author would like to recognize the assistance of Barbora Domcekova in the research for this paper, as well as the insightful encouragement of Dain Borges. [Unattributed translations are my own].
2. (Coutinho,167). [A legitimate presupposition, that these manifestations of the soul of the people serve as a base for literature, at the same time that they are a vehicle for refining Brazilian character through the specific specialization they promote].
3. (Adonias Filho 198). [In all of the Bahian novels of Jorge Amado what is continued is a song book (cycle, repertory). Circulating in narrative orality, then in "ABC" folk verse, finally to become learned fiction, song repertories would be preserved in folk roots through literary constants].
4. Xavier. [The anthropology of Jorge Amado is not that of compendiums for the universities]. With respect to the utility and "learning capacity" of the fiction, see DaMatta, " A obra literária como etnografía . . . ," as well as the bibliographical curiosity of Manzatto.
5. Letter. [Song in my narrative is like a musical background to underline the work, the joy, the misfortunes, the struggles and the love of the people].
6. On varied uses of song texts and other forms of non-literary poetry, see Baden, who considers musical and non-musical examples together. On uses of folk song repertories by Amado and others of his generation, see Perrone, "Cancioneiro." For discussions of Afro-Bahian phenomena, including music, see Hamilton and Nunes.

7. Here operates the basic distinction between folk (mostly rural, "uneducated," anonymous, traditional, variant, orally transmitted) and popular (urban, literate or semi-educated, composed, transmitted by mechanical means [sheet music, recordings, radio], mass-mediated), a distinction that is less clear in the cases of migrant populations and transitional forms in the early decades of the twentieth century, as will be seen in a few examples.

8. (62). [I have only felt Brazilian two times. Once, at carnival, when I danced samba in the street. Another, when I beat up Julie, after she betrayed me].

9. On this figure in Brazilian popular music, see Matos and Oliven. For a study of this and other figures in a representative urban novel of the period, see Perrone "A música popular num romance brasileiro de trinta."

10. Trans. Margaret A. Neves, *Jubiabá* (New York: Avon, 1984), pp. 71–72.

11. Letter from Amado to Baden, 21. The "ABC" genre referred to in the next sentence is the traditional narrative form (whether sung, spoken or written) in which each strophe begins with the next letter of the alphabet. Gilberto Gil (1988) wrote and recorded the title composition of the sound track of the film version of the novel.

12. (Vol. 2, 422, 423). For his part, DaMatta declares that there is in *Dona Flor* "uma relação profunda entre vingança, hierarquia e carnaval" (a profound relationship between revenge, hierarchy, and carnival) ("A obra literária," 47). That relation had been developed in *A Casa & a Rua* (81–112), where he studies *Dona Flor* a "relational" novel.

13. Mazzara illustrates elaborates on the verses of the epigraphs and their connections with the narrative text proper. However, he underplays almost to the point of exclusion the musical substance of the epigraphs. As *rondó* (rondeau) or *cantiga* (song), they are explicitly musical or have, one might say, implicit musical auras. The former type has historical musical origins and maintains intimate association, as does the medieval *cantiga de amigo* (lover's lament). The third epigraph is, in turn, a *cantiga de ninar* (cradle song).

14. On the processes of realization of Afro-Brazilian culture in which both Caymmi and Amado figure, see Risério 21–58. On differences between the two (e.g. synthetic vs. effusive, pragmatic vs. engagé, "masculine" vs. neo-romantic), see 51–52, 86.

15. trans. Barbara Shelby, *Tent of Miracles*. New York: Alfred A. Knopf (1971), pp. 370–371.

16. trans. Gregory Rabassa. *The War of the Saints*. New York: Bantam (1993), p. 294. See discography for recorded versions of the cited song. The title refers to a carnival ensemble whose resurgence was aided by the release (1975) of a recording by pop star Gil, who reprised it (1986) after the phenomenal rise of *afoxé* in the eighties. On the emergence of such neo-Afro Bahian carnival formations, see Crook and, with reference to song, Perrone, *"Axé, Ijexá, Olodum ..."*

17. "Jorge Amado–Axé, Brasil" (Beto s/ Braço-Aluísio Machado-Bicalho-Arlindo Cruz) G.R.E.S. Império Serrano.

## BIBLIOGRAPHY

Amado, Jorge. Letter to the author. April 30, 1979.

————. "O moço Caymmi e a Bahia." Preface to Caymmi, 4th ed.

————. "Obá Onikoyi." Preface to Caymmi, 5th enlarged ed.

————. *O país do carnaval. Cacau. Suor.* São Paulo: Martins, 1959 [1931, 1933, 1934].

————. *Jubiabá.* São Paulo: Martins, 1968 [1935].

————. *Os subterrâneos da liberdade: A luz no túnel.* São Paulo: Martins, 1977, [1954].

————. *Os velhos marinheiros.* São Paulo: Martins, 1961.

————. *Dona Flor e seus dois maridos.* São Paulo: Martins, 1966.

————. *Tenda dos milagres.* São Paulo: Martins, 1969.

————. *O sumiço da santa.* Rio de Janeiro: Record, 1988.

Baden, Nancy. "Popular Poetry in the Novels of Jorge Amado." *Journal of Latin American Lore* 2:1 (1976), 3–22.

Bastide, Roger. "Sobre o romancista Jorge Amado." In *Jorge Amado povo e terra 40 anos de literatura.* São Paulo: Martins, 1972. 39–70.

Beltrão Jr., Synval. *A musa-mulher na canção brasileira.* São Paulo: Estação Liberdade, 1993.

Caymmi, Dorival. 4th ed. *Cancioneiro da Bahia.* São Paulo: Martins, n/d [c. 1967].

————. 5th enlarged ed. *Cancioneiro da Bahia.* Rio de Janeiro: Record, 1978.

Coutinho, Afrânio. *A tradição afortunada.* Rio de Janeiro: José Olympio-Instituto Nacional do Livro, 1968.

Crook, Larry N. "Black Consciousness, samba reggae, and the Re-Africanization of Bahian Carnival Music in Brazil." *The World of Music* 35 : 2 (1993), 90–108.

DaMatta, Roberto. *Carnavais, malandros e heróis: Para uma sociologia do dilema brasileiro.* Rio de Janeiro: Zahar Editores, 1979. Trans. *Carnivals Rogues and Heroes: An Interpretation of the Brazilian Dilemma* (Notre Dame: Notre Dame University Press, 1991).

————. *A casa & a rua: Espaço, cidadania, mulher e morte no Brasil.* São Paulo: Brasiliense, 1985.

————. "A obra literária como etnografia: reflexões sobre as relações entre literatura e sociedade." In Roberto Reis, ed. *Towards Socio-Criticism.* Tempe, AZ: ASU Center for Latin American Studies, 1991. 33–54.

*Enciclopédia da música brasileira: Erudita folclórica popular.* São Paulo: Art Editora, 1977.

Filho, Adonias. "Jorge Amado." In *Jorge Amado povo e terra 40 anos de literatura.* São Paulo: Martins, 1972. 195–202.

Hamilton, Russell G. "Afro-Brazilian Cults in the Novels of Jorge Amado." *Hispania* 50 (1967), 242–252.

Manzatto, Antônio. *Teologia e literatura: reflexão teológica a partir da antropologia nos romances de Jorge Amado.* São Paulo: Loyola, 1994.

Matos, Claudia. *Acertei no milhar: Samba e malandragem no tempo de Getúlio.* Rio de Janeiro: Paz e Terra, 1982.

Mazzara, Richard A. "Poetry and Progress in Jorge Amado's 'Gabriela, Cravo e Canela.'" *Hispania* 46: 3 (1963), 551–556.

Nunes, Maria Luisa. "The Preservation of African Culture in Brazilian Literature: The Novels of Jorge Amado." *Luso-Brazilian Review* 10: 1 (1973), 86–101.

Oliven, Ruben George. " A Malandragem na Música Popular Brasileira." *Latin American Music Review* 5 : 2 (1984), 66–96.

Paes, José Paulo. *De cacau a Gabriela: Um percurso pastoral.* Salvador: Fundação Casa de Jorge Amado, 1991.

Perrone, Charles A. "O cancioneiro popular no romance brasileiro de trinta." *Cultura* 33 (Nov.-Dec. 1979), 40–47.

———. "A música popular num romance brasileiro de trinta: das *Memórias de um sargento de milícias a Marafa.*" *Latin American Music Review* 3: 1 (1982), 73–90.

———. "*Axé, Ijexá, Olodum:* The Rise of Afro- and African Currents in Brazilian Popular Music." *Afro-Hispanic Review* 11: 1–3 (1992), 42–50.

———. *Masters of Contemporary Brazilian Song: MPB 1965–1985.* Austin: University of Texas Press, 1989.

Risério, Antônio. *Caymmi: Uma utopia de lugar.* São Paulo: Perspectiva, 1993.

Tinhorão, José Ramos. *A música popular no romance brasileiro.* Vol. 1. Belo Horizonte: Oficina de Livros. 1992.

———. *A música popular no romance brasileiro.* Vol 2. Belo Horizonte. Oficina de Livros. In press.

Xavier, Raul. "A ficção de Jorge Amado." *Jornal de Letras* #207 (July 1967), p. 4.

## DISCOGRAPHY

Antonio Carlos and Jocafi. *Sing the Music of Jorge Amado.* BMG Milan Latino 35825–2, 1977.

Caymmi, Dorival et al. Fascicule of *História da música popular brasileira.* São Paulo: Abril Cultural, 1970; 2nd. ed. *Nova história da música popular brasileira,* 1976; 3rd ed. *História da música popular brasileira: Grandes compositores,* 1982.

_____ and Jorge Amado. *Canto de amor à Bahia.* Festa Discos, 1958.

Costa, Gal. *Gal Canta Caymmi.* Philips 6349 174, 1976.

Gil, Gilberto. *Gil e Jorge.* Philips 6641–275. 1975.

Gil, Gilberto. *Em concerto.* Geléia Geral 670.9001. 1987.

———. *Soy loco por ti América.* Braziloid BR 4000. 1988.

Various (Costa, Gil, Veloso, et al.). Preface by Jorge Amado. *Bahia de todos os cantos.* 4 Vol. Philips 6328 539–42. 1983.

Various. Escolas de Samba do Grupo 1 A. *Sambas de enredo carnaval 1989.* RCA 122.0002-C. 1988.

Veloso, Caetano. *Caetano Veloso.* Philips 6328 497. 1967.

# Questioning Jorge Amado's Fictional Women-of-Color

## Tereza Batista as Legend or Heroine?

SUSAN CANTY QUINLAN

> *[Feminism] proposes "the individuality of each human soul.... In discussing the rights of woman, we are to consider first, what belongs to her as an individual, in a world of her own, the arbiter of her own destiny ..." This is simply a recognition of the human condition, in which women are included. It is also the precondition for the realization of Marx's greatest ethical idea: "from each according to her need."*
>
> —ANDREA DWORKIN AND ELIZABETH CADY STANTON[1]

> *Representation of the world, like the world itself, is the work of men; they describe from their own point of view, which they confuse with absolute truth."*
>
> —SIMONE DE BEAUVOIR[2]

> *Honey, de white man is de ruler of everything as fur as Ah been able tuh find out. Maybe it's some place way off in de ocean where de black man is in power, but we don't know nothin' but what we see. So de white man throw down the load and tell the nigger man tuh pick it up. He hand it to his womenfolks. De nigger woman is de mule uh de world so fur as Ah can see."*
>
> —ZORA NEALE HURSTON[3]

Opening with the above quotations may seem odd in light of an analysis about a novel by Brazilian author, Jorge Amado, *Tereza Batista, cansada de guerra* [*Tereza Batista: Home from the Wars*] (1972).[4] But it is imperative to reconsider how the representation of women function in his work. The importance of the statements by Andrea Dworkin and Simone de Beauvoir that "this is simply a recognition of the human condition, in which women are included" and "representation of the world . . . is the work of men; . . . which they confuse with absolute truth," probably need little explication as to whether or not Amado's work will establish this precondition. Amado writes from his own point of view, and this is surely the only point of view and the only kind of writing that can be expected from him. Nevertheless, the question, for me, then becomes: does Jorge Amado confuse his own point of view with absolute truth and, if in fact this is the case, in doing so, does he fail to recognize "the human condition," where women are included?

This is not simply a revisionist reading of a male author by a female critic, but rather an attempt to answer the question put forth by Georgio Marotti: "What did it mean to be a woman in a world like that of Brazilian agrarian civilization which had existed for so long on slavery?" (*Black Characters* 341) and to implicitly comment on the words of Elizabeth Cady Stanton as to whether or not women are the arbiters of their own destiny. This study will look at some of the post-1958 stereotypes constant in Amado's work, and more specifically, at the title character in his novel, *Tereza Batista: cansada de guerra,* as a heroine, as a woman-of-color and her relationship to the world around her. Important steps in revealing the intentional formulaic setting of this novel and Amado's quest to write literature for a mass market audience have been raised by Brazilian critics, Walnice Galvão and Silviano Santiago, but neither critic focused primarily on women.

## THE VICTIMIZATION OF TEREZA BATISTA

In order to understand how the character, Tereza Batista, cannot possibly serve as a symbol of either resistance, hope or individuality, we must examine how the telling of her story occurs. *Tereza Batista, cansada de guerra* is the story of a poor but beautiful woman from the Brazilian Northeast who is literally sold into prostitution by her aunt before the age of thirteen. Purchased by a rich, but ignorant, *sertanejo, capitão* Justiniano Duarte da Rosa, she quickly is reduced to the role of a physically and verbally abused sexual slave. Tereza later falls in love with the weak son of a wealthy landowner who promises her much, but in the end fails to rescue her. Having discovered her own sexual pleasure, she manages to kill Justiniano, goes to prison and is again rescued, this time by a wealthy owner of a sugar cane factory, Emiliano Guedes. Even though Guedes, who keeps her as his mistress for six years and dies in the process of making love to her, is apparently more benevolent that the previous lovers, he nevertheless acts exactly like *um dono da casa grande*, a master. Guedes permits Tereza no personal autonomy, no money and no choice. Upon his death, Tereza realizes that Guedes has left her nothing in his will, and his family forces her off the property with nothing.

Tereza then find herself balancing good deeds with earning money as a prostitute or as a dance-hall girl until she is once again rescued by the poor, black sailor, Januário Gereba. Although Amado takes great pains to describe the horror and ruthlessness of the actions of the slave owner and to describe some of Tereza's methods of self preservation, and in as much as he contrasts the loving ministrations by the wealthy landowner and Januário's grief at not being able to rescue her initially, Tereza remains little more than an objectified victim of circumstances whose only action appears to be that of being rescued when her hopes are dissolved by reality. In a seminal study of female characters in the works of Jorge Amado, Ann Pescatello makes these comments about Amado's characters: "This schizophrenia, this dichotomy between *realidade* and *fantasia* is a major concern to me as an observer of historical change and continuity in ... Brazil. How does one separate the image of the mind and heart from the reality of flesh and blood (30)?"

Amado devotes almost too much attention at the beginning of the book to the minute detailing of pornographic and horrific sexual occurrences. The following examples center on Tereza, but I could have just as easily included several of his many sexual descriptions of older women, white women, spinsters, married women, rich or poor. There is a problem with these passages in that both physical and sexual violence miss the mark of censure and become titillating.

> O capitão Justo era tenaz ... Tereza haveria de aprender o medo e o respeito, a santa obediência.... Apanhara sem pedir piedade, ... A menina estava atada de cordas, deitada de barriga para cima. Justiano ... sentou-se no colchão ... Aplicou o ferro de engomar primeiro num pé, depois no outro. O cheiro de carne queimada, o chiado da pele, os uivos, e o silêncio de morte. Tereza por fim obediente. Chupa, ela chupou. Depressa, de quatro e de costas. Depressa se pôs. (118–119)

> [The Captain was obstinate ... Tereza would have to learn fear, respect and holy obedience. . .She had endured the beatings and never begged for mercy; ... the girl was laid belly up on the mattress, bound as she was with cords. Justiano ... sat down ... and applied the iron first to one sole then to the other. There was a smell of burnt flesh, a sizzling of skin, unearthly screams, and then deadly silence ... Tereza had learned obedience at last. Suck! and she sucked. Hurry up and get down on all fours! and she quickly got down on hands and knees.] (141–42)

Lest it be overlooked, Amado is describing the treatment of a not yet thirteen-year-old female victim being physically and sexually abused. The accompanying violence continues throughout the novel even after Tereza finds her soul-mate, her true love, Januário Gereba. Tereza's sexual encounters are marked throughout by violence:

> Nas areias finais, ela se acolhe ao peito do homem para quem nasceu e tarde encontrou: posse com gosto amargo de separação, violenta e irada ela o morde e arranha, ele a aperta contra o peito como se quisesse entranhar-se em sua pele. Nas areias finais da noite de amor, os soluços estrangulados, é proíbido chorar: veio uma onda e os cobriu, veio o mar e o levou. (58)

[On the farthest beach she nestled close to the chest of the man she had been born for but had found too late. Violently, she let him take her; with the bitter taste of separation in her mouth, she bit and scratched him, while he clasped her to his breast as if longing to burrow inside her very skin. On the last beach, on their last night of love, she strangled her sobs. No, she mustn't cry. A wave came and covered them, the sea came and took him]. (68)

The passages indicate a prurient interest and lead me to wonder for whom these fantasies were written? The rape scenes, as well as the apparent love scenes, are so lovingly detailed that they abruptly lose their ability to shock on the one hand, or to be believed on the other. This leaves the readers in a quandary. Do we immediately accept rape as part of the picturesque reality? Does even true, romantic love mitigate violence and separation? To whom do we attribute the lack of an ethical position? Ann Pescatello responds in part observing in a quite chilling way that for Brazilians:

> Moral paraphernalia . . . is quite evident . . . Moral behavior is talked about obviously by the men. . . . It is also guarded by sour spinsters, by harridan mothers, by daughters who resign themselves to a life of apathy and abnegation as wives of "proper" husbands. Men formulate these requirements of women while women see that these requirements are kept—not because they might actually want that to be the case but primarily because they have resigned themselves to their role.
>
> And it is all part of the perceptions of these women—of themselves and their role and responsibilities in life; of their relationships with fathers, husbands, sons, and brothers . . . Most of these women are not in control of their lives; neither do they appear able to dominate the home and the man in actuality. (56)

Sociologist Roberto DaMatta refers to these portrayals as a manifestation of what he calls Jorge Amado's "triadic structure;" where the grotesque blends with the romantic in an attempt to synthesize meaning and reconcile Brazilian reality in a positive manner in order to reflect its hybrid character ("Romance relacional" 3–33). It is not surprising to find readers who want to emulate Justo, Tereza, or her true love, Januário, unless it occurs to them that throughout most of the five hundred page book, Tereza remains unfulfilled, Justiano is killed, and Januário cheats on his dying wife. Discovering the positive messages or meanings here is quite difficult.

## CREATOR OF LEGENDS OR PERPETRATOR OF MYTHS?

In the past forty years, Jorge Amado has done much for stimulating debate about Afro-Brazilian, Bahian culture and literature both inside and outside of Brazil. However, Bobby Chamberlain provides a word of caution to scholarly critics of Amado when he observes:

Amado has increasingly become the target of criticism of younger Brazilian and non-Brazilian scholars. The principal allegations involve such things as populism and the consequent romanticization of poverty, sexual and racial stereotyping, inordinate prolixity and the repetition of episodes and characters, pandering to the values of the marketplace, and failure to break away from timeworn nineteenth-century models. Far from superseding earlier criticisms, such accusations have often been coupled with renewed charges of pornography and Manichean characterization. (100)

Although we cannot include all of Amado's works as examples, caution is ceratinly called for, as the question of pornography and stereotypical representation of women-of-color is of paramount concern in *Tereza Batista, cansada de guerra.*

While there are numerous examples of Amado's varied cultural legacies, none seems more popular or more problematic than his image of the sensual *mulata*, a representation that, for Amado, constitutes the blending of cultures, races and religions in contemporary Brazil and that reinforces the popular theory of *tropicalismo* as explained by Brazilian sociologist, Gilberto Freyre; miscegenation produced the national myth of Brazilian racial harmony. For while some critics attribute Amado with preserving African culture in Brazil (Nunes 101), others view him merely as a populist interested in exploiting social stereotypes (Bosi 457). David Brookshaw notes the following problems with Amado's work in general:

[His] novels may therefore be important vehicles for the preservation of African culture in Brazil, but they also preserve and reinforce white myths regarding the Afro-Brazilian as an individual, and it is this factor . . . [that] illustrates the incongruities of an apparently well-intentioned white writer. (155)

The preservation of white stereotypes about black realities are of paramount importance, because not to acknowledge difference erases individuality.

As part of his prolific cultural legacy, it could be said that Amado has produced a replacement for Hollywood's version of the 1940s and 1950s representative of the exotic, but harmless, *brasileira* popularized through film in Europe and the United States as an alternative image to war footage. Carmen Miranda, with her platform shoes, fruited hat and samba rhythm was superseded by the different, but no-less exotic, image of the sensual and promiscuous *mulata* in the heroines of such books as *Gabriela, cravo e canela* [*Gabriela, Clove and Cinnamon*] (1958), *Dona Flor e seus dois maridos* [*Dona Flor and Her Two Husbands*] (1966) or *Tereza Batista, cansada de guerra.* Amado's novels further the production and dissemination of these female images, so that at least two of them become visual icons in the film versions of these works. The characterizations of Dona Flor and Gabriela, portrayed by the Brazilian *morena* [mulatta] actress, Sônia Braga, have become, for many Europeans and North Americans, the prototype of exotic, Brazilian beauty, both sensuous and erotic. Extending the image, Braga's own career is characterized by many television and film roles where she depicts "the other": a Neo-Mexican woman, a black Puerto Rican, a member of a Central American ruling elite or a German chanteuse, or most recently, Navajo Chaman.[5] (It is interesting to note in passing that Xuxa, one of the few white women to attempt a career in film and/or television outside Brazil met with considerable disfavor and disastrous ratings in the United States). Owing much to Jorge Amado, Brazil, in the eyes of many readers and film audiences, equals lasciviousness, sensuality, and wantonness; in short, unbridled passions.[6]

It is this "verbi-visual" iconization, reflecting an ostensible fascination with the image of the *mulata brasileira*, that attracts so many non-Brazilian readers to the later works of Jorge Amado. But this relationship to the exotic is tinged with the concept of otherness that strengthens conflicts of prejudice, including racial, religious, class and sexual differences.[7]

It is difficult to accept any suggestion of progress, tolerance or even liberal idealism because his images of women, women-of-color, and women struggling in class societies are so unbelievable and lost in the rhetoric of romantic idealism, on the one hand, and so flagrantly demeaning on the other, that they lose any meaningful ability to inform critics about difference. Amado's women are cardboard stereotypes who verge on the obscene and who could hardly have a basis in reality, in Brazil or elsewhere. Amado's heroines are almost always victims of whichever circumstances, usually of a sexual nature, they encounter. Their own self-recognition and the recognition they receive by others regarding their human condition and their human rights are seldom recognized by the author. If we are to seriously consider them as fully human and representative of Brazilian reality, shouldn't the characters portray the individuality so aptly described by Andrea Dworkin and Elizabeth Cady Stanton?

We could begin to theorize the reasons why the consistent victimization of these characters results in these paper images of super-real beings, like Amado's heroines Gabriela, Flor and Tereza, or we can look through the lens of popular culture to see if I can come to terms with Amado's achievements wrought by familiarizing thousands of readers with even a rudimentary knowledge of the Brazilian Northeast and its inherent multitude of social inequities, class distinctions and overt racism. For, in truth, stereotypes are crafted from reality. But the question still remains: are these women representative?

For example, if I were to apply current feminist literary theory, we might be lead farther and farther afield from any but the most token acceptance of Amado's portrayal of race, class and gender as an assuagement of a form of "leftist, liberal, elitist tokenism" (Chamberlain 101) where women function extraordinarily well as contrivances in order to prove Amado's theses. In and of itself, feminist literary criticism reaches an impasse when it creates binary oppositions such as victim/perpetrator: for accepted signifiers (good on the top, evil on the bottom) do not work, in this instance, if we believe that self-hood is important. We know that all women are not victims and do not experience victimization in the same way, just as we know that some women victimize men or other women. If all women were victims, there would be little room for individuality. It is just as easy to see that not all men are perpetrators, just as many men are also victims.

The significant social role of Amado's literary production in the rising consciousness of racial and class discrepancies within Brazilian society before the publication of *Gabriela, cravo e canela* is not being contested. However, we ought to be willing to debate what many critics (Galvão, Santiago, Brookshaw, Chamberlain, Patai, Bosi, to name a few) consider as Amado's entry into the capitalist venture of the mass-production of popular best sellers, even though the critical assessments range from loving portrayals to outright disgust. A better venue might be to look at what is missing given the popularity and interest Amado's women-of-color achieve as main characters within (or in spite of) their guise as victims. Again, Brookshaw draws attention to the problems inherent in the victimization of the poor, *mulata* woman in Amado when he notes that:

> She is not allowed to exist either as a wife or as a mother, for she is the symbol of sexual license. *She is respected neither as a woman nor as an individual* (emphasis mine) Her function is to attract men, to be exploited by them, and to exploit in return by obtaining her own ends through sex. Individual ambition arising from talents outside this realm are consistently destroyed or denigrated in the interests of the stereotype. (*Race and Color* 164–65)

If Tereza, Flor, and Gabriela are seen neither as women nor individuals, then what function do they serve either in the middle-class Brazilian's understanding of racial and class tensions, in the foreigner's new acquaintance with Brazilian reality, or with an increased global conceptualization of women in Brazil? Further, how do they function at all as individuals or as literary prototypes?

Identifying Amado's focus on individuality in her study of *Tereza Batista, cansada de guerra*, Daphne Patai suggests that:

> [Amado's] works are redolent of a nostalgia for a life in which individuals mattered, in which battles were fought between hero and villain in utter simplicity. The very solutions to the problems Amado focuses on, after all, depend upon the divine intervention of the people's traditional "allies": *candomblé* gods and goddesses, and popular heroes. Amado's nostalgia is reflected also in his choice of the *folheto* pattern, for in the world of today

this choice suggests a romantic conceit, distancing the reader from present
reality as entry is made into the modes and conventions appropriate to that
form. (140)

But Patai goes onto contradict this view and to paraphrase Nelson Werneck
Sodré and say that:

> [T]he *folheto* developed in response to particular conditions of production
> and distribution, and reached it peak in the nineteenth century when find-
> ing a public meant doing so via pamphlets and newspapers, not via
> books. The survival and popularity of the *folheto* today is intimately
> linked to the poverty and marginal literacy of the Brazilian masses as
> well as to the relatively recent interest of scholars in preserving this form
> of popular literature. (140)

If the answers to these questions indicate a lack of preoccupation with
social issues and a more intense concentration on romanticized fantasy, what
are the implications for the rest of Amado's social realism and the process of
acculturation in general? My intention in this study then is to approach possible answers to these questions by examining the effects of concentrating on a
central protagonist such as Tereza Batista to see ways in which her identity
benefits or stimulates cultural interest about Brazil.

The role of the Brazilian socialist writer, according to Nelson Werneck
Sodré, should be to destroy fantasies of false hope and express realities that
the future holds. Sodré notes that social artists retain individuality and reac-
tivity while producing for mass viewing or reading. Art should be built on the
liberation of the mind, dedicated to reflecting social conditions, as well as to
encouraging and bringing about change, to foster independence, not to bring
about dependency. Written art, in particular, he views as a form of consciousness; thus writing can contribute to the liberty of the mind and then lead to the
deeds (322).

Amado has been acknowledged to be politically committed to socialism
and communism and, in fact, politically active and even imprisoned on more
than one occasion during the *Estado Novo* (the de facto dictatorship of
Getúlio Vargas, 1937–1945). How then can such a writer in the early 1960s,
during the beginning of the military dictatorship, choose to exalt the status
quo of female victimization and women's lack of bodily rights in a certain
class segment of the Brazilian population? And why is this glorification of
victimization so attractive to the reading public? Does this writing foster
Sodré's notion of independence and eliminate ideas of dependency, and does
it move to create a liberation of the mind that could conceivably lead to the
equality of deed? Georgio Marotti offers an interesting, but flawed explanation when he states that:

Amado managed to avoid the facile trap the advent of the military dictator-ship in 1964 offered to such a writer, the most popular in Brazil. He saw with perfect intuition that the coup d'état carried out by the military was the most obvious aspect of an Establishment that had its roots in a new political world order, in the dealings of the multinationals and in certain structures of Brazilian society. The evil had to be fought at its source; sending the soldiers back to their barracks would be of no use if the Estab-lishment were able to continue its logic through other officials. . . .Tereza Batista who from a thousand adventures and a thousand misfortunes is born again eternally virgin and ready to love and live is perhaps a Brazilian symbol—from slavery to hope. Or perhaps the story is a fable of the char-acter of the woman in a slave-owning and male-chauvinist world who, on the long march of suffering and servitude, finally claims the right to choose and give herself freedom. (341)

It is hard to believe that the character of Tereza Batista ever achieves a right to choose, or that her freedom is possibly secured when she earns money. She only earns money by selling her body, either through prostitution or through semi-nude cabaret dancing. Marotti's logic would lead one to con-clude that Tereza is the hopeful symbol of slavery.

It is doubtful that works like *Tereza Batista, cansada de guerra* can pos-sibly be said to accomplish this most basic of socialist ideals: freedom. Amado does not describe Tereza in a way that presents a person capable of free choice and self knowledge.

## QUESTIONS OF SOURCES

Tereza's story is fleshed out from a variety of perspectives, mostly sympa-thetic, as many critics have pointed out. The tale is primarily crafted with ref-erence to a form of popular art and literature that appears in a *folheto* form, *literatura de cordel*. Cordel literature, in and of itself, preserves the stereotyp-ical qualities of the novel. It almost always makes use of a third person narra-tor; it is almost always limited to repeating a story but without developing psychological insights into motive or purpose. *Cordel* is a literature of the masses that is used primarily for entertainment. Bobby Chamberlain sees the appeal of Amado's use of *cordel* as a way to draw a protagonist as "legendary heroine rather than a 'realistic' or 'mimetic' character" (85). Chamberlain also points to the parodic nature of the work:

Tereza seems to experience few of the psychological contradictions that one would expect of a modern novelistic heroine. Nor does she undergo any major changes as a character. For the most part she is static, opaque, and rather unidimensional from one cover to the other, not unlike many of the epic heroines and heroes of popular legend the world over. (85)

The problem is again one of deciding which heroic qualities Tereza possesses and if these qualities are sufficient enough for her to be seen as an
exemplar of women-of-color and whether parody is an appropriate vehicle to
convey positive meaning to Tereza's life. I suspect that a more realistic version
would be to echo the words of David Brookshaw and question whether or not
Amado continues to perpetuate a white, male myth about women-of-color.

Patricia Hill Collins sees no heroic qualities in this vision of women-of-
color; rather she sees a culturally embedded process of objectfication as she
frankly comments in *Black Feminist Thought*:

> African-American women inhabit a sex/gender hierarchy in which inequal-
> ities of race and social class have been sexualized. Privileged groups define
> their alleged sexual practices as the mythical norm and label sexual prac-
> tices and groups who diverge from this norm as deviant and threatening.
> Maintaining the mythical norm of the financially independent, white mid-
> dle-class family organized around a monogamous heterosexual couple
> requires stigmatizing African- American families as being deviant, and a
> primary source of this assumed deviancy stems from allegations about
> Black sexuality. This sex/gender hierarchy not only operates on the social
> structural level but is potentially replicated within each individual. Differ-
> ences in sexuality thus take on more meaning than just benign sexual varia-
> tion. Each individual becomes a powerful conduit for social relations of
> domination whereby individual anxieties, fears, and doubts about sexuality
> can be annexed by larger systems of oppression. (165)

Collins points out that the social construction of Black women's sexuality is designed to "harness power as energy to the exigencies of power as race,
gender and social class domination" (166). She informs us that rape, pornography and selected breeding reinforce themes of "Black women's passivity,
objectification and malleability to male control" and "reveals pornography's
grounding in racism and sexism" (167).

Bobby Chamberlain approaches Tereza's construction in a different
manner when he points to the intentionally "hyperbolic tenor" of this form of
literature and when he says it makes "specific reference to an allegedly existing text outside the present fictional universe, thus providing a kind of
pseudo-documentation by pseudo-intertextuality of the protagonist's onto-
logical status" (87), and comments that "to the extent that it burlesques the
convention of *cordel* poetry, the style of *Tereza Batista* is a ludicrous exagger-
ation of something that is already itself ludicrously exaggerated" (91). However there is no clear indication that Amado is seriously considering anything
more than "capturing reality." [8]

Several problems quickly become apparent if we more seriously consider the entertainment value of a novel like *Tereza Batista cansada de
guerra*. The first is the social reality that marks this text as one of protest and
the second, the question of victimhood and humor. If the situations in which

Tereza is placed are merely "hyperbole" and a "burlesque" of form and/or content, then we know almost at once that Amado is not presenting us with a serious social commentary. And if he is not commenting on the social problems of women in Tereza's situation, are we to believe she deserves the life she lives? Or that this is the norm for poor women-of-color in Brazil?

In contrast to Chamberlain, Daphne Patai says that "[Amado] rather lovingly creat[es] new versions of [*cordel*] no matter how contradictory it may appear . . . without directing irony toward the literary form from which he borrows, but rather with marked nostalgia" (140). Again, if Amado is playing off a concept of *saudade,* a longing for preserving a paradigm that puts everyone in their places and keeps them there, he leaves little room for a social critique and does not create a sympathetic vision of the underprivileged. Nothing is loving about poverty or abuse. Surely, it is more tempting to be one of the elites than one of the underprivileged. I think it too facile an out to refer to Amado's *povismo* or love of the people as Daphne Patai has suggested, although I agree his characters become objects of consumption (140).

To a certain extent, the oppositional criticism raised in the study of this one novel relates to its popularity both in Brazil and abroad. These critics are correct in their views, but more interesting to me is the side-step around certain central issues, such as child prostitution or child pornography. Tereza Batista has no personal autonomy and never did. She cannot be a heroine, legendary or otherwise, for truly she saves no one nor escapes anything. She is not a heroine of a *Bildungsroman* for there is no evidence of any self knowledge of being a woman in Brazilian society. And more importantly, Tereza Batista offers no way to fight class prejudice, racism or sexism. She does survive, but is that life?

## NOTES

1. Andrea Dworkin, "The coming genocide" in *Right-Wing Women: The Politics of Domesticated Females.* London: The Women's Press, 1988. (90); quoting Elizabeth Cady Stanton, "The Solitude of Self," in Susan B. Anthony and Ida Husted Harper (eds.) *History of Woman Suffrage.* (New York: Source Book Press, 1970 Vol 4).

2. *The Second Sex.* (New York: Knopf, 1952) trans. and ed. H.M. Parshley.

3. *Their Eyes Were Watching God* (New York: Negro Universities Press, 1961, c1937).

4. *Tereza Batista, Home From the Wars.* New York: Avon, 1975. trans. Barbara Shelby. All English translations are taken from this edition.

5. It is interesting to note in passing that Xuxa, one of the few white women to attempt a career in film and/or television outside Brazil, met with considerable disfavor and disastrous ratings in the United States. For more information, see Amelia Simpson's work, *Xuxa, the Mega-marketing of Gender, Race and Modernity* (Philadelphia: Temple University Press, 1993).

6. One only need to consider John Updike's recent silly novel, *Brazil* (1994), to see how Amado's influence is continually corrupted.

7. As a student and teacher of Brazilian literature and culture, an intersting question arises for me as I consider Amado's successes. I want to be impartial and credit Amado's familiarity outside of Brazil as being productive, for example, in promoting interest and knowledge of Brazilian studies. The movie version of *Dona Flor e seus dois maridos*, as an example, is a a film that is continuously shown to Portuguese-language students and often serves as one of the first references to Brazil.

8. See Bobby Chamberlain and Daphne Patai for detailed structural considerations including the insertion of real people as characters, the *folheto* format of the story and the like.

## BIBLIOGRAPHY

Amado, Jorge. *Dona Flor e seus dois maridos: História moral e de amor*. São Paulo: Martins, 1966.

———. *Gabriela, cravo e canela: Crônica de uma cidade do interior*. São Paulo: Martins, 1958.

———. *Tereza Batista, cansada de guerra: Romance*. São Paulo: Martins, 1972.

———. *Tereza Batista: Home from the Wars*. Trans. Barbara Shelby. New York: Avon, 1975.

Bosi, Alfredo. *História concisa da literatura brasileira*. São Paulo: Cultrix, 1970.

Brookshaw, David. *Race and Color in Brazilian Literature*. Metuchen, NJ: Scarecrow Press, 1986.

Chamberlain, Bobby. *Jorge Amado*. Boston: Twayne, 1990.

Collins, Patricia Hill. *Black Feminist Thought: Knowledge, Consciousness and the Politics of Empowerment*. New York: Routledge, 1990.

DaMatta, Roberto. "Dona Flor e seus dois maridos: um romance relacional." *Tempo Brasileiro* 74: 3–33.

Galvão, Walnice Nogueira. "Amado, respeitoso, respeitável." *Saco de gatos*. São Paulo: Duas Cidades, 1976.

Marotti, Giorgio. *Black Characters in the Brazilian Novel*. Trans. Maria O. Marotti and Harry Lawton. Los Angeles: California, University Press, 1987.

Nunes, Maria Luisa. "The Preservation of African Culture in Brazilian Literature: The Novels of Jorge Amado." *Luso-Brazilian Review* 10 (1973) 86–101.

Patai, Daphne. *Myth and Ideology in Contemporary Brazilian Fiction*. Rutherford, NJ: Fairleigh Dickinson UP, 1983.

Pescatello, Ann. "The Brazileira: Images and Realities in Writings of Machado de Assis and Jorge Amado" in *Female and Male in Latin America: Essays*. Ed. A. Pescatello, 29–58. Pittsburgh: University of Pittsburgh Press, 1973.

Santiago, Silviano. "O teorema de Walnice e a sua recíproca" *Vale quanto pesa: ensaios sobre questões politico-culturais*. Rio de Janeiro: Paz e Terra, 1992.

Sodré, Nelson Werneck. *História da literatura brasileira: Seus fundamentos econômicos*. 5th ed. (Rio de Janeiro). Cultura Brasileria, 1969, 322.

# O sumiço da santa
# [The War of the Saints]
## A Postmodern Reconstruction of Racial Dynamics in Contemporary Bahian Society[1]

### CRISTINA SÁENZ DE TEJADA

Acclaimed by scholars, politicians and intellectuals as one of the most socially-conscious Brazilian writers to explore the racial dynamics of Brazil, Jorge Amado has also been recognized for his unique narrative skills. Starting in 1931 with the publication of his first novel, *O país do carnaval* [*The land of carnival*], his prolific literary career has made him widely known for recreating the vitality of the Afro-Brazilian reality in Bahia and for criticizing the racial and political discrimination suffered by this group. His contribution to the defense of the African heritage of Brazil has not been limited to literature, but also expressed through public statements and political activity. As a deputy for the Communist Party in 1946, Amado wrote a bill (projeto de lei) that would guarantee religious freedom in Brazil after a period of virulent persecution during the 30s, a situation described in *Tenda dos milagres* [*Tent of Miracles*] (1969). The Constitution of 1946 included Amado's provision which was in effect until 1964 when the military dictatorship canceled all religious privileges for minorities. This repressive socio-political situation, which entitled that all *terreiros* and their ceremonies had to be reported to the police, remained the same until 1976 when the governor of Bahia "liberated the cults" (Silverstein 140).

His respect for Afro-Bahians, as well as his philosophy that legitimate literary creation only comes from lived experience, makes him a conscious and frequent participant in the *candomblé* ceremonies he so faithfully recreates in his novels. He has been initiated in the "Axé do Opô Afonjá" as an *obá*, one of the twelve ministers of *Xangô*, a title that has been conferred to other intellectuals, such as Caymmi, Caribé, Antônio Olinto, who have also contributed to the expansion of Afro-Bahian religions. All of them are mentioned in one of Amado's latest works, *O sumiço da santa: uma história de feitiçaria.* (1988), a text that is exemplary for the detailed, glorious recreation of the Afro-Bahian traditions. Amado has often described his authenticity in public statements:

Não só posso sentar-me nessa cadeira, mas ali devo e tenho de sentar-me entre as iaôs, as feitas e os ogãs , ao lado da mão-de-santo e dos altos dignatários, porque só assim, na vivência real e profunda, e não na fácil observação de repórter, terei condições para falar dos orixás e da vida popular, dos mistérios, do mundo mágico bahiano, só assim poderei recriar sua verdade, recriar a face desses homens e mulheres que me cercam, cujos pés constroem a dança mais bela, homens e mulheres que trouxeram do fundo da escravidão, nos ombros lanhados, tanta beleza por eles salva e conservada para nós.

[Not only can I sit in that chair [Oba's chair] but I must sit myself among the *iaôs,* the *feitas,* and the *ogãs,* by the *māe-de santo*'s side and at the side of those of high rank, because only in this manner, in this real and deep living experience, and not in the easy observation of the journalist, I will have the proper and conducive environment that is needed to speak of the *orixás* [Afro-brazilian divinities], of the life of the people, of the mysteries, of the magic Bahian world. Only in this manner I will be able to recreate its truth, to recreate the faces of the men and women who surround me, whose feet create a most beautiful dance, men and women who brought out from the depth of slavery, on their lacerated shoulders, such beauty that was saved by them for us]. (dos Santos 87)

It is this direct contact to the Bahian reality and to the dynamics of the racial tensions in his homeland, as well as his socio-political commitment to combat the discrimination against the Brazilian masses, that makes Amado a legitimate witness to the changes experienced by Afro-Brazilians since he began his literary career in 1931. During these sixty years, his ideological positions regarding race relations and definitions of race in Bahia have evolved in and through his novels. His 1935 *Jubiabá* presents the limited Marxist perspective of race interpreted in terms of class, while *Tenda dos milagres*, presents a much-discussed defense of the racial democracy. Amado's later work reveals a more flexible, plural, and cultural definition of race as a result of the socio-political and economical changes brought by the democracy.

In the light of Amado's progressive agenda, this study examines the role of Afro-Bahian culture in *O sumiço da santa* (1988). Attention to the political and the postmodern elements of the text reveals that the re-emergence of civil society after the dictatorship has created new conditions for literature in which previous themes—religion, feminism, race—are encountered by integrating minority and cultural perspectives that provide a more diversified discourse. Significantly, the political criticisms of *O sumiço da santa* are underscored by its postmodern content and form. The content represents a scathing deconstruction of political authority by privileging the power of minority perspectives, as well as magical forces, over the institutionalized discourse of Truth. The form destabilizes history through a pastiche of narratives that interweaves historical events, popular culture and multiple voices.

The text meets the definition of high postmodernism used by the literary critic Adolfo Marín-Minguillón because it questions the relation between history and fiction, between official history and the authenticity of its discourse. Overall, Amado uses the technique of simulacrum to push the limits of journalism, anthropology, essay, and novel in this work.

Written during the beginning of the democratization of Brazilian society, *O sumiço da santa* provides Amado's most open and incisive criticism of the discrimination and authoritarianism that existed in Brazil during the years of the dictatorship. Although the novel is set in the same historical period as *Tenda dos milagres*, Amado's latter work does not resort to allusions and allegories in order to recreate the social history of that time. The end of censorship has clearly influenced Amado's text and its recreation of the racial dynamics of a time when the National Security Council designated any "reports of racial discrimination as subversion" (Kennedy 18). By revisiting a historical moment that tried to erase both the persistence of racial conflicts and the existence of a distinct Afro-Brazilian culture, Amado's *O sumiço da santa* contributes to the political mobilization and organization of blacks into several race pride black movements that reemerged after 1974. This new era in Brazilian society challenges the 'etiquette' of racial relations as traditionally observed in the country, that is, the Euro-centric stereotype about the inferiority of non-whites. In order to achieve his goal, Amado draws heavily upon powerful African forces (music, *candomblé, capoeira*) that both challenge the authority and power of the political institutions of Bahia and change the lives of the Afro-Brazilian characters towards a strong racial consciousness. Committed to political activism, the Brazilian writer tries to re-present the history and heritage of Afro-Brazilians. In this sense, *O sumiço da santa* can be considered a manifestation of the Brazilian "Negritude." Although not written by a black writer, it constructs a black ethos and identity that serves to critique both the official racial democracy and any misinterpretation of blacks constructed for socio-political oppression by any regime.

At this point, I shall present current expressions of Brazilian Negritude, a socio-political concept that has experienced multiple revisions from its first manifestations in 1880 until the most recent wave of black protest in the seventies and eighties. By Negritude, I mean any cultural and political movement that asserts black consciousness and leads towards action that demands the rights of blacks to be at equal terms with any other group in their society.[2] Although it is mainly organized by people of African origin, it can not be limited to this racial group. After 1970, the celebration of black cultural interests and political participation as a distinct ethnic group won intellectual support as well. Alongside this movement of Negritude flows a discourse of resistance against the stereotypes built by the white ideology in order to proudly reclaim an African heritage. Recovering their history, their experience of slavery and their pride in African traditions are crucial elements in the construction of an Afro-Brazilian identity that leads to political action. Historian George Reid Andrews suggests, however, that once blacks are admitted to political participation, as happened during the second Republic (1945–1964), the need for a racially separate, black political movement is greatly reduced (163). What remains, then, is a cultural discourse of *Africanidade* that is based on black literary, theatrical and artistic activities. The power of this cultural discourse in encouraging black political demands became evident during the dictatorship (1964–1985) when the military regime censored any type of discourse or cultural activity that could promote racial awareness (Kennedy 202). This situation started to change in 1984 when several government institutions initiated a series of public debates on the issues of discrimination and inequality as well the publication of "a bimonthly newspaper distributed free of charge in black neighborhoods and the central business district (São Paulo), as well as inexpensive booklets on black history, black literature, and racial problems in Brazil" (Andrews 167). These state initiatives combined with other consciousness-raising activities work to reveal that racial democracy in Brazil does not exist yet until blacks' interests achieve equal status with whites. Unfortunately, according to Andrews, the black political party of the eighties seems to be going through a decline similar to that of the *Frente Negra* (the Black Front) in the thirties due to the risks involved in the current politics of integration (170–171).

If this is the case what is left of the Afro-Brazilian Negritude is a powerful cultural identity based on the traditions and history that Amado faithfully presents in his works. This is one way Afro-Brazilians can remain as a distinctive culture if political solidarity is in danger of being erased by the wave of integration described by Andrews. This is the context upon which Amado's comments in his novel *O sumiço da santa* are to be understood, in emphasizing the relevance of cultural values which are developed within group communities in practices, such as religion, capoeira, and music. In this sense, Amado agrees with sociologist Howard Winant regarding the importance of other expressions of Afro-Brazilian mobilization.

Winant presents an in-depth view of black political mobilization that considers the sociological debates within the movement as well as a lower class perspective neglected by Andrews. Winant explains that black movements from the popular strata are adopting new forms of struggle, such as human rights groups, women's groups, residential associations and ecclesiastical base committees (CEBs), that promote the elimination of racial conflicts and discriminations persisting after the democratization. These new social groups have expanded the terrain of politics to address "issues which had formerly been seen as personal or private—i.e not legitimate themes for collective action—as public, social and legitimate areas for mobilization" (185–186). For the middle and the lower classes, "these new social movements offered a political alternative to leftist and populist traditions which the military dictatorship had effectively stalemated" (186). He explains that many groups and individuals were mobilized: black activists in *favela* associations, in CEBs, and in rural struggles for land (specially in the northeast); blacks who participated in strike activity; blacks involved in cultural activities and organizations; black students; blacks concerned with issues of African liberation; black researchers and intellectuals involved in studying Afro-Brazilian history and culture; and black women involved in feminist activities (187).[3] Each of these types of lower and middle class activists mentioned by Winant are portrayed in Amado's novel in white Padre Abelardo Galvão, who struggles in his parish for the rights of the peasants; in the masters of capoeira; in Nilde Spencer, who coordinated the filming of Brazilian traditions for the French television; in Patrícia, a student who collaborated in the film; in musicians such as Caetano Veloso and Gal Costa; in Mãe Menininha dos Gantois; in the narrator; and, finally, in the author himself. All of them defend the Afro-Bahian culture and, therefore, are protected by their gods as part of the text and subtext of the novel. Thus, Amado's text shows his constant political commitment to the socially dispossessed classes of Brazil.

The narrative scheme, characterization and the inclusion of African traditions are significant in this text because they construct a strong black consciousness that had been erased from the canonical history books. The fact that Amado wrote *O sumiço da santa* at a time of political liberalization allowed him to freely express his condemnation of previous repressive years (106–107) and enabled him to restore a period that is critical in the construction of an Afro-Brazilian history. The socio-political allegories of his earlier works are unnecessary, replaced in *O sumiço da santa* with an open criticism of the political system and its construction of History:

> Dizer que em casa dos pais Manela jamais apanhara seria mentir, falsear os dados da narrativa, mau costume hoje corriqueiro entre os conspícuos senhores que escrevem a História—a grande, com H maiúsculo, acomodando os factos ao bel-prazer dos ditadores. Não se trata, explicam eles, de deturpar a História e sim, de limpá-la de lances e personagens que lhe comprometem a imprescindível pureza ideológica. (58)

> [To say that Manela has never been beaten while living in her parents' home would be a lie, would falsify the facts of the story, today this is a very common and unfortunate custom among the recognizable persons who write History—the big one, the one with a capital H. Thus molding the facts to accommodate the interest of dictators. It is not a question of slanting History, but rather cleansing it of events and characters that compromise its ideological purity]. (49)

Amado's combination of different discourses of journalism, literature, ethnology and history in *O sumiço da santa* has two goals. First, Amado aspires to change previous derogatory representations of Afro-Brazilians. In addition, he documents their cultural contributions in order to give them tools to resist acculturation to white values and to continue the fight begun by runaway slaves in the *quilombos*. This ideological perspective can be considered Amado's defense of the right of Afro-Brazilians to be part of the national identity as a distinct culture. He becomes a cultural reporter who documents and creates different manifestations of the Afro-Brazilian heritage in his hometown.

Through the juxtaposition of history and fiction in which the boundaries of each are erased, *O sumiço da santa* narrates the multiple events that take place in Bahia during the forty-eight hour visit of St. Barbara, also called Iansã or Oyá by Afro-Bahians.[4] On the occasion of a religious art exhibit organized by the German friar and director of the Sacred Art Museum, D. Maximiliano von Gruden, the unique statue of Saint Barbara arrives to Bahia from the parish of Santo Amaro. The relevance of this statue rests on her African attributes, the thunder, in contrast to the traditional Catholic ones, a palm. The function of Maximiliano von Gruden is significant as well because, contrary to the official opinions, he believes that the statue is a work by mulatto Aleijadinho. Thus, his exhibit and his research book on the image contribute to promote the uniqueness of Afro-Bahian artistic heritage neglected by official institutions.

As soon as the fishing boat that transports the image docks in Bahia, the statue of the saint takes on human form as the Yoruba goddess ready to fulfill her mission: to empower the mulattas Adalgisa and her niece Manela to embrace and celebrate their African heritage. Beside the story of their lives, Amado weaves other plots that, as the speaking narrator indicates, can be read pleasurably or subversively according to the reader's wishes. The narrator serves as the touchstone of the different stories that unfold independently in the narrative; however, on several occasions they are brought together through the intercession of the characters' acts and the intervention of Oyá. Such reunions take place within several communal Afro-Brazilian celebrations in the significant neighborhood of Pelourinho, considered the center of the African culture and a symbol of the years of slavery. It is here that Amado's socio-political symbolism shows. By uniting different representatives of the Afro-Brazilian group in a geographical and social environment considered to be characteristically Afro-Bahian, and, therefore, marginalized by Bahian mainstream, Amado creates a bond among all of Afro-Brazilians and their supporters that attempts to recreate a group identity similar to the socio-political consciousness developed in the thirties and expanded in the eighties. This is done by highlighting the function of the "terreiro" and the *candomblé* as a community that identifies itself with the African nations and the Amerindians acting as a channel where Afro-Brazilians can gain self-esteem, social solidarity, prestige and social mobility. According to theologian Joseph Murphy, "the houses offer an alternative to the values of white society and the racism that so frequently underlies them" (47). The critic Fred Hord comments that it is this community bond creates the black ethos and black identity in whose construction literature plays an important role. He believes that literature "can be useful in helping black students to clarify their relationship to the past and thus in making them informed mediators of present issues of racial pride and values" (v). I believe that Amado's intention in this later work goes beyond race to include other socio-cultural sectors of his society which are also marginalized by mainstream interests.

The magical transformation experienced by the statue of Saint Barbara, interpreted as a theft by those who are not Afro-Brazilians, becomes the center of the narrative and Amado's technique to interconnect the lives of all the characters. In various situations, the lives of many Afro-Brazilian characters and those who support their cause and identity become transformed and empowered by the intercession of the saint, acting as Oyá, the Yoruban goddess of winds and storms. According to literary critic Bobby Chamberlain, the presence of Yoruban gods has been characteristic in Amado's later novels as a way both to expand the narrow confines of the empirical world and to create picaresque antiheroes (99). He also suggests that:

> Insofar as they intervene in human affairs in the manner of dei ex machina, the author's supernatural characters, whose existence he regards as metaphorical, perform a wish-fulfillment function, ironically reaffirming the necessity for the dispossessed themselves to redress social abuses, given the unlikelihood of religious or political solutions. (99)

Chamberlain's analysis regarding the socio-political implications of the divine presence is appropriate for O sumiço da santa because the events narrated in the text take place during the most repressive years during the military regime at a time when Afro-Brazilians where excluded from certain social spaces and discriminated against because of their race. As a result Afro-Brazilians were forced to adopt white middle-class values, like the mulatta Adalgisa, or succumb to a folkloric stereotype based on their festivities and Carnivals. The prohibition of the celebration of religious ceremonies, such as the candomblé or the washing of the Church of Bomfim, is an obvious attempt to diminish the racial awareness of the Afro-Bahians. According to the pro-African omniscient narrator, only the necessary intervention of Oyá will contribute to changing the injustices and strengthening the powerful socio-political role of the Afro-Brazilian traditions as a way to resist acculturation. This is clearly explained in the text through the parable of the god Oxalá who, after years of slavery, recovered his position as king and tried to change the injustices in his kingdom:

Oxalá não conseguiu mudar a vida do povo, é fácil conferir. Ainda assim
deve-se reconhecer que nenhuma palavra pronunciada contra a violência e a
tirania é vã e inútil: alguem ao ouvi-la pode superar o medo e iniciar a
resistência. Eis que Manela percorreu os caminhos de Oxalá no pátio da
Basílica do Bonfim na hora em que devia estar chegando em casa. (47)

[Oxalá was not able to change the life of the people, it is easy to bestow.
Even so, one must recognize that no word utter against violence and tyranny
is useless and in vain; someone upon hearing it could overcome fear and
begin to resist. Thusly Manuela walked the ways of Oxalá in the cloister
of the Basilica of Bonfim at an hour that she ought have been getting
home]. (37)

Fiction and characterization occupy the most relevant space in *O sumiço da
santa* because, as Amado has said in regard to his other books, "ser
romancista é essencialmente criar vida [to be a novelist is essentially to create
life]" (dos Santos 107). In this case, Amado recreates the racial dynamics of
Bahia during the sixties and subverts the official whitening policy by engaging African forces and whites forces in a magical war that is won by the former.[5] The story centers on Adalgisa, a middle-class mulatta, whose life is
dedicated to maintaining her status as a traditional decent woman and her
appearance as half Spanish. Under the repressive and ultra conservative education of both her godmother and the Spanish Father José Antonio Hernán-
dez, a defender of Franco's ideology, Adalgisa grows up renouncing her
maternal African heritage. Because she considers this cultural background to
be socially inferior, she is the opposite of her other sister, Gildete, who
strongly inculcates the African traditions in her daughters and sons. Adalgisa's acceptance of the official whitening policies of the sixties are evident in
her marriage to Danilo, a mulatto. His work as a lawyer assistant and his reputation as an ex-football player provides her with the social status she longs
for. Her actions and opinions are also similar to those expressed by local
authorities and some members of the Catholic hierarchy. After nineteen years
together, Adalgisa's marriage has become a social convention in which passion and sexuality have been repressed by her exalting morality. Not having
been able to conceive a child, her life is dedicated to raising one of her two
orphan nieces, Manela, in the same conservative and traditional values. The
other girl, Marieta, lives with her aunt Gildete in a much freer environment,
one that acknowledges and encourages the African heritage of the family.

The narrator's Afro-Brazilian ethics are inferred by his characterization
of these characters in a series of opposites: while Adalgisa is described in
negative terms as a repressed and bitter woman, Gildete and her nieces are
portrayed as caring, free, and lively persons only because they are under the
influence of the African deities they worship. This opinion is clearly stated in
the text when Manela stops being afraid of her aunt Adalgisa after surrepti-

tiously participating in the festivities of Bomfim with her aunt Gildete and her sister and cousins. Manela's decision to break her aunt's rules by being at the African festival is rewarded by the goddess Oyá who gives her the final courage to confront Adalgisa and her severe authority. At the festival, the girl also meets Miro, a black taxi-driver, who later becomes a relevant character in the process of filming the cultural life of Bahia by French television. Manela's new personality and her relationship with Miro distresses Adalgisa who, in attempting to punish what she considers an act of rebellion and subversion, decides to incarcerate her niece at a convent with the help of the Father José Antonio and a legal order from a conservative judge. This unjust decision is finally overruled by Oyá, who appears at the convent under human form to deliver a new legal order. As a result, Manela is freed with the support of the nuns.

Amado avoids suggesting that divine intervention is the only recourse of the Afro-Brazilians in their struggle for cultural independence. For example, Oyá's magical intervention occurs only after Miro and Danilo organize a popular group of Afro-Bahian friends and relatives who react against Adalgisa's authority in solidarity with Manela. It is here that the socio-political symbolism and black identity emerges in the text as subversive. The victory of the Afro-Bahian culture is expressed in Manela's initiation as a daughter of Oyá and in her engagement to Miro. On the other hand, Adalgisa's authority is finally undermined after she is possessed by the African gods Xangô, Oxóssi and Oyá. Her rebirth to her African background brings her a happier personality and a liberated sexuality with Danilo. It is then that Oyá concludes her mission in Bahia and returns to the parish of Santo Amaro, retaking her alter-ego form, Saint Barbara. The symbolism of this act reveals the syncretism of the Bahian culture, that is, the existence and intervention of distinct African forces under the white appearance.

The successful human and divine African intervention in the case of Manela's and Adalgisa's lives is also manifested in the events that take place in the official sector of Bahia after the disappearance of the sacred image of Saint Barbara. Using a journalist voice, Amado presents the rational and objective explanation of the authorities in regard to the icon's disappearance and reports critically about the role of the police, the press, the National Security and the church in Bahia's everyday life during the dictatorship. Adalgisa's fascist ideology in regard to Manela's education is parallel to that of Bahian authorities, who are ready to exert violent methods or invent suspects in order to impose their belief and justify their power. Thus the police accuse the innocent Father Abelardo Galvão after the theft of the icon because he arrived to Bahia on the same boat as the statue. The authorities, including the assistant of the Bishop, already consider the priest a communist and subversive because he defends the rights of the peasants against the oppression of the landowners in the rural areas: "Existem numerosos padres acumpliciados com os comunistas, não estou lhe dizendo nenhuma novidade, o facto é notório. Para mim, para nós, responsáveis pela ordem no País, pela segurança nacional, esses padres são bandidos ainda piores do que os comunistas. Além de inimigos, são traidores" ["There are many priest who have joined cause with the communists, I am not telling you anything new, it is a well known fact. For me, for us, those responsible for the order in our country, for the national well being, these priests are bandits even worse that the communists. More than enemies they are traitors"] (71). The retelling of the humorous and ridiculous persecution of Father Abelardo allows the narrator to dismantle the power of different local authorities and to reconstruct his version of the events. By openly reporting on the inefficacy of the political system, on the distortion of the facts as presented in the press and on the absurdity of the official arguments, the narrator presents how the truth as well as minorities themselves were silenced or manipulated during the dictatorship:

> Recorde-se que os factos narrados nesta crónica, pobre de brilho, rica de veracidade, se passaram nos piores anos da ditadura militar e da rígida censura à imprensa. Havia uma realidade oculta, u país secreto, não noticiados. Gazetas, estações de rádio e de televisão, encontravam-se limitadas, nas secções informativas, a factos em geral pouco palpitantes. Reduzidas nas opinativas ao louvor incondicional do sistema do governo e dos governantes. Proibição total de qualquer noticiário, da menor alusão, a respeito do quotidiano de prisões, torturas, assassinatos políticos, violações dos direitos humanos, de comentários sobre a censura de espectáculos e livros, assim como referências a greves, manifestações, passeatas, protestos, movimentos de massa e tentativas de guerrilha. Nada disso acontecia na pátria feliz sob a égide dos generais e coronéis, a acreditar-se na leitura dos jornais. (107)

> [We must remember that the events narrated in this chronicle, poor in brilliance but rich in truth, happened during the worst years of the military dictatorship, a time of a rigid press censorship. There was a hidden reality, a secret country, not noticed. Newspapers, radio station and television channels, were limited in their news to facts which in general were not very exciting. Opinions were limited to international praises on the government and its leaders. There was a total prohibition of any news, no matter how scant, regarding the daily imprisonments, tortures, political assassinations, human rights violations, commentaries regarding the censorship of spectacles and publications, and also there were no references to strikes, protests, marches, movement of the masses and attempts to guerrilla warfare. Nothing like this was happening in the motherland under the protection of generals and colonels, if one were to believe the newspapers]. (104–105)

Besides this personal opinion on the role of authority during the late sixties, the narrator's account of that period incorporates a humorous characterization of police officers, as Brazilian "James Bonds," who fail to succeed even with the help of sophisticated Japanese technology and CIA methods. At the end, it is Oyá's intervention that impedes Galvão's assassination and destroys the reputation of both the National Security and the police. Supporting the Director of the Museum, she shows up at the Art Exhibit, transformed into the sculptural icon, after the authorities confidently declare to the press and the Church hierarchies that the religious image has been smuggled into Paris by communists, Caetano Veloso and Violeta Arraes. Again, the Afro-Bahian forces win the war against the official discourse defended by the authorities.

Amado's technique in rewriting history and facts which were censured during the sixties—"nestas páginas beatas não se admite a difamação (103) [these pious pages do not accept defamation]—is extended to his narrator's ethnological report on both subversive and official Afro-cultural activities. By incorporating into the narrative an anthropological voice and by quoting real characters who participated in the expansion of the *africanidade,* Amado participates in the contemporary process of Brazilian Negritude based in cultural activities that integrate a varied range of black and white social classes. During the most repressive periods of military rule, when overt political mobilization against racism was almost impossible, cultural movements sustained black awareness and challenged racial stereotypes, making use of "identity politics." Probably the most effective (and controversial) of these currents was "black soul," inspired by the black cultural and political upsurges then engulfing the United States (Winant 189). The importance of this movement to the novel is reflected in Miro's interest in the Black Panther movement. The group support ultimately helps him to act against the unjustice committed against his girlfriend, Manela, by resorting to the political and subversive character of the capoeira. He militantly advocates the need for the powerful and still prohibited *capoeira*:

> Arma de defesa, nascida nas senzalas, criação dos escravos bantos, a capoeira esteve sujeita à mais feroz perseguição: prohibido seu exercício, castigados seus cultores. Considerada, junto a candomblé, expressão de barbaria; toda matriz africana da cultura brasileira era então repudiada, obliterado o seu conhecimento, defesa sua manifestação. Todavia, a capoeira, camuflada em dança coletiva, subsistiu ao som dos berimbaus de barriga, impôs sua eficácia e sua beleza, balé dos passos mágicos, luta de golpes mortíferos, ganhou foros de arte.

> [Defensive weapon, born in the slaves' shacks, invention of the Bantu slaves, the *capoeira* suffered much persecution: its practice was forbidden, its devotees were punished. Together with *candomblé*, an uncivilized expression; all African influence on Brazilian culture was then rejected, any information about it was obliterated, and any outer manifestation was forbidden. Yet, a *capoeira,* submerged in the collective dance, survived under

the sounds of the *berimbaus de barriga* [Afro-Brazilian musical instrument], enjoining its power and beauty, a ballet of magical steps, a contest with deadly blows, prevailed and gained a place in the arts]. (216)

Far from following the official discourse of African tradition as a folkloric element of Bahian society, Amado's description of the Afro-Bahian culture emphasizes its subversive character as a resistance to oppressive and repressive authority since the times of slavery. Therefore, he acknowledges the significant contribution of Africans to Bahian culture, a fact that was internationally recognized when in 1986 the United Nations declared Pelourinho to be a Patrimony of Humanity. Thus, Amado is committed to uncovering the roots of African traditions in order to recover a more authentic and plural Afro-Bahian cultural patrimony that also encourages a distinctive black identity within the national identity. That is why he inserts different manifestations of the African heritage that he has witnessed in his hometown, such as the capoeira, Jacques Chancel's filming of Bahia's traditions, and quotes from hundreds of local Afro-Brazilian artists and intellectuals whose work had been exiled from the national art history. On the one hand, these first person accounts are significant because they represent the Afro-Bahian perspective of their own image and culture in contrast to the folkloric and whitening patterns imposed by the official authority at the time. On the other hand, they represent Amado's use of the postmodernist technique of pastiche that combines fictional and real characters. According to Bobby Chamberlain, pastiche "is a hallmark of the mature Amado, as is the intensified climate of humor, irony, and satire to which it contributes" (70).

For instance, Chancel's film, "Le Grand echiquier," is based on a real event that took place in 1968. Amado describes this film in similar terms in *O sumiço da santa* and in his simulacrum of autobiography, *Navegação de cabotagem [Coastal navigation]* (1992). The documentary was intended to present the richness and vitality of African traditions to the French audience as well as the political commitment of Bahian white and non-white artists and intellectuals. With that intention, Chancel selected different popular cultural activities to film such as carnival, the *afoxés*, several dances, and a "bossanova" concert at the Teatro Castro Alves: "Os maiores do tropicalismo. Movimento musical acusado pela ditadura de acção sediciosa, rotulado de arte degenerada, contestatária, subversiva" [the greatest names of tropicalism. A musical movement accused by the dictatorship of being disloyal, labeled as degenerate art, slanderous, subversive] (212). During the filming, it is in the latter performance that the Afro-Brazilian socio-political ideology becomes more explicit and, therefore, more subversive in the eyes of the authorities, especially because it will be broadcasted out of the country. The participation at the concert of black and white Brazilian composers forced into exile and censorship, such as Caetano Veloso, Gilberto Gil, Gal Costa and Vinícius de

Morães, raises suspicions, as does the presence of George Moustaki, an accused communist who wrote several songs praising the Afro-Bahian culture.[6] The expected political content of the concert attracts the attention of resistance groups (students, intellectuals and fans) and the National Security. Paranoid, the officers stand, ready to interfere with the communication system whenever they consider the lyrics to be critical of the official ideology of racial harmony. Ironically, it is the intervention of Oyá that disrupts attempts to censor the concert by manipulating the National Security's communication system to allow the political comments of the composers to be recorded in Chancel's documentary. Only then does the international community become aware of Brazil's racism as expressed by the music of Gilberto Gil. Gil's political commitment is described by Amado in *Navegação de cabotagem* on the occasion of a later concert in 1990 (447).

The seriousness of the bossa-nova concert is once more balanced in the plot of *O sumiço da santa* by the humorous intervention of Oyá. She disarms both the National Security and the gangster hired by the landowner João Costa to kill Father Abelardo Galvão. The three interventions of the African goddess end in humorous situations that ridicule the authority of those in power and, therefore, question the concept of power itself at a time of extreme violence. It also serves to connect the lives of the different characters, fictional and real, that appear in the text. Her function is parallel to the narrator's text.

The presence of African vital forces, also called *axé* in the Yoruban tradition, in the three narratives that have been discussed, show the author's belief in an alternative power in Bahian society that is only useful for the socially dispossessed and, especially, for Afro-Brazilians. Significantly, in the text, Oyá makes herself visible only to the racially oppressed who are able to recognize and respect her power and authority because it serves to resolve unjustice. As such, she supports Caetano Veloso's music and Father Galvão's theology of liberation although they are both white. Amado's use of African divinities in *O sumiço da santa* suggests that Afro-Brazilians have a distinct culture that is limited neither by ethnic group nor race. This identity culture stands in opposition to the exclusivity of mainstream white culture in which people are defined by race alone.

The role of the narrator, identified with Amado through multiple references and his use of actual facts, is significant because he is not only the spokesman for the Afro-Brazilian community but also the craftsman of the novel. The text interweaves three styles: fiction (the story of Adalgisa and Manela), ethnology (detailed description of the Afro-Brazilian traditions) and journalism (political editorials about restrictions of free speech during the dictatorship), thus becoming a pastiche of discourses that defies any traditional definition of genre. These mutually supporting discourses unveil a period of Bahian history that was silenced, censored and distorted during the military regime as well as revealing forces of resistance that are antecedents to the current movements of *africanidade*. Amado stresses that what constituted *africanidade* in the sixties and seventies and who participated in its construction are necessary to understand the importance of this period to current black politics. His narrator focuses on both the popular and the intellectual, choosing a time when black identity was sustained more vitally by cultural activities than by political ones. For instance, the text links the significant changes in the life of many Bahians following the visit of Oyá/Santa Bárbara to the emergence of multiple and diverse representations of the Yoruban goddess among local artists:

> No início da década de 80, dez anos transcorridos sobre os factos narrados nestas memórias, a museóloga Sílvia Athayde teve sua atenção voltada para o que lhe pareceu coincidência surpreendente, circunstância insólita, digna de pesquisa, esclarecimento e comentário. Debruçou-se sobre o enigma, saiu perguntando, remachando, investigou, moveu mundos e fundos, passou meses amarrando as pontas da meada . . . A museóloga descobriu e comprovou que na década de 70, no curto espaço de alguns dias, os mais importantes artistas plásticos da terra—por mais incrível possa parecer, na Bahia o número de pintores supera o de poetas—conceberam e realizaram esculturas, quadros a óleo, talhas, desenhos, gravuras, monotipias, como temática semelhante, se não idêntica, todos eles se inspirando no mito de Yansã, ou no culto de Santa Bárbara . . . A museóloga foi criticada por não se ter limitado às peças de maior valor. Mas para Sylvia, no caso, a quantidade das obras era tão importante quanto a qualidade.

> [At the beginning of the 1980s, ten years had elapsed since the facts narrated in these memoirs, the museum curator, Sílvia Athayde focused her attention on something that seemed to her a surprising coincidence, an unbelievable set of circumstances, worthy of researching, clarifying and commenting. She immersed herself into the mystery, and emerged questioning, emphasizing, she researched, moved heaven and earth, spent months tying tips and ends . . . The curator discovered and perceived that in the seventies, in just a few days time, the most important plastic artists of the land—no matter how incredible this may appear, there is a greater number of painters than of poets—conceived and realized sculptures, oil paintings, carvings, designs, engravings, monotypes, with a very similar theme, even if not exactly the same, all of them were inspired by the myth of *Yansá* or in the worship of Saint Barbara . . . The curator was criticized for not having limited herself to the most valuable objects. But for Silvia, in this case, the quantity of the objects was as important as the quality]. (186, 190)

Several elements mentioned in this quote should be emphasized because parallels are made to the structure, construction and content of the text itself. First, the narrator praises Sílvia's interest in Afro-Brazilian culture which leads her to do exhaustive and productive research on an apparently insignificant artifact. As a result she manages to organize an exhibit of the myriad representations of Oyá/Saint Bárbara. Her investigation and final product are similar to that of the narrator because his text emerges from an in-depth ethnological research that provided him with innumerable accounts of the presence of Afro-Brazilian forces in Bahia's everyday life and art. Both Athayde's and the narrator's work are important because each manages to explain the connections between the past and the present. Their research is also a manifestation of the interest manifested by various contemporary sectors of Bahia society in recovering relevant aspects of Afro-Brazilian culture that were considered insignificant in previous decades. This ethnological epistemology towards *africanidade* explains the narrator's detailed description of the images presented in Athayde's exhibit as well as his own description of several other cultural manifestations. The narrator also believes that at the current moment of the black awareness process, the quantity of material is much more important than the quality. That is why he quotes hundreds of fictitious and real characters who participated in the maintenance of Afro-Brazilian traditions, including Caetano Veloso, Carybé, Menininha dos Gantois, Amado's brother James Amado, the poet Caymmi and the author, among others. Some of the information included in the narrator's accounts can be verified in Amado's *Navegação de cabotagem.*

Second, Amado's sophisticated technique of combining fiction and reality has created a text that, according to the narrator, has not been very well accepted by literary critics, a comment that Bobby Chamberlain also mentions in his monograph on Jorge Amado (ix). That may explain why Amado included a final section in *O sumiço da santa* where the narrator-author responds to literary critics and to possible questions from his readers. In this post-script, Amado accords equal respect to all categories of readers: professional, pleasure and political. The narrator explains the ideological context in which his revolutionary text was created and how he perceives his own text and writing (303).

Speaking in the narrator's humble fictitious voice, Amado reveals a brilliant view of his own writing, explaining how he has always strived to represent changes in his society, evident in his references to the end of communism. He also sustains his socio-political commitment to shock Bahia and the world through a narrative that evokes contradicting opinions: what may seem superficial and too humorous for some readers is understood as too complicated and stereotypical for others. By responding to the contradictory positions of the literary critics in regard to his writing, Amado ironically reveals the plurality of his text and his writing through which he brings about the end of firmly established categories such as the Real, Meaning, History, Revolution and the Social.

*O sumiço da santa* is a text that falls into the postmodern expression because it opts for the renovation of meaning, literary techniques, social categories and race. It is a text that enters into a lively reconstructive dialogue with the old and the past. Through the use of fact, fantasy, irony and parody, it rediscovers the past by deconstructing the authority and the power of the military regime that inefficiently tried to repress all African elemens of Bahian society. It also incorporates Amado's self-conscious description of his writing and its impact in his society. This innovative technique engenders both complexity and enjoyment. Indeed, Amado's skillfully use of Afro-Brazilian forces in *O sumiço da santa* serves not only to entertain his readers but to inspire political and social reforms. This is done by ridiculing the authorities, by exposing the arbitrariness of their discourse and by uncovering the social and powerful significance of the African heritage of his hometown. Moreover, Amado's balanced combination of both humorous fiction and methodologies characteristic of cultural studies within a multiple narrative limits the theurgical intervention characteristic of his earlier works. This is done by supporting the activities of alternative communal cultural groups, such as *afoxés*, Olodum and neighborhood associations, who are currently engaged in the construction of a distinct and self-sufficient black identity. Finally, it is significant that the novel was finished in Bahia in August of 1988, the 100th anniversary of the abolition of slavery in Brazil when various official celebrations of the *centenário* were organized and contested by Afro-Brazilian groups that wanted to draw attention to the discrimination and racial inequality that they continue to suffer. In this sense, the innovative technique of Amado's *O sumiço da santa,* by incorporating cultural discourses, such as ethnology, sociology, and history, serve to present the need of a plural dialogue about the racial dynamics in contemporary Brazilian society that takes into account Afro-Brazilians' perspective and their historical background. Ultimately, it is a text that celebrates the racial impurity of Brazil.

**NOTES**

1. The research on which this article is based was supported by the Beatrice Atkinson Summer Research Grant from Goucher College.
2. For more information on the different interpretations of Negritude, see the studies of José Montenegro, Kabengele Munanga, Octavio Ianni, Jorge Schwartz and Thales de Azevedo, among others, listed in the bibliography. It is also relevant to point out that, following the recent definitions, Blacks and Afro-Brazilians are used indistinctively in this study as both are based on the affirmation of the African heritage.
3. Among the black organizations recently appearing in Brazil, besides the creation of the political party Movimento Negro Unificado (1978), Winant cites the following: *Grupo União e Consciência Negra*, the *Centro de Articulação de Populações Marginalizadas* (CEAP), the *Centro de Referéncia Negromestiça* (CERNE), the *Instituto Palmares de Direitos Humanos* (IPDH) and the publication of *Jornal da Maioria Falante*. He also mentions the conflict between sectors

of the Movimento Negro Unificado and feminism, and nationalist currents as that of Abdias do Nascimento, *Quilombismo*: "his effort to develop an 'afrocentric' ideology for the black movement" (188).

4. It is important to note that Yoruban deities have different Catholic names depending on the region in Brazil or in the Caribbean. For example, in Cuba, Saint Barbara is identified with a male divinity, Xangô.

5. The English translation of the book has the significant title of *The War of the Saints,* initially given by Amado when he first thought of writing the book during the late sixties.

6. Amado mentions some of the actual songs that were performed in the 1968 concert by Gilberto Gil, "Aquele Abraço," and Caetano Veloso just before they left for London. The concert was authorized in order to collect some money for their expenses during their exile.

# BIBLIOGRAPHY

Ademola Adesoji, Michael. Nigéria. H*istória-costumes, cultura do povo ioruba e a origem dos seus orixás.* Salvador: Tvaratv-Canal 4, 1990.

Amado, Jorge. *O sumiço da santa: uma história de feitiçaria.* Portugal: Publicações Europa-America, 1994.

———. *Navegação de cabotagem.* Rio de Janeiro: Record, 1992.

———. *Tenda dos milagres.* Rio de Janeiro: Record, 1982.

———. *Jubiabá.* Rio de Janeiro: José Olympio, 1935.

Andrews, George Reid. "Black Protest in São Paulo, 1888–1988." *Journal of Latin American Studies* 24 (1): 1992. 147–171.

Azevedo, Thales de. *Democracia racial: ideologia e realidade.* Petrópolis: Vozes, 1975.

Brookshaw, David. *Race and Color in Brazilian Literature.* Metuchen, N.J. & London: The Scarecrow Press, Inc., 1986.

Chamberlain, Bobby J. *Jorge Amado.* Boston: Twayne Publishers, 1990.

Dzidzienyo, Anani y Dr. Lourdes Casal. *The Position of Blacks in Brazilian and Cuban Society.* London: Minority Rights Group, 1979.

Hord, Fred Lee. *Reconstructing Memory: Black Literary Criticism.* Chicago: Third World Press, 1991.

Ianni, Octavio. *Escravidão e racismo,* 2 ed. São Paulo: Hucitec, 1988.

Kennedy, James. "Political Liberalization, Black Consciousness, and Recent Afro-Brazilian Literature." *Phylon* 47 (3): 1986: 199–209.

Luz, Marco Aurélio. *Cultura negra em tempos pós–modernos.* Salvador: SECNEB, 1992.

Montenegro, José. *A Negritude. Dos mitos às realidades.* Braga: Pax, 1967.

Munanga, Kabengele. *Negritude: Usos e sentidos.* São Paulo: Atica, 1986.

Murphy, Joseph. *Working the Spirit.* Ceremonies of the African Diaspora. Boston: Beacon Press, 1994.

Ramos, Artur. As *culturas negras no Novo Mundo,* 3 ed. São Paulo: Ed. Nacional, 1979.

Santos, Itazil Benício dos. *Jorge Amado: Retrato incompleto.* Rio de Janeiro: Record, 1993.

Schwartz, Jorge. "Negrismo y negritud." *Historia y cultura en la conciencia brasileña*. Leopoldo Zea, compilador. México: FCE, 1993: 65–78.

Silverstein, Leni. "The Celebration of Our Lord of the Good End: Changing State, Church, and Afro-Brazilian Relations in Bahia" in *The Brazilian Puzzle: Culture on the Border-lands of the Western World*. Ed by David J. Hess and Roberto A. DaMatta. Columbia U Press, NY, 1995: 134–151.

Vieira, Nelson. "Testimonial Fiction and Historical Allegory: Racial and Political Repression in Jorge Amado's Brazil." *Latin American Literary Review* 18 (34), 1989: 6–23.

Winant, Howard. "Rethinking Race in Brazil." *Journal of Latin American Studies* 24 (1), 1992: 173–192.

# A Postcolonial Reading of a Colonized *Malandro*

CARMEN CHAVES TESSER

What is most bothersome in Amado's writings is that he offers an emphatically view of Brazil: sensual women, Afro-Brazilian religious rituals, spicy food, and so on ... There is a radical populist empathy toward the lower classes and a male-luxurious comprehension of women, who seem to appear in his novel only to make love (if they are black or mestiza) or to serve as a pain in the neck (if they are white and/or middle-class) (Reis 1988, 234).

Although admitting that Jorge Amado "does deserve respect as a writer," Roberto Reis dismisses any analyses of Amado's texts and merely posits the "real problem is with Brazilianists who see Brazilian culture only through the exotic lens of Jorge Amado" (234). As a Brazilian woman and, for many years also a Brazilianist, I, too have dismissed, if not outright rejected, Amado's work. My own view was that Jorge Amado had "sold out" to foreign markets by "selling" exactly what those markets would buy. In other words, I considered Jorge Amado an export author, rather than an expert. In my sheltered world view inside the American academy, I convinced myself that Amado was better known outside of Brazil and that "real" Brazilians did not care for his literature. Like many of us, I, too, fell in the trap of looking for "good" literature in Brazil, of trying to introduce students and colleagues to the "better" writers—those who engage in the postmodern intellectual games of experimental novels and other French models—in my effort to bring them to an understanding of the Brazilian "Other." My mission, I believed, was to point out that Brazil was part of the modern world and its intellectuals knew the discourse and could become part of the theoretical dialogues so common among us in the academy. Jorge Amado, in my opinion, could not be a part of this discourse since his work exemplified all that I, as a Brazilian(ist) woman, wished to forget about the culture that I studied—my own culture of origin. Why, then, have I agreed to contribute to this collection of essays? To answer my own query, I wish to follow the model of Edward W. Said in "Represent-ing the Colonized: Anthropology's Interlocutors" and problematize the four main words in the title of my essay, my purpose being to present questions, not answers, in reading Jorge Amado. In his essay, Said questions the position of the critic in a world that "must contend not only with the consciousness of linguistic forms and conventions, but also with the pressures of such transper-sonal, transhuman, and transcultural forces as class, the unconscious, gender, race, and structure" (206). In problematizing the key words in the title of my essay, I must also contend with all these pressures as must the reader of this essay and any literary critic.

By attaching the adjective "postcolonial" to my reading of Amado, I bring into the essay an emblematic use of a currently debated theoretical stance. Stemming from such central texts as Said's *Orientalism* (1978), Reta-mar's *"Caliban" and Other Essays* (1971 and 1986), and Spivak's *The Post-Colonial Critic* (1990), postcolonial theory describes the writing and the reading of texts that are conscientiously grounded in the colonial experience. This experience may result from European expansion and exploitation or it may be related to repression of minorities and otherwise excluded voices. A "postcolonial" stance problematizes the writer, the text, the source culture, the reader, the critic, and so on. As Walter Mignolo summarizes it, "once again, the basic question is who is writing about what, where, and why?" (122). In his own thinking about the issue of postcolonial discourse, Mignolo posits precisely the issue of Brazilian intellectuals and their voicing of the question, such as Roberto Schwarz's "Brazilian Culture: Nationalism by Elimination." Mignolo posits the question of whether "those of us in exile, when negotiating the intellectual production in our places of origin ... and the intellectual conversation in our place of residence" should be go-betweens (130). As go-betweens, are we to censure what our colleagues who study other literatures learn about Brazilian letters? Hernán Vidal argues that literature in Latin America "has acquired the rank of official high culture with the task of shaping master narratives of national identity" (114). Vidal further concludes that the criticism of Latin American literary production sees "liter-ature as a tool for social construction and an indirect weapon in political struggles" (114). This being the case, then, Jorge Amado's work does not fit nicely into our own social construction of *Brasilidade*. Our primary effort in defining what is, indeed, Brazilian is to point to the hybridity of the Brazilian experience with respect to European values and, as much as possible, to neglect the ever-present African element. How, then, does one take a "post-colonial" stance and neglect Jorge Amado?

In a 1995 study, Santiago Colas argues that in the case of Latin American literature, the "discourse of colonization has accommodated a critique of col-onization" and falls within the realm of internal colonization as well as an external, historical colonization (392). If one looks at Brazilian literature through the eyes of a "postcolonial discourse," one is sure to fall in the trap of a "colonizing discourse," for even this stance is imperialistic in nature and "foreign" to Brazilian culture in origin. In *Against Literature,* John Beverley describes the ambiguous cultural role and legacy of Latin American literature. Since Iberians introduced Latin America to the production of printed books, Beverley argues, "literature (or, less anachronistically, *letras*) is a colonial institution, one of the basic institutions of Spanish colonial rule in the Americas; yet it is also one of the institutions crucial to the development of an autonomous creole and then 'national' (although perhaps not popular-democratic) culture" (2). Beverley goes on to argue that the literary genre of *testimonio* is what will bring together the elite classes composed of those of us in the North American academy with the subaltern communities and classes in Latin America. I believe that if we take a postcolonial view of Jorge Amado and enter into a critical dialogue with his texts, we, too, may come closer to the subaltern classes so favored as subject matter for the Bahian writer. Jorge Amado writes about oppositional elements (European/African) often pointing to the strength of hybridity. Metaphorically, he places the hybrid Brazilian at the center of the text and of his own ideology presenting the struggle toward a balance between what is modern, safe, and often cold and what is savage, exotic, and sensual, as in the case of *Dona Flor e seus dois maridos* [*Dona Flor and Her Two Husbands*]. Within each of his texts, Amado posits the oppositional dialogue and thus breaks with the accepted rules of high literary culture and, at the same time, does not altogether espouse the rules of low literary culture—yet his texts cannot be considered totally an expression of popular culture. Seen in this light, many Brazilianists have found it more expeditious to neglect the study of Amado's texts rather than to engage in the difficult task of entering into a discursive relationship with the subaltern themes of this colonized writer. In my new, postcolonial reading of Amado's work, I must agree with Arif Dirlik who describes the issue that the "appeals of postcoloniality are not restricted to intellectuals of any one national origin, and the problems . . . are of a general nature, born out of a contradiction between an insistence on heterogeneity, difference, and historicity and a tendency to generalize from the local to the global while denying that there are global forces at work that may condition the local in the first place" (341).

Satya Mohanty points to the difficulty of "a discursive and epistemic relationship that will be 'noncolonizing,' that will make possible 'a mutual exploration of difference'" (109). Mohanty concludes that the difficulty lies in the "business of simply interpreting the text (or the other) if the self-other relationship is itself partly constitutive of this 'fabric' or text" (110). In other words, my historical relationship with Amado's work, as well as my ideological stance toward being a spokesperson for all that was positive (if not downright *Positivistic*) about Brazil, did not allow me to enter the admittedly

Afro-Brazilian world described and defined by Jorge Amado. My own development as a "committed" critic did not permit me a "non-colonizing" discursive relationship with Amado's text. In my rejection of his work and words, I
had, in a sense, helped to colonize him. I had helped to keep him in a subaltern position. In problematizing the postcolonial stance, then, I posed the
question: How, then, can a Brazilian(ist) woman who wishes to give voice to
the excluded and to study the (self) Other neglect Jorge Amado's texts? It was
in an attempt at "unlearning historically determined habits of privilege and
privation" (Mohanty 110), that I decided to take a postcolonial attitude and
read Jorge Amado. Had I previously *really* read Jorge Amado? My privileged
position in the North American academy had allowed me to reject and/or
accept whatever best suited my own views of Brazil. Since I agreed with
many of my Brazilianist colleagues that Amado's texts had nothing of value
other than export popular culture, I found it easy and even somewhat smug to
join the many who completely left him out of the program.

In researching Brazilian novels published between 1985 and 1990, I
came across an interesting bit of information in the August 1990 issue of
*Leia.* During the last of these five years—I have elsewhere called them the
"Five Novel Years"—Brazil's 1,859 publishing houses published 73,037
titles by 33, 712 authors. Some of these, of course, are reprintings of the classics; some are translations of works in other languages. However, what
became apparent in my research was that of the some 8,000 new titles published in Brazil each year, the only author who sold steadily and consistently
*in Brazil* was Jorge Amado, thus shattering my myth of the "export Jorge."
My own empirical research pointed me in the direction of a writer who was
not only known outside of Brazil, but who represented, for many Brazilians,
the symbol of Afro-Brazilian culture. Furthermore, a 1994 opinion poll in
Brazil, placed Amado as the "best known and most esteemed man" among
Brazilians. "Real Brazilians" do read Jorge Amado; they know him and they
like him (Vasconcelos 10). With this information, I had to analyze my own
rejection of a man who has made an impact in his own country and abroad. I
realized that I, too, had become part of the "colonial" machinery and had contributed to the colonizing and the marginalizing of Amado's texts. Moreover,
if Jorge Amado is what most foreigners know about Brazil, it seems not only
reasonable but imperative that he be studied, analyzed, and put through a critical screen as have other writers. It seems that now, more than ever, we
Brazilianists must take a postcolonial view of the writer that many of us have
helped to colonize.

What is it about Jorge Amado, aside from his fame and fortune that contributes to many Brazilianists rejection of him? Amado, in his inimitable way
has explained the dilemma: "As for the critics, some like what I write, others
don't. I am not very sensitive to praise nor am I sensitive to critical attack. As
for insults, they have nothing to do with literature but with the success of an

author. Success is unforgivable" (Vasconcelos 11). Can a best-selling author also be a "good" writer? What makes Amado such an easy target for the "colonizer critic"? This question brings me to the last word in the title of my essay—*malandro.*

A *malandro*, according to Roberto DaMatta, is "a being out of place, dislocated from the formal rules that govern the social structure" (208). In the case of the prototypical malandro, Pedro Malasartes, DaMatta states, "we are dealing with a personage who characteristically knows how to transform every disadvantage into an advantage, an ability which is the sign of any good rogue and all good roguery. Persecuting the powerful, he always administers the dose of vengeance and destruction that points up the absence of a more just social relationship between the rich and the poor" (218–9). DaMatta concludes, "to understand him and his destiny, we must get rid of our bourgeois code of prejudices. We must confront him directly and courageously under the strong light of his own particular character. [He] does not reject the social order completely, nor does he act as a completely marginal character. He chooses an intermediate zone, a sphere of inconsistency where not having any character means just the opposite: i.e., being a man of character and never, never pretending or claiming to reform the world by offering oneself as the great example" (238). Jorge Amado, I believe, is an example of a Brazilian *malandro.* He has been an active writer for most of the twentieth century. He has joined political causes and has lived through many Brazilian sociopolitical transitions, but above all, he has crossed the lines of what Lúcia Helena calls the "two competing traditions" in Brazilian culture: "one characterized by rationalism, classicism, realism and referentiality," which she labels *linha do bom senso e do bom gosto* [the line of good sense and of good taste], and the other, dionysian, anthropophagic and carnivalizing, which attempts to demystify, to parody the dominant cultural canon by laughing at it and tampering with its codes" (Chamberlain 14).

Amado has changed the frame of his texts according to the times and to his own taste. What can be seen as a constant is the background of Bahia, Afro-Brazilian culture, and the voice of subalternity through his characters. The very fact that he switches cultural and literary codes makes it virtually impossible to frame him within a school, genre, or ideology. This, I believe, has been one of his greatest *malandragens.* Like Malasartes, Amado has figured what will sell and has produced it, a fact which we, Brazilianists, cannot accept. However, also like Malasartes, he seems to enjoy both his popularity and the critical scorn bestowed on him. More importantly, Amado mixes popular and classical conventions of what it is to be Brazilian—what it means when one discusses national identity—and he breaks with the norms of politically correct "good taste" and normative behavior. As Roberto DaMatta has pointed out, Jorge Amado breaks with all conventions in his first book, *O país do carnaval [The land of carnival],* when the main character, Paulo Rigger states: "I have felt like a Brazilian only twice. Once, at Carnival, when I danced the samba in the street. The other, when I beat Julie after she had betrayed me" (DaMatta 63). In this first novel as well as in other subsequent texts, Amado's definition of what it means to be a Brazilian fit with and broke with the norms of the times. Amado underscores the traditional, patriarchal and authoritarian ideology while at the same time giving action, if not voice, to the subaltern position of the woman. In DaMatta's words, "in the case of finding a more comprehensive Brazilian identity, then, what takes center stage is Carnival and the need for the control over female sexual favors" (63). What many critics have not discussed, and I include myself in this group, is the fact that most of Amado's heroines, or antiheroines, are survivors. They, like their creator, survive the times, the changes, and accommodate themselves as best they can as a true *malandro* might. Thus, Amado gives them the strength to survive even the stereotypical, patriarchal social construct that surrounds them. The woman character in Amado could very well be a metaphor for Brazil, his *pátria*. She is exploited, raped, beaten, controlled, and negotiated; however, through it all she survives and in her hybridity becomes stronger.

Not only are his writing techniques those of a *malandro,* but Amado himself lived, and continues to live the life of a *malandro.* At the age of twelve he ran away from home and from that time has had to make his own life as best he could. At the age of thirteen, he founded the newspaper *A Folha* as a protest against the administration of a literary society. In 1930, at the age of eighteen, he wrote his first book, *O país do carnaval* and published it the following year. 1930 is a significant year in Amado's ideological development. In a recent interview, he claims that the 1930 revolution was of utmost influence in his literary development and in his socio-political awareness, "for it was a movement that had popular support and not simply a coup. Contrary to 64, it was a true revolution because it had popular support. [1930] was so influential that it caused changes in the country and in Modernism, itself" (Gomes 13). Like those who provided the support for the 1930 Revolution, Amado was not the son of rich landowners and coffee planters from São Paulo; he was a member of the marginalized classes.

For the last seventy years, as Brazilian literature moved from Modernism to social engagement, to Postmodernism, Jorge Amado continues to write and publish. For the last seventy years, as Brazil experienced political transitions from Estado Novo, to democracy, to political unrest, to a repressive military dictatorship, to the *abertura*, to a new democracy, to a Presidential impeachment, Jorge Amado continues to write and publish. For the last seventy years, as the Brazilian economy has had more ups and downs and currency fluctuations than ever before in the history of the country, Jorge Amado continues to produce his texts. Like the prototypical rogue, Amado has survived the changes whether in exile, whether banished from publication in some countries, or whether banished from the critical dialogue. Although his own political ideology has changed as he has adapted to each new order, he continues to write about those social classes that have been marginalized but that encompass so much of Brazil. Although his characters are Bahian, the social conditions under which they operate and the cultural codes through which they exist are Brazilian. If we have kept Jorge Amado out of many of our classes, it has been that we, in our position of power have chosen to marginalize him rather than coming face to face with the reality that he depicts—a reality that we choose to ignore but that is part and parcel of Brazilian culture. Whether we agree with the many critics who say that Amado's writing changed completely after *Gabriela, cravo e canela* [*Gabriela, Clove and Cinnamon*] or not, we must recognize that he is known and read throughout the world. For those of use who are concerned with a national identity for Brazilians and with a cultural and ideological identity for ourselves, it becomes imperative that we take another look at this Bahian writer who has so completely filled "foreign" heads with what it means to be Brazilian. If for no other reason than to fight established stereotypes, we must re-read Amado and bring his texts into a critical discussion. To do otherwise is to relegate ourselves to a position of power that comes to us primarily through our elitist perspective, one that makes us the masters that Amado so aptly describes. In our position of authority we have decided to exclude and marginalize one of the most important voices in Brazilian letters—a voice that has had a greater impact in the world than any of our own academic debates.

On July 19, 1995, Jorge Amado received the Camões Prize amidst great fanfare at the Palácio de Belém in Lisbon. Among the many dignitaries from the political and literary arenas were Fernando Henrique Cardoso representing Brazil and Mário Soares representing Portugal and thus symbolically joining the mother country with its largest former colony in honoring "the most universally famous and most read author in our language who, therefore, like no other person has contributed to its dissemination: Jorge Amado" (Vasconcelos 10). Arif Dirlik has suggested that "postcoloniality is the condition of the intelligentsia of global capitalism. The question, then, is not whether this global intelligentsia can (or should) return to national loyalties, but whether, in recognition of its own class-position in global capitalism, it can generate a thorough going criticism of its own ideology and formulate practices of resistance against the system of which it is a product" (356). In this brief "postcolonial view" of Jorge Amado, I realize that I have not analyzed his texts, but rather I have analyzed my own position toward his texts and their message. It is in the analyses of our critical stance that postcoloniality may lead us to understand and begin to accept those thorny issues that involve our cultures of origin and that we have comfortably chosen to ignore. For a Brazilian(ist) woman, a postcolonial reading of the *malandro* Jorge Amado provides me with the kind of (self) Other examination that makes me question my own ideological stance. Perhaps such a reading will place me and other Brazilianists in a crisis of critical consciousness if not of conscience. A crisis, however, is a position that causes a shift, and in resolving the crisis, we may come to understand Jorge Amado's work.

In a recent book, Brazilian anthropologist Ruben Oliven argues that to see Brazil merely as an exotic, tropical country is to deny it of its vast territory—most of which lies outside the Tropics—and to dismiss its modernity. Like many other Brazilian intellectuals, Oliven is concerned about the image of his country that is portrayed abroad, particularly in the United States. Like many Brazilianists, Oliven wants the world—the United States—to see Brazil's European background and modern socio-political ideologies. Brazil is a large and diverse country both in territory and in cultural traditions. "Brazilian music," as most North Americans know it, is the music of Rio de Janeiro; "Brazilian food," as most North Americans know it, is the mixture of black beans and rice typical of the central states in Brazil; and "Brazilian literature," as most North Americans know it, is Jorge Amado. As Oliven argues, a large part of Brazil's population lives in the southernmost states of Rio Grande do Sul, Paraná, Santa Catarina, and São Paulo, yet none of the customs described above apply to all its citizens. More importantly, each of these states represents centuries of European immigration, and each has its own culture that differs slightly from the other states. The point that Oliven argues is that to reach a level of comprehension of national identity, one must first have an understanding of local identity. Then and only then can one understand the other localities within one's country, which allows one to come near to begin to understand the concept of national identity. He concludes that "one can argue the difficulty of accepting cultural diversity in [Brazil] . . . In fact, what we are seeing nowadays is a growing integration [of cultures in the country], but at the same time the affirmation of the most dissimilar types of cultural identity" (136).

To return to a more "colonizing" discourse, I would argue that it is imperative that those of us who study and teach Brazilian literature and culture include in our programs examples of all the different cultures represented in the country. In so doing, we will begin to fight the stereotypes caused by reductionist views of a few members of the academy. To be sure, these views have contributed to a misunderstanding of Brazil as a place of intellectual elitism and European adaptations. And they have often neglected the deep-rooted contributions of African culture that have predominated ideology and thought in a large region of the country. Jorge Amado's writings provide us with a good example of the traditions of the Afro-Brazilian region of the country and its culture. To deny him a place in our courses is to give him more importance, more perhaps, than he should have. To exclude such a prominent figure is to mask—only to ourselves—the impact that he has had in the world.

Students and colleagues have heard of him and wonder why he is forgotten. By including a reading of his texts, we can begin to re-evaluate our own positions and definitions of cultural spaces and identities. We must tackle the question of cultural diversity within national boundaries as well as globally, and, in doing so, create the cultural space—the postcolonial cultural space—that will allow for subaltern voices to be heard, even if they appear in the characters of Jorge Amado. As Homi Bhabha has stated, we must "track the processes of displacement and realignment that are already at work, constructing something different and hybrid from the encounter: a third space that does not simply revise or invert the dualities, but *revalues* the ideological bases of division and difference" (58). Perhaps it is in this "third space" that we will begin to understand—and accept—our cultures of origin as well as the cultures that we currently inhabit.

In this contextual world of ours, all words are representations that defy a static definition. In my own effort to understand the work of an often rejected, forgotten, purposefully left out and misunderstood Brazilian author, I have problematized the words "postcolonial," "colonized," and *malandro*. What is missing from this essay is the problematization of the other word in the title: "reading." Indeed, as I stated in the introduction of this essay, my purpose was to pose questions. I have questioned my own position and that of other Brazilianists, and I have problematized our critical stance. It is imperative that we all engage in some self-questioning. In so doing we will be able to read—deconstruct, essentialize, and revalue—the texts of Jorge Amado.

## BIBLIOGRAPHY

Adorno, Rolena. "Reconsidering Colonial Discourse for Sixteenth- and Seventeenth-Century Spanish America." *Latin American Research Review* 28:3 (1993): 135–45.

Appiah, Kwame Anthony. "Is the Post- in Postmodernism the Post- in Postcolonial?" *Critical Inquiry* 17 (1991): 336–57.

Beverley, John. *Against Literature*. Minneapolis: The University of Minnesota Press, 1993.

Bhabha, Homi K. "Postocolonial Atuhority and Postmodern Guilt." *Cultural Studies*. Lawrence Grossberg, Cary Nelson and Paula Treichler, eds. New York: Routledge (1992): 56–66.

Chamberlain, Bobby J. "Of Charters, Paradigms and Spawning Fish: A Look at Brazilian Literary Periodization and Canon-Formation." *Brasil/Brazil* 6 (1993): 5–23.

Colas, Santiago. "Of Creole Symptoms, Cuban Fantasies, and Other Latin American Postcolonial Ideologies," *PMLA* 110:3 (1995): 382–96.

DaMatta, Roberto. *Carnivals, Rogues, and heroes: An Interpretation of the Brazilian Dilemma*. Notre Dame, Indiana: University of Notre Dame Press, 1991.

Dirllik, Arif. "The Postcolonial Aura: Third World Criticism in the Age of Global Capitalism." *Critical Inquiry* 20 (1994): 328–56.

Gomes, Alvaro Cardoso. *Jorge Amado: Literatura Comentada*. São Paulo: Abril Educação, 1981.

Mignolo, Walter D. "Colonial and Postcolonial Discourse: Cultural Critique or Academic Colonialism?" *Latin American Research Review* 28:3 (1993): 120–34.

Mohanty, Satya P. "Colonial Legacies, Multicultural Futures: Relativism, Objectivity, and the Challenge of Otherness." *PMLA,* 110:1 (1995): 108–18.

Oliven, Ruben George. *Tradition Matters: Modern Gaucho Diversity in Brazil*. Trans. by Carmen Chaves Tesser. New York: Columbia University Press, 1995.

Reis, Roberto, "Who's Afraid of (Luso-)Brazilian Literature?" *World Literature Today* (1988): 231–34.

Said, Edward W. "Representing the Colonized: Anthropology's Inter-locutors." *Critical Inquiry* 15 (1989): 205–227.

Schwarz, Roberto. "Nacional por subtração." In *Que horas são?* São Paulo: Companhia das Letras (1989): 29–48.

Seed, Patricia. "More Colonial and Postcolonial Discourses." *Latin American Research Review* 28:3 (1993): 146–52.

Vasconcelos, José Carlos. "Amado Jorge Amado." *Jornal de Letras, Artes e Idéias* 25 (1995): 10–12.

Vidal, Hernán. "The Concept of Colonial and Postcolonial Discourse: A Perspective from Literary Criticism." *Latin American Research Review* 28:3 (1993): 113–19.

# Hybridity vs. Pluralism
## Culture, Race, and Aesthetics in Jorge Amado

NELSON H. VIEIRA

> *"O que lhe impressiona, prezado coronel, é a cor não a raça . . . Na Bahia, coronel, é difícil dizer quem não é mestiço [Dear Colonel, what impresses you is the color and not the race. . . . In Bahia, Colonel, it's hard to tell who is not a mulatto]."*
> —JORGE AMADO, TENDA DOS MILAGRES
> (TENT OF MIRACLES), 1969

> *". . . me parece indiscutível que o branco no Brasil concebe o negro como um ser inferior . . . O preconceito de côr me parece incontestável entre nós [. . . it seems to me that there is no argument on the question that the white man sees the blackman as inferior . . . Prejudice among us is undeniable]."*
> —MÁRIO DE ANDRADE, "LINHA DE CÔR
> (THE COLOR LINE)," 1939

The epigraphs for this study represent powerful statements on the prejudicial nature of Brazil's color line in contrast to the often-touted explanation that discrimination in this nation is actually based upon class (economic) level and not race. Articulated by Jorge Amado and Mário de Andrade, two significant voices during two different twentieth century time periods of Brazil's literary and cultural history, these statements also point to the importance of the color code in determining social status, acceptance or rejection and to the inherent contradiction between perspectives on race and color.[1] Thales de Azevedo in *Democracia racial: ideologia e realidade [Racial democracy: ideology and reality]* (1975) refers to North American anthropologist Donald Pierson and his 1967 statement about the existence, among racial analysts, of "certa confusão entre discriminação racial e discriminação social, desde quando a cor é, ordinariamente, um índice de classe [certain confusion between racial discrimination and social discrimination, inasmuch as color is normally an index of (social) class]" (37). Of course, Jorge Amado and Mário de Andrade affirm that color represents a form of discrimination directly linked to appearance since the darker the color the stronger the prejudice, at least in terms of "social" or class discrimination. Consequently, for these authors, the sole use of "race" as a category of discrimination appears to be unacceptable since mixture, hybridity and miscegenation constitute a Brazilian reality of racial "transculturalism"[2] that has been on-going since colonial times. In his introduction to Gilberto Freyre's *The Mansions and the Shanties*, Frank Tannenbaum argues the same point when alluding to the sexual unions between masters and slaves: "They are bound together, and Brazil is what it is because of them, because people of many colors, races, and languages mingled, intermingled, absorbed and were absorbed, regardless of theories, views, or notions of superiority or inferiority, of better or worse, of higher or lower" (ix).

Ergo, when Jorge Amado speaks of "racial democracy" in Brazil[3] is he not referring primarily to the flagrant physiological mixture and cultural hybridity that are very apparent in the Brazilian make-up and ethos? Albeit a nineteenth century term used to describe "racialized formulations" (6) which Robert J. C. Young chronicles in *Colonial Desire: Hybridity in Theory, Culture and Race* (1995), hybridity harbors other racial and cultural implications for twentieth century minds seeking the affirmation of difference instead of its erasure via processes of *mestiçagem* and whitening. According to Young, "hybridity . . . implies a disruption and forcing together of any unlike living things . . . Hybridity is a making one of two distinct things . . . Hybridity thus makes difference into sameness, and sameness into difference, but in a way that makes the same no longer the same, the different no longer simply different" (26). But while hybridity may suggest the "impossiblilty of essentialism" (Young 27), it can also subscribe to a notion of sameness (homogeneity) such as "whitening" which diminishes an endorsement of difference (heterogeneity). In other words, a homogeneous ideology can occur when the State promotes the myth of racial democracy while irresponsibly neglecting the individual rights of its pluralistic citizenry. This line of thinking neither reflects Amado's vision nor his depiction of *mestiçagem*. In fact, he challenges the practice of cultural homogeneity.

According to Paula Montero's 1996 essay on culture and democracy, a constructed ideology of mestizo sameness has played an active role in Brazil's modern cultural history:

> por mais paradoxal que isto possa parecer, o Estado brasileiro em sua
> aliança com os intelectuais teve êxito na sua empreitada histórica, que visou
> incorporar as sociabilidades primárias (família, etnia, religião, etc) no *con-*

*structo* de uma identidade nacional "mestiça"; esta acabou, com efeito por enraizar-se profundamente como ideologia popular. Foi portanto o Estado quem, de maneira mais ou menos coerente, harmonizou os elementos étnicos com a democracia [no matter how paradoxical this may seem, the Brazilian State in its alliance with the intellectuals was successful in its tough historical assignment, that strove to incorporate the primary sociable groups (family, ethnic groups) in a mixed blood national identity *construct*; which ended up, per consequence of a deep rooting, as the popular ideology. Therefore, it was the State that, in a more or less coherent fashion, harmonized ethnic elements with democracy]. (113)

Montero presents this case to expose how the State fabricated this "harmony" without actually addressing the rights and belongingness of groups aspiring to socio-political and cultural affirmation.

In his narratives and especially in *Tenda dos milagres* (1969)[4] Amado shows the essential to be frequently or always ambiguous and thus he envisages Brazil's flagrant mestizo hybridity and culture as a signal of the country's historical heterogeneity and national multicultural reality. Amado's fiction actually demonstrates what Young confirms: "Culture and race developed together, imbricated within each other" (28). In this way one may appreciate how for Amado, hybridity may have a physiological *and* cultural connotation by calling attention to the contributions of both cultures to the hybrid form. Moreover, contrary to the proclivity to read hybridity and racial democracy on the broader level of socio-political democratic practices, as suggested by the Brazilian State's former ideological and mythical references to "racial democracy" as well as by the misinterpretation of Amado's usage of that term,[5] Amado does make a very clear distinction between racial (biological) democracy and racism, just as Tannenbaum implies in his introduction to Freyre. For purposes of this study, terms like "hybridity" or "mestizo" capture more accurately the actual combination of race *and* culture rather than the often employed confusing term "racial democracy," used by Amado and until recently by many Brazilians to describe a biological and at times a psychological as well as cultural phenomenon. The term "racial democracy" complicates the cultural meaning because the word "democracy" within this expression also harbors a political connotation that confuses the biological implication primarily stressed by Brazilians and manifested in the country's transracial and transcultural history. In other words, Amado employs the term "racial democracy" to explain and defend miscegenation, but *simultaneously* his fiction directly treats issues of color, status and power along with cultural discrimination to deconstruct the inhumanity of racism and intolerance. In this vein, what do the physiological and cultural signify vis-à-vis a prejudicial color line and the absence of democratic political pluralism in Brazil? Part of the answer lies in Jorge Amado's fiction wherein these issues are dramatized and challenged.

In this study the novel *Tenda dos milagres (TM)* will serve as the corpus for illustrating Amado's conception of hybridity and its implications for pluralism, culture, race, ethnicity, and aesthetics. Allusions will also be made to *A descoberta da América pelos turcos* (1994) for purposes of referring to his view on ethnicity and ethnic cultural mixing. While my theoretical considerations are drawn from several sources, I believe the development of the hybrid in Brazil partially stems from what Young calls "'colonial desire': a covert but insistent obsession with transgressive, interracial sex, hybridity and miscegenation" (xii).[6] The Luso-Brazilian counterpart to this colonial practice, dissected by Ricardo Benzaquen in his study of Gilberto Freyre's *Casa grande e senzala,* describes Brazil's *overt* "colonial desire" in this way: "é justamente uma das modalidades dessa *hybris,* o excesso de natureza sexual, que pode ser apontado como o maior responsável por aquela atmosfera de intimidade e calor que, sem descartar o despotismo, caracterizava as relações entre senhores e escravos em *CGS* [it is exactly one of the modalities of this *hybris,* or excess of sexual drive, which can be pointed out as the main factor responsible for creating an environment of intimacy and warmth, without discarding despotism, which characterized the relationships between masters and slaves in *CGS*]. (59). Since Freyre's pro-mestizo vision during the 1930s and 1940s served to create a gradual shift toward a positive national ideology, a dynamic image of racial hybridity and of a "new [hybrid] world in the tropics," it is not surprising to read Amado's fiction at that time [and later] within this climate, albeit Amado's disagreements with aspects of Freyre's thesis. Moreover, as a champion of miscegenation, Amado's adherence to social scientific developments regarding race, à la Freyre, is even more understandable considering his early interest in race and his link to anthropologists such as Artur Ramos and Edison Carneiro.[7] In fact, in 1962, Amado praised Freyre as a cultural revolutionary and emphasized "a importância de Gilberto Freyre (e de *Casa grande e senzala)* no processo de democratização da cultura no Brasil" [the importance of Gilberto Freyre (and of *CGS*) in the process of the democratization of Brazilian culture] (32).[8] To exemplify Freyre's impact upon Amado, while praising Freyre's accomplishments, Tannenbaum makes the following incisive observation: "This to me is the measure of Gilberto Freyre's achievement. He has given the Brazilian people a quiet pride in being what they are. As a single illustration: Jorge Amado's *Gabriela* could not have been written before *The Masters and the Slaves"* (xi).

In addition to the above theorists and critics, Néstor Garcia Canclini and his *Hybrid Cultures: Strategies for Entering and Leaving Modernity* (1995) will also be consulted for locating the hybrid phenomenon within the Latin American context and especially for demonstrating how the uncertainty about the meaning of modernity in Latin America derives in part "from the sociocultural hybrids in which the traditional and the modern are mixed" (2). Furthermore, in stressing the need to establish concrete recognition of the "hybrid," Canclini declares the following in "The Hybrid: a Conversation": "That is why we don't understand the hybrid if we only look at it as complete dissemination, rather than as something that is ordered, that is experienced as classified or in need of classification in order to contain the dissolution of the signifieds."[9]

Reflecting the views of a white as well as a mulatto writer, the two epigraphs for this study also suggest that color and race have diverse cultural and social connotations and combinations lurking under the rubric of hybridity. Jorge Amado has continually dramatized the mestizo, the *mulato*, and especially the *mulata* in all his fiction, thereby highlighting his argument on the effects of hybridity upon Brazilian society which his mestizo narrator classifies as "amalgamation" in *A descoberta da América pelos turcos* [*The dicovery of America by the Turks*]: "a boa nação turca, uma das muitas que amalgamadas compuseram e compõem a nação brasileira" [the good Turkish nation, one of the many that in a mixing process, made up and makes up the Brazilian nation] (7). But while there is hybridity, there also does exist racism. And thus it is advisable to examine hybridity in Brazilian culture in order to grasp its relationship to democratic pluralism, a phenomenon apparently wanting in Brazil especially for its darker citizens, according to Amado. However, as President Fernando Henrique Cardoso today speaks openly about the existence of racism in Brazil,[10] he appears to be writing a new political and cultural chapter for Brazil, one that becomes part of the text already begun by Jorge Amado, Gilberto Freyre and Mário de Andrade, among others.

In positing "hybridity" vis-à-vis "pluralism," this study distinguishes between ideologies of biological and socio-political representation to illustrate how questions of social, racial, ethnic, sexual, and economic parity are habitually addressed by Amado in terms of culture and power. While hybridity manifests racial mixture or "racial democracy," does it evoke cultural pluralism or individual or social power? In her recent essay, Paula Montero speaks to the questions of power, plurality, and political representation for all Brazilians in the context of contemporary political parties.[11] She criticizes certain political agendas that focus rigidly upon political rights as ultimately undermining the full potentiality and acknowledgement of difference and alterity by the obvious exclusion of a transcultural dialog: "O diferente é apenas aquele que não tem direitos" [Who is different is only the one who does not have any rights] (112), implying that the singular political focus upon rights, on a national basis, does not always enhance the development of cultural differences and cultural pluralism.

Hannah Arendt, in her seminal study, *The Human Condition* (1958), contextualizes the idea of plurality by focussing upon the process of action: "Plurality is the condition of human action because we are all the same, that is, human, in such a way that nobody is ever the same as anyone else who ever lived, lives, or will live" (7–8). Arendt further explains her view by referring to the concept of political and social action with the implication of difference: "Action, the only activity that goes on directly between men without the intermediary of things or matter, corresponds to the human condition of plurality, to the fact that men, not Man, live on the earth and inhabit the world. While all aspects of the human condition are somehow related to politics, this plurality is specifically *the* condition—not only the *conditio sine qua non*, but the *conditio per quam*—of all political life" (8). Therefore, by pointing to the political *and* social implications of plurality, Arendt underscores the need for political action/negotiation for all within a national community. As exemplified in *TM,* whose time structure takes place during moments of social authoritarianism in the early decades of the century through the Second World War and simultaneously juxtaposed with the repressive period of the former military regime of the late '60s, the Brazilian hegemonic social structure based on authoritarian power and the politics of color and class has during different time periods of its history precluded the exercise of democratic political rights and socio-cultural action, also due to the elites' monopoly of socio-economic control.

The following statement by Arendt maps out a prescription that could be applied to the Brazilian reality:

> For though the common world is the common meeting ground of all, those who are present have different locations in it, and the location of one can no more coincide with the location of another than the location of two objects. Being seen and being heard by others derive their significance from the fact that everybody sees and hears from a different position ... Only where things can be seen by many in a variety of aspects without changing their identity, so that those who are gathered around them know they see sameness in utter diversity, can worldly reality truly and reliably appear. (57)

Jorge Amado's fiction repeatedly dramatizes Brazil's "diversity" while simultaneously pointing to the "different locations" of its people and the threat of losing their identity due to their unequal socio-economic-political status and the insidious color code which habitually draws upon authoritarian/hegemonic power to maintain the daily status quo. An example of this threatened loss of identity is illustrated in *TM* in a historical scene where the mulato Pedro Archanjo is defended by a professor who argues with the established academic elite of Bahia's School of Medicine and their authoritarian notion of status and race which does not admit the possibility of academic talent among the poor mestizos: "O talento independe de pigmentação, de títulos, de condição social, tudo isso é tolice" [Talent is independent of skin pigmentation, of titles, of social condition, all these are nonsense] (*TM* 219). Or as Paula Montero states when she alludes to the Brazilian concept of national identity as "uma ilusão porque esconde o corpo fragmentado de uma nação desprovida de direitos" [an illusion because it hides the fragmented body of a nation destituted of rights] (or rather, an) "impostura que denega as desigualdades entre os brasileiros" [a deception that denies the inequalities [existing] among Brazilians] (112).

To illustrate Arendt's view, along with Montero's, in a strategic approach to the issue of "cultural pluralism" for an educational context in the United States, the following definition by the National Coalition for Cultural Pluralism[12] is used here as a definition in concert with Amado's wry perception of Brazil's social reality. Consequently, it harbors relevancy for Brazil's "redemocratization" program, on-going since the mid-1980s. This Coalition defined "cultural pluralism" as:

> . . . a state of equal co-existence in a mutually supportive relationship within the boundaries or frame-work of one nation of people of diverse cultures with significantly different patterns of belief, behavior, color, and in many cases with different languages. To achieve cultural pluralism, there must be unity with diversity. Each person must be aware of and secure in his own identity, and be willing to extend to others the same respect and rights that he expects to enjoy himself. (14)

Albeit somewhat utopian in its vision, this definition of "cultural pluralism" relates to Amado's critical treatment of race and politics in *TM* as well as to ethnicity and gender in *A descoberta da América pelos turcos*, while at the same time championing biological and cultural mixture as "racial democracy." In these novels, readers can appreciate this twentieth-century author's wide historical and social framework of experience and writing in Brazil and its incorporation into his critique of how a "mutually supportive relationship" is still desperately lacking on political, racial, and social grounds. Amado's critical perspective aims at what the above coalition is ultimately fostering: "The concept of cultural pluralism, therefore, must be the perspective used by the different social groups in their attempt to survive as independent, yet interdependent, segments of this society. Pluralism lifts up the necessary and creative tension between similarity and difference. It strongly endorses standards of variety, authentic options, diverse centers of power, and self-direction" (150). Amado's narratives manifest the quest for cultural pluralism by endorsing Afro-Brazilian culture's potential as one of Brazil's "diverse centers of power."

Given the predominance of racial mixture in Brazil, pluralism for Brazil has to include the "mestiço" reality beyond ideological labelling and cultural tokenism. In this vein, Amado adopts an anthropological perspective, embodied in his hero, Pedro Archanjo, a self-made anthropologist who sees "hybridity" as a transcultural phenomenon within Brazil and defines the country's "face" as culturally mestizo in opposition to the elite's "imported" cultural facade: "É mestiça a face do povo brasileiro e é mestiça a sua cultura . . . São mestiças a nossa face e a vossa face: é mestiça a nossa cultura, mas a vossa é importada, é merda em pó" [The face of the Brazilian people is a mixture of races as well as its culture . . . Our face as well as yours are of mixed blood: our culture is also a mixture, but yours is imported, it's powder crap] (*TM* 165). In his trenchant essay, "Brazilian Culture: Nationalism by Elimination," appearing in *Misplaced Ideas: Essays on Brazilian Culture*, Roberto Schwarz refers to this "class" opposition while explaining the practice of cultural copying/importing as an issue predominantly of the white (and at times light mulatto) elite. Schwarz addresses Sílvio Romero's study, *Machado de Assis,* by referring to the Brazilian elites' historical copying of Old World culture, an earlier version of cultural dependency theory, as an example of an imitativeness that is not "essentially" or racially Brazilian, due to class distinctions, but rather a behavior of the elite separating itself from the masses: "It is not copying in general but *the copying of one class* that constitutes the problem. The explanation must lie not in race but in class" (Schwarz 11). In signalling the wide gap between elitist and popular behaviors and realities that fosters alienating and hegemonic practices, Schwarz and Amado are underscoring one of the hurdles cultural pluralism faces in Brazil. Both are also analyzing the complexity of the cultural make-up of Brazil where class simultaneously governs notions of national identity as well as the role of color. For Jorge Amado, Brazil is a racially mestizo country embodied in the "published" words of his mestizo hero-author, Pedro Archanjo: "Formar-se-á uma cultura mestiça de tal maneira poderosa e inerente a cada brasileiro que será a própria consciência nacional e mesmo os filhos de pais e mães imigrantes brasileiros de primeira geração, crescerão culturalmente mestiços" [It will form a mestizo culture, so powerful and inherent to every Brazilian that it will become the very national conscience, that even the children of first generation immigrant fathers and mothers will grow up as cultural mestizos] (*TM* 258). The inclusion of immigrants in this statement refers to questions of race as well as ethnicity, an amalgamation also depicted in Amado's fiction but especially in the two texts treated here. In a similar vein, Benzaquen's assessment of *Casa grande e senzala* appears to support Archanjo's prescription for a mestizo society: "Diferença, hibridismo, ambigüidade e indefinição: parecem ser estas as principais conseqüencias da idéia de miscigenação utilizada em *CGS*" [Difference, hybridism, ambiguity and indefiniteness: seem to be the main consequences of the idea of miscegenation used in *CGS*] (46). For Archanjo, mestizo becomes the *sine qua non* of the Brazilian ethos.

The Amadian work used here for exemplifying the arguments presented above was selected for its "hybrid" focus and conceptualization, incorporated in its narrative discourses and in its mulatto hero, Pedro Archanjo. Our argument stems from Amado's insistent view of racial democracy as a representation of ubiquitous racial mixture or miscegenation, registered among all levels of society, in contrast to the lack of cultural pluralism and human rights reinforced by color prejudice and class status. In this sense, his novels consistently challenge the color code as well as the injustices of the socio-cultural and political practices that reveal the precariousness of the base social positions of Blacks and mestizos in Brazil. Whether or not his novels take place historically in the early part of the century, or during the late '60s or the 1980s and '90s, his vision remains constant. Within the two major discourses that comprise TM, the first person and omniscient voices, Amado discloses the lack of democratic cultural pluralism in Bahia Brazil by highlighting the manipulation of power and cultural issues within the context of hybridity and bigotry. The narrative voices enhance this dual reality of democratic miscegenation and color/class discrimination, the latter tied to the unjust and ruthless dictates of socio-economic status. In other words, while the term "racial democracy" privileges the phenomenon of mixture within the narrative, at the same time, Amado's fiction provides harsh critiques of socio-economic, political, "racial," and cultural inequalities. These critiques of discrimination and prejudice are both embodied in the homodiegetic first-person narrator, Fausto Pena, a white oppressed marginal figure who is responsible for telling his side of the story in 1968, as well as in Pedro Archanjo, the mulatto hero, poet, anthropologist, bon vivant, and writer whose destiny into abject poverty is recounted via a storytelling omniscient narrator who is sympathetic to the characters' marginalization. Both of these characters' fates are shaped by the hypocrisies, prejudices, and greed manifested by cultural and power elites who use myths such as racial democracy and political freedom to serve their own goals of self-promotion in the first half of the century and of commercial advertising in the late '60s. Thus, Amado is coherent in his endorsement of racial democracy as widespread racial mixture, but he is also simultaneously coherent in his challenging the maginalization of less privileged people of all colors as well as the insidious and uneven exclusion of darker skinned people from political participation and economic employment.

In *TM*, Amado illustrates how hybridity unmasks the social inequities engendered by hypocritical practices of race and culture, once inspired directly by notions of eugenics and nobility of class that today have waned but not completely. This view is clearly exemplified when the mulatto, Tadeu Canhoto, Archanjo's son, encounters serious obstacles to marrying the upperclass and blond Lu. In a despotic rage her father orders a lawyer friend to prevent this union by calling attention to the fact that money and class are above the law: "Que me importa a lei! O senhor é advogado, sabe que a lei não é feita para todos. Quem tem posses passa por cima da lei. O senhor está autorizado a gastar o que fôr necessário" [What do I care about the law! Sir, you are a lawyer, and you know that the law is not made for everybody. Whoever has means is above the law. You, sir, have been authorized to spend whatever you deem necessary] (*TM* 298). Here, in the past, we see how power exerts its willful hand, just as it does in the 1968 present when "Fausto" Pena is literally selling his soul in order to achieve an elusive sense of fame.

Also, by using several time frames to reveal historical patterns that keep repeating, Amado underscores how in Brazil hybridity contrasts with cultural pluralism in matters of culture and race because the same social injustices continue to proliferate despite "democratic" racial intermixing. For example, the leftist leaning Professor Fraga Neto during his *concurso* for a chair in the Medical School uses Archanjo's work as scientific authority much to the dismay of the academic elite. This quotation from Archanjo's book not only helps to support Fraga Neto's thesis that Brazil's social structure warrants revamping, but it also reaffirms the significance of maintaining the rituals of Afro-Brazilian cultural difference, while at the same time evoking the novel's central vision and its insistence upon the popular belief in the power of "miracles," also implied in the book's title:

São de tal maneira terríveis as condições de vida do povo baiano, tamanha é a miséria, tão absoluta a falta de qualquer assistência médica ou sanitária, do mais mínimo interêsse do Estado ou das autoridades, que viver em tais condições constitui por si só extraordinária demonstração de fôrça e vitalidade. Assim sendo, a preservação de costumes e tradições, a organização de sociedades, escolas, desfiles, ranchos, ternos, afoxés, a criação de ritmos de dança e canto, tudo quanto significa enriquecimento cultural adquire a importância de verdadeiro milagre que só a mistura de raças explica e possibilita. Da miscigenação nasce uma raça de tanto talento e resistência, tão poderosa, que supera a miséria e o desespêro na criação quotidiana da beleza e da vida [In Bahia the conditions in which the lower classes live are so terrible, the misery is so great, and all medical or sanitary assistance is totally lacking, as is the slightest show of interest on the part of the state or other public authorities, that merely staying alive in such conditions constitutes extraordinary proof of strength and vitality. For this reason, the preservation of custom and tradition, the organization of societies, samba schools, parades, carnival parades, bands, and *afoxés*, and the creation of new dance rhythms and songs—all that signifies cultural enrichment—takes on the character of a veritable miracle which can only be explained by miscegenation. The mixture of races has given birth to a new race of so much talent and endurance, of such power, that is able to rise above misery and despair in a daily creation of beauty and of life itself].[13] (TM 291–292)

Used to combat the aryanism and eugenics of the intellectual power elite in the early part of the twentieth century, this quotation calls attention to the conflicts between Afro-Brazilians and the power elites and also reinforces the cultural and racial attributes of the "hybrid" form by stressing how the richness of its cultural expressions sustains and strengthens Afro-Brazilians despite their miserable socio-economic conditions and periods of despair. This view functions in conjunction with the narrative's popular tone which drives the diegesis by drawing upon the storytelling effect derived from Brazil's oral tradition. By constructing the novel with a popular perspective,

Amado not only uses this view to challenge the indifference of the State and its authoritarian leaders but also emphasizes the power of popular beliefs and cultural difference, an appeal for recognizing, beyond folkloric and patrimonial nods, the "different locations" of diverse peoples that Hannah Arendt discusses in her advocacy for "human action" through political action. Consequently, Amado's novel portrays an incisive drama of subaltern cultural pluralism that begs for democratic or socialist political action. The democracy that results in interracial mixture is not the same as the democracy of political practices. When the narrative reverts to 1968–69 and the post–Gilberto Freyre era of positive mixture, to commemorate the centennial of Archanjo's birth, the reader observes the status quo where the glory of the nation is praised over the importance of Archanjo's work. And while overt statements about the significance of Archanjo's work are presented, they are voiced by the leftist leaning popular lawyer Damião de Souza and the outsider, the supposedly liberal North American Nobel Prize winner, Professor Levenson of Columbia University who rediscovered Archanjo's work. And even though the celebration of Archanjo's work recognizes his contribution to a positive view of racial mixture, it is clear that this serves to nurture the national image of Brazil as *mestiço* but does nothing for rescuing *negros* and *mulatos* from poverty stricken conditions. While, for the State, racial democracy may serve as a national myth, it does not represent in socio-economic terms Brazil's national pluralist reality, albeit the State's proclivity to impart that image. On the other hand, for Amado the need to distinguish between racial democracy and democratic pluralism is repeatedly treated in his novels where the hybrid or mestizo serves as the catalyst for eliciting the interstices and conflicts between black and white in which new formulations of identity not only contribute to the actual racial and cultural diversity within Brazil but also provide inroads toward reevaluationg its national ideology.

By focussing upon mixture, hybridity and conflict, Amado is actually opting for a dialogizing hybridity which Young, in reading Bakhtin, calls "intentional hybridity," a stance that "sets different points of view against each other in a conflictual structure, which retains 'a certain elemental, organic energy and openendedness'" (Young 21–22). In an interpretation of Bakhtin that uncannily parallels Amado's depiction of how hybridity dismantles the notions of power elites, Young states: "For Bakhtin himself, the crucial effect of hybridization comes with the latter, political category, the moment where, within a single discourse, one voice is able to unmask the other. This is the point where authoritative discourse is undone" (Young 22). Thus, we subscribe to the view of Amado's use of "intentional hybridity" via the depiction of racial mixture (racial democracy) to undo the discourse of racism.

Amado closes his novel, not with the pompous and false commemoration of Archanjo's work by the Bahian power and academic elites, but rather by the street celebration of the 1969 Carnaval and a Samba School's theme, "Pedro Archanjo in Four Movements." Besides the euphoria and magic of Carnaval, this last chapter presents a popular and truer picture of Archanjo's glory, merit and accomplishments while simultaneously glorifying, by inference, the Brazilian *mulato* in general: "Glória glória/Do mulato brasileiro/ Contemporâneo/Glória glória" [Glory, glory/of the Brazilian mulatto/Contemporary/Glory glory] (*TM* 372). Interestingly, in the novel's last lines, this strong affirmation of the *mulato*'s hybrid attributes is depicted via the Samba School's multiple encarnation of Archanjo by using a variety of dancers to illustrate the various moments of his life as well as the diversity of his talents which stem from a hybrid form of living between cultures:

> Pedro Archanjo Ojuobá vem dançando, não é um só, é vário, numeroso, múltiplo, velho, quarentão, môço, rapazola, andarilho, dançador, boa-prosa, bom no trago, rebelde, sedicioso, grevista, arruaceiro, tocador de violão e cavaquinho, namorado, terno amante, pai-d'égua, escritor, sábio, um feiticeiro. Todos pobres, pardos e paisanos [Pedro Archanjo Ojuobá's dancing by, not one but several, many multiple: old, middle-aged, young, adolescent; vagabond, dancer, fine talker, hard drinker, rebel, radical, striker, street fighter, guitar and *cavaquinho* player, wooer, tender lover, stud-horse, writer, sage, sorcerer. And everyone of them mulatto, indigent, native of Bahia].[14] (374)

From the singular to the multiple, these lines demonstrate Amado's method of underscoring the *mestiço* way of life that permeates Brazil, especially within the popular classes and, of course, beyond these social parameters.

This mestizo way of life involves race *and* culture which are intertwined, incorporating tradition (rituals) and modern practices that may seem ambiguous and contradictory but which Canclini views as part of the Latin American *gestalt* of cultural heterogeneity that serves as "one of the means to explain the oblique powers that intermingle liberal institutions and authoritarian habits, social democratic movements with paternalistic regimes, and the transactions of some with others" (3). For Canclini, the interweaving of the traditional and the modern has created "an interclass mixing [that] has generated hybrid formations in all social strata" (46). For Amado the Brazilian mestizo's way of life stems from a hybrid form of cross-cultural living, deftly dramatized in a scene where Archanjo debates "teoria e vida," or bookish vs. life experience, or materialism vs. the supernatural, with the sympathetic but somewhat rigid Professor Fraga Neto who cannot understand how Archanjo can reconcile his science with his popular religious beliefs. Archanjo's response is "Meu materialismo não me limita" [My materialism does not limit me] (*TM* 317). Within his world mixture or hybridity exist natural ways of living, whether they be in terms of race, culture or ways of thinking. With mixture, nothing is black and white. Rather, hybridity represents broader cultural living. Cultural parameters are broken down, allowing for perspectives that are not based solely on "referents of legitimacy" (Canclini 243) but on syncretic and cross-cultural experiences. The scene depicting the debate on "theory and life" captures the flagrant mixing that permeates Brazilian culture and thinking because Archanjo recognizes, via his scientific observation, the non-existence of the supernatural, yet cannot prevent himself from calling upon Afro-Brazilian gods and saints during the vicissitudes of daily life. Furthermore, in a prophetic view of the future image of Brazilian culture, Amado has Archanjo herald "mixture" as a national ethos and characteristic:

> Sou a mistura de raças e de homens, sou um mulato, um brasileiro. Amanhã será conforme o senhor diz e deseja, certamente será, o homem anda para a frente. Nesse dia tudo já terá se misturado por completo e o que hoje é mistério e luta de gente pobre, roda de negros e mestiços, música proibida, dança ilegal, candomblé, samba, capoeira, tudo isso será festa do povo brasileiro, música, balé, nossa côr, nosso riso, compreende? [I'm a mixture of men and races; I am a mulatto, a Brazilian. Tomorrow things will be the way you say and hope they will. I'm sure of that; humanity is marching forward. When that day comes, everything will be part of the total mixture, and what today is a mystery that poor folk have to fight for—meetings of Negroes and Mestizos, forbidden music, illegal dances, *candomblé,* samba, and *capoeira*—why all that will be the treasured joy of the Brazilian people. Our music and ballet, our color, our laughter. Do you understand?].[15] (318)

As Canclini's states when referring to Latin American art as transgressive: "always art that is mestizo, impure, that exists by dint of being placed at the crossing of paths that have been composing us and breaking us down" (243). And in rethinking the links between culture and power, Canclini refers to art's "metaphorical struggle" and the importance of cultural analyses which may gradually lead to transformations because he believes that "the search for mediations and diagonal ways for managing conflicts gives cultural relations a prominent place in political development" (261). Amado's vision of hybridity is also in concert with Canclini's plea for a reformulation of the Latin American pluralist patrimony as not a representation of stable goods but rather as a "social process" (Canclini 136). Here, Canclini describes the future role of cultural patrimony, one incisively manifested by Amado in his fiction: "Although the patrimony serves to unify each nation, the inequalities in its formation and appropriation require that it also be studied as a space of material and symbolic struggles between classes, ethnic groups, and other groups. This methodological principle corresponds to the complex character of contemporary societies" (136). And in a similar observation alluding to the global restructuring of society and politics as well as the role of hybridity therein, Neil Larsen cogently declares: "Rather than continuously referring back to a 'patrimony,' or a site of fixed cultural essence or identity, culture now becomes simply a process of 'reconversion,' of constant 'negotiation' and 'hybridization' across the multiple political, economic, and ethnic divisions of Latin American societies (207).

Besides employing the effect of contrast between hybridity and pluralism, Amado also draws upon "contrast" and the notion of conflict, implicated in his use of "intentional hybridity," to juxtapose reality and myth in order to deconstruct the proclivity to read myth as reality. In many instances throughout the novel, the narrative contrasts individual and collective impressions with historical reality to elicit from the reader a recognition of how national myths are constructed and promoted. The novel conveys a keen sense of how cultural realities are manipulated and exaggerated to suit the objectives of the power elites. In this vein, *TM* serves as a fine resource for a cultural studies project showing how "symbolic violence" can occur within what Bourdieu calls the "field of power."[16] In *TM* this process is illustrated via the mythical aggrandizement of Archanjo's life by the powerful cultural producers who create an overblown image for purposes of their own economic or social gains. Amado deftly dramatizes this situation with ingenious shifts in the narrative perspective that are part of the novel's overall narrative of shifting points of view, mainly between an omniscient voice and the dramatized narrator of 1968, Fausto Pena.[17] However, during the 1968 period which is normally narrated in the first person by Fausto Pena, Amado uses the omniscient voice at the beginning of chapter 11 (sub-chapters 1–6, pp.199–214) to expose the reader to various points of view, from Professor Calazans who provides biographical data on Archanjo to the Doping Publicity Agency (perhaps an allegorical allusion to the repressive DOPS, Departamento de Ordem Política e Social, of the military regime). This data is followed by Doping's distorted textual version designed for distribution in primary schools as part of a literary contest and then by a teacher's simplistic and moralistic lecture on Archanjo to students expected to write a composition on Archanjo, exemplified in sub-chapter 6 by a student's totally erroneous version of Archanjo's accomplishments. Chapter 11's title, "Onde Pedro Archanjo é prêmio e assunto de prêmio, com poetas, publicitários, professorinhas e o gaiato Crocodilo" [In which Pedro Archanjo becomes a prize and the subject of a prize, with poets, press agents, lady schoolteachers, and the Crocodile Clown],[18] previews how modern communication can twist reality and create false myths. Amado's critical treatment of this process in *TM* is a tour-de-force of how culture is frequently produced and misinterpreted.

Aesthetically, the aforementioned chapter also signals Amado's deft and complex narrative composition of *TM* in which multiple perspectives serve as examples of a complicated reality that defies the existence of a single cultural paradigm within a national culture. Instead, these sub-chapters, along with the narrative's continual shifts in point of view, affirm the vibrant diversity and multiple realities within Brazilian culture. In fact, as a narrative, *TM* represents a hybrid text in its aesthetic and socio-cultural formulation of diversity within a regional and national context that harbors hegemonic as well as subaltern forces, the latter struggling for the possibility of being one of the nation's diverse centers of power. The hybrid nature of the text in which dominant and subaltern characters battle for cultural space also emerges in the blurring of some narrative perspectives. For example, while the omniscient voice contrasts with Fausto Pena's unreliablity, at times one may interpret the omniscient voice as Pena's formal account resulting from his research for the North American Levenson. While this perspective does not hold throughout the novel, especially when Pena takes leave of Archanjo in jail and the omniscient narrative voice takes over till the end, the reader nonetheless perceives a blending or an approximation of narrative accounts or views that reveal differences yet similarities, suggesting the hybrid experience of multiple identities and situational ethnicity. In other words, one type of discourse is used for formal situations, while another, on a more personal level, reveals vulnerable and intimate realities. In short, Jorge Amado's aesthetics in this novel permeate its form as well as content.

Amado's treatment of race and culture as well as discrimination in *TM* exhibits the ramifications of hybridity, a cultural linchpin that affirms the heterogeneity of culture as well as challenges the hypocrisies precluding the nation's progress toward democratic cultural pluralism. Hybridity questions supposedly stable cultural essences such as the twisted rhetoric posed by the racist antagonist Professor Argolo: "Em que se baseia para defender a mestiçagem e apresentá-la como solução ideal para o problema de raças no Brasil? Para atrever-se a classificar de mulata nossa cultura latina? Affirmação monstruosa, corruptora" [On what do you base the concept of defending miscegenation and presenting it as an ideal solution to the problem of races in Brazil? To dare to classify as mulatto our Latin culture? A monstruous and corrupting assertion] (*TM* 177). Perhaps even the term "*Latin* America" is tyrranical in its insinuation of cultural coherency? Jorge Amado appears to suggest this indirectly, but above all he strives to unmask the tendency to favor sameness over difference. In doing so, he deconstructs national myths and racial hypocrisies that are frequently embedded in such myths and behaviors. His fiction struggles to disrobe embedded behavioral traits covered by the mythical cloak of one national cultural identity. Xavier Albó succinctly articulates what Amado sees as a national problem. In "Our Identity Starting from Pluralism in the Base," from the collection *The Postmodernism Debate in Latin America*, Albó discusses the notion of the plurinational in the context of Black groups "claiming to be recognized in their particular racial and cultural identity" (25). Albó continues his point by describing how pluralism in Latin America may exist biologically but hardly on a socio-political level:

The dominant case in the rest of the countries of Spanish origin and in Brazil, all of which manifest, often hypocritically, unacknowledged forms of racial discrimination. Particularly in Brazil, there is a strong movement to designate a state that accepts and even foments its pluricultural base, but, in general, the African-American populations do not speak of a *nation*. Undoubtedly, their character as a transplanted people brought to the continent as a subordinated labor force substantially modifies their identifying terms. For example, they do not have their own "territory"; their cultural roots and languages remain, to some extent, in Africa (26).

Amado's *TM* portrays the Afro-Brazilian struggle to find its place in the sun, its own cultural "territory" where democratic cultural coexistence is recognized and practiced in the affirmation of national transculturalism.

In conclusion, Jorge Amado traces the obstacles to cultural and sociopolitical pluralism by building his thesis upon the realities of race, culture and hybridity. His treatment involves the deconstruction of violent cultural production and hypocritical racial practices. While his narrative may be misconstrued by the reference to racial democracy, he clearly demonstrates that he is not alluding to mythical ideologies but rather to biological and cultural realities that do not discount the existence of racial discrimination. In fact, his novel repeatedly wrestles with bigotry and prejudice, showing where the important issues lie in relation to the meaning of Pedro Archanjo's life and work: "Importante a descrição de hábitos e costumes, a pesquisa de folclore, mais importante ainda a polêmica contra o racismo, a proclamação da democracia racial" [It was very important his description of habits and customs, a research of folklore, and more important yet, his debate against racism, and the proclamation of racial democracy] (200). Here, within the same sentence, Amado has one of his characters acknowledge the coexistence of racism and racial democracy, thereby belying the notion that he adheres to the myth of racial democracy as a cover-up for the existence of racial discrimination. Amado appears to be fine tuning what Freyre began in *Casa grande e senzala* but, in so doing, he strives to avoid falling into the trap of the "myth" of racial democracy which also stemmed from (mis)interpretations of Freyre's work: "Híbrida desde o início, a sociedade brasileira é de todas da América a que se construiu mais harmoniosamente quanto às relações de raça: dentro de um ambiente de quase reciprocidade cultural" [Hybrid since its very beginnings, Brazilian society is the one among the others in America that built more harmoniously racial relations: within an environment of an almost cultural reciprocity].[19]

These last statements attest to the fact that Amado is not just glorifying Afro-Brazilian folklore and customs but is rather getting to the deep-structural level of Afro-Brazilian reality. He does not repeat what other writers and intellectuals practiced, according to Sérgio Buarque de Holanda in his critical essay "Negros e Brancos" from *Cobra de vidro* (1978): "O erro de parte considerável dos estudos feitos nos últimos tempos entre nós a respeito da influência do negro parece-me consistir no fato de encararem com demasiada insistência o lado pitoresco, anedótico, folclórico, em outras palavras o aspecto *exótico* do africano" [The mistake found in most of the studies made in the last years dealing with the influence of Black man, seem to me that it consists of the fact that they present, with too much insistence, the picturesque, anecdotal, folkloric; in other words, the *exotic* aspects of the African] (13). Amado's *TM* does not treat the mestizo as "exotic" but rather focuses upon the *problem* of race relations in Brazil. Speaking in general terms, Holanda describes the limitations of the debate on race relations in Brazil as exactly this tendency to avoid the discussion of concrete problems: "A limitação que a meu ver encerra esse interesse recente pelos estudos em torno do negro brasileiro vem do fato de encararem a questão não como um problema, mas antes como um espetáculo" [The limitation, as I can understand it, contained in this recent interest for studies regarding the Brazilian Black, comes from the fact that it faces the question not as a problem but rather as a spectacle] (14). Although Amado's dynamic and exuberant writing may be falsely interpreted as a mere celebration of Afro-Brazilian hybrid culture, *TM* belies that notion because it grapples with serious issues of race, culture and politics.

As demonstrated above with allusions to "intentional hybridity," the constant shifts in narrative perspective not only effect a hybrid discourse but also undermine the dominant discourse of the power elites. Amado constructs his novel with the type of narrative hybridity that unmasks the conflictual structure, while presenting a view of mixture that harbors all sorts of permutations from race and culture to ethnicity, also seen in *A descoberta da América pelos turcos*, where Arabic and Brazilian culture, religions, and even languages, are intertwined. Perhaps one can state that, besides the recognition of Afro-Brazilian cultural difference, Amado draws upon the reality of hybridity to impart a notion of openendedness that challenges an imposed ideology of one national image for all, alluded to earlier in Larsen's statement. Interestingly, this line of thinking evokes another reformulation, that is, another reading of Mário de Andrade's novel *Macunaíma*, a hybrid hero if there ever was one, by interpreting the subtitle—*O herói sem nenhum caráter* [The hero without any character]—as the hero without any [fixed] character because he represents a confluence of characters and cultural experiences which is not served by a static national identity.

Amado's picture of Brazilian diversity reverberates Andrade's avoidance of a static image of Brazil's national character. This picture of diversity and mixture is placed at the very beginning of Amado's novel when the omniscient voice describes the Afro-Brazilian Bahian communities as a popular university in which "misturam ritmos, passos e sangue; na mistura criaram uma côr e um som, imagem nova, original" [they mixed rythms, steps and blood, and with this mixure they created a color and a sound, a new original image] (*TM* 15). Thus Amado is coherent in his depiction of racial hyridity or democracy while at the same time being coherent in his exposure of racial discrimination. His view of racial democracy acknowledges and crystallizes the distinction between biological/cultural hybridity and socio-political pluralism as a veritable problem and not merely as a "spectacle."

## NOTES

1. The question of race and color has been treated by many historians, sociologists and anthropologists, but our study aims to focus on how Amado's literary treatment difuses this ambiguity and confusion to show the simultaneity of racial democracy and color disharmony. See Andrews (1991); Azevedo (1975); Dzidzienyo in Sigler (1987); Viotti da Costa (1985); Hanchard (1994); Hasenbalg (1979); and Skidmore (1974/1993).

2. While our usage here of the term "transculturalism" specifically refers to the interactions of various cultures and their influences upon each other within a given nation, this view and other interpretations are explained in Canclini, *Hybrid Cultures* (1995) and Neil Larsen, *Reading North by South* (1995).

3. Amado's statement: "Meu país é uma verdadeira democracia racial" appeared in the daily *O estado de São Paulo* (Oct. 9, 1971) and incited much controversy among intellectuals and academics to the point of Amado being called a racist. In 1983 a protest by Abdias do Nascimento, who believed that Amado did not acknowledge the existence of racial prejudice in Brazil, continued this debate and polemic. For more information on this issue as well as a reading of *Tenda dos milagres* as testimony, see Vieira, "Testimonial Fiction and Historical Allegory: Racial and Political Repression in Jorge Amado's Brazil" (1989).

4. The tenth edition of *Tenda dos milagres* will be used here as the text under study. All future quotes from this novel will be indicated by the letters *TM*, followed by the related pages numbers.

5. Ricardo Benzaquen de Araújo also discusses a misinterpretation of Freyre's distinction between race and culture in *Guerra e paz* which intended to give specific meaning to the African contribution to Brazil. In so doing he alludes to the hybrid and its dialog across traditions: "nosso autor ganha forças não só para superar o racismo que vinha ordenando significativamente a produção intelectual brasileira mas também para tentar construir uma outra versão da identidade nacional, em que a obsessão com o progresso e com a razão, com a integração do País na marcha da civilização, fosse até certo ponto substituída por uma interpretação que desse alguma atenção à híbrida e singular articulação de tradições que aqui se verificou" (30).

6. In Robert J. C. Young's study, *Colonial Desire: Hybridity in Theory, Culture and Race*, the notion of hybridity is posited in a sexual and interracial context of British colonialism. This experience is also manifested in Brazil's history with Portuguese colonialism, according to Benzaquen. See Benzaquen's second chap-

ter "Agonia e extase [Agony and Ecstasy]" for an analysis of Portuguese colonialism and the experience of miscegenation.

7.  For example, in 1930 Amado and Carneiro participated in the movement for cultural renovation symbolized by the Academia dos Rebeldes (Academy of the
Rebels).

8.  This essay by Amado appears in a large volume which contains other pieces
about Freyre's contribution by such luminaries as Antônio Cândido, Alceu
Amoroso Lima, Thales de Azevedo, Fernando de Azevedo, Manuel Bandeira,
and many others. This volume is *Gilberto Freyre: sua ciência, sua filosofia, sua
arte—ensaios sobre o autor de Casa Grande & senzala e sua influência na moderna cultural do Brasil, comemorativos do 25. aniversário da publicação dêsse
livro,* Rio: José Olympio Editora, 1962. Amado's quote from this essay refers to
Freyre's contribution as intellectual as well as in terms of his influence upon
Brazil's cultural production. [This volume was referred to me by Marcos Chor
Maio, Researcher at the Oswaldo Cruz Foundation in Rio and Brazilian Visiting
Scholar at Brown University from 1995–96. I take this opportunity to express my
professional gratitude for our discussions on the topic of race relations in Brazil
and for his suggestions which I have incorporated into this study.]

9.  This statement evolves from a discussion between Canclini, Margarita Zires,
Raymundo Mier, and Mabel Piccini which focuses upon the fact that the hybrid
is not "indeterminate," according to Canclini, and thus demands recognition and
classification. See *The Postmodernism Debate in Latin America,* eds. John Beverley, José Oviedo, and Michael Aronna. Durham: Duke Unversity Press, 1995,
p.81.

10. In his opening statement at the international conference "Affirmative Action in
Contemporaries Societies" held in Brasília July 2–4, 1996, President Cardoso
openly placed the issue of racism in Brazil on the discussion table. I am grateful
to Professor Thomas Skidmore for explaining President Cardoso's remarks since
he participated in this international conference. Cardoso's bold statement followed an earlier one on affirmative action and race in Brazil delivered during the
commemoration of the death of the Afro-Brazilian hero, Zumbi dos Palmares
during November 1995. These speeches serve as a clear indication of President
Cardoso's keen concern for democratic representation of all racial and ehtnic
groups in Brazil as well as his desire to generate more open dialogue on this
issue.

11. This incisive article which appears in *Novos estudos CEBRAP,* 44, março 1996:
89–114, discusses the obstacles to true pluralist representation in Brazil.

12. While aimed at North American cultural and educational issues, the statements
published by the National Coalition for Cultural Pluralism and its Steering Com-
mitte are presented in a universal context that relate to many aspects of the
Brazilian situation. This statement appears in Stent, Madelon D.; William Hazard; Harry N. Rivlin (eds), *Cultural Pluralism in Education: A Mandate for
Change,* 1973.

13. trans. Barbara Shelby. *Tent of Miracles.* New York: Avon Books, 1971, p. 304.

14. trans. Barbara Shelby, p. 395.

15. trans. Barbara Shelby, p. 332.

16. Bourdieu's use of these terms appears in his first chapter of *The Field of Cultural Production: Essays on Art and Literature*, edited and introduced by Randal Johnson. New York: Columbia University Press, 1993, 29–73. Also, Randal Johnson's cogent introduction synthesizes the important aspects of Bourdieu's thesis. Interestingly, Bourdieu's outline of cultural production is aptly dramatized in *Tenda dos milagres*.

17. For an analysis of the complexity of the narrative construct in *Tenda dos milagres*, see Earl E. Fitz, "The Problem of the Unreliable Narrator in Jorge Amado's *Tenda dos milagres*," in *Kentucky Romance Quarterly*, 30, 3, 1983: 311–321.

18. trans. Barbara Shelby, p. 201.

19. This quote is found in the 25th edition of *Casa Grande e senzala*, Rio de Janeiro: José Olympio, 1987, 442–443. The quote is used by Maria Luiza Tucci Carneiro to explain the origin of the myth of racial democracy in her cogent book, *O racismo na história do Brazil: mito e realidade*, São Paulo: Atica, 1994, 35–36.

## BIBLIOGRAPHY

Albó, Xavier. "Our Identity Starting from Pluralism in the Base" in Beverley, et al. *The Postmodernism Debate in Latin America,* 18–33.

Amado, Jorge. *A descoberta da América pelos turcos.* Rio de Janeiro: Editora Record, 1994.

———. "*Casa-Grande e Senzala* e a Revolução Cultural" in *Gilberto Freyre: sua ciência, sua filosofia, sua arte—Ensaios sobre o autor de Casa-Grande e Senzala e a sua influência na moderna cultura do Brasil, comemorativos do 25 aniversário da publicação dêsse seu livro.* Rio de Janeiro: José Olympio Editôra, 1962: 30–36.

———. *Tenda dos milagres.* 10th ed. São Paulo: Livraria Martins Editora, 1973.

Andrade, Mário de. "Linha de côr." *Estado de São Paulo,* March 29, 1939.

Araújo, Ricardo Benzaquen de. *Guerra e paz: Casa-grande e senzala e a obra de Gilberto Freyre nos anos 30.* Rio de Janeiro: Ed. 34, 1994.

Arendt, Hannah. *The Human Condition.* Chicago: The University of Chicago Press, 1958/1989.

Azevedo, Thales de. *Democracia racial: ideologia e realidade.* Petrópolis: Vozes, 1975.

Beverley, John, José Oviedo, and Michael Aronna, eds. *The Postmodernism Debate in Latin America.* Durham: Duke University Press, 1995.

Bourdieu, Pierre. *The Field of Cultural Production: Essays on Art and Literature.* Edited and Introduced by Randal Johnson. New York: Columbia University Press, 1993.

Canclini, Néstor García. *Hybrid Cultures: Strategies for Entering and Leaving Modernity.* Foreward by Renato Rosaldo & Trans. by Christopher L. Chiappari and Silvia L. López. Minneapolis: University of Minnesota Press, 1995.

———. "The Hybrid: A Conversation with Margarita Zires, Raymundo Mier, and Mabel Piccini" in *The Post-modernism Debate in Latin America,* 77–92.

Carneiro, Maria Luiza Tucci. *O racismo na história do Brasil: mito e realidade.* São Paulo: Atica, 1994.

Fitz, Earl E. "The Problem of the Unreliable Narrator in Jorge Amado's *Tenda dos milagres." Kentucky Romance Quarterly*, 30, 3, 1983: 311–321.

Holanda, Sérgio Buarque de. "Negros e Brancos" in *Cobra de vidro*. 2ed. São Paulo: Perspectiva: Secretaria da Cultura, Ciência e Tecnologia do Estado de São Paulo, 1978, 11–14.

Larsen, Neil. *Reading North By South: On Latin American Literature, Culture and Politics*. Minneapolis, University of Minnesota Press, 1995.

Montero, Paula. "Cultura e democracia no processo da globalização. *Novos Estudos CEBRAP*, 44, Março 1996; 89–114.

Schwarz, Roberto. *Misplaced Ideas: Essays on Brazilian Culture*. Edited and with an Introduction by John Gledson. London: Verso, 1993.

Stent, Madelon D., William R. Hazard, and Harry N. Rivlin. *Cultural Pluralism in Education: A Mandate for Change*. New York: Appleton-Century-Crofts, 1973.

Tannenbaum, Frank, "Introduction" to Freyre, Gilberto. *The Mansions and the Shanties: The Making of Modern Brazil*. Trans & ed. by Harriet de Onís. New York: Alfred A. Knopf, 1963, vii-xii.

Vieira, Nelson H. "Testimonial Fiction and Historical Allegory: Racial and Political Repression in Jorge Amado's Brazil." *Latin American Literary Review*, Vol. XVII, 34, July-Dec. 1989: 6–23.

Young, Robert J.C. *Colonial Desire: Hybridity in Theory, Culture and Race*. London: Routledge, 1995.

# The Immanent Imp
## Humor in the Later Works of Jorge Amado

JON S. VINCENT

There are few things in the world more tedious than a joke explained; if the listener misses the point the first time around it is unlikely that any mirth will result from the parsing of the gag. It is also true that we already have a substantial study on humor in the works of Jorge Amado,[1] so it would appear that any further discourse on the topic would be both repetitive and boring. But I think that even Amado's detractors will admit that he has been a remarkably successful comic novelist, perhaps Brazil's most successful, since the publication of *Gabriela, cravo e canela [Gabriela, Clove and Cinnamon]*[2] in 1958, and for that reason alone the topic merits further consideration.

Bobby Chamberlain's dissertation does an admirable job of categorizing the types of humor Amado uses and fitting them into a framework, but I think that there is a sort of comic imperative at work in these novels—a kind of world view that defines scene, situation, and character in terms of an implicit opposite that makes the entire texture of the text comic. Moreover, the dissertation covers only works written until 1975, and I will thus place relative emphasis on those written since then.

A further caveat (in addition to the "never explain a joke" one above) in regard to Amado's humor is that it is impossible to understand it or indeed to speak intelligently of it without considering its political connotation. While in some cases the intention may have an ethical or moral charge, his humor always functions at least on the margin of a political agenda of one kind or another. Although I cannot now go back and reread all the novels published previous to 1958, I would hazard that if Amado had not taken the PCB (Partido Comunista Brasileiro) so seriously these early works would be a lot funnier than they are.

This seemingly bizarre idea occurred to me while I was reading Amado's long-unawaited memoirs (he has promised for years not to write them), *Navegação de cabotagem [Coastal navigation]*.[3] In this remarkably disjointed and achronological account, Amado reveals himself to be an inveterate joker, practical and otherwise. There are abundant examples, but my favorite is the anecdote about Amado and his wife Zélia attending an opera in China in 1952 accompanied by the Cuban poet Nicolás Guillén and his wife Rosa. The Cuban's interpreter had fallen asleep as soon as the opera began, so the monolingual Guillén and his wife had to rely on the retranslation provided by Amado through his French-speaking interpreter. The opera lasted for hours, and, since it was staged without props or sets, was wide open to interpretation. The story, about an Emperor and his "Favorita," was changed by Amado from a medieval tale of derring-do into a pornographic extravaganza, with the Favorita being a nymphomaniac who has sex with men by the battalion and then has at it with their horses. Days later the irate Guillén, in a meeting with Chinese Communist Party officials, rose to lambaste this monument to degeneration and poor taste, much to the bewilderment of the Chinese, until the imp in question made his confession by means of uncontrollable laughter.

This was in 1952, six years before *Gabriela*, and it is merely one of many possible examples, which does indeed imply that Amado had a sense of humor all along but kept it in rein for ideological reasons. The only other explanation I can think of for the remarkable difference between the earlier works and the later ones is that Amado suddenly acquired a sense of humor at the age of forty-six, a phenomenon probably unique in human history.

The year Amado began to uncork his imp's bottle (and, it might be said, simultaneously to put the stopper in the Party's) was 1955. He was increasingly unhappy with the demands made on him by the directorate and had pled with them to let him go back to simply being a writer. When he was a congressman (from 1945 to 1947) he had actually gone into debt with his publisher because of the monetary demands the PCB made on him. He lived in a small country house in the state of Rio de Janeiro, an hour from the then capital. Of his 9,000 cruzeiro salary the Party took 7,000, leaving him with barely enough for transportation. Although he was not part of the leadership, he spent literally all his time working for the Party's aims. He was thus professionally frustrated, in debt, and unappreciated. But what really forced the break was the Soviet invasion of Hungary in 1956 and the Party's steadfast refusal to consider any position divergent from the Moscow line.[4]

Of course not everyone was aware of the degree of Amado's disillusionment with the PCB, and thus when *Gabriela* appeared in 1958 the critical response was nothing short of chaotic. Some critics on the left (those likely to know about the rift) accused him of betrayal; many on the right (most of whom had been ignoring him for years) thought that he had become a more subtle subversive or that he had merely switched allegiance from Stalin to Khrushchev.[5] And a presumably new element seemed to cause as much befuddlement as the problem of political orientation: it was funny. How could a man whose last published work was the tedious *Os subterrâneos da liber-*

*dade [The freedom underground]*[6] have produced a novel of such elegance and charm? Nobody seemed any surer of that than they were about his putative fealty to this or that ism.

People have probably been being funny for about as long as there have been people, but nobody attempted to try to figure out how or why things were funny until Classical Greece, and the word "humor" did not acquire its current meaning until quite recently. Theories of how humor functions range from Plato's theory (based on derision) to Aristotle's (frustrated expectation) to Freud's (pleasure/pain) to Arthur Koestler's (bisociation).[7] These traditional notions about how humor functions are all of at least tangential interest here, but some more recent ideas strike me as particularly useful in discussing humor in Amado's work. I admit to being very attracted to the theory of jokes as violations of Grice's Maxims (of quantity, relation, manner, and quality) but find it so elastic as to be of little use. More interesting is Victor Raskin's script-based theory, in which the opposition of overlapping scripts is the basic matrix for humor.[8]

Script-based humor theory strikes me as a productive way to approach Amado's novels because it is not only broadly applicable to his fiction but also because it so sharply distinguishes between the impish and the impless (or imp-challenged) novels. I have written elsewhere[9] that in some of the earlier political novels Amado was fond of portraying an incident from the perspective of first one character and then of another of a different class. This is particularly notable in *Os subterrâneos da liberdade*, in which events are seen first from the perspective of the power-brokers and then from that of a Communist or sympathizer. And in *Seara vermelha [Red harvest]*[10] there are three separate narrative strands, each the story of one of the brothers—two come to a bad end and one, the Communist, triumphs. The operative word from Raskin's theory here is "overlapping," because in both these novels the variant perspectives are presented in linear fashion, as discrete narrative chunks, and the reader is never given any room to accept any script other than the one being put forth by the narrator. I think this may be one of the keys to the relatively indigestible quality of the more tendentious works and the relative quality of ones such as *Terras do sem fim [The Violent Land]*[11] in which this kind of dialectical scripting is attenuated or absent.

All the novels from *Gabriela* on are comic, and most have overlapping scripts that make the plots, in essence, jokes. At the very least there is a narrator of dubious certainty—at most, a multiplicity of contradictory narrators. This is not only essential to the comic nature of the narratives but is also the source of everything from ambiguity to outright fraud. At the risk of oversimplification, I would hazard that all these later novels share as at least part of the comic structure the overlapping scripts of the bourgeoisie and the *povo*, which is why I insisted at the outset that it is unproductive to talk about Amado's humor without considering the political agenda.

In *Gabriela*, for example, the principal turns of the plot are determined by the differences in perception of Nacib and Gabriela. Nacib's view of marriage as a sacrosanct institution requiring fidelity, proper behavior and the wearing of shoes is totally bewildering to Gabriela. Nacib has adopted a middle-class sense of propriety, while Gabriela's sense of what it right is rather more anarchistic, but neither has ever articulated to the other what the parameters are. For the reader, much of the humor derives from the interplay between his squareness and her innocent hedonism. When he catches her in bed with Tonico he demonstrates the depth of his civility by not killing her (or him), and when he annuls the marriage but eventually takes her back as cook and lover he is essentially capitulating to her script. When his friends show up for lunch and he announces he has taken her back as his cook, Mundinho Falcão remarks, "Esse turco é um mestre do bem viver . . . " [This Turk is a great bon vivant] (349), an observation which indicates a shared value system and a collective ignorance of the other script. All of this is, of course, part of the fun for the reader, since, as in most of these later works, the reader is in on the overlapping scripts but the characters are not.

It is not easy to finish the reading of a 450–page novel and come up with a pithy resumé of the essence of the work, but I have found the notion of Gérard Genette [12] of the basic or nuclear verb to be one enlightening way to approach a text. The verb itself is not usually hard to find, but the discipline in deciding what will be the subject and complement of the central verb is a useful disciplinary exercise because it forces the reader to decide who is really in control of the action, what that action is, and, finally, what the upshot of that action is for the other characters. In the case of *Gabriela* my nuclear sentence is "Gabriela subverts the established order," a somewhat terser version of what I have been discussing here.

The two narratives that comprise *Os velhos marinheiros* [*Home is the Sailor*] [13] are variations of the double-scripting scheme. In "Quincas" the narrator himself confesses that his version of the story is only one version, and that another may also be true:

> Até hoje permanece certa confusão em torno da morte de Quincas Berro D'água. Dúvidas por explicar, detalhes absurdos, contradições no depoimento das testemunhas, lacunas diversas. Não há clareza sobre hora, local e frase derradeira [Until today there is a certain confusion regarding the death of Quincas Berro D'água. Doubts to be explained, absurd details, contradictions in the depositions of witnesses, many gaps. There is no clarity regarding the hour, the place, and the very last words]. (19)

In "Vasco," the narrator claims a similar doggedness to unearth the truth—"Minha intenção, minha única intenção, acreditem! é apenas restabelecer a verdade" [my intention, my only intention, believe me! It's to reestablish the truth] (79), but his narration is undercut by a character, Chico

Pacheco, who throughout the narration offers an alternative version of every episode. In both cases the essential effect, and much of the humor, results from the interplay between the two conflicting versions of the story. In both, there is a banal tale verging on insipidity (Quincas really died in a miserable hovel on the Ladeira do Tabuão; Vasco was just a con man who bought his title and ignorantly had all the lines of the Ita moored) counterpointed by a rather more fantastic tale requiring considerably amplified suspension of disbelief (Quincas refused to die on land and really jumped out of a boat in a storm twenty hours later; Vasco was an old salt who really knew the sea and had the ship moored because he knew a storm was coming). Since in both stories the latter, more bizarre version is what makes them funny, it is they, and not the banal versions, which form the narrative core, so the nuclear verbs would be "Quincas decides when to die" and "Vasco saves the Ita."

*Os pastores da noite* [*Shepherds of the Night*][14] is concocted in a very different fashion. Since the reader must be privy to the ethos of the popular culture to swallow the improbable outcomes, these three stories rely more on the very impossibility of the outcomes for their comic effect. In each of these stories the narrator sets up a conflict with no plausible solution, which of course forces the reader to consider what alternatives there might be, and, as in a good joke, then closes the story with an ending no listener or reader could have conceived of. They thus seem more clearly examples of Aristotelian "frustrated expectation" theory than of overlapped scripts. In the first story the professional bachelor Cabo Martim finally marries Marialva and becomes fully domesticated, which naturally leads to boredom. Curió, who is more than just a friend (they are *irmãos de santo* [brethren in their common Afro-Brazilian beliefs]) lusts after Marialva but of course does not act. Seeing an opportunity to really put the reins on Martim, Marialva encourages Curió, who finally makes a grand speech confessing their shared passion, whereupon Martim, instead of killing or maiming his friend, offers not only his wife but his house and coffeepot as well, at which point Curió of course loses interest. In the second Massu is faced with choosing a godfather for his infant son from among his myriad friends. He is sure to offend anyone not chosen, but, inspired by a vision, decides to ask Ogum, the Afro-Brazilian deity (*orixá*), to accept the honor. At the crucial moment the trickster Exu possesses the hapless Artur (Ogum's go-between), leaving Ogum to search among the congregation for one of his adepts, who turns out to be a Catholic priest. The final episode concerns an "invasion" on the outskirts of Salvador, with the police, politicians, newspapermen, and capitalists all attempting to gain propaganda points by manipulating the situation. Galo Doido, the leader of the invaders, is accidentally killed at the end but returns as an *orixá*. In each episode any plausible prediction of an outcome is subverted by the perverse nature of narrative twists, and even if the plot can be reduced to "Martim subverts a love triangle, Ogum becomes Felício's godfather, and Galo

Doido leads an invasion," a note about the convoluted way in which these things come to pass must be added.

*Dona Flor e seus dois maridos* [*Dona Flor and Her Two Husbands*]$^{15}$ is, after *Gabriela*, one of Amado's most admired novels, and one of his funniest. It is clearly a work of double-scripting, the scripts in this case being those of Vadinho and Dr. Teodoro, the *povo* and the bourgeoisie. The scripts are incredibly convoluted in this novel, encompassing everything from styles of love-making to culinary preferences to politics. The nuclear sentence for this novel is "Flor faz um sanduíche" [Flor makes a sandwich], "sandwich" being the characteristically picturesque Brazilian slang term for a *ménage à trois*. The novel has recipes and musical accompaniments for each of its parts, and it is rich in wordplay and caricature. As Bobby Chamberlain notes, it is also the first novel to extensively exploit "in-group humor." $^{16}$ In addition to the various types of this humor enumerated by Chamberlain (caricature, dissociation, anachronism, disguise, and such), *Dona Flor* has the distinction of being the first novel by Amado to include collaboration by the illustrator in the humor package. The first edition, illustrated by Floriano Teixeira, portrays a group of revelers gathered around the just-expired Vadinho, and it includes, among others, Mário Cravo, Carybé, and Amado himself, plus an obviously American tourist complete with Coca-Cola *cum* girlie shirt and multiple cameras who is obviously Alfred A. Knopf, at the time Amado's American publisher. $^{17}$

*Tenda dos milagres* [*Tent of Miracles*]$^{18}$ shares with the last episode of *Pastores* a plot in which are portrayed the various branches of the power structure attempting to exploit a public event for their own ends. Unlike that episode, however, this novel has not an unexpected turn of events but a double script. This is also an unusual novel in that it is semi-historical, showing the power structure of nineteenth-century Brazil being put on the defensive by Archanjo's publications during his life and that of the twentieth century cynically (and rather witlessly) exploiting an event for personal or institutional gain. The double script is provided by two overlapping narrative tracks, one omniscient and unidentified, the other provided by Fausto Pena, the American professor's paid researcher. *Tenda* has a blatant socio-political agenda which might verge on the ponderous were it not for the bounce provided by the hapless Fausto Pena and the parodic representations of social institutions.

Of the later works *Tenda* probably has the clearest bourgeoisie/*povo* construct, which provides another double script, since the thematic issues of *candomblé*, miscegenation, and indeed the whole issue of Afro-Brazilianness are viewed in counterpoint from the two perspectives. On the one hand are members of the establishment, who view Brazil as a European country which through some massive geological accident has been dislocated to the tropics; on the other, the real folk, who know better. The nuclear sentence, "Pedro

Archanjo finally triumphs," reveals the overriding seriousness of the theme, though even in this grave context the double script allows room for some fun and games, as in the polemic among faculty members at the university about who speaks the best French and the various sendups of the consumer society, including the school contest for the best essay on Archanjo sponsored by Aguardente Crocodilo.

*Tereza Batista cansada de guerra* [*Tereza Batista: Home from the Wars*][19] is a kind of tour de force in terms of multiple scripting. Although on the surface it would appear to be not much more than a romanticized fable about another whore, the five episodes are recounted in fragmentary and often contradictory fashion by at least thirteen different narrators, including the abolitionist poet Castro Alves. What is going on in the book is less a process of canonizing a slut than an examination of the power of gossip and the credulity of those who take it seriously. Every episode has at least two scripts—one based on hearsay, the other provided by a witness or a person privy to the facts of the matter. Since one version is based on the perceptions of persons of limited imagination and the other is based on a far more liberal view of the parameters of reality (which allows for characters like Castro Alves, Exu, Oxalá, and Santo Onofre to appear without evoking the least surprise), the whole narrative is a kind of running gag about appearances. But it is both a melodrama and a love story, and its nuclear sentence would have to be something like "Tereza finally finds love," which gives no indication whatever of the comic flavor of the tale.

*Tieta do Agreste* [*Tieta the Goat Girl*][20] is, in contrast, a much simpler plot, but the apparent simplicity is deceptive. The double script here is essentially a country/city contrast, or, better, a country mouse/city mouse juxtaposition. This is an old trope, widely used in both serious and comic literature. But in the context of Brazilian culture, the plot has the resonance of one of the endless series of *mineiro/paulista* jokes, in which the slick and crafty city dude from São Paulo ends up being flummoxed or ridiculed by the rustic from Minas, who shows himself to be even more cunning. The major differences are the change of venue from Minas to rural Bahia and the unusual character of Tieta herself, since she has both city savvy and country cunning. What is very like the model is the digressive and playful narrator, who seems to assume that we may already know the basic story and thus goes off on various tangents to provide the expected level of entertainment. Since he in fact knows that we don't know the story, these tangential explorations remain inherently interesting but whet the reader's appetite for the return to the regular story.

Two of the principal sources of humor in *Tieta*, then, are the self-indulgent narrator and the characters, all of whom uniformly have erroneous expectations of characters from the other venue. The *paulistas*, at least some of them, are regarded as Martians by the people from Agreste, and the entrepreneurs from São Paulo make totally false assumptions about the townspeople because of their stereotypes about yokeldom. But the main plot line is about Tieta's use of her connections (her profession is a double script, because her "boutique" in São Paulo is a high-class whorehouse) to bring electricity to Agreste and to prevent a titanium dioxide plant from being built there, and so none of this seems to have any real importance. But as in *Tereza*, the nuclear sentence—in this case "Tieta saves Agreste"—does not include the elements which are really the principal threads of the narrative fabric.

In *Farda, fardão, camisola de dormir [Pen, Sword, Camisole]*,[21] the two scripts appear at first to be the agendas of two rival factions in the Brazilian Academy of Letters. But the scripts change because of a series of unforeseen events, so this novel has a combination of overlapping scripts and frustrated expectations. When the beloved poet and Academy member Antônio Bruno dies of a stroke in Paris (his attack being a result of the fall of the city), the academic Lisandro Leite informs the crypto-Nazi Colonel Sampaio Pereira, hoping that with the colonel in the Academy, Lisandro will have a shot at a Supreme Court seat. Another academic who was a friend of Bruno, Afrânio Portela, leads the movement for an opposition candidate, cleverly deciding that what they must do is find a candidate who outranks the colonel. They finally dig up an obscure general who has written a few books and try to groom him for candidacy. The premise here is a juicy one and would have probably been sufficient to carry off the entire novel, but Amado is such an accomplished and perverse storyteller that he subverts his own premise—without foreshadowing, the colonel unceremoniously dies in bed, and the general, who was to be our hero, turns out to be arrogant and authoritarian. Thus, in the middle of the story, the scripts unexpectedly reverse, with the colonel out of the picture and the liberals now campaigning for blank votes or abstentions when the general comes up for election to the Academy. Along with this complex story line, there are also the usual pokes and jabs at the establishment, in this case most notably the army (the general wants a seat in the Academy reserved for the military) and academicians themselves (presumably including Amado, who has been a member since 1971).

As if this were not enough, there is a second set of overlapping scripts involving the deceased poet Bruno and the arrogant General Moreira. The *camisola* of the title, indeed, is also the title of the unfinished sonnet the beloved Bruno intended to write, and the assorted plot complications of the last part are the result of the activities of Bruno's former friends and lovers. As in "Quincas," the protagonist dies in the first sentence of the narrative, and thus the nuclear sentence of the book would have to imply that Bruno, like Quincas Berro D'água, was able to influence events even beyond death— "Bruno wins out over the arrogant General" is not too far removed from "Quincas decides when to die."

*Tocaia grande: a face obscura [Showdown]*[22] is, in terms of structure and theme, something of a throwback in Amado's production. The theme is very close to that of *Terras do sem fim* and *Gabriela*, and indeed the scenario could be situated chronologically between those two books. The structure has an overriding double script which is evident in the title itself—the "face obscura" is the unofficial story of what went on in Tocaia Grande, not the sanitized version available in history books and newspapers. Amado's unidentified narrator then sets about to tell that real story, with lots of nitty and plenty of gritty—not a pretty story, of course, but somebody has to tell it. What makes the larger structure work in terms of humor is the way the not-so-countrified narrator unveils the violent and sordid details of the transformation of a stopover for mules into something like a city. Amado's version of revisionist history is not based merely on oral history—his narrator's version of the growth of *Tocaia Grande* is oral enough, but the saga is also genital, culinary, and, at times, anal.

This is the side of Amado which feminists have highly criticized, especially those who expect a Brazilian male of seventy-two to share notions of political correctness with an American female college graduate fifty years his junior. Part of the problem in this novel is that it is, like *Terras*, a frontier novel, peopled by misfits, adventurers, and those merely trying to survive in a hostile and dangerous environment, not the kind of scenario which is likely to provide room for characters of exemplary morality. The book begins with a bloody ambush carried out by a major character, Capitão Natário, and ends with the same good captain lying in wait to carry out what will be his last ambush, and with this kind of frame it is apparent that the narrator is providing moral lessons only in the most oblique manner.

In terms of humor, in fact, the secondary characters provide more of it than the major ones, most of whom are too bloodthirsty to be much fun. One of the most colorful of these is the *turco* Fadul Abdala, in fact a Maronite Christian from Lebanon, who spends most of the book in a fruitless search for love. Fadul's double script is that of the outlander, attempting to interpret a new and alien culture and to adapt to it, with only his experience from a very different world as a guide. Less assimilated than the similar character Nacib, in *Gabriela*, Fadul is caught in a kind of intercultural bind, which he attempts to solve by switching codes—praying to God, for example, in Arabic, on the suspicion that this God in all likelihood does not understand Portuguese.

*Tocaia* really has two nuclear sentences. The first, which is on the level of characters, is something like "Captain Natário finally has revenge on Venturinha." But this is not a very satisfactory sentence since Venturinha is absent for most of the narrative and because neither Natário nor Venturinha is a very sympathetic character. An alternative would be to posit something like "Tocaia Grande becomes Irisópolis," which is to see the narrative as an epic with a large cast, and which also allows the reader to concentrate more on the secondary, and funnier, characters.

*O sumiço da santa* [*The War of the Saints*][23] has a much clearer double script, this one involving almost all the major characters. Although many of the themes are not new to Amado, the breadth of the scripting makes for a more consistently funny narrative. The story opens with the image of Santa Bárbara being transported by *saveiro* to Salvador for display in the museum. On arrival, Santa Bárbara turns into Iansã and walks away. This scene fore-shadows the two scripts being played out, with the official Roman Catholic church, the hapless Dom Maximiliano, the puritanical Adaljisa, the police commissioner, a *fazendeiro* and his hired gun in one script; in the other *candomblé* (including, as characters, several *orixás*) Manela (Adaljisa's niece), Danilo (her husband), the "subversive" Padre Galvão and his lover Patrícia, *capoeiristas*, and the sound system of the Castro Alves Theatre.

The principal function of the double-scripting in this case is that the reader is privy to much that the characters in the first group aren't— St. George and Exu and Iansä are presented to the reader as any other charac-ter, but we know that they have supernatural powers, while the other characters are trapped in their little world circumscribed by reality, hope-lessly attempting to find logical solutions to problems of supernatural origin. This is a very updated version of Camões, with the classical deities being replaced by African ones, but here the intercession is less to preserve the glory of the race than to be sure all the characters have a good time, even if it is against their will. The nuclear sentence is simply "Saint Barbara comes back," but that only works if we remember all the things that happened in her other incarnation.

*A descoberta da América pelos turcos [The discovery of America by the Turks]*[24] is a joke from the title on: anyone who had the slightest contact with the 1992 Columbus Quincentennial will get half through the title with a sense of "here we go again" and finish it with a laugh, because our expectation might be, well, Columbus, or maybe Leif Ericson, or perhaps somebody who cruised over to South America on a reed raft—but not *turcos*. But this is merely a twist on the tail of the cliché—after all, just because the *turcos* (and he refers here not to Turks but to subjects of the then Ottoman Empire) got to America a little later than some other groups doesn't necessarily imply that they didn't go through the same sense of novelty and alienation that other groups experienced.

This is perhaps Amado's most exotic double-scripted novel to date, because the forces behind the scripting are Allah and Shitan, the Islamic ver-sions of God and Satan. Jamil Bichara is the Syrian-born merchant whom Allah protects (with the collaboration of Jehovah, who enters the scene on behalf of Jamil's Maronite Christian friend Raduan Murad), and if Shitan had triumphed he surely would have married the wretched Adma. As it happens, during Jamil's long absence in the remote town of Itaguassu, Allah has man-aged to find an appropriate suitor for the evil-tempered eldest daughter of the major dry-goods dealer in Itabuna. Jamil, unhappily resigned to marriage, arrives in Itabuna just in time to witness her marriage to Adib, formerly a waiter in a local restaurant.

This is a "Taming of the Shrew" recast and relocated, but it also has other novelties, because the text itself is preceded by a Carybé drawing entitled "*Rondó das Bucetas* [The Rondeau of Pussies]," including the *buceta jaquetão* [Double-Breasted Pussy], the *buceta comum* [Common Pussy], the *buceta boca de sino* [Mouth-of-a-Bell Shaped Pussy], and the *buceta de chupeta* [Pacifier Pussy], the rarest and most prized of all, and the one the otherwise horrible Adma is said to possess. So *Descoberta* is at once a clean joke, a double script and a dirty joke. Further, all the main characters operate in the double-script situation of a Nacib or a Fadul, since they are all *turcos* transplanted to Brazil.

*   *   *

Now that I have gone out on a limb, I will cut it off by confessing that all the previous analysis is really based on what Attardo calls the "canned joke." He makes the crucial distinction between this kind of joke and what he calls the "conversational joke," which he defines as "improvised and contextual."[25] The distinction is an important one, because it distinguishes between those kinds of people we all know who "tell jokes" vs. those who are witty. A joke teller is essentially a theatrical personage with a good memory who has an array (at times vast, at times less) of stories stored somewhere in his memory which he carts out and retells as the occasion arises. I have met prodigies of the genre, as I am sure most prople have. But this is very different from what is going on in Amado, since the "contextual" joke arises from the atmosphere and situation and thus relies on a much more fluid and elusive context than a canned joke. In a novel, of course, the novelist creates a narrator or a number of narrators who determine such things, so in a sense what is going on in Amado's fiction is the exploitation of a context in an invented space, which makes the writer's task both easier (the full control of context can create the ideal situation for a good joke) and more difficult (the invented space has to be accepted by the reader for the joke to work).

Attardo also comments on the differences between texts which are structurally like a joke, which he identifies as a "particularly enriched joke,"[26] and those which are structurally substantially different. It seems to me that some elements I have so far omitted and which are of extreme importance in Amado's later works are such things as register-based humor, sophisticated humor which may be self-contradictory or require "several inferential steps," the technique of systematically withholding information, and what Attardo defines as the "accumulative" joke.[27]

All these proliferate in these novels, and it would be unreasonable to pretend they do not. Register humor, for example, is a technique Amado has used almost from the beginning, in which the linguistic register (usually extremely pompous and often archaic) contrasts with the subject matter or context (most often the small daily doings of fairly insignificant or even marginal characters). His narrators also perversely withhold information, make jokes accessible only to limited numbers of readers, or casually drop the first part of a joke to return pages later with the punch line, which has particular effect because the reader has by that time almost (but not quite) forgotten the premise.

* * *

I began this essay with a caveat about explaining jokes and have so far provided only a few examples of the things I find funny in Amado's novels. It seems appropriate to conclude with a small anthology of examples, if for no other reason to provide a sense of the range and variety of the imp at work:

>—Ela estava nuinha . . .
>—Toda?
>—Inteira?—A voz gulosa do Capitão
>—Todinha . . . A única coisa que levava era umas meias pretas.
>—Pretas?—Nhô Galo escandalizava-se.
>—Meias pretas, oh!—o Capitão estalava a língua.
>—Devassa . . . —condenou o dr. Maurício Caires.
>—Devia estar uma beleza.—O árabe Nacib, de pé, viu de repente dona Sinhazinha nua, calçada de meias pretas. Suspirou. (*Gabriela* 99)

>["She was stark naked."
>"Entirely?"
>"All over?" It was the Captain's greedy voice.
>"Stark naked. The only thing she had on was a pair of black stockings."
>"Black?" Nho Galo was acandalized.
>"Black stockings? Oh, my!" The Captain clicked his tongue.
>"A lewd woman," condemned Dr. Maurício Caires.
>"She must have been beautiful." Nacib suddenly saw Dona Sinhazinha nude, in a pair of black stockings. He sighed].[28]

This is the framing tale from *Gabriela*, an example of the use of an unnecessary detail in an essentially non-essential narrative aside, which, in the context of the atmosphere of rumor, lust, artificial propriety, and scandal the narrator has created, functions as a sort of inclusive metaphor of Nacib's script.

>Não possuía o comandante (comandante uma figa!) nenhum senso do ridículo . . . Só faltavam lamber a bunda do comandante (comandante, uma banana!) . . . Fitava a face risonha e cordial do comandante (comandante, uma ova!) . . . Quem sabe, não saíra jamais o comandante (comandante, um corno!) . . . Enchera-se de esperanças com a chegada do comandante (comandante, uma bosta!) . . . quando o comandante (comandante, um

chibiu!) ... —Pois, seu comandante (de merda ...) ... A voz do comandante (comandante no cu) ... Chico Pacheco iluminou-se quando o comandante (comandante, uma porra!) ... Não punha os pés na casa do
comandante (comandante na puta que o pariu!) [The commandant has no
sense of making a fool of himself (commandant nothing! No sense of
ridicule) ... They only needed to lick the commandant's ass (commandant,
a milk-sop) ... The smiling and cordial face of the commmandant stared
(commandant, like hell!) ... Who is to know, the commandant never went
out (commandant, a cuckold!) ... With the arrival of the commandant one
was filled with hope (commandant, pure crap) ... When the commandant
(commandant, a cunt) ... Well, Mr. (Shitty) commandant ... The commandant's voice (commandant an asshole) ... Chico Pacheco was glowing
when the commandant (commandant sod him!) ... Don't even put a foot in
his house (the bitch who brought him into this world!)]. ("Vasco" 119–126)

The above is part of Chico Pacheco's ongoing attempt to subvert the
other script, which holds that Vasco really is a sea captain. Note that it takes
place over a space of eight printed pages and is thus clearly an example of an
accumulative joke. In this case the reader will likely catch on after the first
three or four references and will be prepared for another epithet every time
the triggering word *comandante* occurs. Also note that the parentheticals are
in ascending order of scatological force (itself a humor form) and that one
(*chibiu*) might not even be recognized by Brazilians not from the Northeast
(an expanded "in-group" joke).

Construa sua casa no morro ou na praia, em terreno comprado ou invadido,
mas adquira os móveis na Movelaria Suprema, na Avenida Sete, número ...
[Build your house either on the hill or on the beach, on a bought lot or an
illegally occupied one, but buy your furniture at the "Suprema" Furniture
Store, Seventh Avenue, number ...]. (*Pastores* 254–5)

During the invasion of Mata Gato, which results in a serious political
confrontation and the death of one of the main characters, the local radio stations report on the gravity of the situation but of course are constrained to
interrupt for the occasional commercial. This is one of dozens of examples of
Amado's roastings of commercial enterprises.

Dona Flor ... recordou um dito do finado seu primeiro esposo, ao voltar do
Rio. Na viagem, dona Flor não sabe onde, ele andara se fartando do tal de
caviar e lhe dissera, quando ela lhe perguntou que gosto lhe encontrara:
—Tem gosto de boceta ... É muito bom! ... Doutor Teodoro procurou
com que comparar o gosto ainda recente da iguaria, nada encontrando:
—Para ser franco não recordo nada com o mesmo gosto
[Dona Flor ... Upon returning from Rio remembered a saying by her
departed first husband. During the trip, Dona Flor does not remember

where, he went on eating such a quantity of caviar and when she asked what
kind of taste it had, he answered:

"It tastes like a pussy. . .it's very good! . . ."

Doctor Teodoro tried to compare the still recent taste of that dainty
delicacy, finding nothing with which to compare:

"To be honest I can't remember anything with the same taste"]. *(Dona
Flor* 403, 406).

Again, the separation by several pages suggests an accumulative joke,
but it is also funny without the second half (as a dirty joke), and it is also a
tidy encapsulation of the double script.

Pedro Archanjo era um órfão muito pobre que fugiu de marinheiro com
uma gringa igual que meu tio Zuca e foi pra os Estados Unidos porque lá
tem dinheiro pra burro mas ele disse sou brasileiro e veio pra Bahia contar
histórias de bichos e de gente e era tão sabido que não dava lição a menino
só a médico e professor e quando morreu virou glória do Brasil e ganhou
prêmio do jornal que era uma bolsa cheia de garrafas de cachaça. Viva
Pedro Archanjo e o Gaiato Crocodilo! *(Tenda* 214)

[Pedro Archanjo was a very poor orphan who ran away to sea with a
gringa like my Uncle Zuca and went to the United States because there's
heaps of money there but he said I'm Brazilian and came back to Bahia to
tell stories about animals and people and he knew so much he didn't give
lessons to children just to doctors and professors and when he died he was
an ornament to Brazil and he got a prize from the newspaper and it was a
bag of bottles of rum. Hooray for Pedro Archanjo and the Crocodile
Clown!][29] *(Tenda* 214)

This is the complete text of one of the entries in the contest sponsored by
Aguardente Crocodilo. It is the fourth version of a historical blurb on Pedro
Archanjo originally prepared by Prof. Calazans (a real person), reissued by
the Doping Promoção e Publicidade (commercial joke) as an information
sheet to be used by schoolteachers, reinterpreted by the somewhat flaky
teacher Dida Queiroz, and seen here in the definitive version, produced by a
nine-year-old. The procedure is of course the same one used in the childrens'
game in which a story is told and retold, but it is also a take on the satirical
bent of the narrative and a gloss on the script's exploitation theme.

Já que pergunta com tanta delicadeza, eu lhe digo, seu moço: desgraça só
carece começar. Começou, não há quem segure, se alastra, se desenvolve,
produto barato, de vasto consumo. Ale-gria, ao contrário, meu liga, é planta
sestrosa, de amanho difícil de sombra pequena, de pouco durar, não se
dando bem nem ao sol, nem à chuva, nem ao vento geral, exigindo trato
diário e terreno adubado, nem seco nem úmido, cultivo caro, para gente
rica, montada em dinheiro. Alegria se conserva em champanha; cachaça só
consola desgraça, quando consola. *(Tereza* 3)

[Well, since you ask me so nicely, young fellow, I'll tell you this: all bad luck needs is a start in life. Once it gets going there's's no holding it; it spreads and it flourishes. Talk all you like, bad luck's a product for mass consumption if ever there was one. Now happiness, on the other hand, is a mighty finicky kind of plant, old pal. It doesn't last long and while it does it doesn't cast much shade; it doesn't thrive in full sun, or in the rain, or where it's windy; it needs feeding every day—just the right amount of fertilizer and soil that's not too wet and not too dry; it's a hothouse flower for rich people with plenty of money to throw around. Happiness is preserved in champagne; all rum can do is ease your misery a little, maybe].[30]

These are the opening words (only about a third of the opening paragraph) of the second narrator in *Tereza*. The first opened with a warning about the impossibility of knowing all the facts, and this second one (also unidentified) launches his version of the story with a metaphor about happiness and catastrophe. Both are voicing, in very different ways, the reality/illusion theme. Although this kind of narrating is less theatrically amusing than other kinds of humor in Amado, I selected it because it is a good example of one of the important sources of amusement in this novel and also an example of the importance of tone, which is a major element of humor in all these novels. Multiple-voicing is crucial to the plural scripting I have been discussing, but here it is obvious that another element of play is going on—the leisurely, misleading, and at times even irritating narrators are having fun with the story, and since the facts themselves are so elusive the narrator thinks it legitimate to indulge in a digressive and metaphorical style which emphasizes the telling of the tale instead of the tale itself.

A economia condiciona o mundo e dirige as ações humanas, ensina Marx aos seminaristas. Ou é o sexo, como aprendem em Freud? ... Após a publicação da *Carta ao poeta de Matos Barbosa*, a explosiva crônica de Giovanni Guimarães, o número de assinaturas (to *A Tarde*, one of Salvador's major dailies) passou de cinco a nove, Dona Carmosina—ela sempre sai ganhando—embolsou polpuda comissão. Polpuda em termos de Agreste, naturalmente. Tudo no mundo é relativo, como diria Einstein, desconhecido dos seminaristas de Aracaju [The economy conditions the world and directs human *actions*, as Marx teaches the seminarians. Or is sex, what they learn with Freud? ... After the publication of *Letter to the Poet by Matos Barbosa* an explosive article by Giovanni Guimarães, the number of subscribers (to *A Tarde*, one of Bahia's main newspapers) went from five to nine, Dona Carmosina—she always comes out a winner—pocketed a fat commission. Naturally, "fat" as far as Agreste understood it. Everything is relative in this world, as Eistein would say. An unknown as far as the seminarians from Aracaju were concerned]. (*Tieta* 334–5)

Another accumulative joke, but also one in perfect keeping with the city/country scripts. The seminarians remain caught in a philosophical battle between lucre and lust, and the enormous (for Agreste) leap in newspaper subscriptions (scandal sells) is a (relative) windfall for Carmosina. But only the narrator views this as related to Einstein.

> Certos críticos, pouco afeitos a obras e autores populares, acusaram sua poesia de fácil e anedótica, mas os leitores encontravam nela a revelação de um universo ao mesmo tempo real e mágico, onde o quotidiano, as insignificâncias do dia-a-dia, fatos aparentemente sem importância, o beco e a cor do céu, o gato na janela e a flor do cacto, adquiriam nova dimensão . . . Os intelectuais de esquerda, em mais de uma ocasião, criticaram o poeta Antônio Bruno pela falta de engajamento de sua poesia num mundo dividido, injusto e conturbado onde outros poetas amargavam o exílio ou morriam fuzilados [Certain critics, not very familiar with popular authors, accused his poetry of being superficial and anecdotal, but the readers found in it the revelation of a universe which was at the same time real and magical, where the everyday, the day-to-day insignificant matters, facts with apparently little importance, an alley the color of the sky, the cat in the window, and the cactus flower, acquired a new dimension . . . The intellectuals from the left, on more than one occasion, criticized the poet Antônio Bruno for the lack of engagement of his poetry in a divided, unjust, disturbed world where other poets either languished in bitter exile or were shot and executed]. *(Farda* 33, 35)

The full array of Amado's comic arsenal is lacking in *Farda*—the principal humorous device is the ridicule of the pompous and pretentious and the irony of outcomes. But there are always little surprises buried in these books, and this quotation describing the fictional poet's work is one of them. The first part of the quote is something you might find in a literary encyclopedia about Amado's work, and the second is Amado's own literary history stood on its head.

> Em troca, não havia ouvinte mais atento do que Tição às narrativas do turco, episódios da Bíblia, fantasias do Oriente, com profetas e tetrarcas, magos prodigiosos e apreciáveis odaliscas de umbigo à mostra. Olhos arregalados, boca em exclamações e riso, o negro acompanhava pelejas e intrigas, passo a passo, apaixonadamente. Não perdia detalhe mesmo quando o levantino, ao referir lance empolgante, para se explicar melhor explicava em árabe [On the other hand there was no listener more attentive than Tição to the Turk's stories, Bible episodes, oriental fantasies, with prophets and tetrarchs, fantastic magicians, and esteemed odalisks showing their navels. Eyes wide open, the mouth either showing amazement or just laughing, the Blackman would go right along with all the fights and intrigues, step by step, full of passion. He would not miss any detail when the Middleasterner, whenever he would narrate a gripping event, to explain it better, would explain it in Arabic]. *(Tocaia* 182–3)

Amado has at least three major characters who are one kind of *turco* or another, and in *Descoberta* even the supporting characters are. All of them find themselves at one time or another in a state of cultural slippage, and they often react, as here, by lapsing into the only language they are certain is real. But the *turco* is just one example of this kind of alienation in Amado's novels—there are also Germans, Gypsies, Italians and assorted other exotics who must make adjustments to a culture which must seem to them a very strange one indeed, and Amado often makes use of the comic nature of these adjustments.

> Inovação em matéria de romance, este Correio dos Leitores, páginas nas quais o Autor responde a perguntas daqueles que se obrigaram à penitência de acompanhar as peripécias do enredo. . . Jamais se ouviu referência a tal recurso jornalístico em obra ficcional, de criação. Este, porém, é um romance baiano e, como tal, atento ao dernier cri da renovação literária, aberto à ventania ideológica desencadeada pela perestroika . . . É notória a incapacidade do Autor de renovar e de inovar . . . de revolucionar a estrutura folhetinesca da narrativa . . . de ser modernoso e chato.
>
> . . . Quem não estiver de acordo com a inovação não é obrigado a ler as páginas que seguem pois, em verdade, a narrativa acabou na página anterior . . . (*Sumiço* 409–10)
>
> [This is an innovation in the novel: Mail from the Readers, pages where the author answers the questions of those who undertook the penance of following the plot . . . Such a journalistic genre is unheard of when it comes to works of fiction, creative things. This is the Bahian novel, however, and as such, it is attuned to the dernier cri in literary innovations, open to the ideological winds unleashed by perestroika . . . The author's own inability to renovate or innovate is notorious . . . To revolutionize the structure of the narrative . . . To be modern and boring . . . No one who disagrees with the innovation is obliged to read the pages that follow. In truth, the tale ended on the preceding page . . . ].[31]

Here is one of Amado's narrators, *modernoso e chato*, commenting on his own narration. The story itself ended on the previous page, but that doesn't deter this long-winded storyteller, who continues on for another twenty-eight pages even though there is no story left. This is, of course, a lie, but it is a common characteristic of the later Amado to comment on his own weaknesses and his tendency to ramble, which are at once part of the tone and a comic device.

> Mocetão fogoso, antes tão bem-visto entre raparigas e mancebas, tornara-se vasqueiro e arredio. Para mantê-lo à noite em casa, no leito matrimonial, de que artes ou artimanhas se utilizava Adma, casapo de canhão, seco bacalhau, tábua de engomar?

... Mas bastariam boas tetas para encobrir o resto? Ou seria Adma por acaso, como suspeitaram e sugeriram alguns no auge das tumultuadas discussões, uma daquelas prediletas a quem Deus concedera a graça de divina xoxota de chupeta a chupitar?

A fiery young man, who was once well accepted among whores and concubines, he made himself scarce and became very aloof. To keep him at home at night, in the couple's bed, what kind of crafts and artifice did Adma used? Adma, an old hag, a dry cod fish, an ironing board?

... Would a pair of big teats be sufficient to cover it? Or, perhaps by chance, Adma, as some folk have suspected or suggested at the high points of heated debates, would be one of those chosen and to whom God has granted the grace of a divine delight of a rarest pacifying pussy?]. (*Descoberta*, 168–9)

This is all gossip and rumor, of course, a favorite source for Amado. And the narrator never tells if it's really true or not, but this is one proof that the genteel writer is frequently a genital one as well, and this is one of a hundred possible examples of Amado having good dirty fun.

*    *    *

The first conclusion that might be derived from all this is that, for a writer so often criticized as repetitive and predictable, there is a lot of variety among these novels. True, there are a lot of unrepentant bums, public-spirited whores, and chauvinist pigs, but I don't think the portrayal of these characters is by any means fortuitous, because they are players in specific and pointed scripts. A second would be that the novels with the most easily identifiable scripts are not only the funniest but also probably better stories. I would include in this group *Gabriela* (Gabriela and Nacib), "Quincas" and "Vasco" (opposing versions of the truth), *Dona Flor* (Vadinho and Dr. Teodoro), *Tieta* (city and country), *Sumiço* (*orixás* and mortals) and *Descoberta* (Shitan and Allah). For a different reason, I would add to this list one more novel, *Pastores*, because it is so successful in frustrating even the most prescient reader's expectations. In many ways all these narratives seem to have facets of the "enriched joke." The other novels are not as clearly scripted, not as funny, and probably less successful as fiction. In each of them, some other element seems to get in the way of the full exploitation of comic potential, leaving the reader if not dissatisfied somewhat disappointed. In *Tenda* the very gravity of the topic of miscegenation makes for a preachy narrator, and the double scripting of nineteenth century/twentieth century seems not to work very well, because the stasis of racism is so unsurprising. In *Tereza*, oddly enough, the scripting seems to get derailed because it is essentially a love story and because the central figure is so static.[32] In *Farda* the script shifts in mid-book, and for some reason this seems to attenuate the comic potential of the story, although I'm not really sure it would have been funnier if this had not happened. In *Tocaia* the scripting is hampered by the fact that the reader really doesn't have the "official" script to contrast with the one being read. It is further hampered by being a story about characters and the epic of the founding of city, which is not a double script but a single one going in two directions. This is probably the reason that the secondary characters in this novel are more interesting than the putative protagonists.

Finally, it must be noted that in addition to scripting and frustrated expectations, all the books on my first list have exuberant blabbermouths as narrators, while those on the second sound more like the earlier Amado—impish, but with more seriousness of purpose than one would expect of a man who retells a medieval Chinese melodrama as a pornographic extravaganza.

## NOTES

1. Chamberlain, Bobby John. "Humor: Vehicle for Social Commentary in the Novels of Jorge Amado." Diss. UCLA, 1975.
2. 71ª ed., Rio de Janeiro: Record, 1987. First ed. by Martins, 1958. Subsequent references are to *Gabriela*.
3. Rio de Janeiro: Record, 1992. The subtitle is "apontamentos para um livro de memórias que jamais escreverei (notes for a book of memoires that I will never write."
4. Santos, Itazil Benício dos. *Jorge Amado: Retrato incompleto*. Rio de Janeiro: Record, 1993, 159–61. He was further alienated from Moscow in 1957, when he received a Lenin Prize to replace the Stalin Prize he had won in 1951. Along with the new parchment and medal was a letter from the Committee requesting that he return the prize containing the now purged name. Amado never answered the letter, and he kept both medals, which are now on display in Salvador. *Navegação* 588–89.
5. This somewhat eccentric view is that of José Carlos Oliveira, in his "Um Romance que não é." *Jornal do Brasil* 25 e 26 de Abril, 1959, Suplemento Dominical. A detailed overview of the incredible variety of critical responses can be found in Almeida, Alfredo Wagner Berno de, *Jorge Amado: Política e literatura*. Rio: Campus, 1979, 245–60. *Gabriela* was Amado's most controversial novel, but since the dust has settled, it has become, like its creator, a sort of national monument. In 1994 fifteen Brazilian intellectuals were asked by *Veja* to produce a list of the twenty-two works that might constitute the Brazilian canon. *Gabriela*, with ten other novels and eleven works of non-fiction, was so consecrated. Gama, Rinaldo, "Biblioteca nacional," *Veja*, 23 nov. 1994: 108–112.
6. 3 vols., 11ª, 10ª, and 11ª eds., São Paulo: Martins, 1964, 1961, 1964. First ed. 1954.
7. A breezy and fairly digestible synopsis of these and other series appears in MacHovec, Frank J. *Humor: Theory, History, Applications*. Springfield, IL.: Charles C. Thomas, 1988, 27–50.
8. Attardo, Salvatore. *Linguistic Theories of Humor*. Berlin; New York: Mouton de Gruyter, 1994, 271–2; 204.

9. "Jorge Amado." *Latin American Writers*. New York: Scribner's, 1989, vol. 3, 1155.
10. 11ª ed., São Paulo: Martins, 1965. First ed. 1946.
11. 14ª ed., São Paulo: Martins, 1964. First ed., 1942. Subsequent references are to *Terras*.
12. in his "Discours du récit," *Figures III*. Paris: Editions du Seuil, 1972, 75.
13. 14ª ed., São Paulo: Martins, 1965. First ed., 1961. The two narratives are "A Morte e a Morte de Quincas Berro D'água" and "A Completa Verdade sobre as Discutidas Aventuras do Comandante Vasco Moscoso de Aragão, Capitão de Longo Curso." Subsequent references are to "Quincas" and "Vasco."
14. 11ª ed., São Paulo: Martins, s.d. First ed., 1964. Subsequent references are to *Pastores*.
15. São Paulo: Martins, 1966. Subsequent references are to *Dona Flor*.
16. Chamberlain,"Humor," 407–21.
17. The illustration follows page 24.
18. São Paulo: Martins, 1969. Subsequent references are to *Tenda*.
19. São Paulo: Martins, 1972. Subsequent references are to *Tereza*.
20. 2ª ed., Rio de Janeiro: 1977. Subsequent references are to *Tieta*.
21. Rio de Janeiro: Record, 1979. Subsequent references are to *Farda*.
22. 3ª ed., Rio de Janeiro: Record, 1985. First edition, 1984. Subsequent references are to *Tocaia*.
23. Rio de Janeiro, Record, 1988. Subsequent references are to *Sumiço*.
24. Rio de Janeiro, Record, 1994. Subsequent references are to *Descoberta*.
25. Attardo 295–96.
26. Attardo 254.
27. Attardo 254, 235, 216, 255–56, 263.
28. Trans. James L. Taylor and William Grossman. *Gabriela, Clove and Cinnamon*. New York: Avon Books, 1978 (108)
29. Trans. Barbara Shelby. *Tent of Miracles*. New York: Avon Books, 1978 (215)
30. Trans. Barbara Shelby. *Tereza Batista: Home from the Wars*. New York: Avon-Books, 1975 (1)
31. Trans. Gregory Rabassa. *The War of the Saints*. New York: Batam Books, 1993 (326–327)
32. Bobby Chamberlain attributes her unidimensionality to the fact that she is a "legendary" figure modeled after the heroes and heroines of *literatura de cordel*. Chamberlain, Bobby J., *Jorge Amado*, Boston: Twayne. 1990, 85,89.

Whenever a translator was not identified, the quote was translated by one of the editors: Enrique Martínez-Vidal.

## BIBLIOGRAPHY

Adorno, Rolena. "Reconsidering Colonial Discourse for Sixteenth- and Seventeenth-Century Spanish America." *Latin American Research Review* 28:3 (1993): 135–45.

Appiah, Kwame Anthony. "Is the Post- in Postmodernism the Post- in Postcolonial?" *Critical Inquiry* 17 (1991): 336–57.

Beverley, John. *Against Literature*. Minneapolis: The University of Minnesota Press, 1993.

Bhabha, Homi K. "Postocolonial Atuhority and Postmodern Guilt." *Cultural Studies*. Lawrence Grossberg, Cary Nelson and Paula Treichler, eds. New York: Routledge (1992): 56–66.

Chamberlain, Bobby J. "Of Charters, Paradigms and Spawning Fish: A Look at Brazilian Literary Periodization and Canon-Formation." *Brasil/Brazil* 6 (1993): 5–23.

Colas, Santiago. "Of Creole Symptoms, Cuban Fantasies, and Other Latin American Postcolonial Ideologies." *PMLA* 110:3 (1995): 382–96.

Dirlik, Arif. "The Postcolonial Aura: Third World Criticism in the Age of Global Capitalism." *Critical Inquiry* 20 (1994): 328–56.

Gomes, Alvaro Cardoso. *Jorge Amado: Literatura Comentada*. São Paulo: Abril Educação, 1981.

Mignolo, Walter D. "Colonial and Postcolonial Discourse: Cultural Critique or Academic Colonialism?" *Latin American Research Review* 28:3 (1993): 120–34.

Matta, Roberto Da. *Carnivals, Rogues, and heroes: An Interpretation of the Brazilian Dilemma*. Notre Dame, Indiana: University of Notre Dame Press, 1991.

Mohanty, Satya P. "Colonial Legacies, Multicultural Futures: Relativism, Objectivity, and the Challenge of Otherness." *PMLA*, 110:1 (1995): 108–18.

Oliven, Ruben George. *Tradition Matters: Modern Gaucho Diversity in Brazil*. Trans. by Carmen Chaves Tesser. New York: Columbia University Press, 1995.

Reis, Roberto,"Who's Afraid of (Luso-)Brazilian Literature?" *World Literature Today* (1988): 231–34.

Said, Edward W. "Representing the Colonized: Anthropology's Interlocutors." *Critical Inquiry* 15 (1989): 205–227.

Schwarz, Roberto. "Nacional por subtração." In *Que horas são?* São Paulo: Companhia das Letras (1989): 29–48.

Seed, Patricia. "More Colonial and Postcolonial Discourses." *Latin American Research Review* 28:3 (1993): 146–52.

Vasconcelos, José Carlos. "Amado Jorge Amado." *Jornal de Letras, Artes e Idéias* 25 (1995): 10–12.

Vidal, Hernán. "The Concept of Colonial and Postcolonial Discourse: A Perspective from Literary Criticism." *Latin American Research Review* 28:3 (1993): 113–19.

# Contributors
## Biographical Notes

**Cathleen E. Anderson** is Assistant Professor of Spanish and Portuguese at Dickinson College. Although her main research area is the Latin American short story of the 20th century, with particular emphasis on women writers, she has also published on José de Alencar's *Iracema*. She is currently studying the short stories of Brazilian women.

**Keith H. Brower**, one of the editors of this volume, is Professor of Modern Languages and Intercultural Studies at Salisbury State University (Maryland). He holds a Ph.D. from Pennsylvania State University (1985) and was Associate Professor of Spanish and Portuguese at Dickinson College for several years prior to returning to his undergraduate alma mater. He is the author of *Contemporary Latin American Fiction: An Annotated Bibliography* (1989) and numerous articles and essays on Spanish American and Brazilian writers and works.

**Bobby J. Chamberlain** received his Ph.D. in Hispanic Languages and Literatures from UCLA. Currently he is Professor of Spanish and Portuguese at the University of Pittsburgh. For six years, Chamberlain was the director of the American Association of Teachers of Spanish and Portuguese Task Force for the Promotion of Portuguese. He was a member of the Executive Committee of the Luso-Brazilian Division of the Modern Language Association of America. He has published widely on Brazilian literature and language and has served on the editorial boards of both the *Revista iberoamericana* and *Chasqui*. He is the co-author, with Ronald M. Harmon, of *A Dictionary of Informal Brazilian Portuguese* (1984) and editor of *Portuguese Language and Luso-Brazilian Literature: An Annotated Guide in Selected Reference Works* (1989), and he is also the author of the Twayne volume, *Jorge Amado* (1990).

**Joanna Courteau** is a "University" Professor at Iowa State University, where she teaches courses in Lusophone and Hispanic Cultures, Languages and Literatures. She is the author of numerous articles on nationality, discourse analysis and feminism. Most recently she has edited a collection of essays on *Mujer, sexo y poder en la literatura femenina del siglo XIX* (1999).

**Paul B. Dixon** has taught Latin American literature at Purdue University since receiving his Ph.D. in romance languages at the University of North Carolina in 1981. He is the author of *Os contos de Machado de Assis: mais do que sonha a filosofia, Retired Dreams: Dom Casmurro, Myth and Modernity,* and *Reversible Readings: Ambiguity in Four Modern Latin American Novels.* He is co-director of *Espelho,* a journal studying Machado de Assis.

**Sandra L. Dixon**, a native of Washington, D.C., completed her B.A. and M.A. degrees at the University of Pennsylvania and earned her Ph.D. in Hispanic Studies at Brown University. Her current position is that of Assistant Professor of Spanish and Portuguese at West Virginia University, where she pursues her fields of interest in Caribbean and Afro-Hispanic literatures. In 1986, she had the opportunity to participate in an N.E.H. Summer Institute on Brazil and in a subsequent research trip during which she worked on a curriculum development project for the teaching of Brazilian culture.

**Ellen H. Douglass** is Assistant Professor of Comparative Literature and Women's Studies at Pennsylvania State University. With specializations in the literatures of Latin America and the Caribbean and in feminist literary theory, she has published articles and translations in journals including *The Luso-Brazilian Review, Brasil/Brazil,* and *The Journal of Afro-Latin American Studies and Literatures.* At present, she is working on a book about feminist recreations of the quest myth in novels by Clarice Lispector and Virginia Woolf.

**Earl E. Fitz,** one of the editors of this volume, is Professor of Portuguese, Spanish, and Comparative Literature at Vanderbilt University, where he teaches courses related to these areas. At present, he is completing a manuscript on the Brazilian writer Clarice Lispector. He is also gathering information on another volume that would compare the development of the novel form in Brazil and the United States.

**Elizabeth Lowe** is Associate Director of the Center for Latin American Studies at the University of Florida. She is author of *The City in Brazilian Literature,* numerous articles and contributor to several books, including *Splintering Darkness: Latin American Women Writers in Search of Themselves.* She translates fiction by Brazilian and Spanish American writers, most recently *Esau and Jacob* by Machado de Assis. Elizabeth Lowe is also co-skipper of the sailing vessel *Dona Flor.*

**Enrique Martínez-Vidal,** one of the editors of this volume, is Professor Emeritus of Romance Languages at Dickinson College. A native of Lyon, France, he has studied in Barcelona, Spain, the United States, and as a Fulbright scholar, he studied culture and civilization in São Paulo, Brazil, in 1982. He has contributed articles and essays on Spanish peninsular literature, culture and civilization to journals both in Spain and the United States. Currently he is completing a manuscript on José Samarago's *O evangélio segundo Jesus Cristo.*

**Gerald Moser** is Professor Emeritus of Romance Languages at Pennsylvania State University. From 1949 to 1978, he taught French language and literature, Spanish language and literatures, Portuguese language and literature, Brazilian and Luso-African literatures. He has published hundreds of book chapters, articles and book reviews. His first book was *Les Romantiques Portugais et l'Allemagne* (1939). His most recent books are *Changing Africa: The First Literary Generation of Independent Cape Verde* (1992), *A New Bibliography of the Lusophone Literatures of Africa* (1993), *Almanach de Lembranças: Textos Africanos* (1993), and *Seven Essays on Joseph Priestley* (1994).

**Celso Lemos de Oliveira** was born in Minas Gerais, Brazil. He is Professor of Portuguese and Spanish at the University of South Carolina, and he also has served as Director of Comparative Literature. His works include *Understanding Graciliano Ramos* (1988) and translations of Ramos' *Childhood* (1979) and Bernardo Santareno's *The Judgment of Father Martinho* (1994). He has contributed translations and essays to many journals in Brazil, the United States, and Europe.

**Charles A. Perrone** is Professor of Portuguese and Luso-Brazilian Culture and Literature at the University of Florida. He first studied musical phenomena in literature as a Fulbright scholar in Brazil in 1978. His critical articles have addressed such topics as interrelations of music and literature, song in neo-regionalist novels, and lyrical passages in João Guimarães Rosa. He is the author of *Letras e Letras da MPB* (1988), *Masters of Contemporary Brazilian Song: MPB 1965–1985* (1989), and *Seven Faces: Brazilian Poetry since Modernism* (1996). He is editor-translator of *Adriano Espínola, Taxi or Poem of Love in Transit* (1992); and co-editor of *Crônicas Brasileiras: Nova Fase* (1994), *Chiclete com Banana: Internationalization in Brazilian Popular Music* (forthcoming).

**Susan Canty Quinlan** is Associate Professor in the Department of Romance Languages and Women's Studies at the University of Georgia. Currently she is Co-Director of the Center for Latin American and Caribbean Studies. Aside from numerous articles on nineteenth-and twentieth-century Brazilian women writers, she is the author of *The Female Voice in Contemporary Brazilian Narrative* (1991) and *Lutas de coração de Inês Sabono,* critical edition (1999). She has co-authored the book *Connected Threads: Brazilian Feminist Discourse* (forthcoming) and the critical edition, *Visões do Passado: Previsões do Futuro* (1995) and is currently co-authoring *Lusosex: Discourses of Sexuality in the Portuguese Speaking World.* She is the recipient of a William Fulbright Distinguished Scholar award for 1995–96.

**Cristina Sáenz de Tejada** is Assistant Professor of Spanish at Goucher College. She has published on contemporary Brazilian and Spanish American literature with emphasis on women writers. She has also co-translated Clarice Lispector's *Uma aprendizagem ou o livro dos prazeres (Aprendizaje o el libro de los placeres)* (1990). She is currently writing about Afro-Brazilian women writers.

**Carmen Chaves Tesser** is Professor of Romance Languages at the University of Georgia. Research and publications in two areas: eighteenth-century Peninsular Spanish literature and Luso-Brazilian literature. Her latest publications are *Tradition Matters: Gaúcho Diversity in Brazil* (forthcoming), and a translation of *A Parte e o Todo* by Ruben Oliven.

**Nelson H. Vieira** Professor of Luso-Brazilian Studies in the Department of Portuguese and Brazilian Studies and Fellow in Judaic Studies at Brown University, is also American founding editor of the literary journal *Brasil/Brazil,* and serves as the current President of the Latin American Jewish Studies Association (LAJSA). In addition to translations of Portuguese articles as well as articles on modern Brazilian fiction, Vieira lists the following among his major publications: *Samuel Rawet: The Prophet and Other Stories* (1998); *Jewish Voices in Brazilian Literature: A Prophetic Discourse of Alterity* (1995); *Construindo a imagem do judeu (1994); Brasil e Portugal: a imagem recíproca* (1991); *Roads to Today's Portugal* (1983); and *The Promise* [translation] (1981).

**Jon S. Vincent** received his Ph.D. at the University of New Mexico. As a graduate student, he spent a year in Portugal as a Fulbright Fellow. From 1967 until his untimely death, he was Professor of Spanish and Portuguese at the University of Kansas and also served as chairperson of his department. He also had visiting appointments at his alma mater, the University of New Mexico, and also at the University of Costa Rica. While at the University of

Kansas he directed the University's Summer Language Institutes in Mexico and Brazil and the K.U. Academic program in Costa Rica. He was a member of the Advisory Board of the K.U. Center of Latin American Studies and Chairman of the K.U. Committee on Luso-Brazilian Studies. He also served as an assistant editor of the *Latin American Theater Review.* He published articles and reviews in *Hispania, Modern Language Journal, Luso-Brazilian Review, Latin American Research Review, Journal of Interamerican Studies and World Affairs,* and the *Brazilian Novel.* He is the author of the Twayne volume on João Guimarães Rosa (1978).

# Index

For Product Safety Concerns and Information please contact our EU
representative GPSR@taylorandfrancis.com
Taylor & Francis Verlag GmbH, Kaufingerstraße 24, 80331 München, Germany